The Prophetic Body

"In this stunningly erudite volume, Anathea Portier-Young has initiated her ambitious project of exploring the textual evidence for the bodily engagement of the prophets of ancient Israel. She has taken into account a vast secondary literature as well as an intense study of the textual material. Portier-Young's book is a seminal work that likely will refocus on-going study of the ancient prophets to show the great extent to which they imposed their compelling bodily reality upon the body politic of ancient Israel. In overcoming a mistaken, even if unintended, dualism, this book opens new vistas in our interpretation and understanding. Portier-Young shows herself to be a major voice in a new generation of interpreters. We will eagerly await the appearance of subsequent volumes in her category-shattering project."
—Walter Brueggemann, William Marcellus McPheeters Professor Emeritus of Old Testament, Columbia Theological Seminary

"This groundbreaking work reframes biblical prophecy as we know it. Rejecting the mind-body dualism that has led to a persistent focus on prophets' words as if separable from their embodied experience, Anathea Portier-Young demonstrates how the prophetic body and word were inextricably interconnected. With remarkable multidisciplinary breadth, Portier-Young examines prophetic experience, action, and affect, and presents a revolutionary new model for understanding prophetic literature. *The Prophetic Body* offers an expansive redefinition of the very nature of biblical prophecy."—Esther J. Hamori, Professor of Hebrew Bible, Union Theological Seminary

"In this stunning exploration of somatic dimensions of prophecy in the Hebrew Bible, Anathea Portier-Young weaves an elegant tapestry of insights drawn from narratology, affect theory, disability studies, gender criticism, and neurobiology. On every page, biblical scholars and homileticians will find fresh wisdom for their theorizing of the synergy of sacred speech, cognition, embodiment, and lived experience in articulations of the holy."—Carolyn J. Sharp, Professor of Homiletics, Yale Divinity School

"In *The Prophetic Body* by Anathea Portier-Young, readers will encounter a thoughtful and insightful exploration of the sheer physicality that went into biblical representations of the prophets' bodily practices and experiences. Drawing on a wide range of studies in neurocognition, social science and cultural theory, this engaging and well-written book demonstrates how biblical prophecy was a fully embodied phenomenon that deeply affected and effected the divine words associated with prophets. An important, fresh contribution, most highly recommended for both old and new students of biblical prophecy."—Mark S. Smith, Princeton Theological Seminary

"Portier-Young's compelling volume weaves together a deft reading of biblical texts and deep engagement with contemporary theory on embodiment, colonialism, and gender to challenge interpretations that reduce prophecy to words. By reclaiming the role of the body—not only for the biblical prophets but also for their readers—she offers us a path beyond the mind-body dualism that feeds ancient and modern systems of oppression. This is essential reading for understanding biblical prophecy and the limits of current paradigms of interpretation. I anxiously await the remaining volumes of the trilogy!"—Julia M. O'Brien, Paul H. and Grace L. Stern Professor of Hebrew Bible, Lancaster Theological Seminary

"In reframing prophecy as fundamentally embodied, Portier-Young lingers over aspects of texts we had previously overlooked, giving fresh understanding of the prophet's relationship to deity, people, and place. With careful exegesis amplified by wide-ranging yet apt insights from fields as disparate as poetry, neuroscience, affect theory, and monster culture, this study is both integrative and innovative. Its subtle argument, clearly and vividly expressed, will prove impossible to ignore."—Ellen F. Davis, Amos Ragan Kearns Distinguished Professor of Bible and Practical Theology, Duke Divinity School

"*The Prophetic Body* is a monumental work that transcends the boundaries of traditional biblical studies. The author's synthesis of cognitive neuroscience, anthropology, and rigorous textual analysis offers a pioneering lens through which to understand the complex interplay between embodiment, prophecy, and religious experience in the Hebrew Bible (the Old Testament). Exploring the profound affective connection between God, people, and place, this book delves into the essential role the body plays in mediating the divine. Insightful, profoundly researched, and elegantly articulated, *The Prophetic Body* serves as a vital contribution to both scholarly inquiry and general understanding of one of humanity's most ancient and revered texts. This book is highly recommended for scholars, theologians, and anyone intrigued by the nexus of spirituality, literature, and the human body. Its groundbreaking insights offer a journey that promises to engage and enlighten readers across a wide spectrum of interests."—Stephen L. Cook, Catherine N. McBurney Professor of Old Testament Language and Literature, Virginia Theological Seminary

The Prophetic Body

Embodiment and Mediation in Biblical Prophetic Literature

ANATHEA E. PORTIER-YOUNG

OXFORD
UNIVERSITY PRESS

Oxford University Press is a department of the University of Oxford.
It furthers the University's objective of excellence in research, scholarship,
and education by publishing worldwide. Oxford is a registered trade mark of
Oxford University Press in the UK and in certain other countries.

Published in the United States of America by Oxford University Press
198 Madison Avenue, New York, NY 10016, United States of America.

© Oxford University Press 2024

All rights reserved. No part of this publication may be reproduced, stored in a retrieval system,
or transmitted, in any form or by any means, without the prior permission in writing of Oxford
University Press, or as expressly permitted by law, by license or under terms agreed with the
appropriate reprographics rights organization. Inquiries concerning reproduction outside the scope
of the above should be sent to the Rights Department, Oxford University Press, at the address above.

You must not circulate this work in any other form and you must
impose this same condition on any acquirer.

Library of Congress Cataloging-in-Publication Data
Names: Portier-Young, Anathea E., 1973– author.
Title: The prophetic body : embodiment and mediation in biblical prophetic
literature / Anathea E. Portier-Young.
Description: New York, NY, United States of America : Oxford University Press, 2024. |
Includes bibliographical references and index.
Identifiers: LCCN 2023056767 (print) | LCCN 2023056768 (ebook) |
ISBN 9780197604960 (hardback) | ISBN 9780197604984 (epub)
Subjects: LCSH: Prophecy—Biblical teaching. |
Bible. Prophets—Criticism, interpretation, etc.
Classification: LCC BS1198 .P58 2024 (print) | LCC BS1198 (ebook) |
DDC 224/.06—dc23/eng/20240206
LC record available at https://lccn.loc.gov/2023056767
LC ebook record available at https://lccn.loc.gov/2023056768

DOI: 10.1093/9780197604991.001.0001

Printed by Integrated Books International, United States of America

Front cover image, *Vision of Chebar* (Ezekiel Detail), Donald Jackson with
contributions from Aidan Hart and Sally Mae Joseph, © 2005, *The Saint John's Bible*,
Saint John's University, Collegeville, Minnesota USA. Used by permission.
All rights reserved.

*To the residents and former residents of the
North Carolina Correctional Institute for Women,
especially my students in the former Canary Unit.
You are prophets all.*

Contents

Preface and Acknowledgments   xi
Abbreviations   xvii
Introduction   xxi

PART I AN EMBODIED PARADIGM

1. The Buried Body   3
   - Word and Body: A Parable (1 Kings 13)   3
   - Modern Biblical Scholarship   8
   - Yes to Words. And Also the Body   14
   - Historicizing a Word-Centered Approach   16

2. Re-Embodying Biblical Prophecy   30
   - A Working Definition   30
   - From Unity to Diversity: Deuteronomy 18:9–22   31
   - Prophecy as Mediation: Key Terms and Concepts   36
   - "A Paradigm of Embodiment"   44
   - Constrained and Shaped by Text: A Challenge, A Caveat, and an Assumption   47
   - Conclusion   51

PART II CALLED IN THE FLESH

3. God's Surrogate (Exodus 3–4)   55
   - Embodied Encounter Sets the Stage for Embodied Mediation   58
   - Moses' Hand as Surrogate of the Divine Hand   61
   - Heavy of Mouth: A Prophet with Disability   68
   - Words and Actions   72
   - Conclusion   75

4. First-Person   77
   - First-Person Narration, Textual Mediation, and Embodied Reception   78
   - Isaiah 6   80
   - Jeremiah 1:4–10   86
   - Ezekiel 1:1–3:15   91
   - Conclusion   97

PART III TRANSFORMATIONS

5. Becoming Other — 103
   Moses, Godlike and Monstrous (Exodus 34) — 104
   Miriam, Debased and Devoured (Numbers 12) — 110
   Conclusion — 116

6. Transformative Practice — 118
   Textual Portrayals of Religious Experience and Bodily Practice — 119
   Askêsis — 123
   Incubation — 135
   Conclusion — 142

7. Ecstasy — 145
   Anxious about Ecstasy: A Century of Debate, 1914–2017 — 146
   A Multidisciplinary Approach — 155
   Induction Techniques — 160
   Spirit Possession — 162
   Conclusion — 167

PART IV (E)MOTION AND AFFECT

8. Mobility and Immobility — 173
   Mobilities: Catalyzing Dynamism in Relation to Deity, People, and Place — 174
   Supernatural Transport — 182
   Immobilities — 189
   The Costs of Mobility and Immobility — 194
   Conclusion — 195

9. Anger and Tears — 196
   Understanding Affect: New Approaches and Relevance for Studying Prophetic Literature — 197
   Jonah: Transforming Affect — 201
   Jeremiah — 208
   Conclusion — 224

10. Devastation and Wonder — 226
    Ezekiel: Devastated and Devastating — 226
    Daniel — 237
    Conclusion — 247

    Conclusion — 249

Bibliography — 259
Index of Modern Authors — 289
Index of Subjects — 293
Index of Ancient Sources — 299

Preface and Acknowledgments

The idea for this book began to crystallize in February 2017 as I listened to a faculty colloquium delivered by my colleague, Lian Xi, entitled "Blood Letters from a Mao Prison: Lin Zhao (1932–1968)." It is to Lian Xi that I offer my first word of thanks, for sharing Lin Zhao's story and sparking the inspiration for this book. Arrested in 1960 during China's cultural revolution, Lin Zhao wrote her testimony — writings her biographer characterized as "prophetic" — in ink and in blood. While imprisoned she wrote often on paper, but also on her sheets and clothing. Preserved by the very government she protested, her "blood letters" participated in a form of embodied resistance that adapted a traditional ascetic practice known from medieval Buddhism to the constraints of her own incarceration. Lin Zhao, like others before her, chose the lifeblood of her own body to be the medium for her letters, poems, memoire, and critique. Did this bodily medium change the "meaning" of the words to which it gave shape? As I heard her story, including the torture she endured and the form she chose for her testimony, the question that took shape for me was this: for the prophet, what is the relationship between word and body? How does each shape the other? My thoughts immediately went to Ezekiel, who is given a scroll to ingest, on which are written the words "lamentation, mourning, and woe" (Ezek. 2:8–3:3). At this climactic moment of Ezekiel's prophetic call narrative, the words entered his body and filled his stomach. The taste was sweet to him, like honey (3:3). The words he would subsequently speak would come not from some abstracted source "out there" but from within his very body.

The artwork featured on the cover of this book captures this moment when Ezekiel receives the scroll to eat and powerfully illustrates the synergy of word and body that is the central focus of this book. I am indebted to the Benedictine community of Saint John's Abbey in Collegeville, Minnesota, to The Saint John's Bible Director Tim Ternes, and to the image use review committee, for allowing this artwork to accompany this project. The featured image is the Ezekiel Detail from the 2005 illumination "Vision of Chebar" by artist and calligrapher Donald Jackson, with contributions from Aidan Hart and Sally Mae Joseph, from The Saint John's Bible *Prophets* volume

(2005). In this detail, Ezekiel sits cross-legged and solitary upon the ground, naked but for a gauzy cloth wrapped about his middle. He faces away from the viewer but is visible in shadowy profile as his arm reaches up to grasp the unfurled scroll that descends to him from the midst of the ophanim, the en-spirited wheels of the divine chariot. The deep indigo silhouette of the prophet's body contrasts with the crisp white vellum of the scroll even as it visually echoes the cerulean triangular and trapezoidal fragments of sky that dapple the field above him. The prophet's inky body also echoes the words of lamentation inked upon the scroll and indeed the very verses of Ezekiel this image illuminates and accompanies. The inbreaking of heavenly revelation thus here solidifies and takes shape in the prophet's humble form. The scroll and the prophet's body form a continuous, zig-zagging line, a single thread connecting heaven and earth, one channel through which word and body together bridge divine and human realms. An inverted rainbow blazes like fire behind the scroll, locating in this moment of sorrow and devastation the glimmer of divine presence and promise of a future beyond destruction and exile. This detail is one part of an illumination that spans two pages; Ezekiel's vision of the divine chariot occupies the upper register of the preceding page and spills into its margins. The two scenes are linked by the repeating motif of the chariots' wheels, stamped across the margins in black and gold, signifying a divine presence that persists in the face of death and is constantly in motion to fill every remote corner where God's people may find themselves cast upon the ground.

Some viewers of this art and readers or hearers of this book may find reflected in the image and story of Ezekiel's commission their own experiences of calling, confusion, wonder, suffering, submission, and encounter with God. Like the mediating body of the prophet, sacred art and text also seek to facilitate such an encounter with God, even, as portrayed in this illumination, at the moment of God's departure from the temple, that is, beyond customary sites and modes of mediation and encounter. This may be meaningful for readers of this book in (at least) two ways. First, for those who normally expect God to "speak" through words on a page or sacred liturgy alone this image may make it possible to perceive divine testimony in the crying of those who have suffered loss, to experience God sitting in the dirt with humankind in places of greatest isolation, to know that God is active for and through God's people in places of rupture and devastation as much as in places of visible order and beauty. Ezekiel's prophetic experience and action testify that just as suffering is experienced in the body, so too will be restoration and redemption.

Second, this book is dedicated to my students at North Carolina Correctional Institute for Women. The bodies of incarcerated people are isolated, strip-searched, and demeaned on a daily basis. During the Covid-19 pandemic, when I taught the course "Prophecy in the Body" at NCCIW, the bodies of my incarcerated students were especially vulnerable. Through their participation in this course, these women have come to know themselves, their bodies, and their experiences as prophetic. It is my hope that this image of the stripped, exposed, and vulnerable prophet can make visible the ways God speaks and acts through those who are incarcerated and make visible also a transformed future for and through them.

The scholarship these pages contain, while technical, also aims to help readers—and by extension those they may teach, minister to and with, and otherwise interact with—perceive the value, dignity, and sacred dimensions of their own bodily experiences, actions, and interactions. In a culture that has so greatly denigrated and abused our bodies and the bodies of others, this feels urgent. The power of sacred art to evoke and facilitate encounter with the divine is a vital complement to what this book's argument aims to do. I thus hope that this book might also operate in synergy with the aims of The Saint John's Bible, for which I have highest regard and deep gratitude.

I owe tremendous thanks once again to the members of the Catholic Biblical Association of America, who supported this project in two ways: through a Grant from the CBA and through opportunities to present portions of the book in progress at annual meetings. It is a special thing for one's research to be funded by the stewardship and generosity of colleagues and friends, by a cloud of witnesses past and present who have invested in and placed their trust in our common work. I do not hold that gift or responsibility lightly. Duke Divinity School, where I have taught for more than twenty years, supplemented CBA grant funding to enable a semester of research leave in Spring 2022. The Divinity School also supported this project through a sabbatical in 2018. The support and insight of my division chair Brent Strawn, Vice Dean Kavin Rowe, and Dean of Faculty (Emeritus) Randy Maddox were invaluable in developing this project and securing time for writing. I offer thanks to my colleagues at Duke and elsewhere, especially Ellen Davis, Chuck Campbell, Mark Smith, Corri Carvalho, and Rod Werline, who offered support, wisdom, and feedback as I pursued grant funding in the project's early days.

Duke Divinity School has the best library team! Katie Benjamin, Lacey Hudspeth, Sigrid Kjaer, Phu Nguyen, Dean Hawkins, and Hildegard the Bunny: I am especially grateful for the extraordinary measures you and your colleagues around the world took to make library resources accessible during the pandemic. You are all-stars.

Numerous institutions afforded opportunities to present and teach portions of my work in progress: Barton College, Princeton Theological Seminary, the Pastoralkolleg Ratzeburg, Sewanee's School of Theology, North Carolina Correctional Institute for Women, St. Vincent College, Union Theological Seminary (New York), and of course Duke. I am grateful to all those whose questions, conversations, and enthusiasm helped sharpen and move this project forward. My students in the class "Prophecy in the Body" at Duke, NCCIW, and Sewanee are partners in this project. You continually expanded my horizons and highlighted for me so many rich aspects of prophetic embodiment I never would have thought to consider on my own. Your ingenuity and creativity are a continual blessing. Sarah Jobe was an invaluable partner in teaching at NCCIW and in developing many of the ideas in this project. It is an honor to learn from you.

David Bosworth, Esther Hamori, Bill Portier, Brent Strawn, and Lauren Winner provided feedback on portions of the book in progress. Brittany Wilson not only provided feedback but also helped me celebrate writing milestones.

In 2018, Jennifer Ahern-Dodson of the Duke Faculty Write Program and Monique Dufour introduced me to the wonderful world of writing retreats and taught me to build social support into the writing process. They and a host of faculty writers have journeyed alongside me as I developed and completed this book project. As this book neared completion, they along with DJ Collie Fulford and Stephanie Norander gifted me with weekly doses of wisdom, compassion, humor, and support. During the pandemic, the London Writers' Salon also provided an invaluable source of inspiration and global companionship in this writing journey.

My research assistants Allison Garde, Caleb Punt, Emily Page, Kálmán (K) Máté, Dean Hawkins, and Jonathan Acosta provided valuable help at different stages of this project. Thank you for your attention to detail and timely aid.

Oxford University Press Biblical Studies Editor Steve Wiggins answered my every anxious question with clarity and calm assurance. Thank you for believing in this project and shepherding it to completion. I am grateful to project editor Egle Zigaite, project manager Vinothini Thiruvannamalai, and copy editor Tim Rutherford-Johnson for your care and diligence in overseeing the technical aspects of manuscript review and preparation for publication. To my anonymous reviewers: your input has helped to make this book better. Even though I was not able to implement every suggestion, I hope you will see the fruit of your labor in this finished product.

I offer my deep gratitude and appreciation to Rabbi Jill Hammer for permission to reproduce lines from the poem "*Pirkei Imahot*/Sayings of the Mothers" and to Julie Moore and John's Hopkins University Press for permission to reproduce in full the poem "Elisha's Bones." Your artistry, wisdom, and generosity humble me.

In 2018, Jaime Clark-Soles and I bonded over a shared love of productivity planners. In short order, we became writing accountability partners. Jaime has journeyed with this project almost from its inception, meeting with me weekly to set goals, strategize, and celebrate progress. I have grown so much through our friendship, not only as a writer, but as a person. Thank you from my heart.

Finally, I thank my family. My sister, Laura Portier-LaLumiere, made revising—dare I say?—fun. You, dear reader, might not be able to tell, but trust me, you're grateful for her interventions. My brother, Phil Portier, gave me a giant computer monitor that lets me write with *three screens going at once* and was a frequent sounding board and perennial voice of encouragement. My parents are the best cheerleaders. My Mom has modeled for me curiosity and wonder that cross disciplines and eras. My Dad retreated with me, wrote alongside me, and even ate my cooking when our daily writing was done. Thank you for always picking up the phone and helping me figure out what that word is, for the thing, and telling me whether "this is something a person can actually say." To Steve and Maxine: your love matters more than all the books and all the pages. I never forget it.

Abbreviations

AB	Anchor Bible
AOTC	Abingdon Old Testament Commentaries
ASC	Altered or alternate state of consciousness
AT	Author's Translation
AYB	Anchor Yale Bible
AYBRL	Anchor Yale Bible Reference Library
BASOR	*Bulletin of the American Schools of Oriental Research*
BBR	*Bulletin for Biblical Research*
BCT	*Bible & Critical Theory*
BETL	Bibliotheca Ephemeridum Theologicarum Lovaniensium
BHS	*Biblia Hebraica Stuttgartensia*. Edited by K. Elliger and W. Rudolph. Stuttgart, 1983.
BibInt	*Biblical Interpretation*
BibS	Biblische Studien
BKAT	Biblischer Kommentar, Altes Testament. Edited by M. Noth and H. W. Wolff
BR	*Biblical Research*
BTB	*Biblical Theology Bulletin*
BThZ	*Berliner Theologische Zeitschrift*
BZ	*Biblische Zeitschrift*
BZAW	Beihefte zur Zeitschrift für die alttestamentliche Wissenschaft
Can J Psychiatry	*Canadian Journal of Psychiatry*
CBQ	Catholic Biblical Quarterly
CBQMS	Catholic Biblical Quarterly Monograph Series
Cult Med Psychiatry	*Culture, Medicine, and Psychiatry*
CurBR	*Currents in Biblical Research*
DCLS	Deuterocanonical and Cognate Literature Studies
DCLY	Deuterocanonical and Cognate Literature Yearbook
DSM-IV-TR	*Diagnostic and Statistical Manual of Mental Disorders*. Text Revision. 4th ed. Washington, DC: American Psychiatric Association, 1994
DSM-5	*Diagnostic and Statistical Manual of Mental Disorders*. 5th ed. Washington, DC: American Psychiatric Association, 2013
E	Putative "Elohistic" documentary source for the Pentateuch
ECL	Early Christianity and Its Literature

EJL	Early Judaism and Its Literature
FAT	Forschungen zum Alten Testament
FM	*Florilegium marianum*
FOTL	Forms of Old Testament Literature
GKC	*Gesenius' Hebrew Grammar*. Edited by Emil Kautzsch. Translated by Arthur E. Cowley. 2nd ed. Oxford, 1910
HALOT	*The Hebrew and Aramaic Lexicon of the Old Testament*. Ludwig Koehler, Walter Baumgartner, and Johann J. Stamm. Translated and edited under the supervision of Mervyn E. J. Richardson. 4 vols. Leiden: Brill, 1994–1999
HBOT	Hebrew Bible and Old Testament, term used when indicating, in aggregate, the overlapping but distinct canonical corpora otherwise known as the Jewish TaNaK or Hebrew Bible and the multiple configurations of the Christian "Old Testament," including the shorter canon used by Protestants and various longer canons used by Catholics and Orthodox Christians
HS	*Hebrew Studies*
HSS	Harvard Semitic Studies
HTR	*Harvard Theological Review*
ICD-11	The International Classification of Disease. Eleventh Revision. World Health Organization, 2019
IECOT	International Exegetical Commentary on the Old Testament
J	Putative "Yahwistic" documentary source for the Pentateuch
J Cogn Neurosci	*Journal of Cognitive Neuroscience*
J Inflamm Res	*Journal of Inflammatory Research*
JAAR	*Journal of the American Academy of Religion*
JBL	*Journal of Biblical Literature*
JCTCRS	Jewish and Christian Texts in Contexts and Related Studies
JE	Putative documentary source for the Pentateuch combining textual strands previously identified as Yahwistic and Elohistic
JECS	*Journal of Early Christian Studies*
JSJ	*Journal for the Study of Judaism in the Persian, Hellenistic, and Roman Periods*
JSJSup	Journal for the Study of Judaism: Supplement Series
JSNTSup	Journal for the Study of the New Testament: Supplement Series
JSOT	*Journal for the Study of the Old Testament*
JSOTSup	Journal for the Study of the Old Testament Supplement Series
JSP	*Journal for the Study of the Pseudepigrapha*
KJOTS	*The Korean Journal of Old Testament Studies*
KUSATU	Kleine Untersuchungen zur Sprache des Alten Testaments und seiner Umwelt
LHBOTS	Library of Hebrew Bible/Old Testament Studies
LNTS	Library of New Testament Studies

LSJ	Henry George Liddell, Robert Scott, Henry Stuart Jones. *A Greek-English Lexicon*. 9th ed. With revised supplement. Oxford: Clarendon, 1996
LXX	Septuagint
MT	Masoretic Text
NICOT	New International Commentary on the Old Testament
NT	*Novum Testamentum*
OG	Old Greek version
OL	Old Latin version
OTE	*Old Testament Essays*
OTL	Old Testament Library
P	Putative "Priestly" documentary source for the Pentateuch
PGM	*Papyri graecae magicae: Die griechischen Zauberpapyri*. Edited by K. Preisendanz. Berlin, 1928
RB	*Revue Biblique*
REN	Dougherty, *Records from Erech, Time of Nabonidus*, YBT vol. VI
RevExp	*Review and Expositor*
SAIS	Studies in Aramaic Interpretation of Scripture
SANt	Studia Aarhusiana Neotestamentica
SBLSymS	Society of Biblical Literature Symposium Series
SemeiaSt	Semeia Studies
SJOT	*Scandinavian Journal of the Old Testament*
STDJ	Studies on the Texts of the Desert of Judah
TDOT	*Theological Dictionary of the Old Testament*
Th	Recension of the Septuagint commonly or historically attributed to Theodotion, including the recension of Daniel now referred to as "Proto-Theodotion" in recognition of its earlier date
TPAPA	*Transactions and Proceedings of the American Philological Association*
TTP	Baruch Spinoza, *Tractatus theologico-politicus/Theological-Political Treatise*
USQR	*Union Seminary Quarterly Review*
VT	*Vetus Testamentum*
VTSup	Supplements to Vetus Testamentum
West J Med	*Western Journal of Medicine*
WUNT	Wissenschaftliche Untersuchungen zum Neuen Testament
ZAW	*Zeitschrift für die Alttestamentliche Wissenschaft*

Introduction

Embodied life is at the heart of the Hebrew Bible and Old Testament (HBOT). It is the ground of biblical imagination and of human relationship with one another, God, and nonhuman creation. Even so, modern culture teaches us to denigrate the body. Western tradition has long conceived of body as separate from mind, spirit, or soul and rated it less important, less valuable, even dishonorable and dangerous. As a result, studies of religion, God, the Bible, and spirituality have often distanced themselves from analysis of what we experience in our bodies.

Shaped by such biases, modern biblical scholarship predominantly conceives of prophecy as a verbal phenomenon. Whether through spoken utterance or written text, the prophet is commonly understood as mouthpiece, spokesperson, or messenger for the deity while prophecy is frequently identified with the word or message the prophet conveys at the deity's behest. In this logocentric model of biblical prophecy, words too often float above the body, while the prophet's embodied experience, affect, actions, and interactions function only to authenticate the messenger and illustrate the message they bear.

A focus on words is partially correct. Christian and Jewish scriptural canons preserve what we have come to call *books* of prophetic *literature*. Oracles, sayings, and speech-acts are central to the work of many biblical prophetic figures. Formulas such as "thus says the Lord" and "word of the Lord" yoke together divine and prophetic speech. The importance of words, speech, and communication for understanding the phenomena we call biblical prophecy is undeniable. Yet they are only part of the picture. A near exclusive focus on words divorces word and body, generating a truncated picture of prophetic experience, action, and reception and an incomplete understanding of prophecy.

A turn to the body in biblical studies has prompted growing attention to diverse aspects of embodiment in the study of biblical prophetic literature, supplementing an understanding of prophecy as word and message with consideration of diverse ways prophecy is also embodied. At the forefront of this movement have been studies of gender and sexuality, most recently including queer approaches, studies of masculinity, and intersectional approaches. Others draw on performance theory to interpret prophecy as interactive drama, while still others have identified the body as a site of individual and collective trauma and healing in such prophetic books as Jeremiah and Ezekiel.

While each of these approaches contributes vital insight regarding the body's role in biblical prophecy, a more fully integrative account of prophetic embodiment is still lacking. The present book builds on the pioneering work that has preceded it with the aim of offering such an integrative account. Yet comprehensive treatment of prophetic embodiment exceeds the scope of what one book alone can do. This book is thus the first installment in a planned trilogy on the theme of "Prophecy in the Body." This broader project aims to correct the logocentric bias governing much modern study of biblical prophecy, including the frequent identification of prophecy as utterance or word (whether spoken or written), by analyzing its embodied dimensions. My thesis is that biblical prophecy is a thoroughly embodied phenomenon whose contours emerge most clearly in the complex interplay of embodied experience, affect, inter/action, and reception. In this understanding, word and body are not to be examined as separate categories, but as intertwined and synergistic. This larger project traces an analytical arc from the body of the prophet outward. The present volume begins this task by attending to the history of biblical scholarship and the factors contributing to a persistent, logocentric approach. It then argues for the synergy of word and body and foregrounds the prophetic body as a node of intersection and mediating bridge between God and human, heaven and earth.

These very intersections and mediations mean that the *prophet's* body is not the sole locus of prophetic embodiment. Prophets' embodied experiences and practices of call, vision, transformation, asceticism, ecstasy, mobility, and affect already entail encounter with embodied *others*: God, other supernatural beings, people, nonhuman creation, place. Prophetic embodiment also extends beyond the prophet's body through actions that invite participation, inaugurate new realities, reconfigure relationships, heal, feed, destroy, and actualize divine power and will. Many of these prophetic actions are also interactions, entailing bodily participation on the part of people and even land. This bodily participation extends also to later audiences of prophetic texts, prompting a reframing of audiences' reception as embodied interaction. The categories of experience and affect that are a focus of the present volume overlap considerably with those of action, interaction, and reception. For this reason, the latter are not absent from the present study. Yet sustained attention to embodiment in prophetic action, interaction, and reception will be the focus of the second and third books in the trilogy, on embodied *prophecy* and embodied *reception* of biblical prophecy, respectively. The overlap between analytical categories and the division of subjects across volumes also means that certain topics, such as gender and sexuality, which have been a major focus of recent scholarship on prophetic embodiment, will receive greater attention in these subsequent volumes than they do in the present one. This is not to deny their vital importance for analysis of prophetic embodiment.

The present study undertakes two primary tasks. In Part I (Chapters 1–2), I assess the prevalence, implications, and origins of a logocentric model of biblical prophecy and propose an alternative, embodied paradigm of analysis. Readers less interested in the history of scholarship and history of ideas may prefer to skim this section and focus on subsequent portions of the book. Parts II–IV (Chapters 3–9) focus on the prophetic body, with attention to portrayals of embodied religious experience and practice in diverse texts from the Hebrew Bible and Old Testament. I argue that the body of the prophet is not accidental but rather vital and necessary to the prophet's mediating role. Specifically, the prophet's embodied religious experience, transformations, mobility, and affect are both *means* (how mediation occurs) and *objects* (part of what is mediated) of prophetic mediation.

Chapter 1, "The Buried Body," makes three main moves. First, I argue for the interdependence and even interanimation of prophetic word and body. I analyze the story of the unnamed man of God from Judah and the old prophet of Bethel in 1 Kings 13 as a parable about prophecy that places both word and body at prophecy's center and inseparably links the two. I document recent turns to the body and religious experience in biblical studies and survey previous works of scholarship that have laid the groundwork for analysis of biblical prophecy as an embodied phenomenon. Despite this work, in modern biblical scholarship word has frequently displaced body, producing a logocentric model that views the prophet primarily as mouthpiece of the deity and prophecy as word or message. After analyzing factors within the biblical prophetic corpus that have contributed to this logocentric model, I trace the further influence of a dualistic hierarchy of mind/word and body in the West in both ancient and modern periods. Recognizing this influence makes it possible to develop an alternate, embodied paradigm of analysis, to which I turn in Chapter 2.

The second chapter, "Re-Embodying Biblical Prophecy," delineates the scope, methodology, and guiding assumptions for the remainder of the study. I offer a working definition of biblical prophecy and argue for the multiplicity of its forms, content, and directionality. A survey of biblical Hebrew terms commonly grouped under the broader label "prophet" and the diverse roles associated with them helps to clarify and illustrate the wide range of mediatory roles biblical prophecy entails. I argue that this breadth and diversity of prophetic mediation requires analysis of similarly diverse aspects of embodiment. Treatment of developments in anthropology and the study of embodied cognition delineate contours of the approach I take in subsequent chapters. I conclude this chapter with a methodological caveat regarding the complex relationship between study of religious experience and practice on one hand and study of texts on the other.

Parts II–IV use examples drawn from the Major Prophets, the Book of the Twelve, and narratives about prophets from elsewhere in the HBOT to examine diverse embodied dimensions of prophetic experience, practice, and affect. These range from multi-sensory encounters with God to visionary ecstasy, transport, and a prophetic pedagogy of wonder.

The study of the prophet's embodied religious experience begins in Part II, "Called in the Flesh," in which I analyze four prophetic call stories or commissioning narratives. Chapter 3, "God's Surrogate," examines the third-person commissioning narrative of Moses (Exod 3:1–4:17), while Chapter 4, "First-Person," focuses on the first-person accounts of Isaiah (6:1–13), Jeremiah (1:4–19), and Ezekiel (2:13–3:15). Earlier studies have asserted the function of these narratives to legitimate or authorize prophetic mission, forge bonds of continuity between prophets and their predecessors, and introduce salient themes found elsewhere in the prophetic book. I argue that the embodied encounter between prophet and deity (or other supernatural agents) enables and shapes the prophet's embodied mediation between deity and people. The perceptible signs given to Moses, including the sign of his own transformed body, are guarantee, precursor, and means for performing future acts of power that transform material and social realities. For Isaiah, an array of sensory stimuli, including vision, sound, vibration, and touch, funds a mission that intertwines sensory perception, cognition, and bodily wellness. Jeremiah's painful encounter with God maps the provenance of his prophetic speech from God's body to his own and anticipates his insistence that the people confront their own woundedness. Interembodiment of God and prophet renders the prophet's body a site of encounter and relationship for God and people as well. Ezekiel's seeing mirrors and participates in God's own while inviting the audience to see, evaluate, and act alongside prophet and God. He further assimilates divine judgment into his body, incarnating the sorrow of loss and displacement God has decreed for the people as well as the possibility of their future restoration.

The third-person narration of Moses' commissioning creates distance, establishing the uniqueness of Moses as privileged and archetypal mediator. The multi-sensory first-person commissioning narratives of Isaiah, Jeremiah, and Ezekiel, by contrast, create a sense of immediacy, transporting the audience into the vision, bringing them to the moment of divine encounter to experience it in their own bodies. Where Moses' call recruited the elders of Israel and his brother Aaron, the first-person call stories recruit the audience, engaging the bodies of readers and hearers in activities of embodied reception.

A motif present in multiple prophetic call narratives is bodily transformation: Jeremiah (Jer 1:18–19) and Ezekiel (3:9) experience bodily transformations that, though not visible, are nonetheless efficacious, providing protection, strength, and resilience that equip them for the tasks to which they are appointed. Jeremiah's transformation aligns him with Jerusalem and anticipates its siege, while Ezekiel's makes him a mirror to the people of Judah. By contrast with these transformations, other prophetic bodies are *visibly* altered and marked as other.

Part III, "Transformations," examines two types of bodily transformation, attending in each case to the relationship between the prophet's bodily transformations and prophetic mediation. Chapter 5, "Becoming Other," examines the visible transformations of Moses and Miriam in Exod 34 and Num 12. Prophetic bodies are border bodies, inhabiting but also crossing the boundary between human and divine realms. The contrasting bodily transformations of Moses and Miriam share a striking feature: each is rendered monstrous. Moses' metamorphoses give visible, bodily form to the liminality and power of the prophetic role. His transformed body paradoxically mediates divine power and presence to the people while isolating him from them. The temporary transformation of Miriam similarly evinces her liminality and isolates her from the people. By contrast with Moses, however, her transformation effectively curtails her prophetic power by denying her access to God, people, and place.

A different sort of bodily transformation is the focus of Chapters 6 and 7, which examine three sets of transformative embodied practices and religious experience connected with the role of prophet, namely *askêsis*, incubation, and ecstasy. Embodied practices such as fasting, withdrawal, and incubation; sensory and behavioral triggers such as music and dancing; and even physical proximity to liminal places could each open channels of contact between human and divine realms. Through these practices, experiences, and resulting contact the prophet's body becomes a locus and conduit of divine power and knowledge and mediates relationship across boundaries of being and possibility.

I begin Chapter 6 by revisiting a methodological matter raised at the conclusion of Chapter 2, here articulating a set of methodological assumptions and insights for analysis of textual portrayals of embodied religious experience and practice. I then turn to the transformative bodily disciplines of prophetic *askêsis*. Portrayals of Moses' withdrawal and ascent to Mt. Sinai, fasting, and abstention from water in Exod 19, 24, and 34, and Deut 9 reveal a range of functions for his ascetic practice. Moses' *askêsis* prepares the prophet to receive and transmit revelation, enables him to intercede and atone for the people, and helps to repair broken relationship and covenant commitments between people and God. Although incubation is less clearly attested as a prophetic practice in biblical literature, the stories of Hannah and Samuel in 1 Sam 1–3 preserve key elements of incubatory type-scenes, assigning to both characters a transformative incubatory practice that has implications not only for their own futures but also for Israel's. These narratives portray incubation as a mediatory modality closely related to prophecy that arises at a time of social change to open new prophetic channels and herald new structures of leadership and mediation.

The liminal states produced by *askêsis* and incubation include altered states of consciousness. Such altered states are also a key to the temporary transformations commonly referred to as prophetic ecstasy, the focus of Chapter 7. After reviewing debates about the existence and nature of prophetic ecstasy in the HBOT, I propose a multidisciplinary approach to its study drawn from neurobiology, psychology, anthropology, and religious studies. I then apply this multidisciplinary approach to assess evidence for the portrayal of certain characteristic (but not universal) features of religious ecstasy in prophetic narratives, namely induction techniques and spirit possession. Narrative portrayals of spirit possession in 1 Sam 10 and 19, Ezek 1–3, 8–11, 37, 40–48, and Num 24 map a strong connection between possession and ecstasy. These possessions may result in oracles, visions, and supernatural transport and may produce experiences of physical and/or psychic distress that both accompany and embody the liminality of ecstatic experience. The prophetic body in ecstasy crosses boundaries of behavior, social norms, consciousness, bodily states, time and place, and realms of being to form an experiential, revelatory, and mediating bridge.

The transformations and practices I examine in Part III highlight a key aspect of the prophetic body: it is not static, but dynamic. Part IV, "(E)Motion and Affect," focuses on two types of movement and change that are crucial to the role of prophet: mobility and affect. Chapter 8 examines prophetic mobilities and immobilities. I argue that prophetic experiences of locomotion and transport are not simply prefatory or auxiliary to prophetic mediation but are a key component of prophetic mediation and mission. Prophetic mobility functions in multiple ways, mobilizing the people, inaugurating changes decreed by the deity, and mediating the presence and power of a God who also moves. Prophets' journeys correspond to multilocal missions and can participate in the work of translocal home-making that links communities together. Supernatural transport may enable prophets to overcome bodily, spatial, and temporal limitations and traverse otherwise inaccessible terrain and boundaries. In other instances, external forces may immobilize the prophet to curtail prophetic agency and power. Like prophetic mobility, prophetic immobility also mediates, embodying divine and human inaction and auguring captivity and exile.

The book's final chapters, "Anger and Tears" (Chapter 9) and "Devastation and Wonder" (Chapter 10) argue that affect is integral to what and how a prophet mediates. I first present my understanding of affect, drawn from the work of scholars in the fields of neurocognition, social science, and cultural theory and emphasizing both its embodiment and its social, interactive character. I then examine prophetic affect in four books: Jonah, Jeremiah, Ezekiel, and Daniel. I argue that in Jonah, affect is a site of transformation, tension, freedom, and pedagogy. Jeremiah's discourse constructs the prophet's body as a node of circulating affect and highlights intersubjectivity and affective entanglement among prophet, God, people, and place. Ezekiel's commission places in his body both the anger of God and the sorrow of his people. Both devastated and devastating, his affective practice variously contrasts, mirrors, counteracts, portrays, presages, and shapes those of the people to whom he is sent. Daniel's affective experience and practice of wonder, divine favor, and fortitude help open pathways for the affective transformation, education, and fortification of characters in the narrative and the book's audience. The analysis of affect in Ezekiel and Daniel further illustrates the synergy of word and body. Ezekiel's body incorporates and transports the words of sorrow from heavenly to earthly realms, while the very text of Daniel becomes the medium through which transformative affect is revealed and transmitted.

The body of the prophet is not incidental or ancillary to the work of prophetic mediation, nor is it an impediment. It is a primary locus of prophetic experience and activity and a crucial means of mediation. Prophetic word and body are not binary opposites. They operate in synergy. Studies of biblical prophecy have long focused on the prophetic word. A more integrated understanding of biblical prophecy widens the focus to include the prophetic body.

Scope and Terminology

The primary sources studied in this book include portrayals of prophets throughout the canons variously identified among Jews and Christians as TaNaK, Hebrew Bible, and Old Testament. These portrayals span material from the Torah or Pentateuch and Nebi'im or Prophets, including the books commonly identified as "Former Prophets" or "Historical Books" and those designated as belonging to the "Latter Prophets." I also consider some material from the Ketubim, or Writings. Among the former prophets or historical books, I give particular attention to narratives in Judges, 1 and 2 Samuel, and 1 and 2 Kings. The Latter Prophets, meanwhile, include in the Hebrew Bible or TaNaK the scrolls of Isaiah, Jeremiah, Ezekiel, and the Book of the Twelve. Christian canons also include the book of Daniel among the prophetic books. For Catholic and Orthodox Christians, moreover, the form of Daniel contained within this corpus reflects a longer Greek text that includes portions commonly regarded by Protestants as apocryphal and by Jews as "outside" the Bible. Where appropriate, I include both Hebrew-and-Aramaic and Greek forms of the book of Daniel in my analyses, but owing to its ambiguous status, I refrain from extrapolating from insights from Daniel to claims about biblical prophecy as a whole.

The diverse canons named above share much in common, but are also quite different from one another, a reality that makes it difficult to find language that accurately and sensitively names the sets of texts under consideration or the wider canonical formations in which they were collected and preserved by Jewish and Christian users. The terminology of Hebrew Bible, for example, elides the presence of Aramaic portions in the book of Daniel and excludes the Greek versions, including such texts as the longer form of

Daniel mentioned above. While TaNaK avoids reference to the language(s) in which the text has been preserved, handed down, and used, it, too, excludes ancient Greek versions and the additional materials they contain.

The common Christian designation "Old Testament," meanwhile, has different referents for different Christian groups, some including only the books contained in the TaNaK, others including a longer list of books contained in some ancient Greek versions, others including still longer lists of books. Beyond this lack of a common referent, the phrase "Old Testament" has been widely recognized as perpetuating negative, supersessionist valuations of ancient Jewish texts. While that which is "old" is sometimes seen as more valuable, in Western cultures it is more commonly associated with being out-of-date, past one's prime, less vital, and less relevant to the present situation. What is old is often viewed as safe (or at least easy) to ignore, as newer generations, models, styles, and ways of thinking and behaving come to replace the ones that have come before. The seemingly contrastive pairing of "Old Testament" and "New Testament" has frequently communicated to Christian believers that the material that matters is predominantly contained in the latter corpus of texts. While the alternate designations "First Testament" and "Second Testament" help to relieve this contrast and sidestep the valuations conveyed by the adjectives "Old" and "New," they have not gained broad traction, and they continue to assert a Christian framework for studying scriptures that are historically Jewish and that have been shared among diverse religious groups.

To navigate this complex terrain, I adopt two locutions, each an imperfect compromise. One is the phrase "biblical literature," the other is the compound "Hebrew Bible and Old Testament," abbreviated HBOT. The first phrase is itself not unproblematic. The adjective "biblical," like the noun "Bible," does not accurately name the way these texts circulated or functioned in their earliest contexts. Rather, these terms arose to describe the collections of texts bound together in codices through new Roman-era book-binding technologies that developed around the first century CE. The terms "biblical" and "Bible" further convey a "canonical consciousness" that has been subject to significant critique among those who study ancient Jewish literature. With these caveats in view, I acknowledge, however, that my own book intentionally enters into conversation with modern users of these texts who have very often engaged these texts as constitutive parts of a collection called "Bible," variously understood. I thus seek in part to locate this book's argument in relation to modern discourses in which these sets of texts have been interpreted by communities of users as collective, authoritative, scriptural witnesses. The stakes involved in interpreting such texts are high. The imprecise but highly charged designation "biblical" thus alludes to this contested history of use in hopes of reshaping modern approaches to the understanding of prophecy as portrayed in these texts. Finally, the abbreviation HBOT engages in similar work while attempting to hold in tension the multiplicity of overlapping canonical collections and different ways that scholars engage with them.

Terms for the region(s) under study pose challenges as well. It has long been conventional in biblical studies and adjacent fields to describe the geographical and cultural scope of study with reference to the "ancient near East." At the same time, scholars increasingly recognize that this terminology is both rooted in and perpetuates an orientalist framework tied to western imperialism, colonialism, and attendant attitudes toward semitic peoples and others who have historically inhabited these regions. The field has not yet achieved consensus on geographic terminology nor even universal acknowledgment of the problems associated with such orientalizing labels. Any solution adopted in the present moment must therefore be provisional. In lieu of "ancient near East," I have chosen in this book to use the phrase "ancient West Asia."

Terminology for the immediate geographic and cultural context of the HBOT is challenging for a different reason. Depending on period and locale, the region, polity, or population group in view might variously be identified as Israel, Judah, Yehud, or Judea. Some authors opt to use the modifier "Israelite" for the corpus as a whole. While this usage does not always conform with that of the sources in view, some form of shorthand is necessary. When referring to a broad swath of source materials, I adopt the locutions "Israel and Judah" and "Israelite and Judean" to refer to the range of contexts and population groups with which these texts are associated.

Gendered Pronouns

In my own writing, I typically avoid gendered pronouns for God.[1] Where a gendered portrayal of the deity is relevant to the analysis of prophetic

---

[1] Several studies have examined ways that the portrayal or assumption of divine masculinity in biblical prophetic literature shapes the portrayal of prophetic embodiment. See, e.g., Graybill, *Are We Not Men*; Carvalho, "Whose Gendered Language of God?"; Carvalho, "Sex and the Single Prophet." For the argument that divine (and correlatively prophetic) speech substitutes for a gendered divine body, see Eilberg-Schwartz, "Problem of the Body," 49–50. For a recent treatment of "gendered god-language" that produces both male and female images of God in the prophetic literature, see Løland Levinson, "Never-Ending Search."

embodiment, I acknowledge this. In the case of human and angelic subjects as well as personified aspects of the natural world, when a gender-inclusive or gender-neutral pronoun is needed, I have often chosen to use the pronouns "they/them/theirs," which may represent plural or singular antecedents.

Translations

Unattributed translations are the author's own.

PART I
AN EMBODIED PARADIGM

1

The Buried Body

"Nothing was beyond his power; and from where he lay buried, his body prophesied" (Sir 48:13 NABRE).[1]

"May the bones of the Twelve Prophets send forth new life from where they lie, for they comforted the people of Jacob and delivered them with confident hope" (Sir 49:10 NRSV).[2]

Word and Body: A Parable (1 Kings 13)

First Kings 13 spins a tale of two unnamed men, one a Judahite "man of God" (איש אלהים), the other "a certain old prophet" (נביא אחד זקן) living in Bethel. W. Boyd Barrick has suggested that this tale be read as a parable.[3] Taking up this suggestion, I read it here as a parable about the embodiment of biblical prophecy.[4] I argue that this story about prophets and prophecy is simultaneously about the word and the body, helping us begin to perceive the multiple ways that biblical prophecy is not simply a matter of words, but is always also a matter of matter, always also in the body.

Throughout the story, word and body are intertwined. The man of God came from Judah to Bethel "by the word of the LORD" and proclaimed

---

[1] Hebrew: ומתחתיו נב[י]א בשרו; LXX: καὶ ἐν κοιμήσει ἐπροφήτευσεν τὸ σῶμα αὐτοῦ.
[2] Hebrew: וגם שנים עשר הנביאים תהי עצמתם פר[ח]ת מתח[תם אשר החלימו את־יעקב וישעוהו בא[מונת תקוה];
LXX: καὶ τῶν δώδεκα προφητῶν τὰ ὀστᾶ ἀναθάλοι ἐκ τοῦ τόπου αὐτῶν παρεκάλεσαν γὰρ τὸν Ιακωβ καὶ ἐλυτρώσαντο αὐτοὺς ἐν πίστει ἐλπίδος.
[3] Barrick, *King and Cemeteries*, 52. Barrick defines a parable as "a short didactic tale with two or more intended levels of meaning" (*King and Cemeteries*, 52). For one example of reading the story as parable, see Bosworth, "Revisiting Karl Barth's Exegesis," who argues that the relationship between the man of God and the old prophet mirrors that between Judah and Israel through multiple stages of their histories.
[4] This is not a claim about *the* key theme of the text. For Noth (*Könige*), the story is about the rejection of the cult at Bethel. For Hens-Piazza, "The role of the man of God is really secondary to this tale, a story that is about Jeroboam and his reign" (*1–2 Kings*, 138). Similarly, for Yoon, "the theme of the narrative is the certainty of God's judgment on the house (or dynasty) of Jeroboam" (*Fate of the Man of God*, 3). By contrast, Dozeman isolates a pre-Deuteronomic layer of which "the unifying theme . . .

4 THE PROPHETIC BODY

against the altar at Bethel at the very moment when king Jeroboam was offering sacrifice upon it (1 Kgs 13:1). When the king sent forth his own hand from the altar toward the man of God, commanding his officers to grab hold of the man's body, the king's hand dried up, so that he could not "return it to himself" (v. 4). The king later asked the man of God to intercede for his healing. The man of God prayed, and the king's hand was restored to him (v. 6).

Now, because of a command issued "by the word of the Lord" (בדבר יהוה 13:9; cf. 13:17, 18), the man of God refused an offer of royal food and water and began his journey home (13:9–10). But when an old prophet in Bethel heard about "every deed the man of God had done" and "the words he spoke" (v. 11), he went to find the man of God and offered him food and drink, deceiving him into thinking the word of the LORD had been instrumental in the issuing of revised instructions for the mission of the man of God (vv. 14–19). After the man of God accepted the prophet's hospitality, the old prophet from Bethel did indeed add a new detail to the instructions the man of God had originally received: by eating and drinking in Bethel, the man of God did not keep the Lord's commandment, and therefore, declared the prophet, "your body [Hebrew נבלה, Greek σῶμα] shall not come to your ancestral tomb" (v. 22 NRSV).

The body, or in Hebrew, more literally, the corpse, of the man of God is mentioned—rather pointedly—nine more times in the remainder of this unusual narrative. When a lion meets the man of God on the road and kills him, the man's body is thrown in the road; a borrowed donkey and the executing lion each stand next to the body (v. 24). People pass and see the body (v. 25). The prophet finds the body, with the donkey and the lion still standing beside the body (v. 28). The lion does not eat the body (or the donkey) (v. 28). The prophet lifts the body (v. 29) and finally lays the body to rest in his own grave (v. 30), mourning him as a brother and declaring "when I die, bury me in the grave in which the man of God is buried; lay my bones beside his bones. For the word that he proclaimed by the word of the LORD against the altar in Bethel . . . shall surely come to pass" (vv. 31–32, adapted from the NRSV).

The absence of names in this story suggests in part that the two men are representative of the set(s) or group(s) their role labels name. At the same time, their differing role labels "man of God" and "prophet" appear not so

---

is true and false prophecy" ("Way of the Man of God"). For an earlier treatment of the latter theme see Crenshaw, *Prophetic Conflict*, 39–62.

much to highlight a difference in prescribed role as allow readers to distinguish one character from the other.[5] The old prophet in Bethel asserts their shared role and status when he tells the Judahite man of God, "I too am a prophet like you"; the man of God finds the prophet's claim persuasive (13:18). This commonality suggests that, in their intersecting stories, both man of God and prophet reveal to us something about the narrator's understandings or constructions of the phenomenon we call "prophecy" and the social and religious role we call "prophet."[6]

As we investigate the portrayal of this phenomenon and role, four sets of repetitions reveal an interwoven thematic focus for the story.[7] The first set of repetitions highlights divine speech. The passage repeats the phrase "the word of the LORD" (דבר יהוה) more than does any other passage in the Hebrew Bible, totaling nine occurrences in a story that spans thirty-two verses (13:1, 2, 5, 9, 17, 18, 20, 26, 32).[8] The similar phrase "the mouth of the LORD" occurs twice in the narrative as metonymy for divine commandment and authority (vv. 21 and 26).[9] In addition to these two noun phrases, the story emphasizes divine and prophetic speech through a series of verbs that make repeated reference to the LORD's speaking (v. 3, 21, 26), the man of God's and the prophet's "proclaiming" or "crying out" (קרא vv. 2, 4, 21, 32), and even the speaking of an angel (v. 18). Together these repetitions highlight for the reader the centrality of "word" and "speech" in prophetic

---

[5] As the story progresses, the man of God and prophet acquire longer, descriptive titles that refer back to their actions in the narrative. The man of God becomes the "man of God who rebelled" (v. 26), the old prophet becomes "the prophet who turned him" (v. 23). See further Dozeman, "Way of the Man of God," 389.

[6] Cf. Wilson, *Prophecy and Society*, 140: "In the biblical traditions that have been preserved, the man of God is synonymous with the prophet (*nābî*) and in fact both titles are sometimes applied to the same individual ... It is possible that the characteristics of the man of God were originally different from those of the prophet, and the two titles may have been used in different geographical areas, but it is now impossible to separate the two figures."

[7] Simon observes that "lengthy repetitions ... distinguish 1 Kings 13 from similar scriptural tales" (*Reading Prophetic Narratives*, 132). Dozeman's analysis similarly recognizes the importance of these repetitions as rhetorical features that unify the tale ("Way of the Man of God," 382–3, 386–7).

[8] In 1 Kings, the phrase דבר יהוה is repeated five times in ch. 17 (vv. 2, 5, 8, 16, 24) and four times in ch. 16 (1, 7, 12, 34). Outside of 1 Kings, the phrase occurs five times in Ezek 12 (vv. 1, 8, 17, 21, 26) and four times in Jer 32 (vv. 6, 8 [x2], 26). A related noun phrase, נאם־יהוה (variously translated "oracle of the LORD" NAB; "says the LORD" NRSV; "declares the LORD" NJPS), does not appear in 1 Kings (see, however, 2 Kgs 9:26; 19:33; 22:19). This phrase occurs 167 times within the book of Jeremiah, with seventeen occurrences in ch. 23, fourteen in ch. 31, and eleven in ch. 49. Haggai 2 combines three instances of "word of the LORD" with ten instances of "oracle of the LORD." Far less common in the Hebrew Bible is the phrase "the word of God" (occurring only five times, with and without definite article: דבר אלהים and דבר האלהים; in three of these instances LXX renders אלהים with κυρίου: 1 Kgs 12:22; 1 Chr 17:3; 26:32).

[9] This phrase is favored in the book of Numbers and commonly refers to divine speech that entails commandment or instruction.

6 THE PROPHETIC BODY

experience, action, and interaction. Given this density of repetition, some scholars have focused on the prominence of the "word of the Lord" in the story. For Kenneth Way the word is "the central theme of the story."[10] Uriel Simon argues that the word is the story's "real hero," "possessing an autonomous existence"; it is "a powerful entity that imposes itself on reality."[11]

An understanding of the story's thematic focus becomes more complicated, however, when we attend to the narrative's other repetitions and their relationship to this first set of repetitions. In a second set of repetitions, the word of the Lord is closely linked to the movements and actions of the man of God and the prophet. Forms of the verbs of motion and conveyance "to go" or "walk" (הלך) occur ten times, "to come" (בוא) twelve times, and "to turn" or "return" (שוב) sixteen times.[12] Granted, these are common words, but there's a lot of movement in this story. Of these thirty-eight occurrences, the man of God is the subject of twenty-two (his dead body is the subject of an additional occurrence), and the old prophet is the subject of eight. Of the latter set, the man of God is the direct object of four, his dead body one. Repeatedly, the command issued by means of "the word" inhibits the man of God from walking or going one route (vv. 9, 16–17) and motivates his going by another (v. 10). Moreover, unusual syntax links the motion of the man of God to the word from the story's beginning, for he "came from Judah to Bethel by [or "in"] the word of the Lord" (v. 1). That is, the divine word is instrumental in or constitutes the modality not only of his speaking (v. 2) but also of his moving (v. 1).

A third set of repetitions further links the divine word to the body of the man of God. The verb-pair "eat" (אכל) and "drink" (שתה) occurs eight times in the narrative (vv. 8, 9, 16, 17, 18, 19, 22, 23), with the verb "eat" repeated two additional times on its own (vv. 15, 28). In each instance but one (v. 28), the man of God is the subject, and the question of his eating or drinking hinges upon the word of the Lord. In the final instance of the verb "to eat," he is no longer the subject (nor living), but remains closely linked to the action, as he is now its direct object (v. 28).

Finally, I noted above that the word נבלה (variously translated into English as "body," "corpse," or "carcass"; rendered in the Old Greek versions of this

---

[10] Way, "Animals in the Prophetic World," 54.

[11] Simon, *Reading Prophetic Narratives*, 136, 150–1. For Simon, the relation between word and prophet is that the word depends "on human messengers." This human dimension also reveals the word's "earthliness" (*Reading Prophetic Narratives*, 150).

[12] הלך: 13:9, 10, 12 [x2], 14, 15, 17 [x2], 24, 28; בוא: 13:1, 7, 8, 10, 11, 12, 14, 16, 21, 22, 25, 29; שוב: 13:4, 6 [x2], 9, 10, 16, 17, 18, 19, 20, 22, 23, 26, 29, 33 [x2].

passage as σῶμα), referring to the dead body of the man of God, occurs ten times in the story.[13] While the man of God is alive, this body is untouchable. When a king dares stretch his hand against it, the king's hand withers. The man of God's body is not to be touched even by the food and water of Bethel. After his death a lion and donkey stood together to guard his body; a prophet sought it, lifted it, and gave it rest; and the same prophet commanded his own bones to be buried beside the bones of this man of God. Three centuries later, even as king Josiah desecrated graves and burned the bones of the dead, Josiah would command that none disturb the bones of the man of God nor of the prophet buried beside him (2 Kgs 23:18).[14]

Interpretations of this passage that focus on the prophetic word are not mistaken to do so. The story thematizes the word of the LORD and begins and ends with pointed references to the proclamation of the man of God. For the prophet, however, the reputation of the man of God was established not by word alone, but by word and deed together (13:11). His concluding assertion that "the word which [the man of God] proclaimed ... will surely come to pass" (v. 32) similarly yokes prophetic word to the prophetic body, not merely by expecting the word to be efficacious, but by linking this expectation to the joining of their bones.

Separately from the wider narrative, it would be possible to explain some of the story's repetitions in terms of discrete, symbolic meanings. For example, the man of God's eating could be analyzed in relation to obedience, walking and turning could be explicated as metaphors for ethical conduct in relationship with God, and care for his body could indicate respect for his office.[15] But even in the face of such explanations, the dense interweaving of verbal repetition and embodied detail continually draws attention back to the body of the man of God.[16] That is, while the word of the Lord animates the story's

---

[13] Dozeman ("Way of the Man of God," 390) argues that this repetition highlights the "folly" (נבלה) of Israel. The latter term, however, is not used in the story.

[14] Compare the attention in this story to the bones and grave of these two prophets to the story of the bones and grave of Elisha in 2 Kgs 13:21: the bones of the prophet Elisha restore life to a man whose dead body is thrown into Elisha's grave.

[15] Regarding obedience, Hens-Piazza similarly observes, "Taken on its own apart from the larger narrative, this peculiar little scene invites us to fix upon the consequences of obedience and disobedience" (*1–2 Kings*, 135). Based on the structure of the passage as a whole, she argues against obedience as a primary focus (*1–2 Kings*, 135, 137–8). Regarding care for his body and the collocation of bones, this explanation would be consistent with his lament for "my brother" (v. 30). Simon argues that the old prophet's burial of the man of God "reflects reverence and awe for the man with whose life and death such mighty portents were associated" but also is motivated by a selfish desire for future protection (*Reading Prophetic Narratives*, 145).

[16] Dozeman recognizes that the dead body is not *other than* the man of God. The prophet declares that they are one and the same ("Way of the Man of God," 391).

action and speech, the man of God's body is the center around which the story's component parts revolve. Taken together, these four sets of repetitions highlight two interrelated thematic foci: word and body. If we take this story, at one level, as a parable about the phenomenon of prophecy, it would tell us this: prophecy is not a strictly verbal phenomenon. In prophecy, word and body meet, interact, and interanimate one another.

Modern Biblical Scholarship

(Re)Centering the Body

Recent decades have witnessed an explosion of interest in embodiment in biblical prophetic literature, helping to recenter the body in contemporary understandings of prophecy. Two shifts in biblical studies have paved the way to bring such theoretical approaches to the study of biblical prophecy: a turn to the body and a (re)turn to experience. Biblical studies have in the past two decades participated in a turn to the body, characterized by engagement with a broad range of theoretical, philosophical, and social scientific discourses in the reevaluation of ancient texts, artifacts, and iconography.[17] Increasingly, this work has moved beyond an early, primary focus on gender and sexuality to encompass such topics as divine embodiment,[18] disability studies,[19] sensory criticism,[20] trauma studies,[21] embodied cognition,[22] and emotion and affect.[23] Second, a dominant emphasis on textuality within

---

[17] In the area of iconography, see, e.g., Schroer and Staubli, *Body Symbolism*.

[18] Hamori, "*When Gods Were Men*"; Kamionkowski and Kim, eds., *Bodies, Embodiment, and Theology*; Smith, *Where the Gods Are*; Sommer, *Bodies of God*; Wagner, *God's Body*; Wilson, *Embodied God*.

[19] Avalos, Melcher, and Schipper, eds., *This Abled Body*; Lawrence, *Sense and Stigma*; Moss and Baden, *Reconceiving Infertility*; Moss and Schipper, eds., *Disability Studies and Biblical Literature*; Olyan, *Disability in the Hebrew Bible*; Raphael, *Biblical Corpora*; Schipper, *Disability Studies and the Hebrew Bible*; Schipper, *Disability and Isaiah's Suffering Servant*; Solevåg, *Negotiating the Disabled Body*.

[20] Avalos, "Introducing Sensory Criticism"; Avrahami, *Senses of Scripture*; Lee, ed., *Sound Matters*; Schellenberg and Krüger, eds., *Sounding Sensory Profiles*; Tilford, *Sensing World*.

[21] Becker, Dochhorn, and Holt, eds., *Trauma and Traumatization*; Boase and Frechette, eds., *Bible through the Lens of Trauma*; Carr, *Holy Resilience*.

[22] Czachesz, *Cognitive Science*; Eastman, *Paul and the Person*; Newman, *Before the Bible*; Nikolsky et al., eds., *Language, Cognition, and Biblical Exegesis*; Shantz, *Paul in Ecstasy*; Thaden, *Sex, Christ, and Embodied Cognition*.

[23] Anderson, *Time to Mourn*; Black and Koosed, eds., *Reading with Feeling*; Egger-Wenzel and Corley, eds., *Emotions from Ben Sira to Paul*; Grant, *Divine Anger*; Kazen, *Emotions in Biblical Law*; Mirguet, *Early History of Compassion*; Kotrosits, "How Things Feel"; Mirguet and Kurek-Chomycz,

the field of biblical studies has recently begun to be counterbalanced by a renewed and critically refined attention to religious experience in antiquity, including experiences portrayed within extant texts and those "behind" and "in front of" those texts.[24] With this shift, space has increasingly opened for critical analysis that acknowledges the complex, dynamic, and pluriform interactions between texts and experiences, including significant attention to the role of the body.

These two developments in biblical studies, the turn to the body and a (re)turn to experience, prompt and make possible a textured analysis of diverse aspects of embodiment in relation to biblical prophecy. Numerous scholars have already begun to do just this.

As noted previously, studies of gender and sexuality were among the first to insist on the importance of the body for biblical interpretation.[25] Feminist and womanist interpreters have thus been at the forefront of studies of embodiment in prophetic literature.[26] The studies of Wilda Gafney on women prophets and Esther Hamori on women's divination frequently bring embodiment to the fore.[27] Others have broadened the focus of gender criticism to include masculinity studies and queer approaches.[28] Two among these who place the body at the center of analysis are Amy Kalmanofsky and Rhiannon Graybill. Kalmanofsky's studies of Isaiah, Jeremiah, and Ezekiel combine a range of postmodern approaches including analysis of gender and horror.[29]

---

eds., *Emotions in Ancient Jewish Literature*; Moore, *The Bible after Deleuze*; Reif and Egger-Wenzel, eds., *Ancient Jewish Prayers and Emotions*; Schlimm, *From Fratricide to Forgiveness*; Spencer, ed., *Mixed Feelings and Vexed Passions*; Thomas, *Anatomical Idiom and Emotional Expression*; Wagner, *Emotionen, Gefühle und Sprache*.

[24] An early example is Johnson, *Religious Experience in Earliest Christianity*. The Society of Biblical Literature's Religious Experience Group has been a seedbed for this work. The group has published two edited volumes: Flannery, Shantz, and Werline, eds., *Experientia*, vol. 1; and Shantz and Werline, eds., *Experientia*, vol. 2. Other relevant work produced by members of this group includes Boda, Falk, and Werline, eds., *Seeking the Favor of God*, 3 vols.; Newman, "Embodied Techniques." For a survey of this approach in New Testament Studies in the early twenty-first century, see Batluck, "Religious Experience." For treatment of this approach more broadly within religious studies, see Martin and McCutcheon, eds., *Religious Experience: A Reader*; Schmidt, ed., *Study of Religious Experience*; Taves, *Religious Experience Reconsidered*.

[25] This pattern is not limited to biblical studies. See discussion in Bynum, "Why All the Fuss."

[26] E.g., Fischer and Claassens, eds., *Prophetie*; Keefe, *Woman's Body*; Maier and Sharp, eds., *Prophecy and Power*; Weems, *Battered Love*. For an overview, see Bridgeman, "Womanist Approaches"; Maier, "Feminist Interpretation," esp. 474–6.

[27] Gafney, *Daughters of Miriam*; Hamori, *Women's Divination*.

[28] See, e.g., Asikainen, "Masculinity of Jeremiah"; Macwilliam, *Queer Theory*; Stökl and Carvalho, eds., *Prophets Male and Female*; Williams, "Queer Readings"; and the commentary essays on the prophetic books in Guest et al., eds., *Queer Bible Commentary*.

[29] E.g., Kalmanofsky, "Israel's Open Sore"; Kalmanofsky, *Terror All Around*.

She explores a variety of ways that prophets "embod[y] the divine word" and participate in "physical and intimate relationship with God."[30] For Graybill, "the body is essential to prophecy."[31] Viewing prophecy as "embodied practice," she asks readers to resist the impulse to focus on "the meaning" of a prophetic action, and instead "remain with the ... body."[32] She argues that, in the Hebrew Bible, prophetic bodies perform an "unstable masculinity" that correlates with disruptions inherent in the prophetic role. Adapting Sara Ahmed's queer phenomenology, Graybill reads prophetic bodies as queer bodies that bring into contact persons, things, and categories otherwise kept apart.

Another significant development in the study of biblical prophetic literature is the use of trauma theory. Advances in scientific understandings of the body's response to trauma combined with new approaches to the study of collective trauma have furnished a range of insights into the context of biblical prophetic literature and the ways it both reflects trauma and functions to help audiences cope with trauma. Two examples include Kathleen O'Connor's use of trauma as a lens for analyzing the book of Jeremiah and Ruth Poser's analysis of the book of Ezekiel as trauma narrative.[33] In a similar vein, Louis Stulman examines the function of prophetic literature both as "disaster literature" and "survival literature." He argues that prophetic word and action operate synergistically to help communities do difficult grief work in the face of loss.[34] Trauma studies help clarify the role of the body in storing and processing memory and similarly highlight the body's importance to the work of healing hidden wounds, for individuals and communities alike. Mary Mills uses a wider and more eclectic theoretical framework to examine the mediating function of prophetic otherness and suffering, constructing a narrative ethics that takes seriously the prophetic body's pain. She finds in "the bodily distortions and pains of the prophetic human being ... the realization of divine speech."[35]

Other scholars have focused on prophecy as performance, attending to such features as setting, characters, audience, and interaction. David Stacey surveys a wide range of prophetic action under the heading of drama, concluding that "prophetic action was essentially the unveiling of an unseen or unrecognized reality" and bore a strong mimetic relationship to the

---

[30] Kalmanofsky, "Postmodern Engagements," 565.
[31] Graybill, *Are We Not Men*, 5
[32] Graybill, *Are We Not Men*, 3, 5.
[33] O'Connor, *Jeremiah: Pain and Promise*; Poser, *Ezechielbuch als Trauma-Literatur*.
[34] Stulman, "Survival Literature."
[35] Mills, *Alterity, Pain, and Suffering*, 9.

actions attributed to the deity or their consequences.[36] William Doan and Terry Giles map a relationship between prophetic and scribal performances, arguing that prophetic literature "preserve[s]" and "abstract[s]" prophetic actions.[37] Traces of a "performance mode of thought" characteristic of oral discourse thus lie "embedded" within the text and continue to engage readers at an imaginative level.[38] Jeanette Mathews applies a similar lens to the study of Habakkuk, noting that "performance theory emphasizes embodiment in all modes of prophetic communication by drawing attention to the whole communication event, not just the words."[39] She asserts a close link between word and action, whether those of the deity, prophet, or audience. Johanna Erzberger's study of prophetic sign-acts, meanwhile, draws on study of modern performance art to highlight the structural relationship between prophet, audience, and context, asserting the importance of spatial, temporal, and social setting and embodied interaction for interpreting prophetic actions.[40] Scholars such as Yvonne Sherwood, Mark Brummitt, and Teresa Hornsby have deployed postmodern and poststructuralist understandings of performance art in their studies of Hosea's, Jeremiah's, and Ezekiel's narrated actions to illuminate the blurring of text and action as well as a subversive capacity of prophetic performance to "circumvent the linguistic."[41]

Finally, scholars focusing on ancient religious experience have brought a range of neurocognitive and sensory critical methods to the study of prophetic dreams and visions. Frances Flannery has argued for "mov[ing] bodies from the periphery to the center of studies on *ancient* religious experience" (italics original), identifying the body as a key "site of religious experience," including that of visionaries and seers.[42] Rodney Werline argues for expanding notions of prophetic experience beyond that of prophetic ecstasy. He considers as one example the prophetic technique of deriving insight by observing ordinary objects, and argues that prophetic symbolic actions invited audiences to participate in a similar revelatory technique.[43] Angela

---

[36] Stacey, *Prophetic Drama*, 223–4.
[37] Doan and Giles, *Prophets, Performance, and Power*, 17.
[38] Doan and Giles, *Prophets, Performance, and Power*, 5.
[39] Mathews, *Performing Habakkuk*, 19–20.
[40] Erzberger, "Prophetic Sign Acts as Performances."
[41] Brummitt, "Broken Pots"; Hornsby, "Ezekiel Off-Broadway." Quoted phrase is from Hornsby, "Ezekiel Off-Broadway," 1. See further the other essays in Sherwood, ed., "Prophetic Performance Art"; Sherwood, "Prophetic Scatology"; Sherwood, *Prostitute and Prophet*.
[42] Flannery, "Body and Ritual," 15–16. See further Flannery-Dailey, *Dreamers, Scribes, and Priests*; Flannery, "Esoteric Mystical Practice."
[43] Werline, "Assessing the Prophetic Vision," 11–12.

Kim Harkins theorizes that the performance of hymns at Qumran, including a richly embodied set of affective practices, was a technique for achieving visionary experience.[44] While Harkins' focus is not on the biblical prophetic literature, her methodology has proved fruitful for the present study.

This brief survey reveals that what I undertake in this book, and will continue in the volumes to follow, is not entirely new. It builds on the previous work of numerous scholars who have pushed boundaries and challenged conventional approaches through an emphasis on varied aspects of embodiment in biblical prophecy.

From a Word-Centered Approach to an Integrative Approach

Despite this diverse and groundbreaking work on embodiment, a logocentric model of biblical prophecy persists. The reasons for this are many. They include the enduring influences of mind-body dualism and colonialism, factors I discuss in further detail later in this chapter and in Chapter 2. A result is that while scholars using a broad range of methodologies increasingly affirm the body's importance to biblical prophecy, definitional understandings of *what prophecy is* have continued to privilege the written and spoken word, such that in scholarship where embodiment is not explicitly made a central category of analysis, the body is frequently relegated to a supporting but subordinate role. This is not to say it is absent. Even approaches that regard prophecy as a primarily verbal phenomenon frequently contain the seeds of a more integrative approach.

General treatments of biblical prophecy commonly define prophecy as a message, communication, or utterance in which the prophet mediates, reports, or proclaims the word of a deity to an intended audience.[45] Such a definitional emphasis on "message" produces a prophet who is understood

---

[44] Harkins, *Reading with an "I"*.

[45] An influential definition by Weippert places strong emphasis on cognition, consciousness, and communication of content: "Prophecy is present when a person (a) through cognitive experience (a vision, an auditory experience, an audio-visual appearance, a dream or the like) becomes the subject of the revelation of a deity, or several deities and, in addition, (b) is conscious of being commissioned by the deity or deities in question to convey the revelation in a verbal form (as a "prophecy" or a "prophetic speech") or through nonverbal communicative acts ("symbolic acts"), to a third party who constitutes the actual addressee of the message" (Weippert, "Prophetie im alten Orient," cited and translated in Nissinen, *Prophetic Divination*, 57). This definition recognizes embodied aspects of receiving revelation and communicating it to others and draws attention to interactive dimensions of prophecy. Yet explicitly embodied aspects of prophecy are grammatically presented as instrumental, and therefore accidental or extrinsic to the phenomenon, rather than intrinsic to its reality.

primarily as a messenger or spokesperson who mediates knowledge through acts of verbal communication.[46] Other aspects of prophetic experience, action, and interaction are sometimes included in such definitions but subordinated to the word or message.[47] Embodied aspects of prophetic experience, action, and performance nonetheless frequently play a significant role in accompanying analyses, suggesting avenues for a more integrative approach. For example, a recent treatment by Martti Nissinen which advances a definition of prophecy as message nonetheless calls attention to social performance and distinguishes between oral prophecy, written records of oral prophecy, and "literary prophecy," noting that many written prophetic texts are secondary to temporally, phenomenologically, or conceptually prior prophetic performance.[48] This category of performance helps to tease out some of prophecy's embodied dimensions. Nissinen further draws attention to such embodied dimensions of prophetic identity, experience, and practice as gender and ecstasy, and identifies for prophecy not only a "transmissive function" but also a "transformative" one.[49] These aspects of Nissinen's work underscore the importance of the body for understanding biblical prophecy.[50] In a similar vein, Walter Brueggemann locates prophecy's socially transformative power primarily "in the act of utterance."[51] Yet he also highlights a relationship between imagination and action.[52] Prophetic voice, utterance, and text reshape imagination and consciousness. [53] From these proceed action that can, secondarily, also be called prophetic.[54] Ellen Davis

---

[46] Nissinen writes, "What makes a prophet different from others is that he or she is believed to have the capacity of acting as the mouthpiece of God, in whatever manner or position" (*Prophetic Divination*, 60). A similar understanding emerges in Stökl, *Prophecy in the Ancient Near East*, where he refers to prophets' role as "speaking for a deity" (1; see also 97, 152), "messengers" (157), and "spokesperson" (229). For Stökl (*Prophecy in the Ancient Near East*, 10), prophets belong (with dreamers) to the category "intuitive [as opposed to technical] diviner," meaning one "who receives his/her messages from a deity without there being any need for a (learned) skill in interpreting the messages." The messages they receive are not for themselves, but for others.

[47] E.g., building on Weippert's definition, Nissinen identifies a "consensus among biblical and ancient Near Eastern scholars" that prophecy refers to the "intermediation of divine knowledge by nontechnical means" and is a "process of communication" with four components: 1) "sender of the message"; 2) "the message, together with its verbal or symbolic performance"; 3) "the prophet," who is "transmitter of the message"; and 4) "the recipient(s) of the message" (Nissinen, "Prophetic Intermediation," 5; see also Nissinen, *Ancient Prophecy*, 13–14, 22–3). See further Nissinen, "Prophetic Intermediation," 14.

[48] Nissinen, *Ancient Prophecy*, 13–14.

[49] Nissinen, "Prophetic Madness"; on gender, see Nissinen, *Ancient Prophecy*, 297–325; "transmissive" and "transformative" functions: Nissinen, *Ancient Prophecy*, 305.

[50] See also Nissinen and Stavrakopoulou, "Introduction: New Perspectives."

[51] Brueggemann, *Prophetic Imagination*, x.

[52] Brueggemann, *Prophetic Imagination*, xx–xxi.

[53] Brueggemann, *Prophetic Imagination*, 7 and 65.

[54] Brueggemann, *Prophetic Imagination*, 125.

advances the model of "prophetic interpreter."[55] This overarching model of prophet as "interpreter" is guided by the analogy between prophet and textual scholar, privileging word, message, and meaning. Yet in her framing of this role Davis helpfully foregrounds not only word and voice but also action and persona, and recognizes prophecy as more than a verbal phenomenon, for it is "an aspect of religious experience."[56] She notes ways in which prophetic experience, such as Isaiah's temple vision, "engages every physical sense," and asserts that the prophets' integrative perspective combines religious, economic, ecological, biological, and social dimensions in ways that "frequently attest to the essential unity of every aspect of human experience in the world."[57] For Davis, this integrative perspective is particularly evident in aspects of prophetic relationality, including the work of healing and intercession, and prophetic participation in both human and divine suffering.[58]

Communication, imagination, and interpretation are key components of prophetic experience, action, and interaction as represented in the textual traditions of ancient Israel and Judah. While a primary emphasis on communicative, cognitive, and verbal dimensions of prophecy risks downplaying or excluding its embodied dimensions, the recognition of prophecy's experiential, performative, and embodied dimensions helps chart a course toward a more explicitly integrative approach.

Yes to Words. And Also the Body

Prophecy has a lot to do with words. For starters, Christian and Jewish scriptural canons preserve what we have come to call "books" of prophetic "literature." These labels remind us that the raw materials we study are made of words and that any ancient phenomenon called prophecy is known to us through textual representations and literary compositions. It also reminds us that across diverse times and places these texts have enjoyed modes of cultural authority accorded to written words, books, authors, and literature in addition to the authority accorded them as specifically religious texts. (In Chapters 2 and 6, I develop further the implications of textuality for

---

[55] Davis, *Biblical Prophecy*, 3.
[56] Davis, *Biblical Prophecy*, xi.
[57] Davis, *Biblical Prophecy*, 11–12.
[58] Davis, *Biblical Prophecy*, 12–16. Regarding relationship and participation in suffering, see also Heschel, *Prophets*.

this study.) Beyond the textual and scriptural character of our sources, we repeatedly find within these and other ancient scriptural texts that oracles, sayings, and speech-acts are central to the work of many prophetic figures. That is to say, it is not only that the stories about the prophets are preserved in literary form within scriptural canons, but that the prophets themselves are portrayed as speakers and sometimes even writers whose oral proclamation and textual testimony is at the heart of their prophetic calling.[59] Finally, within these books and oracles, those we designate prophets often preface or conclude their own writings and speeches with the phrases "thus says the Lord" and "word of the Lord," while narrators similarly implicate the divine word in prophetic experience, action, and speech. These formulas yoke together divine word(s) and prophetic words in a way that many would see as a hallmark of prophecy itself. The importance of words, speech, and communication for understanding the phenomenon we call biblical prophecy is undeniable.

But the prophetic word or words are also embodied. In the narrated, implied, or imagined act of proclamation, muscles, air, vocal chords, tongue, palate, nasal cavities, teeth, and lips combine to create sound waves that bounce off particles of matter and enter into other bodies, while gesture, posture, movement, and facial expression engage senses of sight, touch, proximity, and more. The body is also richly entailed in the act of writing: the human body in motion makes ink from once-living plants and animals, scrapes skin to form vellum, presses reeds into parchment, collects wax from bees, bakes clay into tablets, presses tools into clay and wax, quills ink onto skin and parchment. Prophetic words are embodied also in the actions of hearing or reading and the intertwined sensorimotor, cognitive, and affective responses these create, or in their tangible cultural effects and the embodied actions and interactions prophetic words elicit.

And prophecy is also more than word(s). Regardless of which biblical prophets are chosen to be the most representative of early, classical, or late portrayals of biblical prophecy, biblical narratives testify to richly embodied experiences, actions, and interactions that are constitutive of the prophetic role. Whether we consider supernaturally transportive experiences, prophetic affect, narratives of prophetic healing and revivification, miraculous

---

[59] See Petersen, *Prophetic Literature*. Petersen notes that Aaron's role as mouthpiece for Moses in Exod 7:1 (and cf. Exod 4:30) "presupposes one notion of prophetic activity: God communicates through the prophet to an audience. It is a paradigm of prophecy based on linguistic performance, on the conveying of divine speech" (216).

provision of food or command of bears, or the embodied prophecies that have frequently been analyzed as prophetic "symbolic actions" or "sign-acts," the role of prophet or the thing we call prophecy cannot be limited to the utterance. This thing we call prophecy is portrayed in diverse biblical sources as a lived phenomenon encompassing a wide range of embodied experiences, actions, and interactions.

Historicizing a Word-Centered Approach

Intellectual and social history has shaped how we approach the textual and socio-religious phenomenon we call biblical prophecy. A logocentric approach has roots in a dualism that constructs a binary and hierarchical relationship between mind and body. In this framework, word(s), reason, spirit, and intellect are associated with the mind and dissociated from the body. The latter is subordinated to the former, so that mind, reason, and word(s) are valued while body is devalued. This binary framework has caused us too frequently to view prophecy as disembodied utterance, only accidentally or instrumentally linked to bodily experience, affect, action, or interaction. And this tendency carries with it a harmful legacy.

We have learned from the testimony of feminists and womanists, critical race theorists, queer activists, and others that the valuing of mind and spirit, word and reason over body, and attendant devaluing or denigrating of body and embodiment, continues to play out in modern-day settings. Wealth, education, and technologies can make it possible to mitigate and minimize the perceived negative effects or hindrances of "life in the body"—for some. But a persistent dualism of mind and body attaches to other dualisms. These attachments are not simply conceptual. Time and again, in diverse contexts, variations of the mind-body split have buttressed systems of value that enfranchise some people and disenfranchise others.[60] Freya Mathews argues that "Dualism as a schema of organization is constantly re-applied in new discursive domains to create categories that serve to naturalize and legitimate domination: civilized/primitive, mental/manual, public/private, production/reproduction, self/other."[61] Others have emphasized the patterns of domination supported by the intersecting binaries of mind/body, male/

---

[60] See, for example, Lloyd, *Man of Reason*; Gatens, *Imaginary Bodies*.
[61] Mathews, "Dilemma of Dualism," 58.

female, and white/black+brown. Katie Cannon highlights the pernicious convergence of mind-body dualism with histories of chattel slavery and segregation in the United States:

> The underpinning of anti-body dualism, compounded by chattel slavery and racial segregation, signif[ies] Black bodies, female and male, as inferior, mere performers of brute drudgery; white male bodies as unmarked, normative, full humanity, signifying superior individuality; while white female bodies represent the apex of "genteel" femininity, the prized possession in a privileged masculinist culture.[62]

That is to say, within such a framework, some people are, socially speaking, privileged by the kind of body they inhabit, but that fact is disguised, such that their bodies are less marked. A fiction declares that their bodies are less salient to their identity, identifying these people instead with intelligence, wisdom, nobility, virtue, and power. Other kinds of bodies are regarded as instruments rather than agents. They are viewed as more sexual, dangerous, and dirty, and less noble, less human, or less than human. The dualism of mind and body feeds and supports overlapping systems of human stratification, including colonialism, racism, and sexism.

When we situate modern biblical studies within this wider narrative and landscape, we might begin to see that the fiction of an absent, accidental, decorative, instrumental, problematic, or simply irrelevant prophetic body participates in and perpetuates the same dualisms. A hermeneutic of embodiment rejects schemata that "naturalize and legitimate domination" and rejects binaries that perpetuate hierarchies of human value. In the place of a mind-body dualism, I treat the body not as the other half of a binary pair but as an integral component of the human person, of society, and of relationship. I argue that the body—not only the prophet's body but also bodies with which the prophet interacts—is integral and necessary to prophetic mediation.

But to undertake this work successfully, performative renunciation of mind-body dualism is hardly sufficient. Mind-body dualism and its corollaries enter the framework of modern biblical scholarship from multiple vectors, often shaping our habits of thought and work in ways we do not realize. Before undertaking the integrative work I propose, I therefore trace the

---

[62] Cannon, "Sexing Black Women," 12.

historical roots of the body's burial in much of modern Western thought and, correlatively, in a significant portion of modern biblical scholarship. To do so requires attention to the history and cultural projects of Western philosophy, Christianity, colonialism, and modernity, with particular attention to the construction of such binarized pairs as mind and body and ("true") religion and magic.[63] I do not stand apart from this story but am fully in it and heir to it. It is my hope that bringing to the surface some of the hidden histories, frames, assumptions, and values that have led to the privileging of word over body can help interpreters to recognize, check, and counteract biases that have often shaped our approaches to biblical prophecy.

I wish to be clear: dualism is never the whole story. In the history I trace below, I draw attention to major moments in the construction and entrenchment of mind-body dualism and hierarchy, the elevation of Word/words, and, as appropriate, the understandings of prophecy that follow. But such dualism is not everything and everywhere in the broader historical landscape.[64] Even in the historical movements, moments, and works treated below, there are tensions and complexities, some of which I draw attention to, and some of which, for reasons of economy, I do not. And while I narrate this story of the body's burial in chronological sequence, the real history is not a single line.

Ancient Roots

Western understandings of the human person as consisting of parts that can be divided into body on the one hand and mind, spirit, or soul on the other do not originate in the HBOT nor the ancient West Asian context that is so vital for its interpretation. They have an important predecessor, rather, in the writings of Plato (b. ca. 428 BCE). In the *Phaedrus* (composed between 388 and 367 BCE), Plato uses the analogy of a charioteer in a chariot to elaborate a three-part model of the human person (§246–56). The charioteer is the rational intellect or soul, which seeks truth. Her vehicle to get there is a chariot drawn by two impassioned horses whom she must steer. One horse

---

[63] For an analysis of the persistence of mind-body dualism in post-Cartesian anthropology and study of religion, see Verrips, "Body and Mind."

[64] See, e.g, Cox Miller, *Corporeal Imagination*; Harrison, *Art of Listening*, 33–6; Bynum, "Why All the Fuss." Bynum notes, e.g., that "medieval theologians and philosophers did not discuss anything at all like the Cartesian mind/body problem (any more, by the way, than Aristotle did)"; "knowing, feeling, and experiencing were located in body" ("Why All the Fuss," 13).

is animated by morality and directed by reason, the other is driven by the desires of the body. The former may aid the seeker of truth, while the latter may hinder her. Both must submit to the charioteer if she is to arrive at her moral and intellectual goal. In this model, mind and body must cooperate, but they are fundamentally separate and even alienated from one another. The body is both a necessary engine and an obstacle that threatens to drag the mind down, encumbering the sacred soul on its journey through life and its journey toward truth. The intellect or soul—which for Plato is the part that draws near to God and eternity—must tame and discipline and even dominate it.

In the *Phaedo* (also composed between 388 and 367 BCE), Plato sets forth the idea that every material object has an immaterial form, or essence, that exists independently of the material world. Similarly the intellect—the mind or soul—is not material. That is, it has no intrinsic relationship to matter, to anything that can be seen or touched, smelled, or tasted (*Phaedo* §76). In this dialogue, Socrates further proposes, "the soul is most like that which is divine, immortal, intelligible, uniform, indissoluble, and ever self-consistent and invariable, whereas body is most like that which is human, mortal, multiform, unintelligible, dissoluble, and never self-consistent" (*Phaedo* §80).[65] He imagined the soul as imprisoned in the body (*Phaedo* §81–82).[66] During life, the body is a hindrance to knowledge of what is true and good and beautiful:

> So long as we are alive, we shall continue closest to knowledge if we avoid as much as we can all contact and association with the body, except when they are absolutely necessary, and instead of allowing ourselves to become infected with its nature, purify ourselves from it until God himself gives us deliverance. (*Phaedo* §67)

While the *Phaedrus*, considered above, proposes a tripartite model of the person, the simpler bipartite model described in the *Phaedo* has been more influential. A key to this model is not only its view of body and soul as two separate parts of the person, in some ways cooperating and in others

---

[65] Plato, *Phaedo*, tr. Tredennick in *Plato: The Collected Dialogues*.

[66] The souls of the wicked wander about and "through craving for the corporeal, which unceasingly pursues them, they are imprisoned once more in a body" (*Phaedo* §81e). "Every seeker after wisdom knows that up to the time when philosophy takes it over his soul is a helpless prisoner, chained hand and foot in the body, compelled to view reality not directly but only through its prison bars, and wallowing in utter ignorance" (*Phaedo* §82e).

opposed to each other (*Phaedo* §79, 65–7), but also the way it locates this anthropological dualism within a broader metaphysical framework. In this framework it is not only the parts of the person that negotiate this uneasy tension, but all of reality. Visible, tangible aspects of the material realm provide both a means for recognizing higher, spiritual realities and an obstacle to obtaining them (cf. *Symposium* §210).

Plato's anthropological and metaphysical dualisms were influential in the religious movements commonly referred to under the umbrella of Gnosticism (beginning with Valentinus in the second century CE) and in Neoplatonic thought (third century CE).[67] Classical Greek and Hellenistic philosophical ideas were likewise influential in Hellenistic Judaism (evidenced especially in the writings of Philo) and early Christianity. Daniel Boyarin argues that "[v]arious branches of Judaism ... became increasingly platonized in late antiquity," "adopt[ing] ... a dualist philosophy in which the phenomenal world was understood to be the representation in matter of a spiritual or ideal entity which corresponded to it."[68] A correlate to this understanding was a hierarchical valuation in which the spiritual or inner reality was deemed true and essential while these external, material forms, including the human body, were "non-essential" and of lesser value. According to Boyarin, the views of the apostle Paul were formed in this matrix, but differed slightly: for Paul, the body is necessary, but it is not constitutive of the self.[69] James D. G. Dunn argues that for Paul "body" (σῶμα) names the corporeal dimensions of existence that make human beings, individually and collectively, participants in and with creation in a common social life, awaiting together an embodied redemption (e.g., 1 Thess 5:23).[70] Because redemption is still in the future, to be at home in the body is to be away from the Lord (2 Cor 5:6). Yet the body can be raised in glory and power, in a form no longer terrestrial but spiritual (1 Cor 15:43–44). "Flesh" (σάρξ), by contrast, "cannot inherit the kingdom of God" (1 Cor 15:50) and cannot be transformed into something spiritual, but is rather opposed to spirit (πνεῦμα): "For what the flesh desires is opposed to the Spirit, and what the Spirit desires is opposed to the flesh; for these are opposed to each other, to prevent you from doing what you want" (Gal 5:17 NRSV).

---

[67] For a nuanced treatment of "gnostic" attitudes toward the body, see Williams, *Rethinking "Gnosticism"*, 116–38. For the relationship between soul and body and the mediating "subtle body" in Neoplatonism, see Addey, "Light of the Sphere."
[68] Boyarin, *Radical Jew*, 59.
[69] Boyarin, *Radical Jew*, 60.
[70] Dunn, *Theology of Paul*, 61.

While in passages such as these Paul appears to distinguish body and flesh and to articulate an opposition between flesh and spirit, what he means by each is not always clear. Rodrigo Morales argues that by "flesh" Paul usually means "human frailty" in the era before the anticipated outpouring of the Holy Spirit, and by spirit Paul usually means the Holy Spirit, that is, God, moving and working in and among human beings to lead them in righteousness. In this view, Paul is not talking about an internal dualism at all.[71] While Boyarin offers a somewhat different account of the particularities and peculiarities of Paul's terminology, both highlight the tensions and associations Paul's account of spirit, flesh, and body would create for later interpreters, many of whom would associate flesh with sin and alienation from God.[72] Dunn similarly notes that many modern English translators have avoided the translation "flesh" for σάρξ in Paul's letters because, "consciously or unconsciously, its negative usage seems to carry unacceptable dualistic overtones (materiality as evil)."[73]

The Gospel of John, written a few decades after the letters of Paul, similarly contrasts flesh and spirit. "It is the spirit that gives life; the flesh is useless. The words I have spoken to you are spirit and life" (John 6:63 NRSV; cf. 3:6). Importantly for our understanding of the history of the relationship between (prophetic) word and body, this saying further equates Jesus's speech with spirit, implicitly disassociating Jesus's words from "flesh."[74] By contrast, David Rensberger argues that the prologue to John's Gospel pushes back against a "dualism" in which "the Word, divine reason, was simply incompatible with flesh, human weakness and desire."[75] The prologue's incarnational theology and cosmology positively values and sacralizes flesh or the body (both human and nonhuman) in its assertion that the Word (logos) became or "happened (as)" flesh (John 1:14).[76] For Rensberger the prologue's

---

[71] Morales, *Spirit and Restoration*, 135.
[72] Boyarin (*Radical Jew*, 65–6) cites Jewett's account of later Christian interpretations of σάρξ. E.g., among church fathers, it was commonly construed as "material sensuality which solicited or directly induced sin"; for Augustine it was "man in revolt from God" (quotes are from Jewett, *Paul's Anthropological Terms*, 50).
[73] Dunn, *Theology of Paul*, 64.
[74] Schnackenburg argues that John understands flesh as "that which is earthbound (3:6), transient and perishable (6:63), the typically human mode of being ... in contrast to all that is divine and spiritual" (*Gospel according to St. John*, 1.267).
[75] Rensberger, "John," 340.
[76] See, e.g., Johnson, *Ask the Beasts*, 193–200. In a different vein, Morris (*Theology without Words*, 101) highlights ways that John's Prologue offers to people with deafness "a more accessible picture of God" in which the "word of God ... can be seen and touched." Morris's work draws attention to dimensions of ableism implicit in a word-centered theology. For the translation "happened (as) flesh," see Waetjen, "Logos," 278.

portrayal of the incarnation further entails rejection of existing social and ontological hierarchies.[77] The portrayal of Jesus as Woman Wisdom who offers their own body and blood as life-giving feast similarly cuts across hierarchies of gender even as it underscores the centrality of the body to John's soteriology (John 6:35, 48; cf. Sir 24:19–21).[78]

Despite this valuing of the body (to such a degree that Jesus promises to give his own "flesh for the life of the world" John 6:51), the identification of the Logos with God (1:1) prior to the incarnation could be interpreted as elevating to the status of divine a disembodied word (or faculty of reason) that exists before and above history.[79] Comparing John's prologue to the writings of Philo, Herman Waetjen observes in both an "objectifying thinking [that] converts the word of God into a system of knowledge that transcends the contingencies of historical existence and is therefore universally valid."[80] The theological problem of a disembodied logos is stated well by William Gray:

> Is there not already a paradox in the phrase, "the Word *became* flesh", quite apart from the Christological paradox? Isn't the word *always already* "flesh"? What sense can we really make of a disembodied word, of a discarnate word? Isn't the word always already revelatory, in that it reveals, discovers, makes manifest, the world? But such an insight into the nature of language is suppressed by the Greek metaphysical tradition which, from Plato's *Cratylus* onwards, opposes the intelligible to the physical world . . . [asserting that] true *logos* or language is purely spiritual and intelligible.[81]

Gray challenges this view by way of phenomenology, with attention to the relation between thought and language and the embodied character of language itself. Waetjen similarly identifies logos not with a disembodied reason but rather with "God's activity of speech."[82] He argues that in John "physical organs of sense constitute the epistemological foundation of knowledge of God. Consequently, the words and works of the incarnate Logos should be interchangeable, manifesting the integrity of the Creator whose words are deeds and whose deeds are words."[83] Jaime Clark-Soles focuses on the ways

---

[77] Rensberger, "John," 340.
[78] Douglas, *Jesus as Female Divine*, 15–70.
[79] Jasper, *Shining Garment*. For the relationship between John's logos theology and the contemporary Jewish milieu, see Boyarin, "Gospel of the Memra."
[80] Waetjen, "Logos," 266.
[81] Gray, "Myth of the Word Discarnate," 114.
[82] Waetjen, "Logos," 275.
[83] Waetjen, "Logos," 278.

that the physicality of the incarnation and portrayal of bodily, sensory experience in John's gospel shapes reception of the Bible as Word of God:

> If the Word of God became flesh and dwelt among us—that is, if the Word of God came out of the birth canal of a woman's body, grew, ate, went to the bathroom, bathed, struggled against demons, sweated, wept, exulted, was transfigured, was physically violated, and rotted away in a tomb just before being gloriously resurrected—then the Bible must have flesh on it . . . Any interpretation that denounces the material, created order, including our own bodies, should be suspect.[84]

Such interpretive interventions notwithstanding, and despite the theological significance of incarnation for John's Gospel, as with Paul, so with John's Gospel, subtle innovations and semantic intricacies have often been flattened in the history of interpretation and use.[85] In the process, internal and external dualisms merge, such that a bipartite human, body/flesh, on the one hand, and spirit/soul/mind on the other mirrors the external distinction between material and spiritual, human and God. Despite the incarnation of the Logos, in the history of interpretation Word and words would frequently be aligned with this second category and consequently dissociated from the body.[86]

Modern Developments

More than a millennium later, these bifurcations would be mapped onto cultures and population groups as, beginning in the early fifteenth century CE, European colonizers undertook the conquest of indigenous peoples around the globe. The colonial project was funded by the projection of

---

[84] Clark-Soles, *Engaging the Word*, 32.

[85] Some have argued that the Johannine epistles denounce docetism, the belief that Jesus only *seemed* to have/be a body. One relevant passage is 2 John 1:7: "Many deceivers have gone out into the world, those who do not confess that Jesus Christ has come in the flesh; any such person is the deceiver and the antichrist!" (NRSV; cf. 1 John 4:2–3). For an assessment of these arguments, see Wahlde, *Gnosticism, Docetism, and Judaisms*, 61–81.

[86] For an argument that John's Gospel mediates divine presence by means of "the elimination or shedding of the body" of Jesus, "which the book carries out in the course of its narrative," and subsequent rematerialization of the Logos in textual form, see Pettersen, *From Tomb to Text* (quoted material p. 113). For an analysis of the ways Logos in Philo embodies divine presence, activity, and knowledge, see Orlov, *Embodiment of Divine Knowledge*, 9–15.

ontological and gendered distinctions between colonizer and colonized that constructed European colonizers as the (male) mind, reason, and soul and the indigenous peoples they colonized as the (female, hypersexual) body in need of regulation.[87] Within this racialized and gendered framework, "ideologies of colonial corporeality came to contrast with the rational subject produced by the disciplinary technologies of modern government."[88]

Along with these projected ontological distinctions, colonial discourse similarly distinguished between the religions of colonizers and the colonized. Colonizers adapted and applied the category of "magic" to what they considered to be the barbaric and primitive religious practices of conquered peoples.[89] By attaching the negative connotations of "magic" to a broad array of embodied religious experiences and practices, colonial discourse could dismiss these experiences and practices as belonging to a primitive and false world view. Embodied practices of divination, shamanism, and prophecy were denigrated as vulgar, earthy, even demonic. These practices were contrasted with the "rational" words of scripture, verbal prayer, and the Christian beliefs of colonizers.[90]

Randall Styers notes that religious discourse about magic exerted regulatory force not just in the colonies but also at home.[91] A category closely related to "magic" was "superstition." In the late medieval and early modern periods, European Catholics and Protestants alike critiqued "superstition" in colonial and domestic domains. This critique would help fuel the Protestant Reformation. While Catholics sought to counteract so-called magical aspects of folk-religion focused on protecting body and soul and warding off calamity,[92] "Protestant theological treatises appropriated the

---

[87] On sexualization, see Styers, *Making Magic*, 191.
[88] Rao and Pierce, "Discipline and the Other Body," 4.
[89] Styers, *Making Magic*. This was not entirely new, however. For an overview of medieval attitudes toward "magic," see Page, "Medieval Magic." For the relation to gender, see Breuer, *Crafting the Witch*.
[90] Colonialist structures, attitudes, and practices have persisted into the twentieth and twenty-first centuries and continue to influence biblical scholarship. Styers analyzes ways the category of magic has continued to function in the regulation of piety, reason, inquiry, and desire, observing that "The [modern] scholarly discourses on magic have regularly conformed to the interests of the dominant classes of Europe and America seeking to regulate and control both their colonial possessions and their domestic populations, especially the troublesome groups on the margins of society. In the context of colonialism, non-Western cultural systems were regularly configured by scholars so as to provide a contrasting foil that could bring Western modernity into clearer relief" (*Making Magic*, 16). Styers argues that modern social sciences, including the study of magic and religion in the ancient world, thus inherited these colonizing and regulating biases and continued to rationalize and undergird colonial and domestic regulation of conquered peoples, minoritized populations, and members of lower socio-economic classes.
[91] Styers, "Making Magic," 16.
[92] Cameron, "Reasoned Faith."

arguments of the late medieval superstition-critique and applied them, quite precisely, to Catholic rituals and consecrations."[93] In the process, for Protestants, understandings of religion as ritual or practice gave way to newer perspectives that emphasized belief, faith, and Word.[94]

Indeed, a theology of "the Word" was foundational to understandings of prophecy advanced in the Protestant Reformation (1517–1648). Sujin Pak argues that

> a distinctive element of Protestant conceptions and uses of prophecy was their profound focus on Scripture and its authority, for they insisted that the proclamation of God's Word was the crucial, if not sole, occupation of the true prophet. Prophets and prophecy were tied inextricably to the preaching of God's Word and thereby to the interpretation of Scripture in the teachings of the early Protestant reformers. Such a focal point was the constant, shared factor in the magisterial reformers' understandings of prophecy and the office of the prophet.[95]

Consistent with these emphases, Luther's theology of the Word privileged hearing over other modes of perception and characterized encounter with God as the experience of being addressed.[96] Such understandings of prophecy and Christian vocation led Protestant reformers to find in their logocentric interpretation of Israel's prophets a set of templates for the role of Christian clergy, whose vocation was anchored in the proclamation of Scripture as Word of God.[97] The emphases of the Protestant Reformation had lasting effects on modern study of the Bible, including its portrayal of prophecy. Colleen Shantz observes that, within modern study of religion, these shifts "fueled attention to ideas and propositional knowledge. The methodological companion to the emphasis on belief is the focus on words."[98]

---

[93] Cameron, *Enchanted Europe*, 114.
[94] Smith, "Religion, Religions, Religious," 269–71.
[95] Pak, *Reformation of Prophecy*, 1–2.
[96] Nielsen, "Ritualization, the Body, and the Church"; Laffin, *Promise of Martin Luther's Political Theology*, 61–4; Bayer, *Martin Luther's Theology*, 249–53.
[97] Pak, *Reformation of Prophecy*, 29: "the Protestant reformers employed the prophet and biblical prophecy to frame their reforming work under, within, and in support of the authority of Scripture — for the true prophet speaks the Word of God alone and calls the people, their worship, and their beliefs and practices back to the Word of God"; and *Reformation of Prophecy*, 33: "the Protestant reformers' employment of the prophet and biblical prophecy enabled them to articulate their reformational teachings within the crucial framework of Scripture's prime authority."
[98] Shantz, "Opening the Black Box," 8.

Developments in science and philosophy contributed further to the decentering of the body. In his *Meditations* (ca. 1629), René Descartes distinguished between *res extensa*—body, "the thing that takes up space" —and *res cogitans*— "a thinking thing," the mind, the part of us that thinks and knows (*Meditations* II.8), which can also be identified with the soul. "The mind," he writes, "is completely different from the body."[99] "I am not merely present in my body as a sailor is present in a ship, but . . . I am very closely joined and, as it were, intermingled with it, so that I and the body form a unit."[100] Despite this intermingling, for Descartes the vast majority of the body has no influence on the mind. Only one small section of the brain, where he believed the soul might be resident, could influence the mind, by synthesizing and conveying to it sensory perceptions.[101] Like Plato's three-part model, Descartes' two-part model was not only a division but also a hierarchy.

Descartes' understanding of the relationship and distinction between mind and body is based in part on scientific theories that have since been disproven. It is also the case that Descartes' distinction between mind and body is not absolute. The passions, for example, complicate simplistic accounts of his dualism.[102] His distinction nonetheless continues to exert enormous influence on modern understandings of the human person, yielding a persistent paradigm commonly referred to as Cartesian dualism, in which body is separate from and subordinated to mind or soul.

Descartes' scientific rationalism helped lay the groundwork for the European Enlightenment (1685–1815), also called "the Age of Reason." In addition to the movement's emphasis on reason, it continued an earlier Reformation trajectory that emphasized inner over outer religious expression. For Enlightenment thinkers, religion became "a matter of the private intellect."[103] An important Enlightenment figure for modern biblical studies was Baruch Spinoza, who shared Descartes' rationalism but rejected aspects of his distinction between body and mind. For Spinoza, mind and

---

[99] "mentem a corpore omnino esse diversam." Descartes, *Meditations*, §86, pp. 120–1.
[100] Descartes, *Meditations*, §81, pp. 112–13.
[101] E.g., Descartes, *Meditations*, §86, pp. 120–1.
[102] Hoffman, *Essays on Descartes*, 181. Descartes' account of the passions relies on his prior understanding of the distinction between soul and body (Descartes, *Passions* §3) and on his understanding of human physiology, including how the body processes and responds to external, sensory stimuli (e.g., *Passions* §7–16). In this model, thought is a faculty of the soul alone (*Passions* §4), while the body is like a machine powered by internal heat (*Passions* §6–8). But passion and action are two sides of the same coin (*Passions* §1): a passion is an action of the body that is experienced in the soul (*Passions* §2).
[103] Styers, *Making Magic*, 26. Spinoza famously called religion *viri privati officium* (*TTP* 3.10).

body share an essence, namely "a pattern of activity that can be formed by either thoughts or motions."[104] Yet by contrast with the emphasis on written word/s found in the Reformation's account of prophecy and scripture, for Spinoza, the very materiality of words on the page made possible a form of idolatry and superstition in which written scriptures might be confused with the Word of God (*TTP* 12.3).[105] Rather than identifying God's Word with scriptures, he asserted that the "eternal Word and covenant and true religion are divinely inscribed in [people's] hearts" (*TTP* 12.1).[106] This understanding is consistent with Spinoza's definition of prophecy as revealed knowledge (*TTP* 1.1). The Hebrew noun נביא ("prophet") names a "speaker and interpreter" (*TTP* 1.1) endowed with extraordinary faculties of imagination (*TTP* 2.1).[107] "The nature of mind," then, argues Spinoza, "is the primary cause of divine revelation" (*TTP* 1.4).

Spinoza's emphasis on prophetic imagination anticipated a major focus of late eighteenth- and early nineteenth-century British and German romanticism. Reacting in part to enlightenment rationalism, romanticism responded by privileging individual imagination and inspiration, merging the roles of prophet and poet, and claiming the mantle of prophecy for its own writers.[108] In this process, words and vision were detached from history and context.[109] Biblical scholarship paved the way for the romantic construction of the poet-prophet through literary analysis of the new-found category biblical poetry.[110]

Romanticism influenced biblical scholarship in turn. Max Weber's famous typological contrast between institutional and charismatic authority, in which he associated priesthood with the former and prophecy with the latter, located prophetic authority in "personal revelation and charisma."[111]

---

[104] Morrison, "Spinoza on Mind, Body, and Numerical Identity," 294.
[105] Spinoza, *Theological-Political Treatise*, 145–6.
[106] Spinoza, *Theological-Political Treatise*, 145.
[107] Spinoza, *Theological-Political Treatise*, 10.
[108] See discussion in Balfour, *Rhetoric of Romantic Prophecy*.
[109] Christopher M. Bundock, *Romantic Prophecy and Resistance*. In the first poem of *Prelude* ("Introduction—Childhood and School-time"), Wordsworth relays the experience of being stirred by an internal "creative breeze" that has grown into a storm, "the holy life of music and of verse" (ll. 41–54). The poet "pour[s] out [his] soul in measured strains ... To the open fields I told / A prophecy; poetic numbers came / Spontaneously, and cloth'd in priestly robe / My spirit, thus singled out ... / For holy services" ("Introduction," ll. 57–63). Wordsworth's poet-prophet is passionate ("Introduction," l. 53; "Books" ll. 96–7) and joyful ("Introduction," l. 40; "Retrospect," l. 282), believed by some to suffer madness but knowing himself to possess the ability to see beneath the surface of visible things ("Residence at Cambridge," ll. 151–60).
[110] Balfour, *Rhetoric of Romantic Prophecy*. On the "invention of biblical poetry," see Legaspi, *Death of Scripture*, 105–28.
[111] Weber, *Sociology of Religion*, 46.

In the nineteenth century and early twentieth, biblical scholars would similarly view the prophetic figures they studied as "a unique class of religious individualists with a message focused on the present," such that "a highly distinctive prophetic religion, at once spiritual and ethical, . . . could then be contrasted with the magical and materialistic propensities of popular and priestly religion centered around the sacrificial cult."[112] This contrast owed to the ongoing influence of rationalism as well.[113] Both of these influences contributed to an approach that divorced prophecy from the history and culture(s) in which it and its literary representations emerged and repeatedly separated the thing called prophecy from its embodiment.[114]

Modern understandings of the relationship between body and word have been further shaped by capitalism, industrialism, artificial intelligence, virtual and augmented realities, and other technologies.[115] Weber influentially argued that, following the Protestant Reformation, values of asceticism and bodily denial were applied to an ethic of labor, contributing significantly to the flourishing of industrial capitalism.[116] Industrial capitalism, meanwhile, ultimately generated and relied upon a worldwide network of global slave labor premised on the fungibility, objectification, and monetization of laboring, human bodies. These bodies (people) have been hidden far from the view of the consumer, such that consumers interact with a product, a catalogue, and a cadre of fictionalized users rather than the embodied processes of production. As increasingly sophisticated machines appear to mimic the thing we call "intelligence," the idea that "the thinking thing" might reside outside the human body holds enduring power.[117] And while some highlight the complex interactions of mind and body in the experience and use of virtual reality, for others this digital technology further exacerbates a persistent dissociation between "mind" and body.[118]

---

[112] Blenkinsopp, *History of Prophecy*, 27.
[113] Blenkinsopp, *History of Prophecy*, 29.
[114] Blenkinsopp, *History of Prophecy*, 29; Werline, "Assessing the Prophetic Vision."
[115] Styers argues that capitalism and modern science share a "mechanistic and rationalized manipulation of the material world" and together constitute one key epistemic shift contributing to the modern perception of "magic" (*Making Magic*, 26).
[116] Weber, *Protestant Ethic*, first published in German in 1905.
[117] E.g., Moravec, *Mind Children*.
[118] Stone argues that the distinction between the virtual and the real does not drive a wedge between mind and body but rather represents "a different way of conceptualizing a *relationship* to the human body" (*War of Desire*, 40). On the other end of the spectrum, Tart identifies as a "dualist" who argues that "pure mind is something fundamentally different from the nature of the body and other physical things" ("Mind Embodied," 126).

This story of mind-body dualism and the privileging of the Word in the West reveals numerous contributing factors in the development of a persistent, logocentric model of biblical prophecy and clarifies what is at stake in asserting that biblical prophecy was also richly embodied. The intellectual history charted here is also social and political. Privileging words, writing, mind, or reason has often also meant privileging the people most closely associated with them, including men, white people, and colonizers, and has supported modern systems and structures of domination. Devaluing and obscuring the role of the body has often also meant the subordination and erasure of people with *marked* bodies, including women, people of color, members of lower socioeconomic classes, and people with disabilities. This book participates in a revaluing. It also aims at reintegration. The parable of the unnamed man of God and the old prophet underscores that in biblical prophecy word and body interanimate one another. The alternative I propose to a logocentric model is thus an integrative approach that thematizes the interaction and interdependence of mind, body, and context and the corollary interplay of word, affect, and deed. This approach further emphasizes embodied interaction and relationship between deity, prophet, people, and place. Chapter 2 spells out further contours of this approach, beginning with an understanding of prophecy as a form of embodied mediation.

2
Re-Embodying Biblical Prophecy

The turn to the body and a (re)turn to religious experience in biblical studies and beyond have laid the foundation for a "paradigm of embodiment" that centers the body in the study of biblical prophecy.[1] As documented in Chapter 1, numerous important studies have already advanced this agenda. The present chapter continues this work, delineating the scope, methodology, and guiding assumptions of the analysis I undertake in subsequent chapters. I begin with a definition.

A Working Definition

My working definition of biblical prophecy is this: *mediation proper to personae designated as or widely understood to be prophets within the corpora of the Hebrew Bible and Old Testament.* This definition is meant to encompass portrayed mediation enacted by or enjoined upon characters in biblical texts as well as mediation enacted through prophetic texts.[2] "Personae" is thus chosen in hopes that it has enough flexibility to refer to three groups of people: 1) characters narratively portrayed as prophets; 2) writers (sometimes referred to as "latter prophets") whose books were gathered and preserved under the heading "prophets"; and 3) implied authors or personae constructed by these same books. Including all three of these under one umbrella is perhaps analytically imprecise. But I do so because this is common usage. Moreover, in common (popular) usage those three groups of people are not typically separated out from each other but are considered as one group.

This usage has roots in the biblical corpora: the prophetic literature of the Hebrew Bible and Old Testament (HBOT) does not present us with one

---

[1] The phrase is that of Csordas, "Embodiment as a Paradigm," 5.
[2] I say "enacted by or enjoined upon" because numerous prophetic texts portray the commanding of actions by God or another supernatural being but do not report the completion of the commanded action.

concept or portrait of the role "prophet." Nor, to whatever extent biblical prophetic literature reflects historical roles and practices, does it reflect one consistent social role or set of practices. Readers of these corpora encounter instead a range of roles and practices spanning multiple centuries and geographical regions, interacting with shifting political and religious systems and diverse social and cultural contexts in complex and varied ways.

For these reasons, to intervene in modern understandings of "biblical prophecy" requires not a narrow definition but one that can hold each type of thing commonly placed within this category. Unlike some of the definitions considered in Chapter 1, my working definition does not specify the form, content, or direction of prophetic mediation. Each of these varies considerably among different prophetic figures, within different sources, traditions, and books, and in different times and places. Forms of prophetic mediation range from oracle, sermon, and text to acts of healing and feeding; they include song and dance, confrontation, intercession, resurrection, and childbirth. Biblical prophecy mediates knowledge, affect, power, agency, encounter, and relationship. This mediation is multidimensional and multidirectional, crossing and spanning boundaries of space, time, divine and human realms, and divine and human bodies.

From Unity to Diversity: Deuteronomy 18:9–22

I have stated above that the forms, content, and even directionality of biblical prophecy are not one but many. Yet despite the diversity of representations of biblical prophecy within the corpora of the HBOT, these corpora also contain passages that construct the category of (authorized) prophecy more narrowly. Such passages have shaped the study of prophecy in turn. Perhaps the most influential of these is Deut 18:9–22, a passage that has frequently been viewed as providing a summary of and template for Israel's understanding of the phenomenon of prophecy and by extension the thing called "biblical prophecy."[3] The passage's sharp distinction between authorized prophecy and prohibited forms of mediation contributes to the prevalence of a logocentric model of biblical prophecy. But closer examination helps locate this passage within broader literary and cultural contexts in which the nature of prophecy

---

[3] Cryer, *Divination in Ancient Israel*, 232–43, documents the influence of this passage in the history of the study of Israelite divinatory practices.

itself is contested. Like the account of the separation of word and body in Chapter 1, an appreciation of this inner-biblical contest over what "counts" as prophecy and who is authorized to be a prophet can help interpreters become more aware of how certain biblical perspectives and portrayals have normed modern scholarly understandings toward the privileging of word and decentering of body and toward a unitary understanding of biblical prophecy. Recognizing this contest helps check the effects of such explicit and implicit norming and excavate the diversity of perspectives on and portrayals of prophecy in biblical literature.

In a discourse about the people's future in a land they will come to possess, Moses contrasts forms of prophetic mediation that shall be authorized for Israel with forms of mediation that, he says, are already being practiced in the land the Israelites will come to occupy. Authorized prophecy is here characterized as verbal and auditory only. Prohibited forms of mediation make use of and interact with other bodily faculties, animals, material objects, and spirits of the dead. The proscribed forms of intermediation practiced among "those nations" who have previously inhabited this land are numerous and diverse, but the passage does not provide a disinterested description of what these practices entail. Rather, the list "diviner, omen-seeker, augur, magician, spell-caster, spirit-medium, or necromancer" (18:10b–11; cf. Lev 19:31) is composed of etic (externally imposed) terms and phrases. Some of the labels are derogatory and reductive, designed to discredit and vilify the practitioners they name and to elicit disavowal and disgust from the reader (18:9, 12).[4]

By contrast with these illicit forms of mediation, Moses promises a different kind of mediator. "A prophet from your midst, from your brothers, like me, will the LORD your God raise up for you. You will hear/listen to him" (18:15). The designation "from your midst"—מִקִּרְבְּךָ—idiomatically and metaphorically identifies the future prophet(s) as emerging from internal organs of the body or bodies of the people (18:15, 18). A bodily and spatial belonging thus modifies and amplifies the assertion of kinship, establishing a corporeal, social bond that in some way qualifies the designated future prophet to fulfill a role for their community that the diviners or intermediaries of "those nations" (18:9) shall not be permitted to do (18:14). The prophet(s) will also have a corporeal connection to the deity who establishes them in their role: God will place God's words "in the prophet's mouth" (18:18), and the prophet will

---

[4] See further Fritschel, "Women and Magic," 81–94.

in turn "speak" to the people in the deity's name (18:19).[5] This corporeal connection authorizes and facilitates authentic prophetic speech. Yet its corporeality is overshadowed by an emphasis on the "words" of God. Five times in five verses, "word/s" belonging to or attributed to God are the primary concern of prophets and their audiences (18:18–22). Prophets, whether true or false, "speak" (18:18, 19, 20, 22). Prophetic speech implies divine speech, but false prophets speak words "YHWH did not speak" (18:21–22).

Just as appropriate prophetic activity is here limited to words and speech, so appropriate response to prophetic activity is here conveyed through a term whose primary meaning is auditory reception. The people shall "hear" or "listen to" the prophet (18:15, 19). While it is true that שמע אל means idiomatically "to obey," it also denotes a preceding, auditory experience which functions as a synecdoche for the conditions, dispositions, and actions of obedience.[6] Within this passage, prophecy is circumscribed with regard to content, form, source, and effects. Prophets speak words. Authentic prophets speak God's words. Recipients hear and obey God's words by hearing and obeying the words of God's authentic prophets.

As noted above, readers have often taken the account of prophecy in this passage, differentiating as it does between authorized and unauthorized mediators, or those to be heard (18:19) and those to be abhorred (18:12–13), for a reliable summary of the understanding of prophecy in ancient Israel.[7] Yet this assumption meets with several objections. David Petersen argues, for example, that the designation of Moses himself as prophet was "neither known nor influential in prophetic circles; rather, "the idea of a Mosaic prophet was designed to curtail the power and authority of those whom we know as prophets."[8] Jeffrey Stackert has countered this argument by

---

[5] The image of putting words in someone's mouth occurs also at Exod 4:15; 2 Sam 14:3, 19; Isa 51:16; 59:21; Jer 1:9 (cf. 5:14); 4 Esd 15:1. Multiple occurrences relate directly to prophecy, but some do not.

[6] This act of hearing takes the place of a purportedly more overwhelming and multi-sensorial experience by which the people directly heard the voice of God and saw "this great fire" (18:16). Whereas a prior theophany combined elements of auditory, visual, olfactory, and pallesthetic (sensing vibration) experience in a more direct, communal encounter with God (e.g., Exod 20:18), prophetic mediation here hides God's "fire" from view and tempers the frightening sound of God's own voice by speaking God's words from a human mouth.

[7] See critique of this tendency and lexical test case in Cryer, *Divination in Ancient Israel*, 231–8, 242, 250–63. See also Hamori, *Women's Divination*, 25. Cf. Schmidt's discussion of nineteenth-century anthropological study of ancient magic, which deployed a mixture of etic and emic categories and concepts: "some were nevertheless imitating similar shortcomings or deliberate biases of the ancient writers themselves" (*Materiality of Power*, 7).

[8] Petersen, *Prophetic Literature*, 221. Cf. Minnich's analysis of the Fifth Lateran Council's circumscribing of ongoing prophetic revelation ("Prophecy and the Fifth Lateran Council").

demonstrating that, even though the role-label "prophet" is explicitly applied to Moses only once (Deut 34:10), all major Pentateuchal sources unequivocally portray Moses as prophet.[9] Yet, according to Stackert, "each composition understands Moses's prophetic vocation and practice somewhat differently[,] ... in line with its own ideological and political goals."[10] That is, in different ways both Petersen and Stackert call attention to two aspects of the ways the role of prophet is understood, constructed, and portrayed in the HBOT: 1) sources and traditions differ in their portrayal of the modes, forms, functions, and perceptions of prophetic mediation; 2) in varying degrees these sources and traditions participate in a broader contest over how the role should be defined, how its practitioners and their prophecies may be authenticated, which functions the role of prophet includes, and which modes and forms of prophetic mediation are authorized and by whom.

Indeed, the passage's polemical assault on various "unauthorized" modes of mediation exposes as fiction any assertion of a unitary phenomenon and understanding of prophecy. This unitary fiction disguises a phenomenologically complex and ideologically diverse set of roles, functions, and experiences proper to the broader mediatory phenomena here named, including prophecy, both as projected and constructed within and by biblical literature and as they may have historically occurred among the people of Israel and Judah.[11]

Contrary to the assertions of Deuteronomy 18:9–22, a lexical analysis by Frederick Cryer demonstrates that most of the diverse terminology for divinatory and magical practitioners used in this passage derive not from the "peoples in the land," that is, Israel's northwest-Semitic-speaking neighbors and cohabitants, but either from Mesopotamian terminology or from middle-Hebrew usage. These findings undercut the Deuteronomic claim that the practices described herein are characteristic of "those nations," as written records from "those nations" lack cognate terminology for the roles here listed. Instead, the robust and distinctive Hebrew vocabulary for the practices here condemned by the Deuteronomist suggests that these very practices were popular among speakers of Hebrew: "An almost entirely domestic vocabulary means an almost entirely domestic praxis."[12]

---

[9] Jeffrey Stackert, *Prophet Like Moses*, 39, 69.
[10] Stackert, *Prophet Like Moses*, 39.
[11] See Jeffers, *Magic and Divination*, 123–32.
[12] Cryer, *Divination in Ancient Israel*, 261; see also 277.

Cryer adduces the contrasting example of the root חזה, "to see," which forms the basis for the Hebrew term חֹזֶה, "visionary" or "seer" (on which, see further below) and is also well-attested among other northwest-Semitic languages, to establish that vocabulary describing modes of mediation commonly regarded as prophetic within biblical literature were not distinctive to Israel. Rather, from these and similar comparative linguistic findings Cryer concludes that "prophetic terminology, if not the phenomenon itself, was derived from Israel's 'neighbours', whereas Israel's various forms of magic were in all likelihood domestic."[13]

This disparity between the portrayal and labeling of certain mediatorial roles in the biblical text and their likely historical distribution, origins, and status can be a helpful check on taking such purportedly normative biblical accounts at face value. But even for those who do not consider this passage to be historically accurate, it nonetheless frequently operates as theologically or intellectually normative.[14] Meanwhile, for those who explicitly reject such normativity, it can nonetheless exert *implicit* norming force.[15] This is particularly concerning in light of Deuteronomy's rhetorical deployment of these etic categories to rationalize conquest, regulate subjectivity, and produce docile practitioners of authorized religion in a manner similar to modern colonial discourse analyzed by Randall Styers, discussed in Chapter 1. Yuval Harari argues that Deuteronomic condemnation of unauthorized forms of divination "had a political dimension . . . : a struggle over social assets, which obviously involved material aspects too." Rhetorical condemnation aimed to "displace them beyond the actual (or imagined) boundaries of society."[16]

Two insights for this study emerge from the arguments and observations of Petersen, Stackert, Cryer, Styers, and Harari. First, Styers' analysis of the relation between the categories of magic and religion in contexts of conquest,

---

[13] Cryer, *Divination in Ancient Israel*, 262.
[14] On this, Nissinen (*Ancient Prophecy*, 24) cites Bahrani (*Rituals of War*, 73–74), who refers to this as a "mimetic process" that replicates the biases and ideologies of one's sources. Both scholars note the difficulty of avoiding such mimetic thinking even when adopting a critical, scholarly lens. Beyond this difficulty, Nissinen notes that "mimetic reading of the prophetic books and other texts in the Hebrew Bible is actively encouraged in Jewish and Christian theology," precisely because these books are viewed as scripture (*Ancient Prophecy*, 25). See also Nissinen, "Comparing Prophetic Sources," 17; Hamori, *Women's Divination*, 30.
[15] Cryer notes, e.g., "As far as magic is concerned, and divination in particular, modern Western Old Testament study has tended to follow the lead of the Deuteronomist(s)" (*Divination in Ancient Israel*, 234; see also 242). While Cryer primarily focuses on the understanding of modes of divination apart from prophecy, the same could be said for prophecy (see, e.g., *Divination in Ancient Israel*, 263).
[16] Harari, "Ancient Israel and Early Judaism," 142.

colonization, and domestic social regulation can help scholars to uncover, trace, and evaluate the biases that condition our own analyses of biblical texts portraying diverse forms of mediation, including the presumptive privileging of verbal modalities of mediation and reduction of the role of prophet to that of spokesperson. The fact that ancient and modern discourses share a common pattern of rhetorical othering, displacement, and regulation of religious practice highlights a perennial pitfall for scholars of religion. As noted above, texts such as Deut 18:10–22 exert norming force on present day religious belief and practice and even national ideologies. They also shape categories and frames of scholarly analysis, thus contributing to the biases that scholars, including myself, bring to biblical texts.[17]

In addition, Petersen's observation regarding Moses's shifting status from non-prophet to prophet, Stackert's contrasting analysis of the ways different Pentateuchal sources inflected their portrayals of Moses's prophetic role, and Harari's recognition of political and social dimensions of Deuteronomic rhetoric about prophecy highlight that "prophet" was not a unitary phenomenon or fixed social role, but was understood differently in different social, geographical, and historical settings.[18] It was (and is) also contested and negotiated across time, place, culture, and context.[19] The thing modern scholars call biblical prophecy is thus not monolithic. The differing and even conflicting portrayals of prophecy found across a range of biblical texts press us toward a more expansive understanding of prophetic mediation.

Prophecy as Mediation: Key Terms and Concepts

While earlier biblical scholarship frequently replicated a categorical opposition between diverse divinatory, magical, and other, similar mediatorial

---

[17] The history of the use of Deuteronomic rhetorical and religious othering in narratives rationalizing modern conquest, e.g., the conquest of the Americas by European settlers, reveals that such biases are not innocent. See, e.g., Warrior, "Canaanites, Cowboys, and Indians," 7: "We need to be more aware of the way ideas such as those in the conquest narratives have made their way into Americans' consciousness and ideology."

[18] Nissinen argues that prophecy, as "practice, concept, and category," while found in many times, places, and cultures, is far from an inevitable or universally consistent phenomenon or idea ("Prophecy as Construct," 14). He states: "As socioreligious and political agents, people called prophets execute distinct and culture-specific roles within the social and ideological structure, identity, and narrative of any given society depending on the societal interpretation and appreciation of different types of religious mediation" ("Prophecy as Construct," 11–12).

[19] Stackert (*Prophet Like Moses*) analyzes the differing and at times competing views of prophecy within the Torah.

practices (such as those condemned in Deut 18) on the one hand and authorized forms of prophetic activity on the other, more recent scholarship has positioned prophecy not as a separate category from but rather a subset of divination. Divination, meanwhile, is recognized as a subset of the broader category intermediation.[20] The grouping of prophecy within divination is a salutary development inasmuch as it recognizes commonalities between prophecy and other similar practices and helps to blur the dichotomous distinctions projected by Deut 18. Unfortunately, analysis of prophecy as a subset of divination tends to place primary or even sole emphasis on the mediation of *knowledge*, which is fundamental to the classic meaning of divination.[21] Even those who treat prophecy as a subset of intermediation more broadly still frequently default to a definition of prophecy as verbal communication, orally or in writing, of a message from a deity to a human recipient.[22] For English speakers, the derivation of the English word prophet from the Greek noun προφήτης (m)/προφῆτις (f), literally "one who speaks for" or "one who speaks forth," both reflects this understanding of prophecy and prejudices study of the phenomena and construct(s) it names. Yet the range of titles designating prophetic roles in the Hebrew Bible nowhere includes words meaning "speaker," "writer," or "spokesperson."[23] Unambiguous use of the term "messenger" (מלאך) to designate the role of prophet occurs only once (Hag 1:13), but the same term also designates priestly mediation (Mal 3:1).[24] Indeed, among the four terms commonly accepted as designations

---

[20] See, e.g., Nissinen, "Prophetic Intermediation," 5–22.

[21] Martti Nissinen describes divination as "a system of knowledge and belief that serves the purpose of maintenance of the symbolic universe in a society sharing the conviction that things happening on earth are not coincidental but managed by superhuman agents, reflecting decisions made in the world of gods or spirits . . . its purpose is to become conversant with superhuman knowledge in order to elicit answers (that is, oracles) to questions beyond the range of ordinary human understanding" (*Prophetic Divination*, 75). He then describes prophecy as a subset thereof, saying, "In my language, the word 'prophecy' basically stands for the transmission of allegedly divine knowledge by non-technical means" (*Prophetic Divination*, 77). A somewhat different approach to divination can be found in Rutz, *Bodies of Knowledge*, 2–5, but here, too, the category divination remains primarily focused on mediation of knowledge and interpretation. I do not dispute this understanding of divination, but rather question the aptness of classifying prophecy (or at least "biblical prophecy") as (purely) a subset thereof.

[22] E.g., Grabbe, *Priests, Prophets, Diviners, Sages*, 107: "The prophet is a mediator who claims to receive messages direct from a divinity, by various means, and communicates these messages to recipients." Note that not all definitions revolve around the message. Lindblom, e.g., defines prophet as one "who, because he is conscious of having been specially chosen and called, feels forced to perform actions and proclaim ideas which, in a mental state of intense inspiration or real ecstasy, have been indicated to him in the form of divine revelations" (*Prophecy in Ancient Israel*, 46).

[23] One exception is metonymic use of the word "mouth" to refer to a prophetic role in Exod 4:16.

[24] "Messenger" (מלאך) is also used of the servant in Isa 42:19. "Herald of good tidings" (מבשרת/מבשר) may be used as a prophetic title at Isa 40:9, 41:27, and Nah 1:15, but whether 'herald' in each

38 THE PROPHETIC BODY

for the role of prophet, none etymologically relate to verbal communication, while two relate to visual perception. This terminological evidence does not negate the importance of speech and writing for biblical prophecy but should discourage us from limiting the scope of biblical prophetic mediation to verbal modalities only.

While analysis of the Hebrew terms for prophetic roles does not provide a full or definitive portrait of biblical prophecy, it highlights key aspects of its embodiment that will come to the fore in subsequent chapters and helps to identify the range of roles and figures that will be included in this study.[25] Terms to be considered are, in order of frequency, נביא (m, 316 occurrences)/ נביאה (f, six occurrences); איש האלהים (sixty-four occurrences)/ איש אלהים (six occurrences); חֹזֶה (fifteen occurrences); and רֹאֶה (thirteen occurrences).

Before examining these terms, a caveat is necessary. I noted above that the category "prophet" is not unitary or fixed, but is rather fluid and contested, with differing conceptualizations among different groups and writers in different periods. At the same time, it is not possible to distinguish historical subtypes of prophetic or mediatory figures based solely on the role labels applied to them. Brad Kelle summarizes challenges confronting such attempts at historical reconstruction and differentiation:

> ... the differing Hebrew terms do not permit clear definitions and distinctions of prophetic roles and behaviors. More importantly, for some, the older insights about the secondary redefinition and reapplication of terms such as *navi'* in the biblical texts lead to the conclusion that all such labels are late, artificial standardizations done by scribes in the Persian period. Hence, the scribes may have included a number of things under the label of "prophet" or "prophecy" that were not part of the ancient

---

case refers to a prophet is not clear. On whether biblical prophets were understood to be messengers, see Greene, "Old Testament Prophet as Messenger." Greene concludes, "an investigation of the O.T. produced no concrete evidence that the prophets in general were messengers, or were ever so considered by their contemporaries, especially during pre-exilic periods. The investigation produced evidence to show that only one prophet, the post-exilic prophet Haggai, ... was called a messenger" ("Old Testament Prophet as Messenger," 322). Greene nonetheless affirms the value of comparing Israelite prophets and ancient west Asian messengers through a sociological lens ("Old Testament Prophet as Messenger," 280–301, 334–5).

[25] Grabbe helpfully observes, "although the terminology helps us initially to define what a prophet is, the identity of a prophet ultimately depends on the context—the actions and characterization of the individual in question" (*Priests, Prophets, Diviners, Sages*, 117–18). Petersen (*Roles of Israel's Prophets*, 36) quotes Keesing to similar effect: "Linguistic labels do not turn out to be reliable indicators of social identities" (Keesing, "Toward a Model of Role Analysis," 425).

phenomenon, and this possibility complicates any effort to connect the biblical picture of prophets to a supposed historical phenomenon behind the text ... At the very least, for a wide range of current scholars, ongoing attention to the nature and development of the HB terms has produced an increased recognition that the modern category label of "prophet" overlaps with but is not identical to any one category.[26]

My own focus is not on the historical reconstruction of discrete roles and their evolution or relation to one another, but rather the various *portrayals* of prophetic roles, experience, and activity within biblical literature. Yet scholarly insight regarding the possible evolutions of these roles and labels is nonetheless helpful for clarifying the significance of the body within the range of experiences and activities subsumed under the umbrella of prophecy within biblical literature and its reception.

The central importance of the role label נביא/נביאה for the study of biblical prophecy is not controversial. It is applied to individuals and groups in diverse social locations and is the least marked of the terms considered here. נביא/נביאה, rendered προφήτης (m)/προφῆτις (f) in Greek and "prophet" in English, are nouns appearing to have the form of passive participles literally meaning, "one who is called."[27] Jonathan Stökl concludes from a survey of its uses in Hebrew that נביאה/נביא is "a term for 'diviner' ... including both ecstatic and non-ecstatic forms of divination."[28] He accounts for its broad and varied usage by proposing a historical development in which discrete divinatory roles eventually coalesced into that of the "messenger-type prophet" he argues is typical of the latter prophets. This shift linked prophecy to "Scriptural study, knowledge, and interpretation." In a parallel development, musical modalities associated with ecstatic prophecy found new life in the prophetic activity of temple musicians and singers.[29] Anne Jeffers similarly argues that the role label נביאה/נביא has different features in different periods and sources but expands its functions beyond divination. For Jeffers, this role included at some point(s) "divinatory and/or magical" features

---

[26] Kelle, "Phenomenon of Israelite Prophecy," 280.
[27] See philological analysis in Stökl, *Prophecy in the Ancient Near East*, 157–92. Petersen introduces the phrase "role label" from role theory (*Roles of Israel's Prophets*, 35).
[28] Stökl, *Prophecy in the Ancient Near East*, 175. Stökl also considers a number of Pentateuchal uses of נביא to mean "important person" rather than "prophet," including applications to Moses and Abraham (*Prophecy in the Ancient Near East*, 176), and describes a later sense (found, e.g., in Deut 18:18–22) meaning "leader with a close connection to the deity" (*Prophecy in the Ancient Near East*, 178).
[29] Stökl, *Prophecy in the Ancient Near East*, 175–6.

such as "second sight," supernatural auditory perception of distant or future events, healing, the use of objects imbued with "magical" power, "the creative power of the prophetic word" and deeds, intercession, and cledonomancy.[30] Like Stökl, Jeffers traces a development in which "the later prophets' emphasis was more on the word of Yahweh, an actual message to be delivered, than on physical miracles. But in effect the veil between the magical power of the word and its result is very blurred."[31]

The next most frequent role label, "man of God" (איש האלהים/איש אלהים), has a similarly complex history of usage. But by contrast with נביא/נביאה, its inclusion within the broader category "prophet" has sometimes been contested. Stökl, for example, excludes "man of God" from the set of role labels designating "prophets" in the Hebrew Bible, arguing that it "is not a professional title but denotes a close relationship between a human and a deity."[32] Yet this relationship is in many cases precisely the pre-condition and ground for the fulfillment of a prophetic role. This aspect of the label's meaning does not negate its function as a prophetic role label but inflects it in distinctive ways.

It is commonly recognized that the legends of Elijah and Elisha preserve an earlier use of this role label. Petersen concludes from his sociological analysis of the distinctive features of the role "man of God" in these legends that early uses referred to a recognized social role of peripheral, itinerant prophet with numinous power.[33] Their primary mode of mediation is neither verbal nor visionary: "they themselves personify the world of the sacred in the profane."[34] Petersen argues that over time the role label is applied more broadly to Moses, David, and others. In light of this broader application, Robert Wilson has argued that the role "man of God" cannot finally be distinguished from that of "prophet":

> in the biblical traditions that have been preserved, the man of God is synonymous with the prophet (*nābî'*) and in fact both titles are sometimes applied to the same individual . . . It is possible that the characteristics of the man of God were originally different from those of the prophet, and the two titles may have been used in different geographical areas, but it is now impossible to separate the two figures.[35]

---

[30] Jeffers, *Magic and Divination*, 84–95.
[31] Jeffers, *Magic and Divination*, 95.
[32] Stökl, *Prophecy in the Ancient Near East*, 156.
[33] Petersen, *Roles of Israel's Prophets*, 51–3.
[34] Petersen, "Rethinking the Nature of Prophetic Literature," 28.
[35] Wilson, *Prophecy and Society*, 140.

For the purposes of this study, I include "man of God" as a prophetic role label for two reasons: consistent with Wilson's point above, a number of the same figures called "man of God" in biblical narrative are also called "prophet" (נביא), including the two figures to whom the role label "man of God" is most frequently applied, namely Elijah and Elisha.[36] This functional synonymy, while not complete, indicates that at least some biblical writers considered the role "man of God" as equivalent to or significantly overlapping with the role "prophet." Moreover, while it is widely accepted that Elijah and Elisha are archetypal for the role "man of God" in the biblical corpora, it is also the case that some later biblical writers considered Elijah to be an especially important and even archetypal "prophet."[37] In so doing, they did not separate out acts of power to be assigned to one role and verbal utterance to the other but asserted that Elijah's efficacious prophetic ministry consisted of a combination of action and utterance.[38] For these reasons, analysis of the thing commonly called "biblical prophecy," as defined earlier in this chapter, must include the role "man of God," and not only aspects of that role conforming to definitions of prophecy as verbal utterance, but also aspects of that role encompassing acts of numinous power.

The latter two role labels, "visionary" and "seer," refer at a literal level to the embodied perceptual experience of the prophet. Biblical scholar Colleen Shantz examines embodied dimensions of visionary and other ecstatic experiences from the perspective of neurosciences as well as cultural criticism. She writes,

> while a vision is culturally prepared and interpreted, the fact that it takes place in the body of the visionary is essential to its power. The visionary's neurons, emotions, brain chemicals, and personal associations all root the

---

[36] Elijah: 1 Kgs 18:22, 36; 2 Kgs 1:9; 2 Chr 21:12; Elisha: 1 Kgs 19:16; 2 Kgs 5:8; 6:12; 9:1; cf. 2 Kgs 3:11.

[37] Mal 3:23 MT; Sir 48:1-11; cf. Mark 9:4 and parallels; Luke 1:17. Davis, *Biblical Prophecy*, 56, puts it this way: "Of all the prophets closely associated with Israelite monarchs, Elijah stands as primus inter pares, first among equals—or better, as primus ante (before) pares." With regard to later tradition, she notes further that "the Elijah narrative... is developed... as an indispensable hermeneutical key to the stories and books of the prophets that follow... all the way through to the evangelists' representations of Jesus... [B]iblical tradition consistently reads Elijah as the prophet who is still active in God's service" (*Biblical Prophecy*, 57).

[38] The lengthy praise of Elijah in Sir 48:1-11 is especially revealing on this point. It begins by characterizing Elijah as "a prophet like fire" whose "word burned like a torch" (48:1 NRSV). He withheld rain, produced famine, and raised a dead person to life "by the word" of the Lord (vv. 2-3, 5); he is praised both for his miraculous deeds (v. 4) and for the auditory revelations he received (v. 7).

event *in her* and shape it *as hers*, making it meaningful in ways that doctrine or propositional reasoning is not.[39]

While Shantz is interested here in the experience of the individual, the role labels "visionary" and "seer" suggest that distinctive embodied experiences were at some point central to the *roles* as understood within the cultural contexts of ancient Israel and Judah.[40]

Of these two terms, "visionary" (חזה) is the later and more common in extant literature. Especially favored by the Chronicler, it is overwhelmingly but not exclusively used of prophets functioning in official capacities in relation to the monarchy (e.g., 2 Chr 33:18) and temple service; the latter are Levitical singers credited with composing numerous psalms.[41] "Visionaries" are paired with "prophets" (2 Kgs 17:13; Isa 29:10; 30:10) and are said to "prophesy" (נבא, *hiphil*, Amos 7:12); elsewhere they are paired with "augurs" or "diviners" (קסמים Mic 3:7). Scholars take somewhat differing positions on the salience of the role label's etymology for the role itself. Stökl argues that "as the verbal root (חזה) indicates visual activity, it seems to be reasonably clear that, originally, the חזה was thought to receive divine messages through a חזון, which at first probably referred to a vision, but later became a generic term for 'prophecy'/divine knowledge."[42] Petersen argues for a more persistent correlation between the role-identifier חזה and vision reports and asserts a probability that "the vision reports of Amos, Isaiah, Ezekiel and Zechariah do, in fact, constitute reports of visionary or trance-like experiences."[43]

The second term, "one who sees" or "seer" (ראה), is recognized by the narrator of 1 Samuel as an archaic title; the narrator further asserts its synonymy with נביא (1 Sam 9:9). The role label ראה appears five times in 1 Sam 9 (vv. 9 [x2], 11, 18, 19), wherein the character Samuel applies it to himself (9:19). The Chronicler attaches this role label to Samuel (1 Chr 9:22; 26:28; 29:29) and Hanani (2 Chr 16:7, 10). Petersen has argued that the details of 1 Sam 9 reveal distinctive features of the seer's social role: the seer is honored, non-itinerant, urban, works for hire, and is associated with a public shrine.[44] He further

---

[39] Shantz, "Opening the Black Box," 11.
[40] In later chapters, I examine embodied practices used to induce the visionary state as well as the embodied sensations and experiences attendant upon visionary experience.
[41] Among those called חזה are Gad (2 Sam 24:11; 1 Chr 21:9; 29:29; 2 Chr 29:25), Heman (1 Chr 25:5), Iddo (2 Chr 9:29; 12:15), Hanani (2 Chr 19:2), Asaph (2 Chr 29:30), and Jeduthun (2 Chr 35:15).
[42] Stökl, *Prophecy in the Ancient Near East*, 196.
[43] Petersen, "Rethinking the Nature of Prophetic Literature," 26–7.
[44] Petersen, *Roles of Israel's Prophets*, 38–40.

argues that the seer's intermediation entails a high degree of social interaction.[45] Joseph Blenkinsopp offers a similar description, adding that "the seer is one gifted with second sight or extrasensory perception."[46] Others have countered that the blending of traditions and redactional layers and resulting fungibility of role-labels in 1 Sam 9 make it difficult to tease out characteristic features of the role ראה in this story.[47] A balanced view is that of Anne Jeffers, who posits that the term ראה likely named a specialized mediatorial role that was ultimately enfolded within the broader role of נביא/נביאה.[48] Based on the narratives in which the role label appears she concurs with Petersen's assessment regarding work for hire but remains agnostic regarding association with public shrines. She observes instead that "the seer appears in the texts as someone quite independent, coming and going where and when he wants, not attached to any particular court."[49]

This survey of prophetic role labels in the Hebrew Bible reveals that the category commonly referred to as "prophet" includes a broad range of mediatorial specialists, with differing social locations and modalities of mediation. Some role labels foreground relationship to the deity, others evoke embodied sensory experience of revelation. None of these role labels explicitly names the act of uttering or transmitting a message from God. While this aspect of the prophetic role came to the fore in later periods, it does not convey the whole picture. It is true that a label cannot provide an accurate or complete description of the role itself and should not be regarded as evidence for the content of the role to which it is attached. Other evidence from the HBOT nonetheless prompts us to think expansively about both *how* and *what* prophets mediate. As I stated at the beginning of this chapter and will demonstrate in the chapters that follow, biblical prophecy mediates not only knowledge but also affect, power, agency, encounter, and relationship.

Identifying prophecy as a form of mediation foregrounds its embodied character. Birgit Meyer argues that "Mediation objectifies a spiritual power

---

[45] Petersen ("Rethinking the Nature of Prophetic Literature," 25n.3) credits Overholt (*Channels of Prophecy*, 17–25) for emphasizing "that prophecy involves social interaction, not simply isolated verbal utterance."

[46] Blenkinsopp, *Sage, Priest, Prophet*, 124.

[47] E.g., Stökl, *Prophecy in the Ancient Near East*, 198; Schniedewind, *Word of God*, 44–5.

[48] Jeffers, *Magic and Divination*, 99. Jeffers notes (*Magic and Divination*, 99n.341) that LXX often "fails to take into account any distinction between rō'eh, ḥōzeh, and nābî', using prophētēs indiscriminately for all three. However, the LXX translates ho blepōn for rō'eh in 1 Sam 9:9.11.18; 1 Chr 9:22; 29:29 and prophētēs in 1 Chr 26:28, 2 Chr 16:7.10 (for Hanani)."

[49] Jeffers, *Magic and Divination*, 101.

that is otherwise invisible to the naked eye ... thereby making its appearance via a particular sensational form dependent on currently available media and modes of representation."[50] By "sensational form," Meyer means two things. The phrase can designate "relatively fixed, authorized modes of invoking, and organizing modes of access to the transcendental, thereby creating and sustaining links between religious practitioners in the context of particular religious organizations."[51] Thus, for ancient Israelite and Judean prophecy to function effectively as mediation, the diverse forms of prophetic activity would fall within culturally recognized structures and modalities for conveying access to the divine, including access to the divine realm, knowledge, care, relationship, power, or other aspects of divine realities.[52]

Yet for Meyer the term also refers to ways that "material religious objects—such as images, books, or buildings—address and involve beholders."[53] Meyer is particularly interested in visual media,[54] and so her choice of language ("invisible," "eye," "appearance," "beholders") follows much of Western culture in privileging visual perception and perceptibility in these explanations of mediation and sensational form. Yet her analysis clarifies that mediation produces sensational forms across a broad range of physical experiences: "they call upon the body and tune the senses."[55] These embodied forms simultaneously produce religious subjects and build and shape bonds among practitioners within religious communities. Recognizing this breadth of mediatory forms and their centrality to the study of religion, she writes, "In order to account for the richness and complexity of religious experience, we need theoretical approaches that can account for its material, bodily, sensational and sensory dimension."[56]

"A Paradigm of Embodiment"

In 1990, Thomas Csordas urged scholars in the field of anthropology to adopt as "a consistent methodological perspective" a "paradigm of embodiment"

---

[50] Meyer, *Religious Sensations*, 15–16.
[51] Meyer, *Religious Sensations*, 8.
[52] This is consistent with Blenkinsopp's argument that "prophecy" was "an acknowledged institution" and operated in a primarily cultic religious domain (*History of Prophecy*, 20).
[53] Meyer, *Religious Sensations*, 9.
[54] Meyer, *Religious Sensations*, 18.
[55] Meyer, *Religious Sensations*, 16, 26.
[56] Meyer, *Religious Sensations*, 19.

that would both enable fresh interpretation of familiar data and animate future scholarship by means of new research questions.[57] Building on earlier work by Maurice Merleau-Ponty and Pierre Bourdieu, who emphasize embodied perception and practice, respectively, Csordas examined practices of healing, "resting in the spirit," glossolalia, and prophecy within North American Pentecostal and Roman Catholic charismatic faith communities. Csordas' analysis of glossolalia emphasized the ways this practice reveals "the grounding of language in natural life, as a bodily act," and in so doing "allows for experiential communion of human and divine in a speaking body."[58] Csordas further maps links between glossolalia and "vernacular prophecy" (including cases in which the latter is articulated as an interpretation of the former), arguing that the former manifests "embodied intimacy," while the latter can be understood as a form of "embodied authority."[59] Csordas' analysis of embodied dimensions of modern religious phenomena comprising different types of inspired utterances is suggestive for study of ancient prophecy.[60]

"Even language is body-bound," writes Shantz.[61] But she also argues that study of religious experience enables us to examine more than speech, including "ways of knowing that are not logocentric, even while we work with texts that attempt to put them into words, or ratiocentric, even while we search for the causal links among elements."[62] Like Flannery, Shantz argues further for the importance of attending to the body in the study of religious experience. For Shantz, ritual studies provide one avenue for this work. Another is the study of embodied cognition.[63]

Embodied cognition has been called "the most exciting idea in cognitive science."[64] Early studies of embodied cognition focused a) on ways that body and environment shape and condition cognitive processes, and b) on the relationship between embodied experience and the formation of cognitive and

[57] Csordas, "Embodiment as a Paradigm," 5.
[58] Csordas, "Embodiment as a Paradigm," 25, 29.
[59] Csordas, "Embodiment as a Paradigm," 30.
[60] See critique of Csordas's analysis for its lack of interest in the *material* body per se in Verrips, "Body and Mind," 32.
[61] Shantz, "Opening the Black Box," 13. Shantz here alludes to Fauconnier and Turner, *The Way We Think*, and to Lakoff and Johnson, *Metaphors We Live By*.
[62] Shantz, "Opening the Black Box," 12.
[63] Petersen charts a close connection between Israel's prophets and ritual practice (*Prophetic Literature*, 235).
[64] Wilson and Golonka, "Embodied Cognition," 1.

semantic concepts and structures.[65] Andrew Wilson and Sabrina Golonka argue for a more thoroughgoing understanding of cognition's embodied character:

> Embodiment is the surprisingly radical hypothesis that the brain is not the sole cognitive resource we have available to us to solve problems. Our bodies and their perceptually guided motions through the world do much of the work required to achieve our goals, *replacing* the need for complex internal mental representations. This simple fact utterly changes our idea of what "cognition" involves, and thus embodiment is not simply another factor acting on... otherwise disembodied cognitive processes.[66]

That is to say, it is not only the brain that does cognitive work. This work takes place through dynamic interactions of brain and other parts of the body in relation to their environment. The body is not simply in a supporting role to the brain and the brain is not the only or necessarily primary storage site for the resources that will be activated in interpreting sensory input, making decisions, and directing action.

What are the implications of this dynamic and interactive model of embodied cognition for understanding prophetic literature? First, the prophet's own sensory and affective experience and embodied actions and interactions not only shape the prophet's cognitive processes but are a component part of them. Second, actions performed by prophets do more than reinforce or illustrate the propositional content of their verbal communication. They generate sensory input that will furnish their audiences with new cognitive resources while simultaneously drawing the audience into a shared, interactive set of embodied "cognitive" processes that will produce forms of knowing beyond propositional content. Third, the actions and affective dispositions that prophets enjoin upon their audiences similarly aim to generate forms of embodied knowing that will condition and shape future thought, experience, and action.

We will also see that, as asserted earlier in this chapter, knowing is not the whole picture. Studies of embodied cognition provide insight into certain prophetic experiences, practices, and interactions and are a crucial underpinning for the argument of this book. Other approaches are also needed.

---

[65] Wilson and Golonka, "Embodied Cognition," 1. For the latter, see, e.g., Lakoff and Johnson, *Philosophy in the Flesh*.
[66] Wilson and Golonka, "Embodied Cognition," 1.

Constrained and Shaped by Text: A Challenge, A Caveat, and an Assumption

The primary sources for this study provide artful and artistic representations of religious and social phenomena. Those representations shape the phenomena in turn, as practitioners consciously and unconsciously model their own roles and practices upon exemplars represented within sources available to them.[67] They are also more than representations, for our sources become, for certain audiences, a version of the things they describe or purport to be: channels, mediations, and agents of divine and human power, presence, relationship, words, and deeds. For example, as noted by Stökl and considered earlier in this chapter, a key development within Israel's and Judah's textual traditions is the emergence of "prophetic book" as a literary genre that can both *depict* prophetic activity and simultaneously function *as* prophetic activity.[68] Ehud Ben Zvi has argued that such prophetic books ask their audiences "to construct images of living prophets of the past," while also actualizing prophetic words and roles in new ways.[69] Recognizing the nature of these textual representations, Nissinen proposes a distinction between "biblical prophecy" and "ancient Hebrew prophecy." The former would refer to textual representations and projections. The latter would refer to lived, historical phenomena.[70] The distinction is conceptually a helpful one, though teasing out one from the other is not always a simple matter.

The difficulty in making this distinction arises in part because study of both biblical prophecy and ancient Hebrew prophecy is constrained and shaped by the medium of text, both in terms of the sources available to us and in terms of our own biases. Jürgen Streeck, Charles Goodwin, and Curtis

---

[67] For an analysis of how "classical" prophetic traditions are taken up and reshaped in early Jewish literature, see Jassen, *Mediating the Divine*.

[68] See Ben Zvi, "Prophetic Book." Recognizing the lack of a comparable term in biblical Hebrew, Ben Zvi offers the following definition of "ancient Israelite book": "a self-contained written text that was produced within ancient Israel, and characterized by a clear beginning and conclusion, by a substantial level of textual coherence and of textually inscribed distinctiveness vis-à-vis other books, and that, accordingly, leads its intended and primary readers (and rereaders) to approach it in a manner that takes into account this distinctiveness" ("Prophetic Book," 279–80). Ben Zvi then defines "Israelite prophetic books" as a subset whose members "claim an association with a prophetic personage of the past ... and that are presented to their intended and primary readership as YHWH's word and, accordingly, as such books, claim to convey legitimate and authoritative knowledge about YHWH" ("Prophetic Book," 282). Within this set, Ben Zvi locates Jonah within a further subset that thematizes issues pertinent to the prophetic role and/or understandings and practices of prophecy. He labels this subset "metaprophetic book" ("Prophetic Book," 285).

[69] Ben Zvi, "Prophetic Book," 289, 297.

[70] Nissinen, "Comparing Prophetic Sources," 12.

LeBaron describe both the tremendous value of writing as medium as well as the effects it has had upon how modern scholars conceptualize communication itself. Among these effects, Per Linnell has documented in his own field, the modern study of linguistics, a "written language bias."[71] In the study of biblical prophecy, this written language bias links up with the biases traced in Chapter 1 and at the beginning of this chapter. Streeck, Goodwin, and LeBaron argue that written texts and the logocentrism which their accessibility, longevity, and influence have so broadly engendered make "invisible the embodied frameworks within which language in face-to-face interaction is embedded," including the roles (contributions, experiences, influence) of non-speaking participants, and obscure "many of the crucial forms of semiosis that shape human action."[72] Meaning emerges out of more than words. In cases of interpersonal "face to face" interaction, it emerges within an embodied frame that includes posture, orientation, gesture, facial expression, nonverbal sounds, touch, interaction with landscape, manipulation of objects, and more.[73] The preservation of prophetic literature precisely as literature—as written texts, scriptures—has generated a bias in our own analysis of the texts that often leads us to ignore or discount embodied frames.

Moreover, such biases and the media through which we encounter ancient prophetic speech-forms have frequently contributed to a view of prophetic speech not as an interactive phenomenon but as the product of an isolated, individual subject who operates, speaks, and creates meaning independently of audiences, interlocutors, or bystanders. But prophetic narrative frequently emphasizes "face to face," embodied encounter and interaction as the frame in which prophetic calling, speech, and action unfold. Erving Goffman describes face to face engagement as entailing "preferential mutual openness to all manner of communication"; such mutual openness and shared attention correlatively entails an orientation of body and attention away from other actors.[74] While God's claim to speak "face to face," or more literally "mouth to mouth," with Moses (Exod 33:11) is intended to set Moses apart from other mediators among the Israelites, it also epitomizes the embodied frame for the encounter between God and Moses that allows Moses to function as prophetic archetype within some streams of biblical tradition. This

---

[71] Linnell, *Written Language Bias*.
[72] Streeck, Goodwin, and LeBaron, "Embodied Interaction," 4.
[73] Streeck, Goodwin, and LeBaron, "Embodied Interaction," 4, 9. On the importance of setting, or "extra-bodily environment," see Goffman, "Neglected Situation."
[74] Goffman, "The Neglected Situation," 135. "Preferential mutual openness" need not entail positive feeling but might equally characterize a hostile or anxious engagement.

detail can help alert us to other markers of embodied frames within prophetic literature.

Similarly to prophetic narratives, other forms of prophetic literature, such as oracles or songs, often are framed by or interspersed with descriptors of embodied frameworks within which prophetic speech unfolds. Even when such frameworks are not explicitly foregrounded, we might attend to ways they operate implicitly in the production of meaning and effects. Streeck, Goodwin, and LeBaron remind us, for example, of the role that "co-present hearers" play in the production of speech, action, and meaning:

> in fully embodied situations, utterances are not constituted exclusively within the stream of speech by the actions of the speaker. Instead the visible actions of hearers, including both orientation toward the speaker and operations on the specifics of the talk as it is being spoken, can systematically lead the speaker to change the structure of a sentence in progress.[75]

In addition to the embodied frames for the production of utterance, action, and meaning that are described and portrayed in prophetic literature, a further set of embodied frames takes shape in the complex interplay between orality and writing in the production and transmission of Israel's scriptures.[76] This includes various modes and instances of oral performance of written texts, for purposes as varied as liturgy, entertainment, education, public protest, and commemoration.

Even as we attune our analysis to these dynamics, methodologically, it can never be possible to arrive at a pure, historically accurate account of the religious and social phenomena "behind" or even "in front of" our texts. As Ben Zvi has cautioned, "texts may be evocative [of historical settings], but they are rarely fully mimetic."[77] Indeed, Jeffrey Stackert calls attention to the role of imagination in biblical portrayals of prophecy, arguing that these portrayals entail "creative reimaginations of social conventions and religious practices known to the author and his or her audience."[78] This study does not attempt a historical reconstruction of the phenomenon of Israelite or Judean prophecy. The data presented in our extant sources will not give

---

[75] Streeck, Goodman, and LeBaron, "Embodied Interaction," 5.
[76] See, however, the challenge to scholarly constructions of oral prophecy "behind" biblical prophetic texts in Vayntrub, *Beyond Orality*.
[77] Ben Zvi, "Prophetic Book," 291.
[78] Stackert, *Prophet Like Moses*, 51.

us a clear window into this history, and we must be cautious about confusing literary representation and historical reality.[79] I focus instead on how the texts of the HBOT portray, construct, and instantiate prophecy and the prophetic body.

Having issued this caution, the analyses that follow do assume that, in *varying degrees*, the textual representations in the books of the HBOT both reflect and shape forms of religious experience and lived practice within the cultural contexts in which they were produced and used. The documents convey, in part, what Frances Flannery has called "textual articulations of religious experience."[80] (I develop the implications of this insight in further detail in Chapter 6.) Both Ben Zvi and Stackert recognize that there is a relationship, albeit a complicated one, between *historical* prophetic practices and roles and the *portrayal* of these practices and roles in ancient documents. One aspect of that relationship is that, by literary convention, the writers of the texts analyzed in this book invite their readers to tap into repertoires (shared in varying degrees) of human experience, cultural practices, knowledge, evaluations, and interpretation, even as the writer's art contributes to the construction of a world that is different from the one they each inhabit.[81] This assumption guides a key component of the approach in this book, namely the combination of literary analysis with insights about embodied human experience and social realities from a broad range of fields outside biblical studies or literature, including studies of ritual, religious practice, neurobiology, embodied cognition, embodied interaction, affect, and more.[82] Rather than survey all these approaches here, in the chapters that follow I discuss specific insights and approaches when they are relevant to the argument of the book.

---

[79] Cf. the remarks of Hamori, *Women's Divination*, 36 and Nissinen, "Prophecy as Construct," 26. Nissinen notes that it is often difficult to tell whether a modern critical account regarding a particular prophet or the phenomenon of prophecy is making historical or (only) literary claims.

[80] Flannery, "Introduction," 2.

[81] Gordon, "Mari and Nineveh Archives," 39, considers the feasibility of comparing the phenomenon or concept of "prophecy" in sources from Mari and Nineveh with that found in biblical literature. Responding to the assertion of Knauf that biblical prophets are "literary construct[s]" only ("Prophets that Never Were," 451), Gordon cautions: "We can take account of the current emphasis on prophetic book formation and prophetic literary persona without vaporizing flesh and blood prophets" ("Mari and Nineveh Archives," 39).

[82] Though this book is not a work of phenomenology, my approach is inspired in part by the work of such phenomenologists as Maurice Merleau-Ponty and Gaston Bachelard. See Merleau-Ponty, *Phenomenology of Perception*; Bachelard, *Poetics of Space*. I am especially indebted to Bachelard's interweaving of phenomenology and literary analysis.

Conclusion

An expansive definition of biblical prophecy reflects common (modern) usage as well as the breadth and diversity of types of mediation attributed to figures labeled "prophets," "men of God," "visionaries," and "seers" within the corpora of the HBOT and to the biblical books labeled prophetic writings. Classifying prophecy as a subset of divination risks limiting the content of its mediation to knowledge. I have argued in this chapter and will demonstrate further in subsequent chapters that biblical prophets mediate far more than knowledge. The breadth and diversity of prophetic mediation expands our focus from words alone to include diverse aspects of embodiment. Recent developments in biblical studies, including a turn to the body and (re)turn to experience, furnish tools for this analysis. I draw other aspects of an embodied paradigm from diverse disciplines, including but not limited to the study of embodied cognition and embodied interaction.

Narratively and conceptually, portrayals of prophetic experience often begin with stories of commissioning. I turn to one such story in Chapter 3.

PART II
CALLED IN THE FLESH

3
God's Surrogate (Exodus 3–4)

Among the best-known stories about Israel's prophets is the story in which Moses is first called to his prophetic role (Exod 3–4). The books of Isaiah, Jeremiah, and Ezekiel contain similar stories of commissioning. The similarities among these stories have prompted scholars to analyze them as examples of a shared literary form variously labeled a call narrative (*Berufungsbericht*) or commissioning narrative.[1] These stories of encounter and commissioning establish the prophet as mediator between God and people. They define the scope and content of the prophet's role and mission, introducing the tasks to which God has called them and the challenges they will face along the way. That is to say, they are a starting point, narratively speaking, but they are also more than that: they are programmatic.

The programmatic character of the call narratives frequently prompts scholars to identify in these stories a synopsis of major themes that will be developed in the narratives, oracles, and other prophetic material that follow the story of the prophet's call, such that the call narrative introduces, frames, and interprets what follows. Another approach focuses on their literary form. In an oft-cited study, Norman Habel identified six constitutive features of the form: confrontation, introductory word, commission, objection, reassurance, and sign.[2] Missing from both approaches is recognition of the central role of the body. For example, while Habel occasionally remarks on the body's role in the confrontation, commission, and signs, it is not the focus of his analysis. The other elements—introductory word, objection, and reassurance—are analyzed as verbal. In his analysis of Ezekiel's commissioning, Daniel Block similarly emphasizes the prophet's active role as a speaker, the verbal exchange between the deity and prophet, and the communicative force of the prophet's mission.[3] As stated in Chapter 1, I do

---

[1] It has been argued that Hos 1:2, Amos 7:14–15, and Jonah 1:2 contain partial commissioning narratives. Individuals are also commissioned for roles other than prophet: the stories of Gideon (Judg 6:11–17) and Saul (1 Sam 9:1–10:16) offer the closest parallels. Phinney, "Call/Commission Narratives," 65–6.

[2] Habel, "Form and Significance."

[3] Daniel Block, *Ezekiel* 1–24, 111–31.

not deny the importance of these verbal elements but aim to demonstrate the integral role of the body in relation to them.

A closer look at the stories of call and commission reveals that the prophet's embodied experience frequently occupies center stage. In this chapter and Chapter 4, I argue that the commissioning narratives' emphasis on the bodily experience of the prophet reflects embodied encounter and interaction between prophet and deity. Moreover, as I show in this and subsequent chapters, these encounters transformed and sometimes visibly marked the prophets' bodies. Neither these experiences of bodily encounter nor the bodily transformations that ensue are incidental to the prophetic mission. It is my contention that the prophet's experience of bodily encounter and transformation enables and prepares the prophet to mediate between an embodied God and an embodied people. But the call stories do not isolate body from word. A synergy of body and word in the prophet's encounter with the deity corresponds to a similar coordination of body and word in the articulation of both the prophet's mission (i.e., *what* the prophet is tasked to do) and the means the prophet is to employ (*how* the prophet will do it). That is, the coordination of body and word in the commissioning narratives is itself a programmatic feature, signaling a necessary synergy of body and word in the prophetic mission and activity that follows.

While these commissioning narratives share this programmatic emphasis on the synergy of word and body, they differ in important ways.[4] One key difference is narrative point of view. The call of Moses, narrated in the third person, is the focus of the present chapter. The call stories of Isaiah, Jeremiah, and Ezekiel, narrated in the first person, are the focus of Chapter 4.[5]

The call of Moses is also the most detailed of the prophetic call narratives and has been regarded by some modern scholars as paradigmatic or archetypal.[6] Yet because the book does not call Moses by any of the recognized prophetic role labels (see Chapter 2), some have questioned whether Moses is indeed portrayed as prophet in Exodus. By contrast, Jeffrey Stackert has argued that Pentateuchal sources do not assert but rather presume that

---

[4] Walther Zimmerli placed the commissioning narratives of Moses and Jeremiah in one category and those of Isaiah and Ezekiel in another; the distinction he drew lay in the relative freedom each prophet had to protest. Moses and Jeremiah could argue with the deity; Isaiah and Ezekiel did not have that option (*Ezekiel 1*, 97–100).

[5] I do not here examine the call of Elisha by Elijah, which differs from these four in that the prophet is called by another prophet rather than through encounter with the deity, or the call of Samuel, which does not include a commission.

[6] E.g., Habel, "Form and Significance," 316.

Moses is a prophet.[7] Stackert argues that despite the absence of prophetic role labels, "the basic and persistent portrayal of Moses in each of the Torah sources is prophetic."[8] I follow Stackert in viewing Moses' call in Exod 3–4 as a call to a prophetic role.[9] At the same time, I recognize that Moses is not a typical prophet. He is a liberator, lawgiver, and leader. And even among prophets he is distinguished by his unique intimacy with God, who speaks to Moses "face to face" (Exod 33:11; but cf. Deut 5:4) and "mouth to mouth" (Num 12:8). While Moses does not share these roles and modalities with all prophets, they are nonetheless integral features of Moses' own prophetic role.[10]

Scholars believe that, like numerous other stories in the Pentateuch, the call narrative in Exod 3–4 interweaves material from two originally distinct stories of encounter and commissioning, commonly attributed to the Yahwist (J) and Elohist (E) sources respectively.[11] These sources differ in their portrayals of divine presence, prophetic mission, and the nature and function of accompanying signs. While J provides greater density of detail and focuses greater attention on the prophet's bodily experience, capacities, and interactions, in both sources Moses' commission charges him to perform a range of actions inclusive of but not limited to speaking. In the composite commission produced by the interweaving of J and E materials, prophetic word and body play an equal and mutually reinforcing role as the means by which Moses mediates between an embodied God and embodied people.

This chapter has four main sections. In the first, I argue that Moses' embodied encounter with an embodied God sets the stage for his embodied mediation between God and people. The deity he encounters hears, moves,

---

[7] Stackert, *Prophet Like Moses*, 55.

[8] Stackert, *Prophet Like Moses*, 39. Outside the Pentateuch, Hos 12:14 seems to refer to Moses as prophet: "By a prophet YHWH brought Israel up from Egypt, and by a prophet they were kept safe" (AT).

[9] Meyers proposes that the dialogues between God and Moses in 3:1–4:17 and 5:22–7:7 constitute "the ultimate prophetic interaction with God" by virtue of a "*seven*-plus-one" rhetorical structure that signals totality (*Exodus*, 55).

[10] Graybill argues that Moses can be viewed as "ideal prophet" and thus generalizes from his portrayal to an understanding of prophecy generally: "The example of Moses suggests that prophecy at once depends upon, disturbs, and alters the body of the prophet. If prophecy is written on the body, then the body also displays the transformation of prophetic masculinity" (*Are We Not Men*, 25).

[11] See analysis in Stackert, *Prophet Like Moses*, 56–61. I follow Stackert's delimitation of sources in the analysis below. Stackert (*Prophet Like Moses*, 61) identifies another call narrative, from the P source, at 6:2–13; 7:1–5. I limit my analysis to the JE narrative. The boundaries of the call are debated, with some delimiting the unit at Exod 3:1–4:17 and others extending its boundaries to 4:21 or 4:23.

sees, speaks, and acts in ways that are responsive to the people's suffering; this deity is also dangerous and wholly other. Moses' body will thus mediate between deity and people. Two parts of Moses' body receive particular attention in Exod 3–4 as metonyms for Moses' mediatory agency: his hand and his mouth. This pair vividly illustrates the synergies of action and speech, body and word. The chapter's second section focuses on the hand, arguing that Moses' hand is portrayed as a surrogate for God's own. Within this section, examination of the signs Moses performs further illuminates this portrayal. In addition to their stated function of eliciting belief, the signs both establish Moses' hand (and by extension Moses himself) as a conduit of divine power and mark it (and him) in a way that prevents misidentification of the prophet as an embodiment of God. The third section focuses on Moses' mouth (4:10–16). Moses describes himself as "heavy of mouth and heavy of tongue" (4:10); God's response supports the conclusion that this description implies disability. Just as the performance of signs sets Moses apart from deity and humans alike, Moses' self-description as a person with disability emphasizes difference between Moses and God and between Moses and the human community he serves. I argue that God responds to the perceived insufficiency of Moses' body by extending the boundary of the prophetic body to include a synergistic multiplicity of mediating bodies. I consider the further possibility that Moses employs creative somatosensory and auditory techniques to supplement and extend the abilities of his body. In the chapter's final section, I argue that the portrayals of Moses' hand and mouth find corollaries in the balanced pairing of commands to act with commands to speak and in narrative summaries of the paired speech and actions of Moses and Aaron. Taken together, these textual features demonstrate the body's necessary mediating role in relation to prophetic speech and action alike.

Embodied Encounter Sets the Stage for Embodied Mediation

My assertion that the prophet here encounters an embodied God may seem contradicted by the detail in Exod 3:2 that the being who appears to Moses in the flame of fire in the midst of the bush is initially identified not as God but as an "angel" (מלאך). Yet the "angel" should be understood as an example of what Benjamin Sommer has called "a small-scale manifestation of God" consistent with other portrayals in J and E of fluid and multiple divine embodiment.[12] That is, the angel is not a substitute for divine presence but its partial, bodily expression.[13] God's body remains elusive in this encounter and throughout the book of Exodus (cf. 33:18–23) but is not absent from the narrative. Divine embodied cognition and agency are foregrounded in the subsequent dialogue with Moses, as the deity explains God's presence in this place as a result of divine sensory perception and prelude to action that will include a sending of the deity's "hand." Yet, while sensory perception and the sending of a hand betoken some kind of divine body, the distance established by this small-scale manifestation, coupled with the incongruity of fire that burns but does not consume (3:2) or of a deity calling from a shrub (3:4), emphasizes the need for a human mediator whose body will channel divine power and speech in a way that is more directly and widely accessible.[14]

This encounter between prophet and deity is precipitated by movement (Exod 3:1, 8) and mutual seeing (3:2–4). Upon Moses' arrival at the mountain, dense repetition of the root ר-א-ה portrays sensory reciprocity between prophet and deity: the מלאך "appeared" (וירא), Moses "looked" (וירא 3:2), Moses oriented his body to better perceive (ואראה) the vision (מראה 3:3), and the Lord "saw" (וירא) that Moses turned "to see" (לראת 3:4). Yael Avrahami has argued that in biblical Hebrew usage the senses are "a category of experiencing the world through body organs."[15] This understanding of the senses, including the sense of sight, underscores this encounter's embodied character. Repeated use of the deictic particle הנה marks the visible presence of deity and prophet alike, emphasizing strangeness and immediacy in their encounter (3:2, 4).[16]

God's subsequent instruction to Moses establishes a physical boundary, placing a limit on proximity. At the same time, Moses is instructed to eliminate a barrier that separates him from the ground (Exod 3:5). Upon removing his sandals, Moses comes into direct contact with the same earth in which is rooted the shrub that hosts the divine presence. In a manner akin to grounding, this holy ground now functions as both buffer and conduit between prophet and deity.

---

[12] Sommer, *Bodies of God*, 42. Exod 3:2 is generally understood to be from the J source.
[13] Sommer, *Bodies of God*, 43.
[14] Polak notes a dialectic tension here: "The more the narrator reduces the gap between the human and the divine, the more he has to emphasize the distance" ("Theophany and Mediator," 120–1).
[15] Avrahami, *Senses of Scripture*, 127.
[16] Merwe, "Cognitive Linguistic Perspective," demonstrates the function of הנה to denote "immediate proximity." Miller-Naudé and Merwe, "Mirativity," identify a core (but not sole) function of the particle in expressing surprise or calling attention to something unexpected.

In electrical engineering, grounding establishes a physical connection to the earth, taking advantage of earth's electrical conductivity to protect against life-threatening and system-destroying electrical shock. This practice acknowledges a role for earth as conduit, with the capacity to energize and stabilize. Organic matter that makes contact with earth, including plants and animals, shares this conductivity.

Grounding is known to have applications beyond electrical engineering. James Oschman and colleagues document the physiological effects of direct contact between the human body and the earth's surface, including contact with bare feet.[17]

> Such effects relate to inflammation, immune responses, wound healing, and prevention and treatment of chronic inflammatory and autoimmune diseases . . . Grounding reduces pain and alters the numbers of circulating neutrophils and lymphocytes [white blood cells critical to the body's immune response], and also affects various circulating chemical factors related to inflammation.[18]

While modern principles of electrical engineering and studies of grounding's anti-inflammatory effects would have been unknown as such to ancient storytellers, these storytellers might well have had some awareness of the earth's conductive, protective, and even healing properties. The removal of sandals from Moses' feet might then do more than signal respect or mitigate impurity.[19] In removing this covering from his feet, Moses would enable direct contact with a medium through which divine power could more safely be channeled, from flame to bush, through the bush's roots into soil, from soil to Moses' feet, and from his feet throughout the remainder of his body. Divine self-disclosure follows upon this commanded act of grounding, suggesting that Moses' grounded state prepares him for the next stage of his commissioning.

The deity's subsequent assertion of having seen, heard, and known the people's suffering (Exod 3:7, 9; cf. 3:16) further develops the portrayal of

---

[17] Oschman, Chevalier, and Brown, "Effects of Grounding."
[18] Oschman, Chevalier, and Brown, "Effects of Grounding," 83.
[19] Meyers connects the removal of sandals with priestly practice (*Exodus*, 53). The removal of sandals can also be associated with shifting social obligations: "The books of Deuteronomy and Ruth explain rites in which removing one's sandal(s)—or having them removed by another—nullified previously binding legal and social ties (Deuteronomy 25:9–10; Ruth 4:7–8; cf. Amos 2:6, 8:6), creating the conditions for new claims, new relationships, and new responsibility" (Portier-Young, "Commentary on Exodus 3:1–15"). On sandals in New Kingdom Egypt, see Hagen, "New Kingdom Sandals."

divine embodied cognition first limned in the mutual seeing of God and Moses. In each case, God's embodiment is portrayed in relational terms. In a similar way, the deity's descent to the terrestrial realm is portrayed as a direct response to this embodied knowing of the people's pain. The commissioning of the prophet is a second component of this divine response, with the intended result that the prophet will implement the actions of liberating and leading that God has now determined to do (3:10).[20]

In the subsequent dialogue between God and Moses, two body parts receive significant attention: the hand and the mouth. The prophet's hand and mouth will be surrogates for God's own. They will likewise each have surrogates in the form of Moses' staff and Aaron's mouth.

Moses' Hand as Surrogate of the Divine Hand

The motif of hand is first introduced through the device of metonymy, which refers to one thing (target) by the name of a (variously) related thing (source). As the body part with which people most efficiently and effectively wield tools (including weapons), grasp and touch, make things, and otherwise interact with and transform their material environment, the hand (source) can metonymically name what it effects, possesses, and demonstrates: agency, power, and strength (target).[21] The "hand of the Egyptians" thus denotes the coercive power by which the Egyptians oppress the Lord's people (3:8). The Lord surmises that it is only ביד חזקה, "through the instrumentality of a strong hand" (i.e., compelled by *divine* power), that the king will allow the people's departure (3:19; cf. 6:1). The Lord therefore resolves to intervene by supplying the hand (power, agency, instrument) and forceful action that will free the Lord's people: "I'll send my hand and strike" (3:20).[22]

David Seely emphasizes the central role of the divine hand in Exodus, where, he argues, it is "a metaphor of God's power to intervene in history"

---

[20] Promise of deliverance is also accompanied by concrete promise of land and food, emphasizing the people's embodied experience and physical needs, while the promised land is itself figuratively portrayed like the body of a mother and female sexual partner, flowing with milk and honey. Meyers notes that the land is portrayed as "explicitly fertile" (*Exodus*, 54).

[21] Schroer and Staubli assert that "human action is concentrated in the hands" (*Body Symbolism*, 161).

[22] According to Ackroyd ("*yād*," 425) there are five passages in the Hebrew scriptures where God is the subject of sending the hand: Exod 3:20; 9:15; 24:11 (all J; note that in 24:11 the narrator remarks on God's *refraining* from sending the hand); Ps 138:7; Ezek 8:3.

(e.g., Exod 15:6).[23] He contrasts the prominence of the divine hand in Exodus with its near absence in Genesis (occurring at Gen 49:24 only) and notes that an association between the hand of God and the deliverance from Egypt persists in numerous other books of the Hebrew Bible. Seely further acknowledges that what he describes as the hand's metaphoric function should not obscure the anthropomorphizing portrait of God that it projects.[24] This blurry boundary between seemingly metaphoric usage to indicate power and seemingly anthropomorphizing portrayal of an embodied attribute of the deity militates in favor of seeing these uses of hand not as metaphor but as metonymy: the divine hand is a part of the divine body which metonymically conveys divine agency, power, and strength.[25]

Elsewhere in Exodus the divine hand is portrayed as a literal part of the divine body that shapes material reality and interacts with other bodies. The deity's finger engraves words upon stone tablets (Exod 31:18; cf. Deut 10:2; Ps 8:4 MT/LXX, 8:3 NRSV); the deity's hand shields Moses from seeing the full glory of God (33:22–23). Yet the present passage does not portray the divine hand's direct interaction with Moses nor direct shaping of material circumstances. Rather, three sets of narrative details combine to portray Moses himself as an instrumental embodiment of the divine hand: 1) five references to the Lord's sending Moses (3:10, 12, 13, 14, 15) precede the promise to send the Lord's hand (3:20); 2) the Lord then directs attention to *Moses'* hand, which becomes in part a visible sign of divine transformative power (4:2–8); and 3) God instructs Moses to "send your hand" to initiate the wondrous transformation of staff to snake (4:4). As I explain further below, these and other narrative details construct a set of functional correspondences between the hand of God and Moses' own by which the prophet's hand mediates divine power and agency.[26]

---

[23] Seely, "Image of the Hand," 38. Ackroyd documents close association between the hand of God and power ("*yād*," 418–22), including military might, especially when paired with "forms of the root ḥzq" (420). He further notes the use of this root "in connection with prophetic inspiration" (421; e.g., Ezek 3:14, examined below).

[24] Seely, "Image of the Hand," 52.

[25] Littlemore (*Metonymy*, 14) notes that recent approaches to metonymy situate it in the middle of a "continuum ranging from literal language through to metaphor."

[26] Noting that the "hands of Moses and Aaron [often] represent the hand of God," Seely argues that this embodied agency finds a parallel in more generic and figurative use of ביד ("by the hand of") elsewhere in scripture to denote God's use of prophets to carry out God's purposes, whether through speech or action ("Image of the Hand," 40). As Ackroyd notes ("*yād*," 410), "the boundary between literal usage . . . and . . . extended senses [of hand] . . . is very difficult to define"; he includes at least one instance of ביד in this fuzzy category. These extended senses include "personal responsibility" and "possession and control," wherein ביד "designate[s] the agent through whom a particular action

The verb "to send" occurs sixty-one times in Exodus, with a majority (thirty-nine, or 64%) of occurrences pertaining to Pharaoh's releasing or refusing to release God's people.[27] These repetitions focus attention on the people's release from slavery and exodus from Egypt, a narrative telos and goal of Moses' commissioning (3:16–22). Here and throughout Exod 3–9, the "sending" action God desires from Pharaoh finds a parallel and precipitating action in the sending actions of God, such that God's sending of agent(s), hand, and blows or plagues mirrors and aims to elicit the sending God desires from Pharaoh, that he "send" the people from Egypt.[28]

Among the twenty-two occurrences of the verb "to send" in Exodus that do *not* refer to Pharaoh's releasing or refusing to release God's people, nearly half (ten) occur in the story of Moses' commissioning.[29] In half of these ten instances (3:10, 12, 13, 14, 15), Moses is the object of God's sending. In two, Moses asks God to send a different person (4:13 x 2). In the remaining occurrences, noted above, God vows to send God's hand (3:20) and instructs Moses to send Moses' hand, which Moses then does (4:4 x 2). The narrative thus focuses attention on three parallel actions: God's sending an agent, God's sending God's hand, and the prophet sending his own hand. These parallels contribute to a portrayal of the hand of Moses as a surrogate for God's own.[30]

The hand of Moses (and in a similar way, the staff it holds) will channel and implement divine destructive, transformative, and saving power. Yet just as the hands of God and Pharaoh function metonymically to denote power, agency, and strength, so does the hand of Moses. As metonym, the literal functions of Moses' hand are not displaced by figurative meanings of power,

---

is performed"; "the dividing line between such expressions and those referring to an actual hand is not always clear" (Ackroyd, "*yād*," 410).

[27] The first of these occurs at Exod 3:20.
[28] In Exod 3–9, God sends Moses: 3:10, 12, 13, 14, 15; 4:28; 5:22; 7:16; divine hand: 3:20; 9:15; blows or plagues: 8:17; 9:14. The sending actions of God and Pharaoh are directly paired in 3:20; 7:16; 8:17. On the association of the hand with plague or calamity, see Roberts, "Hand of Yahweh."
[29] 3:10, 12, 13, 14, 15, 20; 4:4 x 2, 13 x 2.
[30] The phrase "send my hand and strike" (3:20) will be repeated in a negative form at 9:15 (cf. 9:3). This repetition links God's sending the hand with Moses' mediatory role in announcing (9:1) and summoning the plagues against Egypt (cf. 9:8–10). Later, in the story of the Reed Sea crossing, at the Lord's command (14:16, 26), the prophet twice stretched out (ויט) his hand (14:21, 27). In the first instance, the direct consequence is narrated as divine action: "The LORD drove the sea back by a strong east wind all night, and turned the sea into dry land; and the waters were divided" (14:21b NRSV). In the second instance, divine action follows ("the LORD tossed the Egyptians into the sea," 14:27 NRSV), and it is the Lord (not Moses), who is credited with effecting salvation: "Thus the LORD saved Israel that day" (14:30 NRSV). While this later passage uses a different idiom to describe the gesture of extending the hand, it further reinforces a relationship between the hand of the prophet and the actions of the deity.

agency, and strength. The two levels of meaning are integrally connected. This helps to clarify the function of the three signs in 4:1–9: they do not merely demonstrate Moses' power or God's. The first sign establishes the hand and staff of Moses as instruments of divine power to destroy, transform, and save. The second sign retains an emphasis on the hand of Moses in order to make visible the distinction between human mediator and deity. The symbolic enactment of enslavement and liberation on the prophet's body clarifies that the prophet who channels divine power also represents the people. The abjection of his body corresponds to this dual role that paradoxically locates him both at the intersection of and outside of divine and human realms.

Signs

In response to Moses' concern that the people will not believe him or listen to his voice (4:1), God instructs Moses to perform "signs" (4:8–9) that aim to elicit belief (4:5, 8–9). The signs share a common structure of divine command, action, transformation; command, action, restoration; purpose statement.[31] The parallels are shown in the following table.

God commands Moses to perform action	"Throw it on the ground" 4:3	"Put your hand inside your cloak" 4:6
Moses performs the action	"he threw the staff on the ground" 4:3	"he put his hand into his cloak" 4:6
Object is transformed	"it became a snake" 4:3[32]	"when he took it out his hand was leprous as snow" 4:6
God commands Moses to perform second action that mirrors first	"Reach out your hand and seize it by its tail" 4:4	"Put your hand back in your cloak" 4:7
Moses performs the second action	"he reached out his hand and grasped it" 4:4	"he put his hand back in his cloak" 4:7
Object is restored	"it became a staff in his hand" 4:4	"when he took it out it was restored like the rest of his body" 4:7
God states sign's purpose, to elicit belief	"so that they may believe that the Lord . . . has appeared to you" 4:5	"if they will not believe you or heed the first sign, they will believe the second sign" 4:8

---

[31] A third commanded action (4:9) does not share the same structure, is not performed at this juncture in the text, and is not here referred to as a sign.

[32] Not represented in the table is Moses' reaction to the snake: "he drew back from it" (4:3). A similar reaction is not present in the story of the second sign.

While both signs have the same structure and explicit goal of eliciting belief from witnesses, their symbolic functions differ.

The first sign demonstrates the channeling of divine transformative power through Moses and maps functional parallels between the hands of Moses and God. God initiates the first sign (4:2–5) by asking Moses "what is in your hand?" (4:2). The question draws attention both to the prophet's body and to the object he holds, which Moses identifies as a staff, human artifact that functions as physical support, protective weapon, and tool for shepherding.[33] The staff is imbued with supernatural power, such that when Moses throws it upon the ground it transforms into a living, creeping being; when he grasps it, it transforms back into a staff.[34] As noted above, the second action which God commands Moses to perform, "send your hand" to grasp the snake, mirrors God's own promise to send God's hand to strike Egypt (3:20), suggesting that the hand of Moses is a conduit for divine power.[35]

The staff, elsewhere referred to by the narrator and Moses alike as "the staff of God" (Exod 4:20; 17:9), similarly mediates divine power, as will be made explicit at 9:23 and 10:13.[36] While in this first sign the staff is itself transformed, it will later mediate divine power to summon lightning, hail (9:23), and locusts (10:13); divide the sea (14:16); produce water from stone (17:5–6); and aid Israel in battle (17:9).[37] Yet the first sign is not simply the staff, but rather an interactive combination of Moses' body, his hand, his actions ("throw it onto the ground" 4:3; "send forth your hand and grasp its tail" 4:4), and the staff's serial transformations, as the staff first becomes a living body in its own right, namely that of a snake, and then reverts to its seemingly inert form as a "staff in [Moses'] hand" (4:4).

---

[33] As Glazov notes, the staff also had royal connotations, including in the Egyptian cultural context (*Bridling of the Tongue*, 92).

[34] Noting the magicians' attribution of agency for the wonders later worked by the staff to the "finger of God" (Exod 8:15 MT/LXX; 8:19 NRSV), Glazov proposes that the staff "seems to function as a symbol of Yhwh's hand" (*Bridling of the Tongue*, 92).

[35] The staff-serpent may anticipate the שרף (identified in 2 Kgs 18:4 as נחשתן) Moses will later make and erect upon a pole at God's command as prophylaxis against disease (Num 21:8–9).

[36] Cf. the surmise of the Egyptian wonder-workers that the staff wielded by Aaron is (or owes its efficacy to) "the finger of God" (8:15 MT/LXX; 8:19 NRSV). See Couroyer, "Doigt de dieu."

[37] Trimm views the staff as a "divine weapon" ("God's Staff," esp. 205–6). On a separate note, the relation between the staff Moses wields and the staff Aaron wields is unclear. Some commentators distinguish them on the grounds that Moses' staff transforms into a land serpent (נחש) and Aaron's into a sea serpent (תנין; Dozeman, *Exodus*, 212). At 7:15–17 God commands Moses to "take in your hand" the staff that transformed into a serpent (נחש 7:15), and Moses speaks for the Lord in saying "With the staff in my hand I will strike upon the waters . . . " (7:17). Then the Lord instructs Moses to command Aaron to "take your staff and stretch your hand over the waters . . . " (7:19). Moses issued the command and Aaron performed the action (7:20). Aaron's staff also brings forth frogs from the waters (8:5) and insects from the dust (8:16–17).

The first sign establishes that Moses wields divine transformative power and maps a parallel between the hand of God and the hand of the prophet. Once this parallel is established, the second sign distinguishes the human hand of Moses from the divine hand of the Lord by marking Moses' flesh for death. The affliction and restoration of Moses' flesh further signals divine power to cause death and life. Insight into how the sign accomplishes this can be found in Jacob Milgrom's analysis of the symbolic meaning of scale disease within the priestly theology of purity in Lev 1–16. Milgrom argues that visible scale disease has the "appearance ... of approaching death" (cf. Num 12:12) and "symbolizes the death process," which he contrasts with the life-principle associated with the deity and with holiness.[38] While I do not posit the influence of priestly theology on Exod 4, I propose that the symbolic associations between scale disease and death as well as whole flesh and life here operate in a similar way, emphasizing and making visible the distinction between Moses, who is human, contingent, finite, and subject to death and disease, and the deity whose power he (conditionally) channels. Similarly to the Deuteronomic refusal to identify the location of Moses' remains, the sign of צרעת ensures that even when the prophet's body functions as a surrogate for God's own Moses will not be mistaken for an embodiment of the deity.

The motions Moses performs, "leading" his hand into and out of his חיק,[39] include two *hiphil* verbs that will be used for leading the people out of Egypt: הבא (4:6) and יוצאה (4:6, 7). While both verbs are common, the latter verb has unique connotations in the book of Exodus, where it functions stereotypically to denote both the mission of Moses (6:6, 7, 13, 26–27; etc.) and God's action of leading the people out of bondage in Egypt (Exod 7:5; 12:17, 42, 51; 13:3, 9, 14, 16; 16:6; 18:1; etc.). This includes three occurrences in the present story, wherein the verb summarizes the action Moses is being commissioned to perform on God's behalf (3:10, 11, 12). While *hiphil* forms of the very common verb בוא do not function in this stereotyped way in Exodus and do not otherwise appear in the commissioning of Moses, their use elsewhere to describe God's action of leading the people out of Egypt (19:4) and into the land of promise (6:8; 13:5, 11; 15:17; cf. 23:20, 23) strengthens the likelihood that Moses' "leading" his hand in and out

---

[38] Milgrom, *Leviticus*, 12.
[39] Referring either to the "lower, outer front of the body," often translated bosom or lap, or to the "fold of the garment, above the belt where hands were placed and property kept," akin to a modern-day pocket ("חיק," *HALOT* 1.312).

of his חיק should be seen as homologous to Moses' and God's leading the people out of Egypt and into the land God has promised them. That is to say, the actions do not merely provide a gestural trigger for the transformation of Moses' body. They also anticipate and correspond to the liberating work Moses will perform at God's behest. By means of a third verb (השב), "return" or "restore," the healing of Moses' hand both anticipates the liberation of the people and portrays it as a restoration to a previous (free) state (4:7; cf. Isa 42:22). The people's change in status from free to enslaved and enslaved to free/d is thus symbolically enacted upon the body of the prophet.

As the one leading out/in and the one whose hand is afflicted and restored, Moses simultaneously embodies the power and agency of the deity and the condition of the people. This dually representative role paradoxically positions Moses apart from God and people alike. It was noted above that the intermittent scale disease that afflicts his hand marks him as subject to death and disease and thus fundamentally distinct from, subordinate to, and contingent upon the deity. It also marks him as other in relation to God's people. As Rhiannon Graybill argues, "impurity staged on [Moses'] body ... thematizes the alterity, abjection, and power of his body."[40] By this reading, the transformation of Moses' hand—the appendage that symbolizes power, agency, and action—into a source of impurity and contagion (cf. Lev 13; Num 5:2-4) may be viewed as partially analogous to the later affliction of Miriam (Num 12:10-15; Deut 24:8-9; see further analysis in Chapter 5), with the result that Moses is, however briefly or temporarily, marked for exclusion and isolation. The restoration of his hand to a state of wholeness and purity would similarly restore Moses himself to a state that permits his access to and belonging within the social body. Yet this restoration is not once for all. To fulfill his prophetic role and elicit belief in his voice, Moses must submit his body to a recurring cycle of abjection and restoration.[41]

According to the deity, the two signs speak with a "voice" (4:8) that elicits belief that God has "appeared" or become visible to Moses. The operative logic is that God's reality, presence, and intentions can be deduced from other phenomena that are more directly apprehended and confirmed by the senses.

---

[40] Graybill, *Are We Not Men*, 30. A different interpretation is offered by Propp, *Exodus 1-18*, 210, who connects Moses' affliction with that of Miriam (Num 12) and argues it is a "penalty for doubting Moses' authority."

[41] A third commanded action (4:9) receives less attention in the narrative, and while Moses is to perform a sequence of actions with his body ("take some water ... pour it on the dry ground"), his body is not thematized as it was in the two signs. The commanded transformation of water into blood anticipates the first "plague" (7:17-25).

Yet the metaphoric attribution of voice to Moses' actions and the transformations they effect might contribute to a reductive interpretation, by which the signs are viewed as (simply) analogous to prophetic speech and their purpose primarily for communication. Following NAB, one could then attempt to render the "voice" of the sign as a "message," such as, "God will work through Moses to create change." Yet the repeated non-synonymous pairing of words and signs noted above suggests that prophetic words and signs are not simply analogous. They are different in kind and complement, supplement, and interact with each other. The signs commanded and performed in this narrative are complex enactments and demonstrations of divine power through and on the body of the prophet. They entail action and interaction, alter and construct reality, and are guarantor and precursor of future acts of power. These recurring, efficacious, and transformative manifestations of power are thus different from a message. They are "signs" not because they are reducible to linguistic (semiotic) content, but because they provide visible and tangible evidence of the deity's power, work, and intention. The attribution of voice to the signs further conveys a dynamism by which the performance of divine transformative power and promise "addresses" those who witness it, inviting belief and active response.[42]

Heavy of Mouth: A Prophet with Disability

While earlier portions of the commission focused attention on Moses' hand, 4:10–16 focus on the mouth. Near the conclusion of the commissioning narrative, Moses raises the problem of the insufficiency of his own body, specifically his mouth and tongue, for the work to which he has been called (4:10). The deity's response asserts both divine agency in the creation of the human body and ongoing divine presence and agency in the prophet's work. The deity further expands the structure of mediation to include a third mediating body, that of Aaron, who will be Moses' mouth and will enact Moses' commission with and for him (cf. 4:30). The resulting model of prophecy is interactive and collaborative, enlisting multiple bodies within a single prophetic commission.

---

[42] The portion of the narrative containing these signs is commonly attributed to J. In the material commonly attributed to E, a different sign is promised that seems to embody the very response these two signs aim to elicit: the people will worship God "on this mountain" (3:12).

Moses' objection that he is "not a man of words" and is "heavy of mouth and heavy of tongue" (4:10; cf. 6:12, 30) has been variously interpreted as a description of ineloquence, language loss, and disability. Based on his interpretation of YHWH's response at 4:12, Gregory Glazov argues that the "root cause of the impediment cannot be medical but is implicitly intellectual."[43] Adducing ancient West Asian parallels for "opening of the mouth," Carol Meyers similarly argues that "this is metaphoric language and not the description of a speech impediment."[44] Kristine Garroway has recently argued that Moses refers to Hebrew language loss ("attrition") due to his adoption into a royal Egyptian household in which the Egyptian language would be taught and used while Hebrew language would be associated with an enslaved group of people.[45]

Other details in the text lend weight to the interpretation that Moses describes a condition commonly regarded as a disability.[46] God's immediate response frames Moses' objection in relation to the human body and to a triad of disabilities, namely muteness, deafness, and blindness: "And the Lord said to him, who gives a human a mouth? Or who makes [someone] mute or deaf or seeing or blind? Is it not I, the Lord?" (4:11).[47] God's response first makes an implicit claim about the specific body part that is the focus of Moses' objection, declaring, in effect, "I put it [there]. You have this particular mouth because of my choosing, my doing."[48] By including an example of

---

[43] Glazov, *Bridling of the Tongue*, 77.

[44] Meyers, *Exodus*, 61.

[45] Garroway, "Moses's Slow Speech."

[46] Graybill argues that even a metaphorical reference to lack of eloquence "represents the interference of the body in the transmission of meaning" (*Are We Not Men*, 29). While acknowledging the portrayal of disability in this text, Junior and Schipper ("Mosaic Disability") shift attention away from a diagnostic approach that relies on and perpetuates a medical model of disability toward a cultural approach that examines how disability functions in the discourse of the text as a marker of identity and difference. In Moses' case, they argue that his focus on his physical disability enables him to deflect questions about loyalty that may be occasioned by his embodiment of multiple ethnic identities and is consistent with "literary use of disability as a means of expediting resolution while obscuring a more socially complex rendering of the experience of characters with disabilities" (Junior and Schipper, "Mosaic Disability," 441).

[47] Tigay counters that God's response could be taken as a "maximal expression of [divine] powers," arguing a fortiori for God's power over human faculties ("Heavy of Mouth," 61). While God does here seem to respond to Moses' objection by arguing from a stronger example of divine power to a lesser one, the example chosen is not random or loosely connected to Moses' objection. Rather, God has chosen examples of difficulty that are in the same category as the one Moses has just named—physical disability—in order to make plain that God will not be deterred in overcoming the limitations Moses experiences.

[48] Tigay argues that "the most natural reading" of God's response is that God is the author of Moses disability: "If your speech is defective, it is because I have made you that way" ("Heavy of Mouth," 62). Junior and Schipper summarize God's argument as an assertion that "God controls all physical conditions" ("Mosaic Disability," 431).

non-disability, namely sightedness, among conditions commonly regarded as disabilities, God's second question rhetorically disrupts and destabilizes the condition or category of "disability" even as it invites Moses to view his own "heaviness" of mouth and tongue within this framework. The form of God's questions mirrors those the Lord poses to Job in the speech from the whirlwind, which foreground both the awesome creative power of the deity and the limits of human understanding of how creation works and God's role and actions within it.[49] This parallel helps illuminate the logic of God's speech in Exod 4:11: Moses' experience of "heaviness" of mouth and tongue is only part of the picture. God does not offer to remove Moses' heaviness of mouth and tongue, but rather to come alongside and work with and through this mouth: "I will be with your mouth and I will teach you what to speak" (4:12). God further offers to supply another "mouth" in the person of Aaron (4:16).[50] The particularity, contingency, and limitations of the prophet's body necessitate extending the boundary of that body to include a multiplicity of human bodies acting together in synergy.

Disability studies illuminate further social and cultural aspects of the portrayal of Moses' mouth/speaking. Saul Olyan attends to "ways in which textual castings of disability function to realize and communicate patterns of social inequality," noting that "texts create categories of stigmatized persons whom they seek to marginalize, as well as their antitype: categories of privileged persons who lack negatively constructed, stigmatized characteristics and possess valued traits."[51] In this story, Olyan argues, Moses' body is stigmatized, while the priestly body of Aaron is privileged. Both together mediate between a deity whose body is inaccessible in the narrative and a people who are disempowered. Graybill similarly notes that as culturally marked physical difference, the heavy mouth and tongue of Moses mark his body as other, placing him in a category of exclusion and drawing attention to the ways he does not meet expectations.[52] For Olyan, Moses' disability draws attention to the difference in power between deity and prophet and emphasizes the prophet's dependence on divine ability.

Yet dependence does not render Moses passive. A further aspect of the portrayal of Moses' embodied experience as a person with disability may yield insight into the portrayal of the embodiment of prophecy in this text.

---

[49] E.g., Job 38:5–6, 25, 36, 41; 39:5.
[50] Graybill argues that God supplies a prosthesis in the person of Aaron (*Are We Not Men*, 30).
[51] Olyan, *Disability in the Hebrew Bible*, 3.
[52] Graybill, *Are We Not Men*, 29.

Fidias Leon-Sarmiento, Edwin Paez, and Mark Hallett contribute a perspective from modern neuroscience. Arguing that the portrayal of Moses is consistent with that of a person with a stutter, they further interpret Moses' staff and singing (Exod 15; Deut 32) as examples of somatosensory and auditory "tricks" that Moses uses to promote "sensorimotor integration" in the motor cortex and consequently increase or facilitate speech fluency.[53] A caution must be raised before building on this hypothesis. Nyasha Junior, Jeremy Schipper, and others critique a medical model of disability that "approaches disability as an individual medical or health care issue that must be corrected or cured through treatment by healthcare professionals or lifestyle changes by persons with disabilities," noting that this approach "locates the so-called 'problem' of disability in the body of the individual."[54] Consistent with the approaches of Olyan and Graybill above, they advocate instead for a cultural model that focuses on the representation of disability in diverse forms of media and analyzes the ways these representations convey "a range of values, ideals, or expectations that are important to that culture's organization or identity."[55] They note that such representations "might include medical issues and social discrimination" but do not necessarily provide an accurate representation of those aspects of the experience of a person with disability. Rather than adopting a cultural model, Leon-Sarmiento, Paez, and Hallett seem to view Moses as a historical person (a "patient") about whose disability the biblical texts provide reliable medical data. While I do not share this approach to the text, the scientific knowledge they bring to bear may nonetheless shed light on the ways that the textual portrayal of Moses as a person with disability shapes the text's portrayal of prophecy as an embodied phenomenon. Put another way, similar to the argument made regarding grounding, above, storytellers both draw on and shape existing knowledge, both experiential and cultural (and these are also mutually shaping). In crafting the story of Moses' commissioning, the (composite) narrator of Exodus may have drawn on their experiential and/or cultural knowledge and/or activated experiential or cultural knowledge in their readers regarding the kinds of "tricks" Leon-Sarmiento and colleagues identify in Moses' story. If so, then the observations of Leon-Sarmiento, Paez, and Hallett regarding the use of

---

[53] Leon-Sarmiento, Paez, and Hallett, "Nature and Nurture."
[54] Junior and Schipper, "Disability Studies," 22.
[55] Junior and Schipper, "Disability Studies," 23.

these tricks can be helpful for understanding the text's portrayal of prophecy as an embodied phenomenon.

With these caveats in place and recognizing that the possibility raised above remains just that, a possibility, the insights of Leon-Sarmiento, Paez, and Hallett have heuristic value, helping to uncover aspects of the interaction of word and body in Moses' prophetic ministry. The possible use of "tricks" would mean that Moses' disability is not simply removed or remedied by God's presence and teaching or by God's supplying of Aaron as oral prosthesis. Rather, while Moses' subsequent prolific speechmaking implies that he does achieve some measure of verbal fluency, the argument of Leon-Sarmiento, Paez, and Hallett suggests that he might do so in part through an ongoing process entailing attunement to the experiences of his body, interactions with his environment, a creative process of trial and error, and practice. By drawing attention to his difficulty and portraying his success, the narrative highlights the ways that even spoken prophecy requires somatic integration across multiple domains: sensory, motor, rhythm, and speech. Moses' possible use of staff and song to enhance sensorimotor integration to produce fluent and efficacious prophetic speech further suggests a role for material artifacts and other, diverse forms of artistic expression in the production of prophecy more generally. Finally, Leon-Sarmiento, Paez, and Hallett acknowledge that Moses' staff and singing each have multiple functions, including "performing divine signals and guiding" the people.[56] If the staff is a triggering stimulus for sensory integration, it is also, as noted above, physical support, lever, device for striking or signaling, and object imbued with supernatural power to transform itself and its environs. As such, the staff extends the capabilities of Moses' own body, enhancing the functions of his body both internally and externally. The singing that may help Moses achieve verbal fluency may also aid the audience in memory retention and access. It may enhance their sense of wonder and beauty, both marking and generating an experience of shared transcendence.

Words and Actions

Thematic focus on Moses' hand and mouth is matched by the repeated pairing of actions and words in YHWH's instructions to Moses, emphasizing

---

[56] Leon-Sarmiento, Paez, and Hallett, "Nature and Nurture," 236.

both in equal measure. In the E source, two pairs of commands to act frame a two-fold commission to speak.

> ACT: "So now **go**. I will send you to Pharaoh to **bring out** my people, the Israelites, from Egypt." (3:10)
> SPEAK: "This is what **you will say** ..." (3:14)
> SPEAK: "This is what **you will say** ..." (3:15)
> ACT: "And this staff **you will take** in your hand; with it **you will perform** the signs." (4:17)

The first pair of commanded actions functions as a summary. In a literal sense, the verb "go" denotes the prophet's motion to the site of his mission, a physical precondition for the subsequent speech and actions. In relation to the mission as a whole, it is the first action from which the others follow. As such, through the device of synecdoche, it signals volitional acceptance of the mission. The command "bring out" identifies the mission's telos. The command thus uses the device of merism, naming the mission's first and final action to refer to the mission in its entirety. Speaking (3:14–15) and acting (4:17) will both be necessary to accomplish the goal of bringing out the people from Egypt.

In the J source, commands to speak twice frame commands to act, creating an interlocking structure of speech and action. Their overlapping functions are neither identical nor simply complementary, but synergistic.

> ACTION + SPEECH: "Go and **assemble** the elders of Israel and **say** [s] to them ..." (3:16)
> ACTION + SPEECH: "you will **go** and the elders of Israel to the king of Egypt and **say** [pl] to him ..." (3:18)
> ACTIONS: "Throw (4:3)
>   "Send ... grasp" (4:4)
>   "Lead in" (הבא 4:6)
>   "Return" (4:7)
>   "Take ... pour" (4:9)
> ACTION + SPEECH: "So now **go** and I will be with your mouth and teach you what you will **speak**." (4:12)
> SPEECH: "You will **speak** to him and you will **put** the words in his mouth ..." (4:15)

ACTION: "**see** all the wonders that I have put in your hand and **do** them before Pharaoh." (4:21)[57]

SPEECH: "**Say** to Pharaoh . . ." (4:22)

The synergy of speech and action is further brought to the fore in the direct pairing of commands to act and commands to speak. In 3:16 and 3:18, commands to act immediately precede the commands to speak. While it may be tempting to view their function as formulaic scene-setting, the commands to "go and assemble the elders of Israel" do more than set the scene for the first commanded speech of Moses (3:16). They enlist an active audience who will receive in Moses' first speech a corresponding commission of their own. That is, the pairing of actions ("go and assemble") with words ("say to them . . .") makes it possible for the prophet to recruit leaders of the people as coworkers in the prophetic mission of liberation. The second speech-command is accordingly not addressed to Moses alone but is a plural form whose subjects are Moses and the elders together: ואמרתם (3:18).

Similarly to the recruitment of elders into the prophetic commission, Moses' speaking to Aaron will equip him to participate in the prophetic mission (4:15). A later summary report of Moses' completing this command uses parallel structure to emphasize that Aaron, too, is enlisted for speech as well as action:

"Moses told Aaron
    all the words of the Lord   which he had sent him,
    and all the signs   which he had commanded him." (4:28)

Moses' speaking to Aaron results in Aaron's speaking and acting in accordance with Moses' commission:

"Aaron spoke all the words   that the Lord had spoken to Moses,
and performed the signs   in the sight of the people." (4:30 NRSV)

These pairings emphasize the conjoining of word and action at the heart of Moses' mission. In the interweaving of the J and E sources to form the present narrative, these interlocking structures of words and action become knotted

---

[57] The dual command, "see . . . and do" (4:21) might be more idiomatically translated "make sure that you do." At the same time, the syntax of the instruction emphasizes the dual role of Moses, in the role of people who witness the wonders, and, because God has put them in Moses' hand, in the role of the deity's surrogate who performs them in the sight of others.

together. Metonymic use of mouth (4:12, 15) and hand (4:21) anchor both aspects of this prophetic commission in the prophetic body, linking speech to the mouth and actions to the hand. In the case of the elders, the pairing of word and action makes it possible for the prophet to recruit coworkers into the prophetic mission. The summary statements that follow Moses' commissioning narrative illustrate the recruitment of another individual, Aaron, into the prophetic mission. Through parallel structure, these summaries of the content of the mission shared by Moses and Aaron place words and actions on equal footing.

Conclusion

Moses has often been viewed as a prophetic archetype and paragon; his commissioning narrative has similarly been regarded as a paradigm that other examples of the genre may have followed. While Moses' commissioning story was not determinative of subsequent portrayals of biblical prophecy, it nonetheless exerted lasting influence within the biblical corpus and later tradition. My analysis of Moses' commissioning narrative has aimed to supplement a prior focus on verbal address, dialogue, and the task of communication with greater attention to embodiment.

I have argued that emphasis in the narrative on the body of the prophet is not incidental but programmatic. The portrayal of divine embodiment emerges as a key starting point for understanding the importance of the prophet's body for the commission they receive. The narrative portrayal of embodied encounter between deity and prophet emphasized paradoxical nearness and distance, presence and inaccessibility. The third-person account of Moses' commissioning, often regarded as paradigmatic for later call narratives, first emphasizes the strangeness and immediacy of the encounter between deity and prophet before establishing both boundary and connection between their bodies. The portrayal of divine embodied cognition then accentuates relationality and interaffectivity, beginning to map a complex relationship between divine and human beings (and their bodies) that structurally requires a mediator.

Two body parts, hand and mouth, receive equal attention in the interaction between deity and prophet, signaling the pairing of action and word in the divine response to the people's suffering and in the prophet's corresponding commission. After establishing the hand's metonymic function in conveying agency, power, and strength, I have argued that Moses' hand is portrayed as a surrogate for the deity's, able to channel divine transformative power. The signs in 4:1–9 both confirm this surrogacy and reinforce the distinction between human mediator and deity, locating the prophet in the space between divine and human realms. The concluding dialogue (4:10–17) focuses primarily on Moses' mouth and tongue, drawing attention to the capacities and incapacities of his body for prophetic speech. In the face of possible disability, Moses' staff and singing may simultaneously enhance the prophet's verbal fluency, aid the prophet in carrying out the actions he is charged to perform, and contribute to comprehension and retention on the part of his audience. Aaron and the elders similarly supplement the capacities of Moses' body. Their synergy mirrors the synergy of word and deed in their shared commission.

4
First-Person

Like the story of Moses' commissioning analyzed in Chapter 3, the commissioning stories of Isaiah, Jeremiah, and Ezekiel each foreground an experience of bodily encounter with the deity that is both intimate and distanced. Such bodily encounters—and their resulting bodily transformations—prepare each prophet to mediate between deity and people in specific ways. The stories themselves also have mediatory power.

Isaiah's commissioning narrative projects a physical environment richly populated with sensory stimuli ranging from sight, sound, smell, and touch to movement, vibration, and emotion. Isaiah's mission holds a corresponding sensory complexity and intertwines sense perception with cognition, decision making, and bodily and social wellness. Temporal and spatial markers, sensory detail, and the portrayal of responsive liturgy invite audiences to locate themselves with Isaiah at a moment of consecration and purification that may mediate their own future restoration and healing.

Jeremiah's call narrative provides fewer details regarding exterior physical setting, delving instead within the body of the prophet and the womb of the woman who bore him. In a jarring physical encounter, God strikes Jeremiah's mouth and places God's words within it, mapping the provenance of Jeremiah's future prophetic speech from God's body to the prophet's.[1] This painful commissioning marks the beginning of a prophetic ministry wracked with suffering and lament for a people who must learn to confront their mortal wound. Divine touch also opens a door for reciprocity and surprise. These portrayals of interembodiment reveal a simultaneous intertwining and differentiation of subjectivity, will, and agency, making the prophet's body a site of encounter and node of mutually shaping relationship between God and people.

---

[1] Contrast Jer 5:13: "The prophets are nothing but wind, for the word is not in them" (NRSV). See further 5:14, "I am now making my words in your mouth a fire, and this people wood, and the fire shall devour them" (NRSV).

Ezekiel's commissioning narrative, like his later visions, invites the audience to see, evaluate, and act alongside God and prophet. Interactions of the divine hand, spirit, and word with the prophet's body further thematize the interembodiment of prophet and deity and portray the interrelationship of word and body. In eating divine words of judgment and lament, Ezekiel becomes oracle, sign, and incarnation of the future he shares with God's people. As host to God's spirit, he also incarnates the conditions for their restoration. Ezekiel's transformed body witnesses to the people's trauma and makes their future both visible and possible.

First-Person Narration, Textual Mediation, and Embodied Reception

A distinctive feature of Moses' commission was its recruitment of other actors—elders and Aaron—into the prophetic mission. This interactive, collaborative, and multiply embodied commission finds an analogue in a different feature shared by the commissioning stories of Isaiah, Jeremiah, and Ezekiel: first-person narration. The use of third-person narration to relay Moses' call created distance, contributing to the portrayal of Moses' uniqueness as archetypal prophet whose intimacy with God set him apart even from his own siblings. By contrast, first-person narration of the call and commissioning of Isaiah, Jeremiah, and Ezekiel heightens audience identification, immersion, and affective engagement, opening pathways for audiences to participate in the embodiment of encounter, revelation, call, and mission.

Georg Fischer has compared the first-person narration in the books of Isaiah and Jeremiah to the poetic stylistic device described in German as "das lyrische Ich," "a literary technique that brings the author's message more closely to the feelings of his audience and enables them to identify with the 'I' of the text."[2] Such identification can be heightened through sensory detail and references to the speaker's own body, emotions, movement through space, experiences, and interpretations. In an analysis of vision signals in prophetic discourse, Daniel Carver argues that first-person narration of visionary experience invites the audience to likewise "experience the vision, in a small way, like the prophet did, thereby heightening the

---

[2] Fischer, "Riddles of Reference," 278.

reader's emotive and cognitive connections to the revelation God gave the prophet."[3]

This assertion is supported by scientific studies of physiological and neuromotor responses to first-person narrative. A recent study of cognitive processes activated during reading has demonstrated that, by comparison with third-person narrative, first-person narrative creates measurably higher levels of what are referred to as "immersion", "flow," and "transportation."[4] The experience of immersion is characterized by a variety of factors, including imaginal and sensorial simulation, emotional engagement, an experience of being transported into the story-world, and altered attention that can lead to a "subjective experience of losing self-awareness, awareness of the surroundings, and losing track of time."[5] In another study, it was noted that neural "circuits" activated while exposed to first- and third-person narrations were located in different areas of the brain, such that first-person "action language" produced motor simulation responses, but third-person action language did not.[6] The researchers concluded that third-person narration is less likely to engage motor processes in the brain, whereas first-person narration is more likely to do so, including possibly producing kinesthetic sensations associated with "internal rehearsal of a motor act."[7]

The findings of these studies suggest that, by comparison with the third-person call narrative of Moses, the first-person call narratives of Isaiah, Jeremiah, and Ezekiel have greater potential to activate the reader's or hearer's sensorimotor cortex in distinctive ways, creating heightened immersion, transportation, affective response, identification, and internal simulation.[8] Moses' call expanded to recruit elders and Aaron to his mission. First-person call narratives of Isaiah, Jeremiah, and Ezekiel expand to recruit the audience. Through such embodied reception of the prophetic text, the audience comes to participate in the embodied experience the prophet reports, internally simulating the prophet's movements, seeing the vision, registering sensations of vibration, touch, smell, and sound, feeling awe and

---

[3] Carver, "Vision Signals," 4–5.
[4] Hartung et al., "Taking Perspective," 1.
[5] Hartung et al., "Taking Perspective," 2.
[6] Papeo, Corradi-Dell'Acqua, and Rumiati, "'She' Is Not Like 'I.'" The study does not exclude the possibility that third-person accounts *could* produce motor simulation under other conditions, but only notes that it did not in their experiment.
[7] Papeo, Corradi-Dell'Acqua, and Rumiati, "'She' Is Not Like 'I,'" 3945.
[8] Some scholars consider Isa 6:1–13 not a call narrative (i.e., not the story of Isaiah's initial summons to the role of prophet) but rather a commissioning pertaining to a specific task. See discussion in Sweeney, *Isaiah 1–39*, 135–6.

fear and wonder with the prophetic narrator. Modern neuroscience helps us to understand how and why this is so but did not discover the phenomenon. Readers have long spoken of being "lost in a good book," and audiences have long enjoyed being caught up in a story, identifying with its characters, and entering the imaginative world it portrays. That the first-person prophetic commissioning stories should facilitate such immersion and transportation is supported by evidence that readers in the ancient and medieval periods studied and meditated upon the vision report in Ezek 1 precisely to achieve their own similar visionary experiences.[9] Through such embodied reception the text itself has the capacity to mediate encounter and relationship.

Isaiah 6

Isaiah's commissioning story introduces a short section in the book of Isaiah (6:1–8:18) sometimes referred to as the Isaiah memoir, partly in recognition of the first-person narration in Isa 6 and 8 of a series of deeply personal experiences, actions, and interactions that frame and ostensibly inaugurate Isaiah's prophetic ministry.[10] While scholarly interest in this portion of the book has often focused on what it was thought to reveal about the historical prophet Isaiah, I bracket that question and focus on aspects of embodiment in the portrayal of prophetic experience, mediation, and mission.

The story locates prophet and God together in time and place, after the death of a Judahite king, Uzziah, and in the temple of YHWH in Jerusalem (Isa 6:1). Such temporal and spatial markers are not incidental to the prophet's embodied experience but are a crucial component of embodiment itself. In his analysis of divine embodiment in the Hebrew scriptures, Benjamin Sommer defines "a body" as "something located in a particular place at a particular time, whatever its shape and substance."[11] While this definition has been critiqued as "too broad," its insistence on location in place and time accords with the approach in this study.[12] Manuel Vásquez similarly

---

[9] Rowland, "Visions of God," 152–3; Wolfson, *Speculum that Shines*.
[10] See Jong, *Isaiah among the Prophets*, 17–24, for literature review and reassessment of evidence regarding the composition and dating of these chapters and their relationship to a reconstructed historical prophet Isaiah. See also Becker, "Book of Isaiah," esp. 50.
[11] Sommer, *Bodies of God*, 2. A different definition can be found in Knafl, *Forming God*, 72: "the physical or material frame of some being." Yet Knafl also emphasizes place. See especially Knafl, *Forming God*, 158–214.
[12] For critique see Wilson, *Embodied God*, 16; Smith, *Where the Gods Are*, 14.

emphasizes the necessary interrelation between embodiment, spatiality, and temporality.[13] With these understandings in view, the scene-setting details in Isaiah's commissioning narrative emerge as more than window-dressing and more than symbolic. They locate in space and time the prophet's embodied encounter with an embodied deity. In so doing, they also supply to audiences' imaginations a framework in which they may themselves imagine, re-create, and participate in that encounter.[14] The detail of Uzziah's death evokes a contrast between the vital energy emanating from the divine glory and the contingency and finitude that characterize the now inert body of the deceased, earthly king. The temple setting evokes a history of relationship that includes the election of people and place and the worship of YHWH enacted through repeatable rituals of procession, song, and sacrifice. The built environment thus carries with it the memory of earlier encounters and the promise of future ones, even as it frames the unfolding drama of the prophet's present commissioning.

Markers of time and place are followed by vivid sensory detail, beginning with visual perception of the deity's posture, size, height, and clothing (Isa 6:1). In this way, Isaiah's seeing provides a template for the reader and hearer, who may envision the deity in turn. The deity is stationary, exhibiting a posture of authority, stability, and sovereignty. Two participles, "high" and "lifted up," describe the deity's position relative to the prophet and to the rest of the scene. Vertical height is associated with power and strength (Exod 15:2, Deut 1:28; 9:2), honor (1 Sam 2:8), triumph (Exod 14:8), and rule (1 Kgs 14:7). It further suggests great size, a possibility confirmed by the description of YHWH's garment, a robe so vast that its edge fills the temple.[15] The great size of the deity creates an impression of smallness in the beholder, increasing the awareness of contingency and finitude evoked by the reference to Uzziah's death.

The stationary deity contrasts with the six-winged seraphim whose "standing" (עמדים, connoting attendance upon the deity) is paradoxically characterized by aerial motion (יעופף 6:2). They embody paradox and

---

[13] Vásquez, *More Than Belief*.
[14] Mills, *Alterity*, 37–62, highlights the importance of spatiality for Isaiah's vision, but places greater emphasis on the chaotic landscape of destruction in 6:11–13, which, she argues, "deliver[s] a dynamic of annihilation of meaning, an evacuation of significance within human beings and within the land of their habitation" (53), thereby pressing the reader to "come to terms with a physical reality" of social and political collapse (56).
[15] Smith estimates the deity's size portrayed here as "about ten times human size" ("Three Bodies," 481).

liminality. With two of their six wings they cover their faces, concealing the part of the body most closely associated with identity and encounter. With two they cover their feet, perhaps a euphemism indicating concealment of the body parts most closely associated with intimacy, or perhaps a literal image meant to evoke mystery pertaining to their locomotion. With two they fly. Their composite form combines the characteristics of creatures elsewhere viewed as belonging to separate categories of creation, including winged creatures of the sky, swarmers on the ground, and human beings.[16] Their name suggests a further feature: they are "burning ones," creatures of venom or flame.[17] Physical form that defies human approach, resists full perception, combines categories of created order, and wields destructive power emphasizes their role as guardians and mediators of sacred power. They both protect and open the boundary between human and divine realms.[18] God and prophet meet at the threshold.

The next detail is auditory, but quickly expands to include a multitude of sensory details that mark the transformation of the temple into a new kind of liminal space. Isaiah hears "the voice of the one who was calling" (Isa 6:4). Seraphic sound inaugurates a moment when divine reality breaks into human reality in a form that is not only visible and audible but also tangible and breathable. And with that in-breaking, the very boundary shifts. The voice causes the posts of the temple doorways (or "thresholds" NRSV) to shake, totter, or lift (וַיָּנֻעוּ; ἐπήρθη). This tottering or lifting of the architectural boundary will symbolize and effect a shift in which it is temporarily possible for Isaiah both to witness the theophany and worship of God and to interact bodily with other participants in this sacred scene.

The voice further causes the temple ("the house" or divine dwelling) to fill with smoke (6:4). Readers might associate the smoke with the brazier from which a seraph will take a burning coal. Smoke is elsewhere a hallmark of theophany (Gen 15:17; Exod 19:18) and, together with quaking, marks God's descent from heaven within the temple (2 Sam 22:8–10; Ps 18:8–10).[19] Here

---

[16] Hartenstein presents the arguments for considering these seraphim to be "serpent-like beings" with anthropomorphic features in addition to their wings ("Cherubim and Seraphim," 164).

[17] Hartenstein, "Cherubim and Seraphim," 164, 172.

[18] See Cohen, "Monster Culture," thesis 3: "The Monster is the harbinger of category crisis" ("Monster Culture," 6); thesis 4: "The monster dwells at the gates of difference" ("Monster Culture," 7); and thesis 5: "The monster polices the borders of the possible" ("Monster Culture," 12). Cohen describes the monster as "difference made flesh" ("Monster Culture," 7).

[19] On the possibility that YHWH was a volcanic deity, see Dunn, "God of Volcanoes." Hartenstein associates the smoke with judgment ("Cherubim and Seraphim," 171–2).

the sound, shaking, and smoke are part of an interactive, co-operative liturgy in which the very architecture responds to God's existence and presence.[20]

The seraph's declaration of worship— "Holy, holy, holy is YHWH of armies! The fullness of all the earth is [YHWH's] glory" (Isa 6:3)—draws attention first to the absolute otherness of the divine being who sits on the throne above the prophet, then to the great extent of the divine glory in relation to the inhabited world. Sommer argues that, while the precise meaning of "glory" (כבוד) varies among sources, its range of meanings includes "body" and "substance." According to Sommer, when applied to the deity it can variously refer to an exceptionally bright and massive divine body, a quality of God that "embodies God's presence but does not exhaust it," or "to an abstract characteristic, such as the honor due to the deity."[21] Mark Smith understands glory in this vision as an attribute or quality that emanates from the divine body.[22] Whether the term here connotes the divine body itself, a quality it possesses, or something that radiates from it, the preponderance of concrete sensory details in this vision, including the deity's garment and seated posture, suggests that "glory" here refers to a similarly perceptible, physical manifestation of God's divine being.

The sensory stimuli described above—singly and together—might disorient, elicit movement or loss of balance, constrict airways, impede breathing and seeing, or produce distinctive smells and tastes.[23] Yet Isaiah glosses over such effects in favor of asserting the inadequacies of his body and the bodies of the people to whom he belongs: "Woe to me, I have been cut off! For a man of impure lips am I and amid a people of impure lips I dwell; for the King, YHWH of hosts, have my eyes seen!" (Isa 6:5). The verse emphasizes both lips and eyes, the first through repetition, the second through emphatic final position. Juxtaposing them expresses a contradiction between the functions of speech and sight, embodying on the one hand a mortal state of impurity and on the other the means by which this human has perceived the deity.

Transformative touch will engage yet another sense to resolve the contradiction between the faculties of seeing and speaking, making it possible for the mortal prophet to speak and act on the deity's behalf. A seraph grasps

---

[20] For a later set of texts (e.g., 4Q403 frag 1 I.41, II.4–16) that envision the temple architecture participating with heavenly beings in praise of the deity, see Newsom, *Songs of the Sabbath Sacrifice*.
[21] Sommer, *Bodies of God*, 60–2.
[22] Smith, "Three Bodies," 481.
[23] Grey similarly notes that the prophet "was overwhelmed, not just cognitively but physically. All his bodily senses were engaged: his sight ... hearing ... sense of smell and taste" ("Embodiment and the Prophetic Message," 432)

tongs, picks up a glowing stone (MT) or coal (LXX) from the altar, and, touching the prophet's mouth, declares, "See, because this has touched your lips, your guilt has departed and your sin will be atoned" (Isa 6:7).

The verb here translated "touch," נגע, used twice in this verse, also means to strike. This touch can hardly be reckoned as tender. In a later portion of Isaiah, the *qal* passive participle from this root denotes the affliction of the suffering servant: he is accounted as נגוע, there translated "stricken" by NRSV and NAB and "plagued" by NJPS (Isa 53:4; cf. 53:8). An ancient translator there interprets the servant's having been "touched" or "struck" according to the perceived effect: the servant is accounted "in pain" (ἐν πόνῳ Isa 53:4 LXX). In the present context, the coal that touches Isaiah's lips is either so hot, so holy, or both, that a sacred creature of fire does not touch it directly but uses tongs to grasp it and apply it to the prophet's mouth. Applying a live coal or glowing stone to the prophet's lips could burn the skin. Jacqueline Grey describes this action as "painful purging by fire."[24] The blazing serpent has effectively branded the prophet for service to the deity.[25]

The seraph's touching the prophet with the glowing stone or coal has a further connotation. The stated effect of this action is the removal of guilt and atonement of sin (Isa 6:7). The combination of the temple setting, seraphic liturgy, the seraph's use of tongs from the altar, implied searing of flesh, and the resulting purgation of guilt and atonement of sin suggests that a form of sacrifice has taken place. Overwhelmingly, the Hebrew scriptures speak of atonement of sin in the context of animal sacrifice, specifically burnt offerings. In this instance, the flesh that is burned belongs not to a substitutionary animal, but to the prophet, suggesting that the prophet is himself, in a sense, an offering of or for the people whose impurity he names. An analogy is the consecration of Levites in a manner consistent with a wave offering (Num 8:11). A further comparison may be made to the portrayal of the suffering servant in Isa 53:5–7, 10–12, yet it must be noted that there is no reference in Isaiah 6 to vicarious atonement. Isaiah is purified and his own sins atoned for, but not (yet) those of the people. Rather, his mouth is made

---

[24] Grey, "Embodiment and the Prophetic Message," 432. Rhiannon Graybill similarly writes of Isaiah's "painful transformation" (*Are We Not Men*, 10).

[25] For the use of branding to mark service to a deity in the Neo-Babylonian and Persian periods, see Dougherty, *Shirkûtu of Babylonian Deities*. Dougherty's study focuses on a group of temple servants or slaves, some of whom received star-shaped brands/marks on their hands, arms, or heads. A likely reference to heat-branding is found in *REN* 224, yet Dougherty acknowledges that it is difficult to ascertain for certain whether the mark described there and in other texts is produced by heat-branding, tattooing, or scarification. See detailed discussion at Dougherty, *Shirkûtu of Babylonian Deities*, 81–9.

pure and, through sanctifying, burning touch, his sin removed, to prepare and possibly mark him for a ministry that will at times prevent the people's turning (6:10) and at times declare and urge it (30:21; 31:6).

The density of paradoxical and conflicting sensory detail that characterizes Isaiah's encounter with the deity and seraphim also characterizes his mission. These parallels suggest that the mission is not simply tacked on to the story of encounter; they are thematically linked.

Following the seraph's declaration of atonement, Isaiah hears another voice, the deity's, requesting a candidate for mission. Emboldened by the purification of his mouth, Isaiah immediately volunteers and, in response, receives his mandate. A doubly emphatic construction—two finite verbs each paired with cognate infinitive absolutes (וראו ראו/שמעו שמוע)—highlights the faculties of seeing and hearing. But paradoxically, Isaiah must encourage the people to see and hear without knowledge (6:9). Mary Mills finds here "a deliberately excessive depiction of the human senses" deployed to underscore their failure and the attendant failure of comprehension and meaning-making.[26] Isaiah must fatten their hearts, make their ears heavy, and gum up their eyes to prevent these organs from understanding, hearing, and seeing (6:10). If they do perceive, they will "turn" (שוב). Though translators frequently render the verb שוב metaphorically in relation to repentance, its basic meaning is physical turning, suggesting an about-face that will reorient the people to God, bringing them face to face with their deity so that they might better see; better hear; encounter the deity who is present, sovereign, acting, and speaking; and understand.[27] If they turn, ורפא לו (MT): "It will heal for them"; or ἰάσομαι αὐτούς (LXX): "I will heal them" (v. 10).

In this passage the faculties of heart, eye, and ear are more than metaphors for the cognitive work of perceiving and understanding. These organs were understood to mediate knowledge and facilitate encounter and relationship. To inhibit their function would inhibit perception, understanding, and decision-making, and in the process also encounter and relationship with the deity. The healing that would take place if the people did perceive, understand, and turn similarly is not merely metaphoric. Bodily restoration of God's people was part and parcel of their restored relationship with God. It could also symbolize restoration of health to the social body.[28] In a manner

---

[26] Mills, *Alterity*, 52.
[27] For detailed treatment of the ways repentance has been retrojected onto diverse biblical texts, see Lambert, *How Repentance Became Biblical*.
[28] Uhlig, *Theme of Hardening*, 109–10.

86   THE PROPHETIC BODY

consistent with the prophet's own painful experience of atonement and purification, Isaiah's commission defers bodily and social healing until after desolation and expulsion from the land (6:11–12). At such a moment, the narrative coordinates of time and space and vividly immersive sensory detail may facilitate the audience's transport to the throne of glory and their own atoning, healing transformation.

Jeremiah 1:4–10

The book of Jeremiah begins with layered authentication formulas that highlight the divine origin of Jeremiah's prophetic calling and of the words presented in his book (1:1–4). The two-fold assertion of the divine word-event occurs first in third-person narration, then in simpler first-person narration. Once this initial authorizing framework is established, "Jeremiah" continues to use a first-person perspective ("I") in relating his call-narrative.[29] Further, a reported dialogue within the call narrative results in *three* actors, rather than one, using first-person speech. They are Jeremiah-the-narrator ("the word of the Lord came to me" 1:4), YHWH, and Jeremiah-the-boy. This multiplicity of speaking, first-person subjects invites the audience to participate in a dialogue that thematizes interpersonal encounter, relationality, experience, and agency.[30]

Like Isaiah's temple vision, Jeremiah's commissioning narrative emphasizes time and space. It begins with a flashback that replaces the temple's quaking pillars with the fleshy walls of a womb and a king's death with gestation of new life. Growth and differentiation of human tissues are the embodied temporal boundary God chooses to mark God's relationship with Jeremiah. God's role as the one who formed the prophet in the womb echoes the shaping of the first human (Gen 2:7), subtly imaging God as a potter who molds life like clay in God's hands. Yet, according to the deity, Jeremiah's creation is not for his own sake. Before he journeys through the birth canal, when his body will separate from that of his mother, he is sanctified and appointed as a prophet (Jer 1:5).[31] This

---

[29] Carvalho ("Drunkenness, Tattoos, and Dirty Underwear," 601) writes that "the book's introduction invites the audience to see the world through the eyes of the eponymous prophet who functions on and off as a first-person narrator starting in 1:4."
[30] On the multiple first-person speakers, see further Fischer, "Riddles of Reference," 281.
[31] Roshwalb, "Lost and Found," 357, argues that he has been consecrated as a "warrior-prophet." She writes: "Jeremiah understands the meaning הקדשתיך as 'set you apart as a warrior' (not 'set you apart for a sacred task')" ("Lost and Found," 360). While linking Jeremiah's prophetic role to that of

prenatal consecration sets him apart for an office and role he did not choose.[32] The temporal and spatial dimensions of this commission thus combine to emphasize the inevitability of Jeremiah's call. Josefa Raz notes the significance of this temporal detail:

> The parallel verses of the commission set up a chronological paradox. How can a prophet be commissioned before being "formed"? If prophetic calls are meant to be answered, Jeremiah's call to prophecy is impossible—he could not answer it because he did not yet exist. He could not be "consecrated" or set apart because he was still completely united with and dependent on his mother's body.[33]

Moreover, while imagery of the maternal womb and divine potter have intimate connotations, elsewhere in the book their associations are not strictly positive. Lamenting his lack of freedom and self-determination, Jeremiah later curses the day of his birth (Jer 20:14). Homology of womb and tomb elicits a wish that his mother's body had been a site of death and burial instead of (temporary) nurture and protection (20:17–18). Jeremiah's exit from the birth canal awakened his senses ("to see" לראות) to a world filled with stimuli, but the objects of his seeing were "toil and grief" (עמל ויגון 20:18; cf. Job 3:10). Jeremiah's lament over this passage into pain follows his account of his prophetic experience as bodily compulsion (Jer 20:7–9). Amy Kalmanofsky links these two passages, arguing that Jeremiah uses "body-language" related to the experience of birth to "protest ... his mission." He expresses "his desire to be freed of his body" precisely because the body is "the medium through which God exercises control over the prophet."[34]

Divine control similarly colors the later references to God as potter in the book of Jeremiah (Jer 18:6–11; cf. 19:1–15), there referring to control over the fate of the people rather than prophet: "See, like clay in the potter's hand,

---

a warrior opens up an interesting set of interpretive possibilities, Roshwalb does not offer sufficient evidence to exclude reference to a sacred role.

[32] Berquist notes, "The birth imagery emphasizes that Jeremiah's call came when he was unable to protest. He is helpless before Yahweh" ("Prophetic Legitimation in Jeremiah," 131). For an analysis of the womb's role as a site of revelation and pedagogy in a later text, see Flannery, "Woman's Womb."

[33] Raz, "Jeremiah Before the Womb," 94. Noting parallels with Mesopotamian royal "uterine commission[s]," Raz speculates that the combination of authorizing tropes from multiple domains (prophetic and royal) amplifies the intended legitimating effect of Jeremiah's commission in the face of both monarchic instability and prophetic conflict that made it difficult to rely on civil and religious leaders alike ("Jeremiah Before the Womb," 97–8).

[34] Kalmanofsky, "Postmodern Engagements," 562.

so are you in my hand, house of Israel" (18:6). Yet there is more to the metaphor than simply control. The shaping work of the potter includes planning, making, and unmaking that correspond directly to Jeremiah's own mission: "at one moment I may declare concerning a nation or a kingdom, that I will pluck up and break down and destroy it . . . and at another moment . . . that I will build and plant it . . . I am a potter shaping evil against you and devising a plan against you" (18:7–11 NRSV). The interweaving of five of the six infinitive constructs (לבנת ולנטע 18:9; לנתוש ולנתוץ ולהאביד 18:7) that constitute the core of Jeremiah's prophetic commission (לנתוש ולנתוץ ולהאביד ולהרוס לבנות ולנטוע Jer 1:10) with the metaphoric imaging of God as potter colors the description of God's "shaping" Jeremiah at 1:5. The actions of plucking up, tearing down, building, and planting are outcomes the potter shapes for the people. At one level, the shaping of a prophet commissioned to enact precisely these outcomes portrays the prophet's instrumentality and lack of independent agency, suggesting he is a vessel shaped for whichever purpose the deity shall determine.

Yet God's invocation of the prenatal context of Jeremiah's consecration has a further connotation: interembodiment. This motif reveals a simultaneous intertwining and differentiation of personhood, subjectivity, and agency. Pregnancy offers an obvious and even extreme example of interembodiment. The maternal body surrounds and nourishes the fetus; they are physically joined even as the tissues of one body differentiate within the other. For Eva Simms, "A great paradox rules pregnancy: Are there two bodies or one? Two beings or one?"[35] Yet the evident separation that takes place at birth masks a reality from view: the phenomenon of interembodiment extends well past the moment of birth. Bodily systems of parents respond to stimuli provided by infants and vice versa. Cells of a fetus can remain "for decades" within the mother's "marrow and other organs,"[36] while maternal cells similarly pass into the bodies of their children.[37] These biological data provide a cellular analog to broader, bio-social realities that characterize diverse types of relationships.[38] "Bodies," writes Deborah Lupton, "are a dynamic and complex admixture of the social, the cultural and the biological, in which none of these elements can be effectively disentangled from the others' influences."[39]

---

[35] Simms, *Child in the World*, 14.
[36] O'Donoghue, "Fetal Microchimerism."
[37] Lo et al., "Two-Way Cell Traffic."
[38] Lupton, "Infant Embodiment and Interembodiment," 39–40.
[39] Lupton, "Infant Embodiment," 38.

In this understanding, embodiment is—from beginning to ending—relational. Thus, even bodies that are often regarded as independent or autonomous are experientially intertwined and mutually affecting and shaping. God asserts both that God participated in the intercorporeality that defined Jeremiah's infancy and that this experience and reality of interembodiment is the matrix of his prophetic vocation.

Jeremiah's reply to the deity's declaration of his prenatal consecration echoes Moses' protest in Exod 4:10, asserting his lack of knowledge and skill for the prophetic work of speaking. Yet while Moses appears to describe a lifelong experience of verbal difficulty, Jeremiah highlights a lack of life experience all together: he is "a boy" (Jer 1:6). The Lord's corresponding promise to be with Jeremiah to deliver him (1:8, 19) further echoes the encounter between Moses and the Lord ("I will be with you" Exod 3:12; cf. 4:12, 15: "I will be with your mouth") but raises the stakes. Where Moses' concern was that the people would not believe him, the Lord's promise to Jeremiah acknowledges a different concern: the prophet's need for protection from harm. Yet while divine presence may partially insulate the prophet from human harm, it does not mitigate Jeremiah's vulnerability to the deity.

Jeremiah reports that after promising divine protective presence, "the Lord sent [the Lord's] hand and touched/struck against my mouth" (Jer 1:9). As previously with Isaiah, so here the nature of this touch is ambiguous, but clues from elsewhere in scripture may illuminate its force. Two other biblical verses pair the actions of sending (שָׁלַח) God's hand and touching/striking (נָגַע): Job 1:11 and 2:5. In the narrative introduction to the book of Job, the accuser cajoles God: "send your hand and touch/strike all that [Job] has"; then, "send your hand and touch/strike his bone and his flesh." When a "great wind/spirit/breath" subsequently "touches" the house that sheltered Job's children and causes their deaths, the translators of NRSV and NJPS choose "struck" rather than "touched"; NAB renders the verb "smashed" (Job 1:19). Later, Job would say to his friends: "pity me, pity me, you my friends, because God's hand touched/struck me" (Job 19:21). Another figure well known for contending with God was also "touched": "When the man saw that he did not prevail against Jacob, he *struck* [וַיִּגַּע] him on the hip socket; and Jacob's hip was put out of joint as he wrestled with him" (Gen 32:25 NRSV). Jeremiah's relationship with God in the book that bears his name has close similarities with the wrestling of Jacob and the railing lament of Job. Jeremiah will later accuse God of seducing, overpowering, and prevailing over him (Jer 20:7). In line with this later description of the deity's manner of interacting with the prophet, God's touch here may have been less like a tender caress and more like a punch in the jaw. Like the affliction of Job's body or Jacob's limp, and like the coal that touches Isaiah's lips, this touch may have left a scar or wound upon the prophet's body.

Whether violent, tender, or otherwise, the Lord's sending the Lord's hand to touch Jeremiah's mouth continues the theme of interembodiment introduced in Jer 1:5. Penelope Deutscher's study of touch sheds further light on ways the tactile encounter between the Lord and Jeremiah relates to Jeremiah's mediating prophetic role.[40] For Deutscher, skin is more than the body's fleshy container and more than a sense organ. "It is the locus of a subjective project of relation to the world, and illustrates how physiological and psychological domains cannot be separated."[41] Deutscher places in conversation two accounts of touch, one by Jean Paul Sartre and the other by Simone de Beauvoir. Sartre articulates an understanding of touch as possession, an "appropriation of the Other's body" that is also a shaping of the Other.[42] Beauvoir focuses rather on "a complex reciprocity, in the simultaneous assertion and undermining of bodily and subjective boundaries."[43] In Beauvoir's understanding, touch does not seek to appropriate or possess but remains open to surprise by the Other. Deutscher's placing the accounts of Sartre and Beauvoir in conversation yields insight for interpreting Jeremiah's encounter with the Lord. The deity's touch of Jeremiah might likewise aim at more than possession and shaping, and instead open up the possibility of reciprocity and surprise. While with this touch God placed God's words in Jeremiah's mouth (Jer 1:9), the call-narrative's first-person narration and dialogic structure, the prominence of the subsequent first-person "confessions" of the prophet, and God's later injunctions against Jeremiah's intercession (7:16; 11:14; 14:11) suggest that, despite the instrumentality implied by the metaphor of potter and clay, in the relationship between deity and prophet, Jeremiah nonetheless retains his subjectivity and self-differentiation and the deity may yet be capable of surprise.

Finally, the focus on the mouth of the prophet and the placing of the deity's words within it should not be seen as reducing Jeremiah's mission to a strictly verbal role. Esther Roshwalb argues that the story foregrounds two themes "repeated throughout this encounter between God and Jeremiah," namely

---

[40] Deutscher, "Three Touches."
[41] Deutscher, "Three Touches," 146.
[42] Deutscher, "Three Touches," 144.
[43] Deutscher, "Three Touches," 145.

"verbal skill and physical strength," which together constitute "the skills required of Jeremiah to qualify as a messenger-prophet of God."[44] God appoints him destroyer, uprooter, and overthrower, as well as builder and planter (Jer 1:10). Jeremiah will frequently enact his mission through the declaration of oracles. He will also undertake a series of prophetic actions.

Beyond the actions he performs with his body, Jeremiah makes present deity and people alike in and through the experiences of his own body. Else Holt draws on the work of Timothy Polk to argue that in Jeremiah, "The word of God and the prophet merge into one persona, and the prophet's *vita* serves as an authorization of the divine word-become-flesh." She thus locates the placing of God's words within Jeremiah's mouth within a wider frame in which "the prophetic persona represent[s] and incarnat[es] the divine persona."[45] The prophetic persona also participates in and shapes the bodily experience of the people. Louis Stulman writes, "In the opening chapter of the book, a symbiotic relationship between the life and destiny of Jeremiah and Judah begins to take shape ... Jeremiah mirrors and fully participates in the fate of his countrymen."[46] Just as Jeremiah's later captivity will symbolize, prefigure, and participate in the captivity of the people, so his wounding may correspond to that of the people—from the site of his own injury Jeremiah would help God's people to acknowledge the wound they preferred to ignore (Jer 6:14; 8:11). The prophet consecrated in the matrix of interembodiment is not an incarnation of the deity's persona only or a representative of the people only. His body is a site of encounter, intersection, and relationship between God and people and a means by which he simultaneously participates in, is shaped by, and shapes divine and human realities.[47]

Ezekiel 1:1–3:15

The commissioning of Ezekiel (Ezek 2:1–3:15) follows closely on the book's opening, first-person, theophanic vision-report (1:1–28). Key details from

---

[44] Roshwalb, "Lost and Found," 352–3. Roshwalb further argues that these verses do not constitute the call narrative but introduce it.

[45] Holt, "Prophet as Persona," 313, drawing on Polk, *Prophetic Persona*.

[46] Stulman, *Jeremiah*, 44. According to Stulman, these correspondences are consistent with a portrayal of the prophet that "is less concerned with actual personal experiences than theological construction" (*Jeremiah*, 44).

[47] An avenue for further study that lies outside the scope of the present chapter but is nonetheless relevant for understanding the prophet's intermediary role is the implication of interembodiment for understandings of moral agency. For one sounding, see Zarhin, "Emergence of Agency."

the opening vision report set the stage for the commission, including the reference to visions of God and the cooperative activity of the word and hand of the Lord. After analyzing these details, I turn to the commissioning story, focusing on its portrayal of the interembodiment of deity and prophet, the interrelationship of word and body in the opening vision and subsequent commission, and the significance of those interrelationships for the mission he receives. I examine affective dimensions of the commission in greater detail in Chapter 9.

From the book's incipit, the narration of first-person visionary experience links the body of the prophet with that of the deity: "I saw visions of God" (Ezek 1:1). While interpreters commonly understand this phrase to mean that God was the object of Ezekiel's seeing, Edgar Conrad has argued that the phrase should be interpreted as a subjective, rather than objective, genitive, such that Ezekiel sees "what God sees."[48] To support his argument, Conrad notes the pointed repetition of the noun "eye" throughout the vision in descriptions of the divine chariot and one like a human being (1:4, 7, 16, 18, 22, 27). Interpreters commonly opt for the literal sense of "eyes" to describe what covers the rims of the wheels (Ophanim) (1:18) but translate the other instances metaphorically with reference to the luminous and reflective properties of the stones and metals to which Ezekiel likens the appearance of the deity and chariot. Whether understood literally, metaphorically, or mystically (i.e., somewhere imprecisely in between), the repetition underscores a key detail: Ezekiel sees one who also sees.

The thematic significance of shared sight emerges into sharper focus as Ezekiel is "shown" visions in which the deity is not the object of vision but a partner in the act of viewing. Conrad notes that the phrase "visions of God" occurs in only two other passages in the HBOT, both in Ezekiel (8:3; 40:2).[49] Its second occurrence is similarly paired with description of a theophanic or angelophanic "eye" (8:2; cf. 40:3) and entails the transport of the prophet in order to see the abominations in the temple. Ezekiel is there shown "what the elders of the house of Israel are doing in the dark" (8:12). That is, he is granted a vision of realities that, apart from the vision, God alone is able to see.[50] Divine seeing is here linked with divine judgment and mercy, as the

---

[48] Conrad, "God's Visions."
[49] Conrad, "God's Visions," 54–5.
[50] Seeing is thematized throughout the passage, with forms of the verbal root "to see" (ראה) occurring thirteen times (8:2, 4, 6 [x2], 7, 9, 10, 12 [x2], 13, 15 [x2], 17) and, from the same root, the noun "appearance" (מראה) occurring five times total, at (8:2 [x3], 4 [x2]). Seeing is similarly thematized in 40:4, with four forms from the root "to see" and a reference to "your eyes."

temple visitation concludes with God's pointed declaration that "my eye will not spare" (8:18). The third occurrence of the phrase introduces the book's final vision of the new temple, city, and land (40:2, introducing chapters 40–48). These three occurrences of the phrase "visions of God" map a thematic arc for the book, with Ezek 1:1 and 40:2 forming endpoints through which the prophet is inaugurated into divine visions of present and future.

The prophet's own embodied emplacement is a further key to how these endpoints establish the arc of the book as a whole. Adriane Leveen argues that "Ezekiel's dramatic enactment of the return of his body to its proper place in that restored temple logically emerges from a preoccupation with using his body to enact the intolerable situation of being uprooted in the first place."[51] Leveen documents the book's attention to the location and movement of the bodies of prophet and God alike and the diverse ways in which the prophet's body is used to portray the fate of people and place. Yet the prophet does not simply move about on his own. Rather, as portrayed through a set of narrative details that further develop the theme of interembodiment, he will be propelled and conveyed through the locomotive agency of the divine hand and spirit.

As the incipit continues, the hand of the Lord's physical relationship to the prophet is described in conjunction with the arrival of the word:

The word of the LORD came
    to Ezekiel the son of Buzi, the priest,
        in the land of the Chaldeans by the Chebar river.
And the hand of the LORD was upon him [MT]/me [LXX]. (Ezek 1:3)

Divine word and hand enclose and surround the prophet in the place of exile. Through this framing device, the word and hand of the Lord are placed in parallel, each moving toward or positioned in relation to prophet and place. This framing establishes dynamic and persistent interrelationship between divine efficacious speech, embodied agency, and the person and place of the prophet.[52]

The deity's hand has already featured in the call narratives of Moses and Jeremiah, each in distinctive ways. Yet the hand has a more persistent role in

---

[51] Leveen, "Returning the Body," 387.
[52] For Mills, God moves Ezekiel like a puppet. This manipulation "mirrors the ways in which God can and will pull apart the fabric of society" (Mills, *Alterity*, 65).

relation to Ezekiel's prophetic experiences. The hand of the Lord directs and shapes the prophet's commission and transformation. It is "strong" on him (Ezek 3:14), "falls" on him (8:1), grabs him by the hair (8:3). The hand initiates visionary experience (1:3; 8:1), gives him a scroll to eat (2:9), transports him to Tel-Abib, to Jerusalem, to a valley filled with bones, to a high mountain in Israel (3:14–15; 8:3, 37:1; 40:1–2), initiates dialogue and movement (3:22), and opens his mouth (33:22).

To understand the significance of this divine hand in Ezekiel, J. J. M. Roberts looks to parallel examples in ancient West Asian literature. In idioms identical to those found in biblical texts, the hand of the deity most frequently brought calamity such as defeat in battle or illness. Roberts argues that the broader usage of the phrase "the hand of [the god]" both outside and within the Bible suggests that for prophets as well the experience of the "hand of the god" had "concrete manifestations of a physical or psycho-physical nature" that were similar to the symptoms of various illnesses.[53] David Garber builds on Roberts' work to suggest that Ezekiel's experience of the hand of God corresponds to the prophetic task of witnessing to traumatic realities.[54]

As I discuss further in Chapter 7, the experience of the divine hand as physical and/or psychic distress is consistent with reports of illness or distress accompanying religious ecstasy.[55] The idea that "hand of the Lord" here denotes a prophetic ecstatic experience akin to physical illness would correspond well with Ezekiel's response of prostration (Ezek 1:28) and his correlating the experience of the hand of the Lord upon him with "bitterness in the heat of my spirit/breath" (3:14). Yet an understanding of the hand as the physiological symptoms of distress that accompany ecstatic experience does not fully account for the hand's doing things in its interactions with Ezekiel that hands typically do: grabbing, offering, directing, conveying. Accompanying the understanding of hand as ecstatic illness is another, perhaps more obvious sense: the hand is a part of the divine body. Robin McCall has argued that Ezekiel portrays God's body "with franker anthropomorphism than any earlier biblical description, but at the same time obscure[es] that physicality from human sight" (1:26–8).[56] In similar fashion, the hand of the Lord portrays divine agency in a manner that acknowledges divine embodiment but hides the vast majority of the divine body from view. Ezekiel's account of

---

[53] Roberts, "Hand of Yahweh," 251.
[54] Garber, "I Went in Bitterness," 354.
[55] Lewis, *Ecstatic Religion*, 59–89.
[56] McCall, "Body and Being," 378.

interacting with the hand of the Lord thus utilizes the familiar trope of the divine hand—conventionally likening aspects of prophetic experience to physical ailment—in novel and creative ways, allowing him to record a series of embodied encounters with a partially anthropomorphic—and only partially perceptible—deity.

The book's incipit is followed by a first-person report of Ezekiel's initial vision of the chariot-throne and the (partially) anthropomorphic divine figure seated upon it (Ezek 1:4–28). The details of the vision assign and disrupt categories and invite and confound perception. The form of the living beings who comprise and move the chariot combines human, lion, ox, and eagle (1:5–14). The chariot's wheels are ringed with eyes and animated by spirit (1:15–21). The deity's glorious body has the appearance of human, amber, and fire, but is also none of these (1:26–28). These details simultaneously map connection and difference between deity and creation, emphasizing in the moments before Ezekiel receives his commission the immense gulf between God and mortal prophet. Ezekiel's first-person narration relays a dizzying array of sights and sounds, including meteorological phenomena, spatial arrangements, and movements. This detailed narration invites the audience to imagine and experience Ezekiel's vision along with him; it also highlights the inadequacy of human language to describe such an encounter with God. Throughout this initial vision Ezekiel himself is more observer than participant, until finally, upon beholding the appearance of divine glory, he falls to the ground. His act of prostration signals reverence and human smallness while contrasting the earthy location and limitations of his mortal body with the exalted, mobile, and glorious divine body he has both seen and not seen.

The gulf between deity and human is bridged first by a voice, then by a spirit. The voice directs the earth-bound prophet to stand. He does so, but not through his own power: "And a spirit entered me when he spoke to me and it stood me on my feet; and I heard the one speaking to me" (Ezek 2:2). Ezekiel's report highlights both the conjoining of Ezekiel's body with a supernatural animating force and the close connection between that animating force and the act of speaking.[57] Repetition of the verb דבר, to speak (2:1, 2x2, 6x2, 7x2, 8), thematizes speech, linking the voice that addresses the prophet

---

[57] Mills argues that Ezekiel's possession is both a fusion and a fission: divine and human are fused within the body of the prophet, but their "contradictory elements" remain discontinuous, such that Ezekiel embodies difference and dislocation (*Alterity*, 66–7).

to the spirit that enters him and to Ezekiel's commission to "speak my words" to the people of Israel.

Those words, like the animating spirit, will also enter the prophet's body. The voice commands, "open your mouth and eat what I give to you" (Ezek 2:8). A hand then extends a scroll to the prophet (2:9) on which is written, "Dirges and moaning and lamentation" (2:10), and the prophet opens his mouth and swallows the pages of pain, obeying the command to "feed your body and fill your inner parts with this scroll" (3:3).

As Susan Niditch has argued, by ingesting these words, "the prophet is transformed into a medium through his literal absorption of God's words."[58] Niditch further draws a parallel between Ezekiel's swallowing the scroll and the ritual for the woman accused of adultery in Numbers 5:11–31.[59] In this passage, words of accusation and curse against an accused woman are recorded on a scroll by a priest (Num 5:23) and then rinsed off into a potion of bitter water that contains holy water mixed with dust from the tabernacle floor on which she has been made to sit (5:16–17). The accused woman must then imbibe the liquid that combines holy matter with the dust of the earth and with liquefied words of accusation and curse against her body (5:24). The effect of the potion upon her body is meant to be probative, determining her guilt or innocence. If she is guilty, it is also meant to punish, not only causing intense pain, but also transforming her body from the inside, swelling her womb and causing her sides to collapse, likely discharging from her body any child she might have born to a man who was not her husband (5:27). Her inflating and deflating body parallels and signals her change in status "in the inward parts" of her people. Her own welfare is now aborted as she herself becomes an oath (האשה לאלה 5:27), a physical embodiment of the words she has imbibed. Like the accused woman, Niditch asserts, Ezekiel's "future status is determined by the words within him. The words are transformative in a real, physical sense."[60]

Ezekiel's ingestion of the prophetic word incorporates into his very body the judgment upon the people and their response to it, making of his own flesh a participatory oracle, sign, and incarnation of their collective future. Yet he incarnates more than their judgment. He also incarnates the conditions of possibility for restoration and new life. The divine hand that directs and shapes the prophet's commission and transformation acts in tandem with the

---

[58] Niditch, *Oral World*, 83.
[59] Niditch, *Oral World*, 83.
[60] Niditch, *Oral World*, 83.

spirit or wind of God three times in Ezekiel. The first two occasions are at the conclusion of Ezekiel's commission (Ezek 3:12, 14) and the beginning of his temple visitation (8:3), both examined earlier in this section. On the third occasion, on his journey to the valley of dry bones, "the hand of the Lord came upon me and brought me out by the spirit of the Lord" (37:1).[61] It is that same breath or spirit of the Lord to which Ezekiel is commanded to prophesy, commanding it to enter the bodies of Israel's people so that they may live (37:9). When the spirit entered them, the people "stood on their feet" (37:10). This vision of the people's restoration closely mirrors the prophet's own experience at the time of his commissioning, when a spirit entered him and stood him on his feet (2:2). The animating force of spirit here links the body of the prophet to the bodies of the people and links both to the divine power of movement and possibility that animated God's own chariot-throne in Ezekiel's first vision. Ezekiel is more than the people's watchman and more than God's messenger. He undergoes in his own body transformations and translocations that make possible and show forth the judgment, confrontation, transformation, and revivification of God's people.[62]

Conclusion

The first-person commissioning narratives of Isaiah, Jeremiah, and Ezekiel draw their audiences into the experience of divine encounter, facilitating narrative immersion, flow, and transport that engage not only the imagination of the reader or hearer but also their body. That is, the text itself mediates a form of divine encounter and relationship, and its embodied reception opens a door to modes of active participation and engagement in the prophet's experience and mission.

In Isa 6, spatial and temporal cues supply coordinates for audiences to locate themselves within a liturgical scene of encounter, while vivid but

---

[61] The spirit moves and transports Ezekiel on four other occasions: after Ezekiel's first journey, "the spirit entered me and set me on my feet" (3:24). Later the spirit transports Ezekiel to the temple gate (11:1) and "falls" on him. The spirit then lifts him and brings him back to Chaldea "by the spirit" (11:24). Finally, toward the book's conclusion, the spirit lifts Ezekiel and brings him to the inner court where he sees the glory of the LORD filling the temple. This last journey forms a chiasm with the first one, wherein Ezekiel's journey coincided with the rumbling departure of the chariot throne that carried the appearance of the likeness of the glory of God.

[62] Similarly, note the connection between the spirit entering Ezekiel and the command to get a new heart and spirit, and the repeated promise that God will give the people a new heart and spirit (11:19; 18:31; 36:26; cf. 39:29), which culminates in God's promise to put God's spirit in them (36:27).

paradoxical sensory details, including sight, sound, smell, and vibration, enhance the experience of immersion, flow, and transport. Isaiah's reference to his own lips and eyes highlights a felt contradiction between his sensory experience of encounter with divine glory and the state and capacities of his body and the bodies of his people. The embodied paradox and contradiction of Isaiah's divine encounter are matched by the embodied paradox and contradiction of his mission. The contradiction in his own experience is resolved through transformative touch that purifies, dedicates, and marks his body for service to the deity. Yet this does not eliminate the paradox of a prophetic commission to prevent the people's turning, understanding, and healing. Resolution of that paradox, and with it the bodily and social healing of his audience, is deferred until after a period of desolation. On the heels of such devastation, the audience's immersion in Isaiah's vision may ultimately facilitate their transformation in a manner corresponding to Isaiah's own.

Jeremiah 1's dialogic character enrolls the audience as participant while foregrounding themes of encounter, relationship, and agency. In the context of Jeremiah, images of womb and clay connote inevitability and instrumentality. They also assert for his call and mission a formative matrix of interembodiment and relationality. The theme of interembodiment is further developed in God's touching or striking Jeremiah and placing God's words in Jeremiah's mouth. Whether violent or gentle, touch temporarily dissolves bodily boundaries, thereby enabling Jeremiah to represent the deity in speech and action but also opening to reciprocity and surprise. Paradoxically, then, this divine touch does not negate the prophet's subjectivity or agency. They persist even in the face of divine shaping, possession, and prophetic incarnation of the divine persona. The prophet also continues to participate in the life of the people, embodying and prefiguring their fate. As such, the prophet's body is an enduring site of encounter and mediating node of relationship between deity and people. By drawing the audience into this narrative space of dialogue and relationship, the first-person prophetic text has an analogous mediating function.

The theme of interembodiment introduced in the analysis of Jeremiah's commission takes on new contours in the opening chapters of Ezekiel. Ezekiel sees a God who also sees; this faculty of sight is linked to judgment and mercy. The modality of shared seeing will extend to Ezekiel's later visions, creating a mode of visionary experience and action that opens to both readers and hearers the possibility of seeing, evaluating, and acting alongside prophet and God. Through the cooperation of divine word and speech with hand and spirit, the body of the prophet becomes a host for the spirit and judgment of God and a visible and active incarnation of the people's future. The emplacement and spirit-driven mobility of the prophetic body witness to the trauma of the people's displacement and map their present and future reality. These movements and transformations of the prophet's body thus prefigure and make possible the people's own.

PART III
TRANSFORMATIONS

5

Becoming Other

The mediating prophetic body occupies border zones and margins. To do so it becomes other: other than human, other than God, other than what it was before. Chapters 3 and 4 focused on the commissioning narratives as stories of embodied encounter between prophets and deity that set the stage for the prophets' embodied mediation, sometimes, and in part, through the transformation of prophetic bodies.[1] In the case of Moses, I argued that the temporary transformation of Moses' hand modeled the captivity and liberation of the Israelite people and provided a visible sign that Moses' body was a recipient and conduit of the transformative power of YHWH even as it distinguished Moses' mortal body from the incorruptible body of God. Isaiah's body was transformed through the branding of his lips, a purifying and atoning action that marked him for service to the deity. Jeremiah's experience of the divine touch may have also been a wounding; this temporary dissolution of bodily boundaries enabled the prophet to incarnate divine words and the divine persona while simultaneously opening the relationship between deity and prophet to dynamics of reciprocity and surprise. Ezekiel received into his body both animating spirit and words of lament and judgment, incorporating the people's future into his very person. In Chapter 9 I additionally examine the transformation of Ezekiel's forehead into adamant, hardening his face to match the stubbornness of the people. Each of these transformations has a bodily component. But not all were or would remain visible, even if their effects endured.

The present chapter leaves the call narratives to focus on the visibly transformed bodies of Moses and Miriam in Exod 34 and Num 12. When Moses returns from his sojourn with the deity, his face terrifies his beholders, prompting him to wear a veil for the remainder of his days. His bodily transformation simultaneously mediates divine presence to the people and separates him from them. Miriam's transformed body similarly separates her from the

---

[1] Koosed writes of Moses that his body does not simply bear the traces of encounter with the deity. Rather, he is "the embodiment of the encounter" between God and the people ("Face of Fear," 415).

community, but her altered skin conveys not glory but shame. Marked by disease, her rotting body becomes punishment and warning. Both prophets are portrayed as monstrous. Their bodies occupy and police boundaries between divine and human realms and roles. Yet the contrasting portrayals of their transformations limns and enforces a hierarchy. Moses is partially assimilated to the deity; his luminous or horned visage reflects and participates in divine glory. Miriam's affliction distances her from the deity, embodying her shame and emphasizing her mortality. She is not only bound for death; she is its visible manifestation. The transformation of Moses does not prevent him from mediating: it is rather the hallmark of his unique mediatory status. But while Miriam's transformation is temporary, within the narrative it puts an end to her role as prophetic mediator. From the time her sentence is decreed and her body transformed she neither speaks nor acts again.

Moses, Godlike and Monstrous (Exodus 34)

By contrast with the temporary transformation of Moses' hand in Exod 4, Exod 34 (vv. 29, 30, 35) reports a more lasting transformation that results from Moses' extended, face-to-face interactions with the deity. A dual textual tradition produces a prophetic body that is productively ambivalent, made simultaneously godlike and monstrous by his proximity and relationship to God. Moses' mediating body now bridges and polices the boundary between human and divine. His luminosity reflects the glory of God's body; his monstrosity reveals the danger of divine presence. In both streams of tradition, his veiling stoppers the terrifying flow of divine power into the people's midst.

Key details from the preceding chapter (Exod 33) set the stage for this transformation and clarify its significance.

1) By their own volition and by God's command, the people abstain from and remove ornamentation from their bodies as an expression of lament in the face of their disobedience and God's refusal to accompany them (33:4–6).
2) The rift between God and the people finds a counterpoint in the intimacy between God and Moses (33:9, 11–14, 17).[2]

---

[2] Britt examines the function of Moses' transformation and veiling within a covenantal "reordering" (*Rewriting Moses*, 85).

3) Moses leverages the intimacy between God and Moses to negotiate with God to ensure God's continued presence with the people (33:12–17).

4) Moses seals this negotiation by requesting to see God's ways and glory, pushing up to and beyond the boundary between mortal and divine. God responds to this request with a proposal to reconstellate the bodies of prophet and deity. In this creative accommodation, the divine body will interact directly with the prophet's mortal body in a painstaking and care-filled choreography of prophylaxis and revelation. God's body will shield and place the prophet's body, then turn, pass, and reveal Godself (33:22–23).

On the heels of this promise, Moses ascends Sinai a second time (34:2). God reveals Godself to Moses (34:6), and the prophet spends a further forty days and nights upon the mountain with the Lord (34:28). As Moses descends from this experience of intense and prolonged encounter with the deity, he is unaware of a change to his body.[3] According to MT, קרן עור פניו (34:29; cf. 34:30, 35): the skin of Moses' face is transformed, but how precisely? The verb is denominative, deriving from the noun קרן, meaning "horn," but in other contexts it has the meaning "to shine" or "radiate." While many interpreters have regarded the meaning of קרן as ambiguous (or simply unclear), Seth Sanders has made the case that what is envisioned is a corporeal radiance that encompasses both meanings of the word.[4] Ancient versions nonetheless differed in their interpretations of the nature of Moses' transformation, interpreting the verb as denoting radiance or glory, on the one hand, or the formation of horns, on the other.

According to LXX, "the appearance of the skin of [Moses'] face was charged with glory" (34:29 NETS; δεδόξασται[5] ἡ ὄψις τοῦ χρωτὸς [V: χρώματος][6] τοῦ προσώπου αὐτοῦ LXX). Similar readings are attested in the Peshitta and Targums.[7] The LXX translation makes two key interpretive moves: 1) it emphasizes that the change is visible to others; and 2) it links

---

[3] Koosed writes, "Moses moves across the divide between human and nonhuman, himself constituting a 'modulating field of myriad becomings,' perhaps most strikingly realized in his second trip up and down the mountain to convey the words of God. Moses is the only prophet in the tradition to see God 'face to face,' and this intimate contact transforms his very body" ("Face of Fear," 416).

[4] Sanders, "Old Light," 403–4 argues that the two meanings were connected in ancient West Asian astronomical texts and literary and iconographic portrayals of deities, monsters, and astral bodies.

[5] Another possible meaning of δοξάζω is "magnify."

[6] Vaticanus's variant reading χρώματος ("color") rather than χρωτὸς ("skin") is preserved in OL's *color*.

[7] Propp, "Skin of Moses' Face."

Moses' transformed appearance with a quality most typically associated with the deity, namely glory. Apart from its use in the descriptions of Moses' transformed face, uses of the verb δοξάζω in LXX Exodus cluster in one other chapter (Exod 15), characterizing God and God's actions in the Song of the Sea and Song of Miriam (15:1, 2, 6, 11, and 21). These songs deploy various forms of the verb to praise the awesome, overwhelming, and incomparable power YHWH exhibited in the victory over Pharaoh's army at the Reed Sea. In them, forms of the verb δοξάζω render forms of the Hebrew roots גאה, נוה, and אדר, whose meanings encompass exaltation, splendor or glory, and praise. In Exodus, the related noun δόξα most commonly translates כבוד and in each such instance refers to the deity or a property of the deity (16:7, 10; 24:16, 17; 29:43; 33:18, 19, 22; 40:34, 35).[8] It is the δόξα of YHWH that Moses asks to see in Exod 33:18 and the δόξα of YHWH that fills the tabernacle when the cloud descends upon the tent of meeting (40:34–35). As a property of the divine person, glory is sometimes portrayed as luminous and overwhelming. At 40:35 it prevents Moses' entry into the tabernacle. By translating קרן in a manner that links the transformation of Moses' face to this luminous, overwhelming, and forbidding aspect of God's own visible appearance, the LXX translator suggests that Moses' body has partially assimilated to God's own, however incomparable, paradoxically immaterial, or unapproachable that divine body may be. Targum Pseudo-Jonathan makes explicit the idea that a quality of the divine body has now been communicated to the body of Moses; possible substitution of אור ("light") for עור ("skin") may account for the further detail that Moses' own face was now also luminous: "the splendid aspect of his face, which he had received from the splendor of the glory of the Lord's Shekinah, was illuminated."[9] Among other effects of these translations, the translator-interpreters provide an implicit rationale for the fear that characterizes the Israelites' response to Moses' transformation: the danger that inheres in the glorious divine body (cf. Exod 33:20) now adheres to the body of Moses.[10]

---

[8] In each of these instances, כבוד is translated "glory" by NRSV and "Presence" by NJPS.
[9] Propp, "Skin of Moses' Face," 377, Propp's translation.
[10] Sommer, *Bodies of God*, 58–68, notes that in priestly texts, glory is not only a property of the divine body but also a term used to denote the divine body. Moses' body is thus made like God's body. Targum Pseudo-Jonathan's interpretation of Exod 34:29–35 plays an important role in Orlov's argument that early interpreters regarded the glorification of Moses' face as a restoration of the glorious image of God (*Embodiment of Divine Knowledge*, 55–57). This tradition, he argues further, is a key to the portrayal of Moses in the gospels' transfiguration narratives (*Glory of the Invisible God*, 123–8).

A different Greek version, Aquila's recension, interpreted קרן with a more literal connection to the noun "horn": κεκερατωτο.[11] Jerome's Latin Vulgate translation followed Aquila's recension: Moses' face was *cornuta*, "horned."[12] Moses' encounter with the deity entails a shift in spatial position; it produces a corresponding shift in relation to categories of being. In Aquila's and Jerome's readings, Moses descends the mountain as though emerging from a cocoon, in a form that is no longer human only but crosses the boundary between human, nonhuman animal, and God.[13] Jennifer Koosed locates Moses' transformed body "at the nexus where the human, the animal, and the divine meet and converge."[14] Sanders similarly characterizes Moses' transformation as "a physical mark of inhumanity" that, in assimilating his body to the divine persona, may have rendered him unrecognizable to the people.[15] The horns mark Moses as a possessor of power, virility, and strength.[16] They also mark him as categorically other, even monstrous.[17] Asa Mittman writes that "the monstrous ... calls into question our (their, anyone's) epistemological worldview, highlights its fragmentary and inadequate nature, and thereby asks us ... to acknowledge the failures of our systems of categorization."[18] Jeffrey Jerome Cohen describes the cultural roles of the monster as one who embodies liminality and inhabits the border zone between familiar and

---

[11] Wevers, *Exodus*, 383; Foster and Marzouk, "Horns of Moses." For analysis of this interpretation in relation to ancient iconography, see Strawn, "Shining or Horned Face?"

[12] Cf. Jerome, *In Amos*, 3.6: *unde et in exodo iuxta hebraicum, et aquilae editionem, legimus: et moyses nesciebat, quia cornuta erat species uultus eius*. For the legacy of Jerome's translation in later art, see Mellinkoff, *Horned Moses*, and the well-known later works of Michelangelo and Marc Chagall. Mellinkoff argues that Jerome did not simply "mistranslate" as is commonly asserted. Rather, he was aware of a range of interpretive and translational options and translated in a manner consistent with lexical knowledge available to him that allowed him to activate/make explicit the metaphorical meanings he perceived in the text (77–8).

[13] See also Sasson, "Bovine Symbolism."

[14] Koosed, "Face of Fear," 416.

[15] Sanders, "Old Light," 404.

[16] Jerome interprets Moses' horned visage as a capacity to overcome enemies (*In Amos*, 3.6) and links horns to royalty (*In Abacuc*, VI, 639 ad Hab 3:4): *moris est scripturarum, ut semper cornua pro regnis ponant*.

[17] Propp proposes an alternative interpretive option, arguing that the MT should be interpreted not as glorification or growth of horns, but rather as a disfiguring injury resulting from exposure to the fiery radiance of God's own glory: "the skin of his face was burnt to the hardness of horn" ("Skin of Moses' Face," 386). The benefit of this gradual hardening was protection from further injury. A factor weighing against this interpretation would be that readers might easily infer that while the character Moses would not have had the opportunity to see his own face, he would surely have felt the pain of burns and would likely have had occasion to touch the skin of his face and perceive its hardened state. His ignorance of this condition, which, according to Propp, would have developed gradually over the period of repeated exposures, seems to defy narrative conventions of plausibility.

[18] Mittman, "Impact of Monsters," 8.

108 THE PROPHETIC BODY

forbidden spaces, surveilling and enforcing the boundary between realms.[19] By inhabiting the middle space, epistemologically and bodily, Moses simultaneously mediates and protects.

The monstrous horning of Moses' face—whether luminous radiance, overwhelming glory, spiky rays, unsettling blisters, or protrusions of keratin and bone—elicits fear from the congregation, prompting even Aaron to turn away and hold himself distant from his brother (34:30–1). Nor is the alarming condition a transitory after-effect.[20] Moses' visage is permanently altered, prompting him to wear a veil when he is outside the tent of meeting so the people will not fear to approach him (34:33). A further detail suggests that Moses removes the veil to convey to the people the commandments of the Lord (34:32). While this verse does not make the veil's removal explicit, the following verse portrays Moses' replacing the veil after speaking in his capacity as prophetic lawgiver.

Moses' veiling positions his body across and between categories in a further way. Rhiannon Graybill highlights gendered connotations of veiling, a practice that in the HBOT and ancient West Asian culture was typically associated with women.[21] If horns convey virility, a veil communicates and performs feminine propriety. Carolyn Alsen notes that, in the West Asian context, veiling conveyed status, both the liminal status of women "promised in marriage but not yet married" and the high social status of certain married women.[22] Moses' veiling marks his similarly liminal status as prophet. It does so in a way that is markedly gendered. His resulting gender identity is accordingly "outside of normative masculine embodiment."[23] The narrative portrayal of the horning and veiling of Moses constructs for Moses a mediatorial persona that continually alternates between masculine and feminine gender identities.[24] His identity now encompasses both.[25]

---

[19] Cohen writes, "the monster is dangerous, a form suspended between forms that threatens to smash distinctions" ("Monster Culture," 6); "the monster is difference made flesh . . . an incorporation of the Outside, the Beyond" ("Monster Culture," 7); "the monster of prohibition polices the borders of the possible . . . exists to demarcate the bonds that hold together that system of relations we call culture" ("Monster Culture," 13).

[20] See Baker, "Did the Glory Fade?" It should be noted that no other Pentateuchal texts comment on Moses' transformation or veiling. While this passage exerted significant influence in the interpretive tradition, within TaNaK its portrait of Moses is limited to Exod 34.

[21] Graybill, *Are We Not Men*, 32.

[22] Alsen, "Veiled Resistance," 67.

[23] Graybill, *Are We Not Men*, 33.

[24] According to Koosed, this alternation "make[s] Moses' gender utterly unintelligible" ("Face of Fear," 420).

[25] Grabbe offers examples of "gender transformation" among prophets in varied cultural settings, wherein "male prophets take on some female features and vice versa" ("Her Outdoors," 23). See also

The function of the veil both intersects and exceeds its cultural associations with gendered identity. Alsen notes that conventional social meanings of veiling went hand in hand with a social function of resisting or undercutting social hierarchies and expectations.[26] It does so in part by creating a physical barrier that denies sight and touch. In this narrative, the veil simultaneously enables proximity and inhibits intimacy.[27] It reveals that a cost of Moses' intimacy with and assimilation to God is his bodily alienation from the people.[28] According to Jennifer Koosed, Moses' veil further signifies his "unique status" in relation to God and people, "constantly calling attention to his role as prophet even when, especially when, he is not acting as such; and constantly calling attention to the frightening face it is worn to hide."[29] That face, whether glorious, monstrous, or both, mediates divine presence to the people, accompanying divine speech with an embodied manifestation of the deity's strange and alien nature.[30] Akin to the cloud's withdrawal from the tabernacle (or, as in Ezek 1 and 10, the glory's departure from the temple), the veil effectively stoppers the visible and affective flow of divine energy that threatens to emanate from the face of Moses. While his transformation is neither temporary nor intermittent, Moses' practice of veiling and unveiling mirrors and participates in the alternating rhythms of divine revelation and hiddenness, presence with and withdrawal from the people.[31]

The physical transformation of Moses results from, embodies, and effects his bodily separation from the people on whose behalf he mediates. It simultaneously results from and embodies his experience of divine presence and mediates that presence to the people. In the passages examined above, the theme of separation is developed in four stages: 1) Moses sequesters on the mountain and in the tent to encounter the presence of God; 2) his body is transformed by this encounter to an other-than-human state; 3) frightened

---

Hamori, "Childless Female Diviners," 185–90; Graybill, "Body of Moses"; Carvalho, "Drunkenness, Tattoos, and Dirty Underwear."

[26] Alsen, "Veiled Resistance," 68.
[27] Survivors of the Covid-19 pandemic have experienced this paradoxical combination of connection and barrier in the protective facemask.
[28] Graybill, *Are We Not Men*, 31, similarly accentuates Moses's social and physical distancing from the people. Propp likewise emphasizes "the price [Moses] paid" for his nearness to God but interprets that cost differently ("Skin of Moses' Face," 386).
[29] Koosed, "Face of Fear," 419. See also Britt's assertion that the veil "signifies Moses' work as a prophet" even as it "dissociates Moses [as person] from his prophetic office" (*Rewriting Moses*, 82).
[30] See also Britt, who labels Moses' transformed visage and consequent veiling "a kind of theophany" (*Rewriting Moses*, 85).
[31] On the veil in relation to presence and absence, see Britt, *Rewriting Moses*, 82–115.

by his transformed state, the people flee from him; and 4) he dons a veil to mask the transformed state of his body. While the specific form of Moses' transformation is unique within the biblical prophetic literature (cf., however, the transfiguration of Jesus, Matt 17:2), it is emblematic in the same measure that Moses is regarded as a prophetic paradigm. The ambiguity of MT's קרן produced a dual textual tradition that emphasizes the ambiguity, liminality, and even monstrosity of the prophet's body. Mediating between human and divine produces a prophetic body that is no longer strictly human but pushes against and crosses over boundaries and categories of humanity, animality, and divinity.[32] Even upon returning to the human community, this body is barricaded from "normal" interactions by the fear it produces and the veil that separates Moses from the people. To be face to face with God and speak on God's behalf changes the prophet's face and place forever.

Miriam, Debased and Devoured (Numbers 12)

Moses' bodily transformation is paralleled by that of his sister Miriam. For both, their transformation sets them apart, locating them outside of ordinary social structures and rendering them visibly other in ways that elicit fear (Moses) and shame (Miriam). Yet while Moses' transformation betokens closeness to the deity whose otherness he reflects and mediates, Miriam's calls attention to her human fallibility and finitude, and distances her from the deity's chosen site of mediation. Moses is marked as a prophet of highest standing; Miriam's flesh signals her subordination. Indeed, their status relative to one another is a central concern of the story.[33] While the deity confirms Moses' special status as the trusted prophet who speaks with YHWH "mouth to mouth" (12:8), the visible abjection and exclusion of Miriam's body prevents her from accessing communal and sacred space and, consequently, from mediating between God and people.

A passage in Micah suggests that some of Israel's traditions grouped together and even placed on equal footing the liberatory leadership and mediating authority of Moses, Aaron, and Miriam: "For I brought you up from

---

[32] Orlov sees this transformation instead as a precondition of mediation. He analyzes traditions about Moses' transformation in Exod 34 in the context of early Jewish pseudepigrapha, noting there a pattern in which "the reception of divine mysteries, especially theophanic knowledge, coincides with the visionary's dramatic metamorphosis." The visionary's human "nature must undergo changes so that s/he will be able to receive and carry the revelation" (*Embodiment of Divine Knowledge*, 57).
[33] Burns, *Has the Lord*, 41–2.

Egypt, and from a house of slaves I ransomed you, and I sent before you Moses, Aaron, and Miriam" (Mic 6:4).[34] Numbers 12 settles the question of status very differently. Miriam and Aaron challenge an implicit assertion of Moses' exclusive mediatorial status, asking, "Has YHWH not also spoken through us?" (Num 12:2). While the triggering event or pretext for their challenge seems to be Moses' taking (or sending away) a Cushite wife (12:1), the narrative thematizes neither marriage nor ethnicity, focusing instead on prophetic status and modes of revelatory mediation. Moses' unique status is evidenced by (or results from) God's expressed choice to speak with him directly, "mouth to mouth," and likewise to appear to him in person, such that he sees the very form of YHWH (12:8).[35] Other prophets—based on their question in 12:2, readers might reasonably infer that this group is meant to include Miriam and Aaron—see and hear the deity not directly, but through vision and dream (12:6).[36]

Indeed, consistent with the deity's claim that Moses alone perceives the deity's form, in this encounter the Lord stands at the opening of the tent but has descended within a column of cloud, present and powerful but obscured from view (12:5). YHWH condemns Miriam and Aaron for their lack of fear in response to Moses' unique status as the prophet closest to God (cf. Exod 34:33) whom God has entrusted with the deity's very household (12:7). YHWH implies that the challenge to Moses' authority is an affront to the deity whose glory Moses has perceived and mediates. The heat that stirs within YHWH's nostrils consequently takes aim at Miriam and Aaron (12:9) for failing to honor their brother's status; when the cloud departs from over the tent, Miriam's transformation becomes visible: she is מצרעת, afflicted with scale disease, "like snow" (12:10).

---

[34] Kessler, "Prophecy of the Persian Period," 77; Kessler, "Micah," 469; Tervanotko, *Denying Her Voice*, 112–15. Kessler argues that this passage "stresses the equal rank of the three" even as "the order implies a certain hierarchy" (Prophecy of the Persian Period," 77). In Kessler's view they stand for "Torah, cult and prophecy," respectively. Thus (by contrast with the position of Burns, *Has the Lord*), Kessler sees Miriam as representative of prophetic mediation in both Micah 6:4 and Num 12 ("Prophecy of the Persian Period," 81). Trible, however, invokes a different order to argue for a flattening of hierarchy in Mic 6:4: the passage prophetically "acknowledges the full legitimacy of Miriam . . . who was designated 'the prophet' even before Moses. The recognition undercuts a hierarchy of authority with a male at the top" ("Bringing Miriam," 181).

[35] Burns, *Has the Lord*, 55, notes that Moses' "direct encounters with the Divinity . . . were unequivocally connected with Moses' role as mediator of Yahweh's word."

[36] Burns, *Has the Lord*, 42, argues that Miriam was not regarded as belonging to such a prophetic group, but rather a priestly one: "A later writer used the early (pre-Deuteronomic) divine declaration of Num 12:6–8 to settle a struggle for oracular authority between an Aaronic group of priests (represented by Aaron and Miriam) and the Levites (represented by Moses)." She acknowledges, however, that Miriam is here portrayed as "an oracular figure" (Burns, *Has the Lord*, 48).

112   THE PROPHETIC BODY

Indeed, the narrator twice joins Miriam's name to the emphatic phrasing, והנה מצרעת, pairing deictic particle and passive participle to convey immediacy and surprise as Miriam herself is stripped of agency and status. With this repetition the narrator demands the reader join Aaron in looking at Miriam's transformed body.[37] The skin condition that afflicts her makes of Miriam both *monstrum* and *monitum*, a bodily warning against insubordination.[38] The visible permeability and disorder of her body symbolically asserts that their challenge to Moses' sole authority has threatened the accepted order of the social body. In modern terms, we might say that her body both hosts and sheds contaminating microbes and, as it fights her infection, simultaneously wages inflammatory battle with her own tissues. This modern understanding of a body at war with itself is consistent with the portrayal of Miriam's affliction as something incurred through her own act of rebellion.

Upon seeing this *monstrum*, Aaron's discourse toward Moses undergoes a transformation as well, reversing the discourse of rebellion by acknowledging Moses' authority through a title reminiscent of God's own: אדני, "my lord" (12:11). Indeed, the petition Aaron directs to Moses would more logically be directed to the deity, causing the person of the prophet to recede from view as the deity's power and will move to the fore.

After begging forgiveness for the transgression Aaron shares with his sister, he compares her transformed body to "one who is dead," a fetus expelled from its mother's body with "half its flesh eaten" (Num 12:12). Extensive maceration is a visible indicator of death prepartum, that is, before the time of delivery.[39] Miriam's punishment for challenging Moses' authority renders her as an aborted and decomposing fetus, never born living into the world, unviable, unable to achieve independence as a human agent. She is vulnerable even in the most protected space.

The paradoxical linking of birth and death contributes to Miriam's status as *monstrum* and *monitum*, an embodied prophecy warning of the

---

[37] Interpreters have asked why Miriam is punished in this way, but not Aaron. Some have argued that it is because of Aaron's priestly status (see, e.g., Davis, *Biblical Prophecy*, 50); others see Miriam's gender as the most salient factor. Exum opines that "as a man, Aaron poses no threat to the symbolic order" ("Second Thoughts," 86). Fischer allows for both: "the impossibility of telling a story about a leprous high priest in no way diminishes the palpable misogyny of the text" (Authority of Miriam," 169). A minority view, attributed to Rabbi Akiva in *b. Šabb.* 97a and more recently argued by Gafney (*Daughters of Miriam*), holds that Aaron was also afflicted. Keys to this interpretation include the detail that God's anger kindled against them both (Num 12:9) and Aaron's acknowledgment of shared responsibility and plea not to place the sin "on us" (עלינו 12:11).

[38] Ahmed and Stacey note the dread that arises when "the skin falls away, revealing the subject's vulnerability to external scrutiny" ("Introduction: Dermographies," 17).

[39] Gold et al., "'Fresh' versus 'Macerated.'"

peril of uprising, of asserting unauthorized prophetic power and challenging revelatory hierarchies.[40] The subsequent silencing of her voice—no further words of Miriam are recorded in the Hebrew Bible—suggests that to some extent her prophetic role is likewise aborted, the fruit of her prophetic womb withers and enters the world without capacity for life.[41] Deuteronomy 24:9 interprets her leprosy as admonition, cautioning those who would challenge the authority of God's intimates or the instruction of God's priests lest they meet a fate similar to hers. While priestly authority is not thematized in Num 12, this interpretation is nonetheless consistent with the way Miriam's body functions there. To borrow language from Cohen, Miriam's monstrous body "polices the borders of the possible, interdicting through [her] grotesque body some behaviors and actions, envaluing others."[42] Monster Miriam marks the lines "that cannot ... be crossed."[43] Her embodied warning reinforces structures of hierarchy and authority.[44]

The consequence of her affliction will be her confinement and exclusion from the camp for seven days. While it may be tempting to harmonize the instructions for Miriam's confinement in Num 12:14 with similar instructions for purification after identification of skin disease (Lev 13:4), the focus here is not on purity but shame.[45] David Jobling has argued that Miriam is not made ritually impure but rather "is marked with the whiteness of a skin disease that has run its course."[46] In this reading, her exclusion from the camp does not result from impurity.[47] It is a social expression of the shame that is marked upon her body. Dennis Olson concurs: "The seven days, however, do not appear to be a period of quarantine or ritual purification in accord with the laws in Leviticus; the seven-day banishment is a sign of the shame she has brought

---

[40] Trible writes, "Aaron unites birth and death in describing the horror God has inflicted on Miriam" ("Bringing Miriam," 177).

[41] Graybill observes, "what should not be said (at least by women) corresponds to what should not be born" (*Are We Not Men*, 135).

[42] Cohen, "Monster Culture," 13.

[43] Cohen, "Monster Culture," 13.

[44] Rapp, *Mirjam*, 388, 392, and passim, finds in this text evidence of an effort to refute "democratic" claims to prophetic authority within post-exilic Judea.

[45] As Baden and Moss observe, the Levitical purity laws are "literally unrelated" to Num 12. These independent traditions are evidence "of two conceptualizations of ṣāraʿat, similar in many ways but distinct in the crucial area of etiology. These two concepts ... exist[ed] simultaneously and independently, each representing the different worldview of its particular author" ("Origin and Interpretation of ṣāraʿat," 653).

[46] For why this condition should not be interpreted as "whiteness" see Gafney, *Daughters of Miriam*, 83–4.

[47] Jobling, *Sense of Biblical Narrative*, 1.38.

on herself."⁴⁸ The deity's articulation of her shame (תכלם) accentuates her lower(ed) status by comparing God's inflicting scale disease upon her flesh to her father's having spit on her face (Num 12:14). Esther Fuchs observes, "The somatization of Miriam's transgression and punishment is rendered in graphic metaphors that elicit revulsion."⁴⁹ The analogy emphasizes, moreover, that she is subordinate to a familial male figure whose authority is accepted by social convention and supported by the very structures of a primary social institution—family—which that authority shapes.⁵⁰

The act of spitting in her face would be a public performance of violation, marking the daughter's violation of social norms by violating the boundaries of her body in return. In the scenario God invites these interlocutors (and the audience) to imagine, the excess of her father's body—and by extension of his power and authority—is launched at her visage, threatening to enter and contaminate her orifices, including the organs of speech vital to the work of prophecy and the points of entry for the breath she needs to live. His saliva also coats her skin, making of his excess a barrier, real and symbolic, between her body and the material and social worlds she inhabits. This coating emphasizes the subordination and contingency of her social status, which is now erased (she "loses face") by one with greater power. Her resulting exclusion would punish her violation of social norms with a further act of ritual humiliation designed to produce "social invisibility" and non-recognition.⁵¹

The divine invitation to imagine Miriam with her father's spit on her face calls attention to Miriam's body in order to degrade and exclude it. God's afflicting her flesh with scale disease does so to an even higher degree, covering her not with saliva but with the stigma of infection and covering not just her face but her entire body.⁵² The hypervisibility of her (diseased) body similarly covers over her assertion of personhood and dehumanizes her, stripping away identity, attributed and actual agency, and access to

---

⁴⁸ Olson, *Numbers*, 74. Note that Num 12:1–16 is commonly attributed to the E source rather than P. Strathern theorizes the relation between skin and shame: As the "immediate point of contact with the physical world," skin "can also conveniently symbolize the point of contact between [self] and the social forces that surround" a person ("Why is Shame?" 348).
⁴⁹ Fuchs, *Feminist Theory*, 99.
⁵⁰ Tervanotko posits that traditions of Miriam as "challenger" predate those portraying her as a member of Moses' and Aaron's family (*Denying Her Voice*, 90). If this is the case, it would be consistent with the use of an analogy drawn from the domain of family to "bring Miriam into the fold" and subordinate her authority to that of her male family member(s).
⁵¹ Kuch, "Rituality of Humiliation," 54.
⁵² On the hypervisibility of Miriam's afflicted body, see Yoo, "Healing Stigma and Trauma," 158.

community.⁵³ Her exclusion furthers this process, mapping her otherness in relation to the spatial and social structures of Israel's camp. In this new map, her temporary location outside the camp emphasizes her distance from the deity whose tent occupies its center. This exclusion thus does more than cut her off from the social matrix of her prophetic work: it refutes her claim to prophetic relationship with the deity and resulting authority.⁵⁴ The period of seven days designated for her humiliation (Num 12:14) symbolically links her exclusion, lack of access, and degradation to the ordering of creation, implicitly asserting that the constellation of power, privilege, relationship, and prophetic authority is both ordained by God and consistent with the fundamental ordering of the world God has created. As such, it permits no further challenge.

The bodily marking of Miriam establishes her subordinate position within a mediatory hierarchy while emphasizing the contingency and even precarity of her access to God and people.⁵⁵ Some later traditions circumscribed her prophetic authority in a further way, judging her speech to have violated gendered cultural scripts and relocating and limiting the scope of her prophetic activity to domains of life commonly associated with women, namely the household and childbirth.⁵⁶ Other interpreters have imagined Miriam's body transformed in other ways, each a prophecy in itself.⁵⁷ Still others engage in creative practices of remembrance and poiesis that aim to contribute to the healing of Miriam and those who follow after her.⁵⁸ Jill Hammer's poem "*Pirkei Imahot*/Sayings of the Mothers" affirms Miriam's status as mediator, placing her at the beginning of a chain of transmission that originates with God at Sinai. The poem's three stanzas each map a different chain. In one, Miriam receives Torah directly from God, transmitting it across generations to daughters and granddaughters. Public proclamation by women prophets, teachers,

---

⁵³ Kelman focuses on the loss of identity and community produced by dehumanization ("Violence Without Moral Restraint," 48). Oliver focuses on the role of the body. She argues that discourses of dehumanization portray "groups such as women . . . and disabled people . . . as 'too fully embodied'" ("Dehumanization," 94).

⁵⁴ This is contrary to the view of Fischer, who argues that Miriam's prophetic authority is not negated but confirmed ("Authority of Miriam," 168).

⁵⁵ On her subordination, Exum writes, "Miriam is put outside the boundary of patriarchal order, symbolized by the camp, where she becomes, literally, the outsider, the other—until she is allowed to come back *inside* the camp/symbolic order in her proper, submissive role" ("Second Thoughts," 86).

⁵⁶ Siquans, "Miriam's Image."

⁵⁷ Bach, "Dreaming of Miriam's Well," analyzes a modern midrash by Leonard Angel, in which Miriam dances before Pharaoh and embodies each plague of Egypt in turn, becoming fog, a cloud of gnats, and a bloody, limping child.

⁵⁸ Yoo, "Healing Stigma and Trauma"; Dame, "Paradoxical Prophet."

and mothers is sanctified and affirmed as part of oral Torah. In another, Miriam and her daughters are excluded from this chain of transmission; they nonetheless hold fast to one another and fight to create space where their own wisdom is honored and preserved. In the third stanza, Miriam steals Torah at Sinai and gives it away. It is lent and lost, scattered and stolen, repurposed and multiplied. Housewives, jazz musicians, midwives, and teachers feed Torah to hungry masses. Their precepts are not statements but questions, simultaneously challenging the very salience of Miriam's status as other and transferring her prophetic and teaching authority to all who share her otherness: "What if I'm not you? / Why are those your questions? / Who will transmit *my* Torah?"[59]

Conclusion

The body that bridges human and divine realities becomes other. In the process, it is sometimes *visibly* altered. In this chapter I have argued that the visibly altered skin of Moses and Miriam conveys divine glory and human shame respectively, making the siblings into monsters who police boundaries between categories of being, warning of the danger of the divine power and presence the prophet mediates and advertising the punishment for transgression of mediatory roles. In so doing the transformed bodies of brother and sister prophet also make visible their status relative to one another, establishing and enforcing hierarchies of mediation.

As I argued in Chapter 3, Moses' earlier, momentary, and partial affliction with scale disease temporarily marked his body as other than the deity's, to prevent himself and others from confusing him with the deity whose power he mediated and to signal his status as representative of the people whose liberation he was sent to achieve. By contrast with this earlier transformation, the transformation of Moses' face at the time of his descent from Mount Sinai resulted from his *closeness* to the deity. The ambiguity of the phrase קרן עור פניו in Exod 34:29 MT spawned a dual textual tradition. In LXX, similar to the Peshitta and Targums, "the appearance of the skin of [Moses'] face" was understood to be "charged with glory" (NETS). This interpretation emphasized both the visibility of the transformation and its connection to divine glory and presence. Aquila's Greek recension, followed by the Vulgate, instead interpreted קרן to mean that Moses face was horned. The tradition of

---

[59] Hammer, "*Pirkei Imahot*/Sayings of the Mothers," © Jill Hammer 2000, 2016, quoted with author's permission.

Moses' glorification bridges the boundary between human and divine. The tradition of his horning makes of him a composite creature, incorporating in his body features of nonhuman animals that mark him as virile and powerful, not only mediator but also guardian. In both traditions Moses has become permanently other. In both, his form elicits terror. Both the fear he elicits and the veil he dons separate prophet and people, placing him outside the boundaries of normal social relationships and locating him instead in the space between. Whether shining or horned, Moses is monstrous, simultaneously bridging and reinforcing categories of difference. Yet Moses' monstrosity is not portrayed as shameful. It testifies to his unique and elevated role as mediator between divine and human realms.

Miriam's scale disease, by contrast, manifests her mortality and shame. She is like one born dead. She is like a daughter whose father has spit in her face. The decay and contamination of her skin is the marking, containment, and regulation of a transgressive body. Miriam's monstrous body does not attest to her mediatorial role but interrupts and possibly refutes it.[60] Her transgression was to challenge the primacy or uniqueness of Moses' prophetic authority. The deity refutes her challenge and with it her claim to authority equaling Moses'. God's response neither verbally affirms nor denies Miriam's ongoing prophetic role, leaving her future status ambiguous. Yet her punishment, this othering of her body and the spatial and social exclusion it demands, unequivocally puts her in her place, now outside the boundaries of the community. This act of dislocation deprives her of access to deity and people alike, symbolically and practically stripping her of mediatory standing and cutting her off from the spatial and social loci of mediation. While that ritualized act of exclusion is temporary, it may effect a more lasting reconfiguration of roles and relationships. Within the HBOT, she never speaks nor acts again. Her death is marked (Num 20:1), her birth is remembered (Num 26:59), and her transgression stands as a warning (Deut 24:9). Her marking and exclusion solidify a mediatory hierarchy. Miriam is simultaneously *monstrum* and *monitum*, an embodied prophecy warning not of the danger of the deity but the danger of prophetic insubordination. Yet subsequent interpreters have not always accepted this hierarchy. Many have instead found confirmation and authorization for their own prophetic activity in the very otherness of Miriam's body.

---

[60] Tervanotko, *Denying Her Voice*, 84, argues that Miriam's question in 12:2 makes sense only if she did possess prophetic authority. I agree with this assessment and also remain agnostic as to whether Miriam should be imagined as possessing some measure of prophetic authority after her reintegration in the camp, as no biblical narrative portrays her in that role after this one.

6
Transformative Practice

The mediating body of the prophet proves to be a malleable one. Moses' and Miriam's transmuted skin visibly marked their altered status. But these are not the only prophetic transformations recounted in the HBOT. Other transformations—both visible and invisible—resulted from a range of embodied practices and religious experiences. In this chapter and Chapter 7, I analyze textual portrayals of three types of transformative embodied practice and religious experience connected with the role of prophet, namely *askêsis*, incubation, and ecstasy. These three practices could alter both the prophetic body and consciousness. Although none are viewed within the biblical corpus as a *necessary* component of prophecy, analysis will show that they nonetheless establish a close and sometimes causal linkage between bodily praxis, bodily transformation, and prophetic mediation.[1] The present chapter focuses on *askêsis*, or formative discipline that shapes both the prophet's person and the relationships in which the prophet participates, and incubation, or the ritualized practice of sleeping in a sanctuary in hopes of receiving a revelation or encountering a supernatural being.

Before analyzing these sets of practices, I first pose a broader question: What is the relationship between what putative historical prophets did and experienced and the literary portrayals found in the HBOT? The results of this inquiry guide my analysis of portrayals of prophetic transformative practices in biblical literature. I then analyze prophetic *askêsis*. The bodily disciplines of *askêsis* transform the prophetic body while preparing the prophet to encounter the deity, receive revelation, or intercede for the people. They also hold power to reshape social and even cosmic structures. The stories of Moses' ascent to and sojourns on Mt. Sinai provide an example of prophetic *askêsis* in the form of withdrawal, physical exertion, prolonged fasting, and abstention from water. I argue that these practices make of Moses' body a

---

[1] In light of the growing body of research on embodied cognition, I include altered states of consciousness (ASCs) as a form of bodily transformation, however temporary. See Chapter 7 for more detail.

bridge between human and divine realms that also bridges life and death, possibility and impossibility. Moses' *askêsis* contributes to the transformation not only of his own person but also of his people's future, intervening to reshape and make possible life in covenant with the deity and one another.

Closely related to prophetic *askêsis* is the practice of incubation. While incubation is less clearly marked as a *prophetic* practice in the HBOT, I argue that it emerges as a liminal therapeutic and divinatory practice in a time of political transition. Hannah's incubatory practice positions her body at the threshold of a new prophetic era and participates in its inauguration through the birth of her son Samuel. Hannah's experience finds a parallel in Samuel's: As he sleeps beside the ark, the Lord speaks to him, mirroring the opening of her body in the re-opening of mediatory channels between God, prophet, and people.

Textual Portrayals of Religious Experience and Bodily Practice

Asceticism, incubation, and ecstasy are forms of religious experience entailing a range of bodily practices. Studies of narratives portraying prophetic religious experience sometimes seek to determine whether Israelite and Judean prophets historically experienced such phenomena and whether "actual" religious experience lies behind a particular narrative being studied.[2] For example, if we posit a historical Ezekiel and posit that he is the author of the book of Ezekiel, should we infer that he experienced—with his senses, in his body—anything like the visions, transport, or physical restraint he describes in the book?

A rationalist approach to the study of ancient prophecy has frequently ruled out the possibility of "genuine" encounter with a deity or semi-divine being. One alternative has been to analyze reported experiences of encounter, vision, ecstasy, or transport as a product of mental illness, stress, or trauma.[3] Biblical evidence suggests that allegations of mental illness or incapacity were a weapon in the toolbox of prophetic conflict, lobbed at opponents by a canonically authorized prophet (Jer 29:26) and at canonically authorized prophets

---

[2] On the relationship between experience and expression, see Hardtke, Schmiedel, and Tan, eds., *Religious Experience Revisited*. For a history of the study of Israelite and Judean prophecy as a phenomenon (i.e., not simply a literary representation) and current state of the question, see Kelle, "Phenomenon of Israelite Prophecy."

[3] Strawn and Strawn, "Prophecy and Psychology," 615–16.

by skeptical audiences (Hos 9:7). Designations of mental health and illness are in significant measure culturally constructed and contested. As I discuss further in Chapter 7, experiences, mind states, and behaviors that in one context may be regarded as signs of illness may in another context and under certain conditions be attributed to possession by a spirit or deity. Behavior and experience pathologized in one setting may be honored in another.

While psychoanalytical approaches have fallen out of favor in biblical studies, an alternative approach underscores the literary quality of a book like Ezekiel and proposes that we understand these narrated events as fictions designed to persuade. Recognition (and critique) of such fabrications can be found even in the book of Jeremiah: "I have heard what the prophets have said who prophesy lies in my name, saying, 'I have dreamed, I have dreamed!'" (Jer 23:25 NRSV; cf. 23:32). While much twentieth- and twenty-first-century biblical scholarship has regarded the literary quality of such reports as contraindicative of "genuine" religious experience, some scholars have called for a more nuanced approach that acknowledges the shaping force of genre and literary convention while noting that these conventions, including specialized language, type-scenes (such as call narratives), seemingly stock responses, and a shared lexicon of symbol and metaphor do not betray a phenomenon that must have been literary only (though this is always a possibility) but rather suggest the important role of tradition in shaping religious experience, including that of the visionary or prophet. Ellen Davis offers such a model for the oracles of Ezekiel, arguing the likelihood "that Ezekiel composed his oracles in writing, yet in a manner that was deeply imbued with the forms and practices of traditional oral prophecy."[4]

Beyond providing narrative and conceptual frames, evidence suggests that the contemplation and study of specific, earlier prophetic texts and visions could also provide a catalyst for new visionary experience. Such a phenomenon is narrated in Dan 9, where Daniel studies the scroll of Jeremiah and receives a vision in response to his professed inability to understand the scroll he reads. In his study of apocalyptic visionary texts, Christopher Rowland has emphasized the interplay of text and experience, noting that earlier literary and oral traditions *about* prophetic experience, likely paired with inherited (learned) and adapted practices, helped to shape a framework in which new visionary experience could take place.[5]

---

[4] Davis, *Swallowing the Scroll*, 37.
[5] Rowland, "Visionary Experience."

We in the twenty-first century will not determine whether specific accounts of prophetic experience reflect "genuine" experiences of their writers. Yet it seems unlikely that such experiences and behaviors existed solely within Israel's and Judah's literature and not in the embodied lives of historical prophets. If we posit the existence of prophets at various moments in Israel's and Judah's histories (whether or not they are the same ones named in the texts that became the scriptures of Israel and Judah), then it would be logical to assume that their range of religious experiences would in some measure be reflected in (and shaped by) Israelite and Judean prophetic literature.[6] As discussed in Chapter 2, while my goal is not to reconstruct historical prophetic practice and experience, this assumption nonetheless guides my use of anthropological, psychiatric, and neurobiological study of religious experience in analyzing biblical texts.

Three additional suppositions shape my analysis of prophetic religious experience. First, as noted above, biblical texts do not give us unmediated access to or necessarily accurate depictions of the religious experience of ancient, real-life prophets. In light of this limitation, Frances Flannery proposes that the appropriate object of study is not the experience per se but its "textual articulation."[7] Second, religious experience is not simply passive experience that "happens to" biblical prophets. Rather, prophetic religious experience includes diverse sets of *practices*.[8] Third, these experiences are part of shared cultural repertoires. They shape and are shaped by convention, tradition, and other aspects of culture.[9]

Yet practices belonging to a cultural repertoire are not necessarily universal within that culture. Some practices I consider are shared with other

---

[6] This position is similar to that of Husser: "Whatever the literary genre of the text in which the dream report appears, it is necessary, if the report is to be understood by the readers, that they should be able to recognize in the description an experience known to them. To the extent that the dream report, however fictitious, means something to the readers, it avoids being conditioned solely by literary forms and necessarily retains something of common psychological [I would add neurological/biological] experience. In other words, the historical authenticity of the experience related in the dream report is less important to the reader than its psychological plausibility. On the other hand and inversely, the strongly traditional character of the texts means that they unavoidably acted as paradigms. However stereotypical the dreams reports, they in turn determined to a certain degree, the actual dream experience of the individuals to whom they were addressed. Literary forms apart, it would appear possible, by reason of this inevitable and necessary collusion between author and reader, to assume a degree of formal analogy between the intimate dream experience of individuals and its stereotypical literary expression, however fictitious" (Husser, *Dreams and Dream Narratives*, 17–18).
[7] Flannery et al., "Introduction," 2.
[8] See Werline, "Experience of Prayer," 59–61.
[9] Flannery et al., "Introduction," 5.

kinds of religious practitioners. Others are portrayed as unique to certain prophets or certain *kinds* of prophets. For example, Jonathan Stökl notes that the categories of ecstatic and prophet overlap but are not coterminous: "there are prophets who do not go into ecstasy and ecstatics who do not prophesy."[10] Thus, none of the embodied religious experience studied in this chapter or Chapter 7 are shared by all biblical prophets and none are a necessary qualifying credential for the role of prophet. Yet collectively they demonstrate the interrelation of the prophetic body, experience, practice, and mediation.

Embodied practices shape cognition, concept formation, and theological propositional content; they also shape social and cultural realities. Thus, the bodily practices integral to *askêsis*, incubation, and ecstasy contribute to and in some cases "trigger" religious experience and mediation, but they are not merely a set of levers. In his analysis of the role of embodied cognition in religious experience, Tobias Tan builds on findings from cognitive neuroscience and related fields that link concept formation to modes of perception (i.e., sensory input and processing) and movement: "[T]he concepts do not become separated from the perceptual systems, but the visual, gustatory, olfactory, auditory, tactile, proprioceptive perception, as well as the motor movements which accompany and support them, also *constitute* these concepts."[11] These embodied practices also shape social realities. In an analysis of "convention in ritual," Roy Rappaport argues that participation in ritual both "indicate[s] aspects of performers' contemporary states" and "impose[s] transforming decisions on those states."[12] Rituals are composed of conventional elements arranged in a shared, agreed upon structure or choreography. To the extent that this choreography and its attendant meanings pre-exist the performance of them and to the extent that the performer aligns their performance with shared conventions, the performer "accepts" and "conforms" to the "social contract and morality" encoded within the ritual. But within that framework, the ritual also signifies a thing and "brings [it] into being."[13] This insight extends beyond the framework of ritual in the strict sense to illuminate the simultaneously conventional and creative praxis inherent in prophetic religious experience.

In the remainder of this chapter, I argue that prophetic *askêsis* employs culturally coded bodily disciplines to transform the prophetic body and for

---

[10] Stökl, *Prophecy in the Ancient Near East*, 14.
[11] Tan, "Corporeality of Religious Experience, 215, italics original.
[12] Rappaport, *Ritual and Religion*, 107.
[13] Rappaport, *Ritual and Religion*, 108.

the purposes of encountering the deity, receiving revelation, or interceding for the people. These disciplines also hold power to reshape social and even cosmic structures. While less clearly attested among Israel's prophets, incubation invited encounter with the deity to transform existing structures of leadership and mediation during a time of national transition.

Askêsis

In the apocryphal *Martyrdom and Ascension of Isaiah*, a community of prophets including Isaiah, Micah, Joel, and Habakkuk withdraws to a mountain in the wilderness for two years. They forsake possessions, wear only sackcloth, eat "wild herbs," and lament the turning away of their people (*Mart. Ascen. Isa.* 2:7–11).[14] Influenced by biblical and Greco-Roman traditions alike, this later text (composed between the first and second centuries CE) merges the practices of various biblical prophetic figures into a composite portrait of prophetic asceticism and ties that ascetic practice to their role as mediators between people and God. It would be wrong to retroject that composite portrait onto the HBOT. Yet this later narrative intuits a close connection both between the biblical portrayals of the transformative practices of Israel's prophets and their mediatory role and between such prophetic transformative praxis and the practices that modern scholars study under the label of religious asceticism.

Definitions of asceticism vary widely, depending in part on whose asceticism is being discussed, the forms it takes, and the goals it has in view. Asceticism is a modern analytical construct within the study of religions—it is not a word writers in the HBOT used to describe religious practice.[15] The English noun asceticism derives from the Greek noun *askêsis*, meaning "exercise, practice, training" and more broadly "mode of life, profession," deriving in turn from the verb ἀσκέω, meaning to "work raw materials" such as wool or wax, "form by art," and, in an athletic context, "practice, exercise,

---

[14] Thiering ("Biblical Source," 444) observes, "In the same writing, Isaiah's stance at his death shows the admiration of mastery of physical suffering that is implied in ascetic discipline" (see *Mart. Ascen. Isa.* 5:7–14). While Thiering attributes some of this portrait to "hellenistic influence," she also finds antecedents in biblical portrayals of Elijah, the suffering servant, Jeremiah, and Ezekiel.

[15] Fraade, "Ascetical Aspects," 253. An exception is 4 Macc (included in the canon of the Georgian Orthodox Church), which refers to people "trained in piety" (τοὺς τῆς εὐσεβείας ἀσκητὰς 12:11 NETS) and to "discipline in divine law" (ἐν νόμῳ θεοῦ ἀσκήσεως 13:22 NETS). In a somewhat similar vein, 2 Macc 15:4 uses the verb ἀσκεω to refer to observance of sabbath.

train."[16] This extended meaning of practice or training effectively applies the idea of "form[ing] by art" to the human body and to the person more broadly. Raw materials—the unpracticed body, the wandering mind—are molded and transformed through repeated action. Within the context of the ancient gymnasium, *askêsis* denoted "a rigorous program of physical and mental training and discipline" comprising the body techniques of a visible and publicly acknowledged transformation from boyhood to adult male citizen.[17] That is, in *askêsis* the malleable body becomes the site for the creation, performance, and (in the case of the gymnasium) maintenance of cultural and social values.[18] At both individual and collective levels, learned and regularly repeated disciplines and the skills they support mold the body inside and out, shape affect, language, modes of discourse, desires, habits, and patterns of thought, and create procedural memory. Practice embeds a value system within neurons and muscle tissue. Viewing and interacting with a body, a person, molded by *askêsis* can subtly embed aspects of the same value system in the bodies of beholders and interactants.

Modern study of asceticism rarely has the practices of the ancient gymnasium directly in view but recognizes a similarly formative power in bodily and spiritual disciplines undertaken for the purpose of achieving personal transformation and accessing or activating spiritual power.[19] Already in antiquity, the loci of *askêsis* expanded to include "philosophical schools and religious sects," wherein it took on a specialized meaning oriented not toward citizenship but toward greater access to and participation in divine realities.[20] The modern analytic construct "asceticism" generally has this type of *askêsis* in view.

Within religious studies, the type of practice most commonly identified as characteristic of asceticism is a rigorous "self-denial," abstention, withdrawal, or renunciation.[21] Focusing on early Christian ascetic

---

[16] "ἀσκέω," LSJ, 257.

[17] Nijf, "Athletics," 272.

[18] Nijf, "Athletics," passim. Nijf cites as examples of the encoding of value systems in relation to bodily performance "judgment contests [that] included events in *euexia* (comportment), *eutaxia* (discipline), and *philoponia* (endurance)" ("Athletics," 273).

[19] Clark observes, "Early Christian ascetics assumed that humans were transformable: the human person could be improved by ascetic practice" (*Reading Renunciation*, 17). In her study of asceticism at Qumran, Thiering ("Biblical Source," 435) similarly emphasizes the goal of "*transformation*, of a new kind of human life, that appears in a close study of the [ascetic] practices."

[20] Goehring, "Asceticism," 127.

[21] There is significant literature on various aspects of gender, sexuality, and embodiment in relation to Christian asceticism. See, e.g, Bynum, *Holy Feast and Holy Fast*; Burrus, *Sex Lives of Saints*; Clark, *Reading Renunciation*; Clements, *Sites of the Ascetic Self*; Gager, "Body-Symbols"; Hunt, *Clothed*

practice, James Goehring thus defines asceticism as "the voluntary exercise of self-denial designed to separate the individual from the human world and thereby facilitate access to the divine."[22] Steven Fraade similarly emphasizes disciplined denial, noting the tensive pairing of "abstention (whether total or partial, permanent or temporary, individualistic or communalistic) from the satisfaction of otherwise permitted earthly, creaturely desires" with "the exercise of disciplined effort toward the goal of spiritual perfection."[23] Within Judaism and Christianity alike, such practices of "self-denial" did not typically aim to negate the body or cut ties to the material realm per se. Instead, they presumed a close connection between material and spiritual realms and created a pathway for the transformation of the whole (embodied) person.[24]

The transformation of the individual through ascetic practice could also have wider ramifications. That is, while ascetic practice might entail modes of withdrawal from existing social structures and networks, this transformation often aimed to shape the self in ways that might also reshape the world. In this vein, Richard Valantasis defines asceticism as "performances within a dominant social environment intended to inaugurate a new subjectivity, different social relations, and an alternative symbolic universe."[25] Valantasis' definition sets up his analysis of a feature he regards as characteristic of asceticism, namely its resistance to "a perceived or a real dominant context."[26] For Valantasis, this intentional distance and resistance distinguishes asceticism from the *askêsis* of the ancient Hellenistic gymnasium, which reinforces the values of a dominant culture.[27] The ascetic, by contrast, aims to embody not existing cultural values, but alternative ones. While Valantasis has identified

in the Body; Martin and Miller, eds. *The Cultural Turn*; Miles, *Carnal Knowing*; Miller, "Blazing Body"; Miller, "Desert Asceticism"; Miller, *Corporeal Imagination*; Perkins, *Suffering Self*; Schroeder, *Monastic Bodies*; Shaw, *Burden of the Flesh*; and Vos and Geest, eds. *Early Christian Mystagogy*.

[22] Goehring, "Asceticism," 127.
[23] Fraade, "Ascetical Aspects," 257.
[24] Clark, *Reading Renunciation*, 17.
[25] Valantasis, "Constructions of Power," 797. Crucial to Valantasis' definition are configurations of power, which he understands as "the capacity to change and the capacity to affect the productive environment of another subject" ("Constructions of Power," 793; the other subject can be an altered self). Asceticism renounces some forms of power in order to achieve "empowered alterity" (Valantasis, "Constructions of Power," 792).
[26] Valantasis, *Making of the Self*, 102.
[27] Valantasis pithily summarizes the difference between what he categorizes as formation and asceticism: "Formation orients itself toward dominance; asceticism orients itself to alterity and subversion" (*Making of the Self*, 87).

a prominent feature shared by many examples of asceticism, ascetic practice should not be read as intrinsically resistant.[28] Dale Launderville offers an understanding of asceticism that relates more favorably to existing social structures:

> Ascetical practices have as their initial goal the shaping of an individual's behavior into a form that is compatible with a larger social body. Beyond conformity, however, such practices usually aim to effect a deeper, more enduring transformation of a person's character that will contribute to the harmony required for a healthy social body.[29]

It is true that ascetic practice may occur within an alternative social body that exemplifies values contrary to those of the dominant culture, making it possible to conform (to the values of an alternative social body) and resist (the values of a dominant social body) simultaneously. But even within an alternative social body asceticism may aim to participate in the transformation of the wider culture and cosmos in a mode that is seen as contributory and healing rather than resistant. Recognizing this range of postures toward existing social systems and structures will be helpful for analyzing the functions of prophetic ascetic practices.

A further feature of ascetic practice emerges from Valantasis' understanding of asceticism. To the extent that asceticism is performance, it is also revelatory: it communicates what it embodies.[30]

> Ascetics reveal the inner working and effects of dominant structures. They open to analysis and discernment the social, religious, political, and personal dynamics operative at any particular point in time, and they reveal the way those dynamics affect the person, the religious community, the society at large, and the physical environment. Ascetic communication reveals both the actual and the potential, both the lived reality and the possible new realities, and both the limits of the old and the expectation of the new.[31]

---

[28] Clark cites Rousseau, who pushes back on the idea that the ascetic was always positioned outside of and against a dominant cultural system, noting that within early Christianity ascetics were often admired within broader society (Rousseau, "Structure and Spirit," 2–3, cited in Clark, *Reading Renunciation*, 16).
[29] Launderville, *Celibacy*, 373.
[30] Valantasis, *Making of the Self*, 115.
[31] Valantasis, *Making of the Self*, 115–16.

While prophetic ascetic practices are recognized as a mode of preparation for receiving revelation, an understanding of ascetic practice as performative and revelatory *in itself* suggests a wider range of functions. In this understanding, ascetic practice does more than prepare someone for the work of mediation. It can also be a mode of mediation through which the prophet "reveals both the actual and the potential" in their practice and person. They might show forth a present reality, reveal the contours of a possible or inevitable future, or contribute to the outworking of divine plans.

Goehring observes that groundwork for early Christian and Jewish asceticism was laid both within Greek philosophy and the literature of the HBOT.[32] Within the latter corpora, biblical prophetic literature has been identified as a key source for later asceticism. Barbara Thiering links the transformative bodily and social practices described (and prescribed) in the literature of the *yaḥad* (the religious and social movement responsible for the composition of the Community Rule [1QS] and several other documents discovered at Qumran) to those portrayed in biblical prophetic literature. Thiering argues that ascetics in the *yaḥad* "attempted to anticipate in their own bodies and within the community the altered state of humankind."[33] In her view, biblical prophetic traditions portraying ecstatic behavior as well as those "concerned with the renewal of creation, the manifestation of the divine within the material world" were important antecedents of this later, more structured and systematic asceticism.[34]

Yet the very structured and regulated nature of ascetic discipline in the literature of the *yaḥad* highlights the lack of a unified or thoroughgoing prophetic asceticism in the HBOT. While biblical prophetic literature furnishes important sources for the patterning and articulation of later asceticism, the bodily disciplines portrayed in prophetic literature are less obviously a way of life in themselves. They are often occasional or episodic, prompted by specific, time-bound circumstances.[35] I propose that biblical prophets do indeed

---

[32] Goehring, "Asceticism," 127. A biblical antecedent outside of the prophetic literature is found in the Nazirite vows (Num 6:1–21). See Fraade, "Ascetical Aspects," 273–7, for analysis of differing rabbinic evaluations of this set of practices.

[33] Thiering, "Biblical Source," 444.

[34] Thiering, "Biblical Source," 440, 444.

[35] Leyerle and Darling Young write that "asceticism is defined by a series of sustained bodily practices." "Introduction," 8. While they do not specify a duration, a practice sustained for forty days (as in perhaps the clearest example of prophetic ascetic practice, Moses' sojourn on Mount Sinai) seems to differ in kind from one sustained for years, or for the remainder of a lifetime. Wills observes

engage in "performances within a dominant social environment intended to inaugurate a new subjectivity, different social relations, and an alternative symbolic universe" (Valantasis' definition of asceticism, considered above), and these performances include practices of withdrawal, abstention, or renunciation characteristic of later asceticism. But these performances should also be distinguished from the thoroughgoing asceticism of later religious movements like the *yaḥad*. To maintain that distinction, I refrain from using the term "asceticism" to describe the practice of bodily discipline portrayed in biblical prophetic literature, preferring the terms "*askêsis*," "ascetic practice," and "ascetic praxis." I use "*askêsis*" in the broad sense of "formative discipline" common to the term's ancient uses in the context of the gymnasium, philosophical schools, and religious movements. I use "ascetic practice" to refer to a specific practice (such as fasting) or to a constellation of practices undertaken by one individual or group. I use "ascetic praxis" to signal the capacity and intent of such practice/s to effect change within a wider social, relational (I here include the people's relationship with God), or even cosmic matrix. I will apply insights from the scholarly study of asceticism to the study of prophetic *askêsis* but will test and verify their applicability rather than assume it.

I noted above that the portrait of prophetic asceticism in the *Mart. Ascen. Isa.* is composite, reflecting not one biblical model of prophetic ascetic praxis but assembling topoi from diverse accounts. It is also anachronistic, projecting into an earlier period a symbolic framework and narrative tropes associated with asceticism in the time of its composition. With respect to biblical topoi, the wilderness community of foraging, weeping, and penniless prophets imagined by *Mart. Ascen. Isa.* evokes (among other traditions) Moses' sojourn on Mount Sinai, Elijah's reliance on food provided by ravens in Wadi Cherith (1 Kgs 17:4–9), the abstemiousness of Daniel and his companions (Dan 2:11–17), Jeremiah's abstention from marriage and children (Jer 16:2), and Jeremiah's laments (Jer, *passim*). The examples just cited underscore both the degree to which biblical prophetic *askêsis* is linked to specific circumstances and goals, such as preparation for entering the deity's presence, prophetic inquiry/seeking a revelation, intercessory petition, and actions commanded by the deity, and the close connection between prophetic *askêsis* and mediation.

---

that "The ascetic practices found in the Hebrew Bible, for example, are few. There is at most an occasional, *ad hoc*, or preparatory asceticism" ("Ascetic Theology Before Asceticism?" 904).

Moses on the Mountain

Perhaps the most familiar and archetypal example of prophetic *askêsis* occurs during Moses' sojourns on Mt. Sinai.[36] The prophet ascends the mountain multiple times in Exod 19, 24, and 34. On two occasions (chs. 24 and 34), he remains on the mountain with the deity for a period of forty days; during the second forty-day period he abstains from food and drink. In Deut 9, Moses asserts that he fasted during both forty-day sojourns and offers commentary to explain the reason for his fast. In addition to fasting, the physical climb to Sinai's peak is itself a form of *askêsis*, linking approach to the deity with arduous exertion across dangerous terrain. In Exodus, this climb also exemplifies the theme of separation developed across the ascent cycle, which links Moses' withdrawal to the holiness of the deity. This separation is also a joining, as withdrawal from the company of other humans enables entry into the deity's presence ("Moses entered the cloud" Exod 24:18 NRSV) and assimilation of divine attributes (34:30, 35; see further Chapter 5). Moses' withdrawal, ascension, and abstention from food and drink makes of his body a bridge between life and death, human and divine, charting a space of possibility for the renewal of broken covenant.

Exodus 19 juxtaposes Moses' ascent with the people's summons to holiness, establishing a parallel between his separation and theirs. The chapter portrays Moses' ascending the mountain at least twice (19:3, 20); another ascent is implied by his descent in v. 14. The first time Moses ascends the mountain, God calls the people to be "a priestly kingdom and holy nation," set apart through their covenant obedience (19:5–6 NRSV). They are to sanctify themselves for this priestly calling and for their own encounter with God by washing their clothes (19:14) and refraining from contact with women

---

[36] Moses' practice has numerous features in common with the ritual practice of incubation, considered further later in this chapter. A close parallel to Moses' forty-day period of withdrawal and abstention is found in 1 Kgs 19. Scholars debate the direction of literary dependence between these texts. For an argument against literary dependence and in favor of shared dependence on an earlier tradition, see Seidl, "Mose und Elija." Jesus' withdrawal to the wilderness in fasting and solitude (Matt 4:2; Mark 1:13; Luke 4:2) bears a typological relationship to both of these narratives (cf. the appearance of Jesus, Moses, and Elijah together on the mount on the occasion of Jesus's transfiguration: Matt 17:1–8; Mark 9:2–8; Luke 9:28–36) and provides a basis in turn for Christian observance of Lent as a forty day period of sacrificial preparation for the feast of Easter; fasting is historically one of the characteristic disciplines of Lent. PGM XIII.1–646 (part of the "Eighth Book of Moses") instructs the reader in a forty-one-day fast. Dietmar Neufeld surmises that "The forty days plus one of abstinence from food in the PGM suggests a common practice among prophets, exorcists, magicians, and thaumaturges" ("Eating, Ecstasy, and Exorcism," 160).

(v. 15).[37] These instructions exhibit concern for spatial and social boundaries that allow the (male?) people to encounter a deity who is holy, other, and dangerous. Moses' repeated ascent, descent, negotiation of boundaries, and conveying of instructions constitute a rigorous and fraught shuttle diplomacy. His motion back and forth foregrounds his mediatory role at the same time that his withdrawal embodies and exemplifies the people's preparation to encounter the deity and the state of being set apart for relationship with God that their covenant will entail.

While Exod 19 links Moses' repeated withdrawal to the holiness of the people, a later episode more closely links his separation with the holiness of the deity. Moses is singled out from among a group of priests and elders to ascend the mountain of the Lord (24:1–2) to receive the stone tablets containing the law for the people (24:12). He makes his ascent in stages (24:9, 13, 18), first ascending partway with the group. Together they are granted a vision of the deity, whose feet are visible on a pavement of translucent stones, a detail suggesting the deity stands above them while they perceive the soles of the feet from beneath the translucent pavement. The narrator's comment that the deity does not "send [God's] hand" to the leaders, that is, does not attack them, paradoxically assures the reader of their safety while emphasizing the danger posed by divine presence. The leaders behold the deity, eat, and drink (24:10–11). Following this meal, Moses separates himself from the group. While he and Joshua set out together (24:13a), at this juncture Moses alone is the subject of the verb "ascended" (24:13b, 15, 18) and only Moses is said to have "entered the cloud" (24:18). The deity, meanwhile, no longer appears in anthropomorphic form but speaks from the cloud (24:16); the appearance of the Lord's glory is now "like a devouring fire on the top of the mountain" (24:17). Moses remains "on the mountain forty days and forty nights" (24:18 NRSV). By comparison with the theophany in vv. 9–11, this second theophany portrays an increasing level of distance, danger, transcendence, otherness, and holiness. Moses' progressive withdrawal and lengthy separation bring him gradually closer to the dangerous deity whose holiness he now mirrors.

When Moses returns to the people following this forty-day sojourn on the mountain (Exod 32:15), his body and affect likewise mirror the deity's.

---

[37] Meyers proposes that "The phrasing of verse 15 may simply be conventional male language referring to sexual intercourse, typical of the androcentric orientation of the Hebrew Bible but not intended to exclude women from the experience of the theophany or from being party to the contents of the revelation" (*Exodus*, 154).

Upon perceiving (ראיתי) the people's worship of the golden calf, the Lord's nose burns hot (ויחר־אפי) against the people (32:9–10). Moses similarly sees (וירא), and his nose burns hot (ויחר־אף 32:19, cf. v. 22). But this alignment of Moses' seeing and feeling with God's own is not a total absorption. As mediator, Moses aligns also with the people, seeking to atone for their sin (32:30). His invitation to the Lord to blot him from the Lord's book if the Lord declines to forgive them stakes out for Moses a position outside and in-between, risking erasure to preserve and heal the relationship between deity and people (32:32).

As their negotiations continue, the Lord commands Moses to ascend Mt. Sinai yet again (Exod 34:2). The Lord reveals the Lord's self to Moses (34:5–7), Moses again intercedes for the people (34:9), and the Lord responds favorably, renewing the covenant and repeating certain promises and stipulations (34:10–27). The Lord commands Moses to (again) write the words of the covenant (v. 27), which Moses does. The narrator concludes the story of Moses' second sojourn on Mt. Sinai with a summary of Moses' actions: "He was there with the LORD forty days and forty nights; he neither ate bread nor drank water. And he wrote on the tablets the words of the covenant, the ten commandments" (34:28 NRSV).

The second forty-day sojourn differs from the first in one key detail: at this moment of covenant renewal, Moses deprives his body of nourishment and hydration. Forty days is nearly twice the length of Mohandas Gandhi's longest fast.[38] More crucially, it is more than five times longer than scientists estimate a human can survive without water.[39] As a multiple of four and ten, two numbers signaling totality in biblical literature, the number forty certainly has symbolic significance, but it here symbolizes more than "a very long time" and more than totality. Forty days without food and drink exceeds what is humanly possible. Moses exits society and abandons both the rites and rhythms of social life and the bodily practices necessary to sustain human (biological) life. He enters a border-zone between life and death and in so doing becomes other, his body a bridge between human and divine realities and possibilities.[40] This transformation of Moses' body prefigures,

---

[38] "Previous Fasts," 1.

[39] Piantadosi, *Biology of Human Survival*, 51–3.

[40] Writing in the first century CE, Philo emphasized the transformative effect of Moses' abstention from food and drink, possibly linking it with Moses' altered appearance on his descent from the mountain. For Philo, the revelation was itself a superior nourishment: "He had more excellent food than that in those contemplations with which he was inspired from above from heaven, by which also he was improved in the first instance in his mind, and, secondly, in his body, through his soul,

prepares for, and helps inaugurate a new social reality whose contours are limned in the law Moses receives and mediates.[41] To understand how it does so requires further analysis of the social and religious function of fasting in the HBOT, insights from studies of fasting in other contexts, and analysis of the motif of food and drink in this narrative cycle.

Fasting may prepare an individual or group to encounter the deity or receive revelation, whether through purification, sacrificial propitiation, focusing attention, desire, and will, producing an altered mind-state, or a combination of these.[42] The use of fasting as a "spiritual technique . . . to gain . . . illumination" is attested in Dan 9:3 and in rabbinic literature.[43] Fasting could "induce an ecstatic state," prepare a practitioner for receipt of a vision or oracle, and prepare someone to act and speak on behalf of a deity.[44]

Further insight emerges from analysis of the symbolic function and social meanings of food and drink in Exod 24–32. In Exod 24, the meal shared by Moses, Aaron, Nadab, Abihu, and the seventy elders follows a rite of animal sacrifice accompanying an act of covenant commitment (24:4–8). While not explicit in the narrative, the plot sequence suggests that the meal may be "a formal element in the conclusion of a covenant."[45] A "meal event [is] a ritualized act displaying the microcosm, or model of the universe, upon which the community is established."[46] Notably absent from this meal is the deity, who is the recipient of sacrifice and covenant partner but does not eat with the group of elders. Divine abstention marks eating as a human social ritual that may be oriented toward the deity but does not include the deity, suggesting that Moses' later abstention on Sinai may be an imitation of the deity and partial participation in divine nature.

---

increasing in strength and health both of body and soul, so that those who saw him afterwards could not believe that he was the same person" (*Mos.* 2.69, trans. Yonge in *Works of Philo*, 3.89).

[41] Neufeld, "Eating, Ecstasy, and Exorcism," 159, finds a similar purpose to Jesus' abstention from food, including declining commensality in certain social settings and with certain groups: "By not eating Jesus was using food as the medium through which he wished to communicate an alternative vision of life and death, a negative reciprocity that, though not normally practiced on members of one's family or village, nevertheless challenged the contours of social structures and transformed social relations."

[42] Neufeld, "Eating, Ecstasy, and Exorcism," 160.

[43] Hecker, *Mystical Bodies*, 73. A further example may be found in 1 Sam 28, wherein Saul consults the medium of Endor. After she has raised Samuel for him and Samuel finishes speaking, Saul falls to the ground with no strength because he has abstained from food for a day and night (1 Sam 28:20).

[44] Neufeld, "Eating, Ecstasy, and Exorcism," 158, 160.

[45] Sarna, *Exodus*, 153.

[46] Belnap, *Fillets of Fatling*, 37.

The people's worship of the golden calf is also accompanied by a meal (32:6). Dan Belnap observes that "Often, relationships are made, maintained, or destroyed through the ritualized actions associated with the meal."[47] The feast that follows sacrifice to the golden calf exchanges the elders' microcosmic map for a different one, effectively undoing the covenant commitment ritualized in that earlier meal (cf. 34:15). The landscape charted by this new map will have abundant food and drink, but not the Lord (33:3). The remedy for food and drink without God is to spend time with God without food and drink. That is, seen in the light of the meal-events in Exod 24 and 32, Moses' abstention from food during his second sojourn on God's mountain (34:28) does more than imitate God in order to experience divine presence, receive revelation, and more fully participate in divine nature. It walks back the people's inappropriate sacrifice and feasting, negating the commitments these entailed in order to make possible a re-commitment to their covenant with the Lord. The prominent role of food praxis within the heavily abbreviated repetition of covenant stipulations (34:15, 18–22, 25–6) underscores its importance in marking and maintaining this covenant relationship.

Like Exodus, Deuteronomy portrays Moses' fasting as preparation for revelation that helps inaugurate a new reality. But where Exodus emphasized separation and holiness, Deuteronomy emphasizes diligent repetition and observance, suggesting a link between Moses' *askêsis* and observance of the law. Deuteronomy further makes explicit the atoning function of Moses' second fast, highlighting the power of this practice to repair the ruptured relationship between God and people.

By comparison with Exodus, Deuteronomy doubles Moses' fast, asserting that he abstained from bread and water on both occasions, for a total of eighty (possibly consecutive) days. On the first occasion, Moses reports, "I remained on the mountain forty days and forty nights; I neither ate bread nor drank water" (Deut 9:9 NRSV). On the second occasion, Moses continues, "I lay prostrate before the LORD as before, forty days and forty nights; I neither ate bread nor drank water" (9:18a NRSV). Deuteronomy links Moses' fasting directly to his receiving the law (9:10–11). The subsequent speech of Moses further portrays the commandments of the law as the foundation for a different kind of *askêsis*: diligent repetition and observance of the law (11:18–22 and passim) that locates the divine words in the heart and life of each person (v. 18). Moses' repeated description of his own *askêsis* on the mountain offers

---

[47] Belnap, *Fillets of Fatling*, 35.

his audience an example of diligent practice that allows them to appreciate the seriousness of the observance to which they are called.[48]

Yet Deuteronomy also emphasizes the function of Moses' fasting as a form of petitionary mourning.[49] As a practice of mourning, fasting is a "[reversal] of day-to-day behaviors" that "function[s] to separate mourners from the rest of society."[50] That is, the person who is fasting refrains both from consuming food and drink and from participating in social rituals that form the rhythm of daily life in community.[51] Fasting thus effects an interruption in time corresponding to the rupture caused by death, sin, or exigency. In the context of petitionary mourning, fasting amplifies and displays human weakness, accentuates mortality, and performs dependence. The visible weakening and shrinking of the human body and ego magnify the deity in turn, acknowledging that the deity has power to accomplish what humans cannot. The voluntary surrender of human status and agency is offered in hopes of gaining the deity's attention and prompting divine forgiveness, healing, or rescue. For Saul Olyan, pairing petition with fasting and/or other practices of lament, self-denial, and obeisance aims to increase the odds of a favorable outcome: "The point . . . is to get noticed and elicit a positive, active response from Yhwh."[52]

In Deuteronomy, Moses identifies the people's sin as the reason for his fast: "I neither ate bread nor drank water, because of all the sin you had committed, provoking the Lord by doing what was evil in his sight" (9:18b NRSV). His fasting is accompanied by a posture of self-abasement, reverence, and submission before the deity. Moses twice reports that he "prostrated himself before the Lord" (9:18, 25) and remained in this position throughout the forty days and nights. Later Moses adds that throughout the time that he lay

---

[48] In a similar vein, in Jeremiah the Lord calls attention to the example of the Rechabites, who abstained from wine and lived in tents in accordance with a command received from their ancestor (Jer 35:1–19). God contrasts their diligent observance with the people's failure to observe the law (35:16).

[49] Examples of fasting as a practice of mourning include a) mourning the dead: 1 Sam 31:13; 2 Sam 1:12; b) individual petitionary mourning: 2 Sam 12:22; c) individual petitionary mourning on behalf of the people: Ezra 9:5; 10:6; 11:4; Neh 1:4; and d) communal petitionary mourning: 1 Sam 7:6; Jonah 3:6–8; Esth 4:16; Joel 2:12; Isa 58:3. This list is not exhaustive.

[50] Olyan, *Biblical Mourning*, 33.

[51] This abstention can create social friction, as reported by the psalmist at Ps 69:10–11.

[52] Olyan, *Biblical Mourning*, 76–7. See also Hecker, *Mystical Bodies*, 72. Both Esther and Jonah include abstention from food and drink as practices of petitionary mourning. Esther and the Jews of Susa undertake a fast before she risks her life to save her people (Esth 4:16). While the deity is not mentioned in MT Esther, implicit in the timing of this act is the hope that it may improve Esther's chances of success. See Seidler, "Fasting." Est OL explicitly links the fasting to practices of prayer. See Bellmann, "Theological Character," 10.

prostrate he prayed on the people's behalf (9:25). Moses' prayer intercedes between people and God, petitioning the deity not to destroy the people God has already saved, invoking their ancestors, and appealing to God's reputation and the special relationship between God and the Israelites (9:26–9). The words of prayer and the practices of Moses' body function in tandem. By withdrawing from the people to spend forty days and nights in stillness and isolation with God, the prophet effects an interruption that corresponds to the magnitude of the rupture the people's sin has caused. By bringing his own body to the brink of death, he displays their vulnerability before God. By prostrating himself before the deity he surrenders status and agency, acknowledging God as the one with power to forgive and save. By trading bodily sustenance for nearness to the deity, he reorders desire, need, and will. Moses' petition is successful. God responds by reissuing the commandments (10:1–5), and Moses reports: "I stayed on the mountain forty days and forty nights, as I had done the first time. And once again the LORD listened to me. The LORD was unwilling to destroy you" (10:10 NRSV). Moses' act of petitionary mourning elicits grace from the deity and the possibility of a new beginning.

Religious experiences and the practices that constitute them can alter body and consciousness even as they shape reality. I have argued that one mode of religious experience and practice, prophetic *askêsis*, disciplines the body in preparation for revelation, intercession, and mediation of divine power. It is also revelatory and efficacious, with a capacity to heal broken relationship and help inaugurate new beginnings in the covenant between God and people.

Incubation

Closely related to prophetic *askêsis* is incubation, a practice that entails "preparing oneself ritually by means of diverse observances (fasting, purification, sacrifices) and of spending the night in a sanctuary or in a natural holy site, in order to receive either a visit or a message in a dream from the divinity invoked."[53] While evidence is insufficient to declare with certainty that incubation is portrayed as a prophetic practice in the HBOT, I argue that the

---

[53] Husser, *Dreams and Dream Narratives*, 21. Isaiah 65:4 may refer to a practice akin to incubation at gravesites. See Renberg, *Where Dreams May Come*, 1.32, 68.

use of incubatory type-scenes to portray Hannah's petitionary praxis and the revelatory experience of her son Samuel demonstrates a close connection between incubation and prophetic mediation. These portrayals allow us to describe the actions of Hannah and Samuel as forms of incubatory practice even if they do not unambiguously conform to scholarly definitions of incubation. Hannah's incubatory practice decenters existing authority to claim her own. The liminality of this revelatory practice mirrors the liminality of her body; the prophet and prophetic song that issue from it herald and inaugurate new structures of governance and mediation for Israel. The portrayal of Samuel's practice of sleeping by the ark in the Shiloh sanctuary and attendant interactions with the deity similarly evokes formal characteristics of incubatory type-scenes. Samuel's incubatory practice results not only in a personal encounter with the deity but also in the restoration of mediatory channels that had previously been closed. This liminal mediatory modality occupies a space both adjacent to and intersecting with prophetic mediation. It emerges at a moment of national transition to enable a reconfiguration of leadership and mediatory structures.

Gil Renberg distinguishes two types of incubation, therapeutic and divinatory, based on their differing aims. Therapeutic incubation seeks healing intervention in the face of personal disease, injury, or disability as well as assistance with reproductive fertility. Divinatory incubation seeks revelation about any other matter.[54] In either type of incubation petitioners could consult a deity either indirectly, that is, with the aid of a cultic functionary or other proxy who would receive and mediate the revelation, or directly, that is, receiving the revelation or healing through their own dream or vision, depending in part on the ritual norms for a given deity or sanctuary.[55] Cultic functionaries could also assist by verifying and interpreting dreams received through direct revelation.[56]

While divinatory incubation is thought to have its origins in ancient West Asian and Mediterranean religious practice,[57] evidence of incubation in the Old Testament is slender. Jean-Marie Husser takes a cautious approach, noting that "the only element of which we are certain is that oneiric experiences are numbered among divinatory techniques."[58] A. Leo

---

[54] Renberg, *Where Dreams May Come*, 1.21–3, 29. Among Mediterranean religions, a particular subset of incubation sanctuaries (e.g., *Asklepieia* and *Sarapieia*) were primarily devoted to bodily healing.
[55] Renberg, *Where Dreams May Come*, 1.6; Kim, *Incubation*, 43.
[56] Renberg, *Where Dreams May Come*, 1.27.
[57] Renberg, *Where Dreams May Come*, 1.72.
[58] Husser, *Dreams and Dream Narratives*, 168.

Oppenheim went a step further, theorizing that theophanic dream visions containing details regarding the physical space of the sanctuary reflected incubation practices.[59] If this is correct, then reports of theophanic visions such as those found in Isa 6 and the book of Habakkuk might be influenced by incubation practices and/or their literary representations. And while Husser critiques overly enthusiastic interpretations of Old Testament texts that fill in missing details in order to reconstruct supposed incubatory practices, he concurs with those who find reflexes of incubation rites in texts such as 1 Kgs 3:4–15.[60]

Despite the paucity of evidence, a few texts may portray prophetic revelatory praxis that is similar to or consistent with incubation.[61] I focus here on 1 Sam 1–3. Koowon Kim argues that incubation practices familiar to ancient Israelite audiences furnished the *Gestalt* for a literary type-scene found twice in 1 Sam 1–3.[62] Drawing on Kim's work, I argue that the narrator of 1 Sam 1–3 deploys tropes related to both therapeutic and divinatory incubation in order to portray a transferal of authority from an established priestly line to a new prophet-priest who will form a bridge to the era of monarchy in Israel. While Samuel is the primary prophetic figure in this story, his mother Hannah occupies a quasi-prophetic role. Her incubatory praxis carves out a liminal space in the Shiloh sanctuary, opening a previously closed circuit so that new revelation might issue forth from the sanctuary to and for Israel. Her prophetic prayer, the transformation of her body and birthing of the prophet, and her bringing the child to the sanctuary and providing for his physical needs all set the stage for Samuel's own theophanic encounter.

---

[59] "We would like to propose that the incubation dream, the dream experienced in a sanctuary or a sacred locality—whether the dream is sought or not—is to be considered the prototype of most of the dreams discussed so far.... The traditional circumstances of a theophany experienced in a dream furnish the mold into which all dream-experiences containing a message from supernatural powers were cast" (Oppenheim, *Interpretation of Dreams*, 190).

[60] Husser, *Dreams and Dream Narratives*, 172–6. Cf. Renberg, *Where Dreams May Come*, 1.68: "Despite numerous references to dreams and dreaming, the description of Solomon's visit to Gibeon is the only passage in the Hebrew Bible that clearly describes incubation." Renberg (*Where Dreams May Come*, 1.69–71) also considers Gen 28:10–22. Of course, neither Solomon nor Jacob is identified in these narratives as prophets, nor do they mediate the revelations they receive. Later traditions, however, including *midrashim* and the Quran, do identify Solomon as a diviner and/or prophet. For analysis of midrashic traditions, see Shemesh "God Gave Solomon Wisdom." For relevant texts from the Quran, see Wheeler, *Prophets in the Quran*, 266–79.

[61] Stökl, "Ready or Not," 129–30, argues for the likelihood that Balaam practices incubation in Num 22, but allows that "the text also makes sense without this" (130).

[62] Kim, *Incubation*. Given the lack of nonliterary evidence for incubation practices in ancient Syria-Palestine, Kim (*Incubation*, 60n.133) allows that this familiarity may not have been firsthand and may even have been distant cultural memory. Kim builds on Michael Nagler's understanding of type-scenes as furnishing not a fixed pattern but rather a *Gestalt* that generates scenes related to one another by "family resemblance" rather than shared formulae (Nagler, "Oral Formula").

Samuel encounters the deity in a manner that is similarly liminal: in lamp light but in the dark of night, next to the ark of divine presence, and in a state of consciousness between sleeping and waking.[63] As a mode of divination, incubation is liminal in a further sense, as it can be direct or indirect, related to domains public or private, with epiphanies granted to cultic functionaries and lay people alike. Thus, even when tied to a specific sanctuary, incubation theoretically has the capacity to decenter existing mediatorial authority, to shift that authority to the edges, and, in the case of Hannah and Samuel, to transfer it from representatives of an old institution to the inaugurators of a new one. This liminal practice is portrayed in fuzzy outline rather than clear detail. It is not a trusty arrow in the quiver of Israel and Judah's prophets, but instead shimmers into view at one moment of crisis and transition, manifesting destabilizing powers of interruption and change.

In Kim's analysis, Hannah's story contains several "component motifs" of the incubation type-scene.[64] These include "clear movement of plot from problem to solution"; ritual practices including sacrifice, abstention from food, and weeping; pilgrimage to a holy place and repeated reference to her location in the sanctuary and in the presence of the deity; an implied nocturnal temporal setting; petitionary prayer and vow; divine blessing that includes the healing transformation of her body and resolution of her predicament; change of mood in the petitioner; fulfillment of the divine promise; and fulfillment of the petitioner's vow.[65] Given that the resolution of Hannah's predicament ("the Lord had closed her birth canal" 1 Sam 1:5) entails the conception and birth of a child (v. 20), it would stand to reason that Hannah's incubation type-scene would be understood as an example of therapeutic incubation. Yet key details suggest that, while the aim of her incubation may have been therapeutic, the result combines features of therapeutic and divinatory epiphanies.

Hannah's status as prophet is not explicit in the Hebrew Scriptures, yet her victory song or prayer in 1 Sam 2:1–10 shares features with the songs of the

---

[63] Oppenheim argues that ancient sources considered dreaming "a *sui generis* state of consciousness, a hovering between the eclipse of sleep and the stark but dull reality of day" (*Interpretation of Dreams*, 190).

[64] Kim, *Incubation*, 276.

[65] Kim, *Incubation*, 276–328 (quoted phrase, 276). Kim argues that Hannah's "simple act of refraining from eating and drinking out of distress had taken on a quasi-cultic nature, namely, it had become a cultic fasting and abstention from wine for the purpose of winning divine favor" (*Incubation*, 289). Her tears follow a similar trajectory, shifting from an expression of distress (1 Sam 1:7d) to "a means of inducing divine mercy" (1 Sam 1:10; *Incubation*, 291).

prophets Moses, Miriam, and Deborah. It also foretells God's future victories and the rise of Israel's monarchy. The prophetic character of her song is made explicit in Targum Pseudo-Jonathan, which, according to Daniel Harrington, further "transforms Hannah's song into an apocalypse that charts the course of Israel's future history and climaxes in a vision of the eschaton."[66]

The targum clarifies in v. 1 that Hannah prays ברוח נבואה, "in a spirit of prophecy," and deploys a fourfold repetition of the verb אתנביאת, "she prophesied," to introduce a series of oracles against Assyria, Babylon, Greece, and the sons of Haman.[67] She declares her own son a prophet and links his lineage to a further prophetic tradition present in Chronicles by identifying her descendants through Samuel as including Heman (1 Chron 6:33; cf. 1 Sam 8:2; 1 Chron 15:17) and his fourteen sons who will "speak with song" in temple worship (אמרין בשירה על ידי נבלין וכנורין עם אחיהון ליואי לשבחא בבית מקדשא Tg. Ps.-J. 1 Sam 2:1). According to the Chronicler, the music of the sons of Heman was a form of prophecy (1 Chron 25:1) performed in the presence of the ark (1 Chron 6:16–17). Eveline van Staalduine-Sulman theorizes that this link between song and prophecy drives the targum's identification of Hannah's song as prophetic.[68] She also notes that, similar to the interpretation of *Targum Psuedo-Jonathan*, the Talmud names Hannah among seven women prophets, providing explanation as to how her prayer was prophetic (*Megillah* 14a). While these traditions apply later exegetical methods to Hannah's story and song, they arguably grow from seeds already present in the biblical text. As van Staalduine-Sulman writes, "Within the Hebrew Books of Samuel, Hannah's song already functions as a prophetic, proleptic song, anticipating the throne of glory and the anointed king. It is therefore not surprising that TJon understood the prophetic nature of some verses and extended this nature to the entire song."[69]

---

[66] Harrington, "Apocalypse of Hannah," 147. Harrington argues that this portion of the Targum likely circulated as an independent composition before being included in the Targum at the time of its "final redaction." Based on *Tg. Ps.-J.* 1 Sam 2:5, he dates this composition sometime after 70 CE in the period of Roman hegemony, stating, "It is hard to be more precise than that" ("Apocalypse of Hannah," 152). On dating of *Targum Pseudo-Jonathan*, see further Flesher and Chilton, *Targums*, 151–66. Cook notes that in *Targum Pseudo-Jonathan*, "Hannah herself expands from the faithful woman who rejoices in her motherhood to prophet who predicts the divine military might and judgment. She joins the ranks of the women who sing victory hymns, but differs from Miriam and Deborah in predicting divine success rather than celebrating the accomplished facts" (*Hannah's Desire*, 85).

[67] For *Targum Pseudo-Jonathan*'s view of prophets and prophecy, see Staalduine-Sulman, *Targum of Samuel*, 170–1.

[68] Staalduine-Sulman, *Targum of Samuel*, 171; cf. 199.

[69] Staalduine-Sulman, *Targum of Samuel*, 199.

140 THE PROPHETIC BODY

What became full blown in later tradition was thus present *in nuce* in 1 Samuel. The biblical Hannah charts a prophetic border zone or growth edge. That is, while her story does not provide definitive evidence for the portrayal of Israelite prophetic incubation, it occupies a domain closely adjacent to prophetic divination and from there inserts a wedge into existing structures of authority to create avenues of access and mediatory power for herself and her son. Within the story-world of 1 Sam MT and LXX, her praxis is portrayed as unorthodox and unwelcome. The priest Eli occupies a gate-keeping position "by the temple doorpost" (1 Sam 1:9) from which he surveils the locus and manner of her speaking (שׁמר את־פיה/ἐφύλαξεν τὸ στόμα αὐτῆς "watching/guarding her mouth" v. 12) and attempts to regulate both her observable affect and the bodily practice he assumes she has engaged in prior to entering the sanctuary (1:14). The Septuagint preserves the further detail that he commands Hannah's departure from the Lord's presence (πορεύου ἐκ προσώπου κυρίου 1:14 LXX). This attempt to exclude her from the sanctuary and to dismiss her ritual praxis and transformed state as inebriation (1:14) suggests that incubation (or a practice very close to it) here provides an avenue for an outsider to lay claim to divine revelation and transformative power. In so doing, Hannah sets the stage for her son Samuel to step into his prophetic role.

Hannah's body is itself a site of liminality: she is a woman, and thus barred from access to cultic roles and spaces; she is favored, and thus elevated; but she is infertile, and thus deprived of status. Her affective practices of fasting, weeping, and praying transgress behavioral norms and expectations even as they form a petitionary bridge between human and divine realms.[70] Her body forms a double gateway: from her birth canal, first closed then opened by the deity, will issue the prophet; from her mouth, opened wide against her enemies (1 Sam 2:1), will issue an oracle of salvation. The liminal body

---

[70] In Philo's treatment of Hannah's story, she is an even more liminal figure, straddling and holding together dualities of masculinity and femininity and soul and body while journeying from the human to the divine realm "under the influence of divine inspiration" (*Ebr.* 1.147): "Having broken all the chains by which it was formerly bound, which all the empty anxieties of mortal life fastened around it, and having led it forth and emancipated it from them, he has stretched, and extended, and diffused it to such a degree that it reaches even the extreme boundaries of the universe, and is borne onwards to the beautiful and glorious sight of the uncreate God" (Philo, *Ebr.* 1.152, trans. Yonge in *Works of Philo*, 1.484–85). Mackie argues that in Philo's account, "Hannah does not transcend her embodied existence in order to ascend to the vision. Rather, her sensual body cooperates perfectly with her masculine mind as she attains the *visio Dei*. In so doing, she not only models the Edenic intent for humanity, she also effortlessly and fluidly transcends the ontological and metaphysical dualisms that rigidly structure Philo's thought-world" (Mackie, "Passion of Eve," 146).

of Hannah participates in a liminal practice that creates a threshold to a new prophetic era.

The second incubatory type-scene follows in 1 Sam 3, after Samuel has come to reside in the sanctuary of YHWH at Shiloh. The young prophet sleeps in the temple near the ark, at a time when "the word of the Lord was rare and vision was uncommon" (1 Sam 3:1–2) and "before the word of the Lord had been revealed to him" (v. 7). Three times the deity calls Samuel in his sleep, and Samuel mistakes the deity's voice for that of Eli, priest of the sanctuary.[71] Eli then directs Samuel to sleep once more and reply to the deity (in the dream-state) with words that signal attentive listening (v. 9). Samuel follows Eli's instructions (v. 10) and receives a revelation (vv. 11–14). At Eli's prompting, Samuel reports to him the content of his revelation, and the priest confirms its veracity (v. 18).

Husser resists classifying 1 Sam 3 as incubation but observes that v. 9 suggests a "technique of self-conditioning permitting the disciple to perceive a divine word 'heard' in the night." In Husser's interpretation, Samuel engages in a learned practice of guided or lucid dreaming, "awakening to a particular form of consciousness *in sleep*, permitting the *nabî* not only to listen to an oneiric oracle but also to solicit it." The concluding reference to the Lord's repeated self-revelation to Samuel at the Shiloh sanctuary (3:21) suggests to Husser that this form of revelatory dream-vision became the habitual medium through which the deity communicated with Samuel.[72] Samuel's later statement to Saul, "I will tell you what the Lord said to me last night" (1 Sam 15:16), potentially supports this hypothesis (cf. 2 Sam 7:4; Jer 31:26; Dan 2:19, 4:10).

In Kim's analysis, 1 Sam 3 "contains an ancient literary pattern drawing on the actual practice of incubation," with the result that the revelation Samuel receives "may be something very close to an incubation dream."[73] Given that the revelation to Samuel remedies a broader lack identified by the narrator at the story's beginning, namely the scarcity of God's word, Kim further ventures that Samuel's practice might be a form of "surrogate incubation" in which Samuel receives a revelation not for his own benefit but on behalf of an implicit petitioner, Israel.[74]

---

[71] Oppenheim regards the calling of Samuel's name (3:4, 6, 8) and the deity's standing posture (3:10) as characteristic features of incubation narratives (*Interpretation of Dreams*, 189–90).
[72] Husser, *Dreams and Dream Narratives*, 177.
[73] Kim, *Incubation*, 335.
[74] Kim, *Incubation*, 335. Kim notes that while, from the standpoint of analyzing the actual religious practice, it would be necessary to demonstrate such intent, when examining a literary representation

It is not only the form of Samuel's revelatory encounter that is relevant for understanding this liminal practice but also its content. The oracle Samuel receives from YHWH and reports to Eli declares an end to the leadership of the house of Eli (1 Sam 3:11–14). This ending is also a beginning. The narrator here labels Samuel a prophet, linking recognition of his prophetic role to the oracle he received at the Shiloh sanctuary and to YHWH's continued appearances to him there (3:19–21). The practice is thus liminal in one further way. Its availability not only to appointed functionaries but also to petitioners, including women and children, affords it a unique power to disrupt and even displace existing systems of mediatory authority. That is, not despite the fact but rather *because* it is not the "usual" mode of prophetic mediation, it is able to participate in a reconfiguration of power and relationship. Samuel's epiphanies occur in between: in between days, darkness and light, sleeping and waking, authorized modalities of mediation, eras, and institutions. His incubatory experience does not provide a template of prophetic praxis but rather opens a previously closed prophetic channel at a time of national and cultic transition.

Conclusion

The transformative, bodily practices examined in this chapter, namely *askêsis* and incubation, are forms of religious experience. A caveat bears repeating here: in this book, we are focused not on the lived experiences of historical prophets but rather on the portrayals of prophetic experience, and, more narrowly, the portrayal in biblical literature of the body's central role as locus and means of prophetic mediation. But these portrayals are not unrelated to what human beings experience(d) "in real life." For this reason, before digging into portrayals of ascetic and incubatory practice, I asked how the narrative portrayal of prophetic religious experience might relate to the experiences of (putative) actual ancient Israelite and Judean prophets in the world "behind the text" and why this might matter for analysis of the ancient texts themselves. This inquiry produced a set of working assumptions to guide my analysis in this chapter and in Chapter 7. I argued that although we lack evidence to map direct connections between specific historical individuals and

---

this is not the case. Kim cites Oppenheim's treatment of "unintentional incubation" as "literary category" rather than a "practice in reality" (Kim, *Incubation*, 334–5).

specific texts, the types of religious experiences characteristic of the *lived* role of prophet in the various sociohistorical contexts of ancient Israel and Judah would to some degree both be reflected in and shaped by prophetic *literature* now preserved in the HBOT. This reflexive relationship between lived experience and its textual articulations means that insights from anthropology, psychiatry, and neurobiology can illuminate these textual articulations even when the primary focus of these fields of study is on phenomena in the "real world." This assumption opened the door for engagement with studies of religious experience, including ritual. A key insight emerged: religious experience is not simply passive but includes a wide range of religious practices constituting a shared cultural repertoire. These practices are both conventional and creative, with power not only to transmit and reinforce shared values but also to shape and reconfigure self and world.

Having established this framework, the remainder of the chapter focused on two types of transformative practice: *askêsis* and incubation. While the HBOT does not portray the thoroughgoing asceticism characteristic of later religious movements, prophetic *askêsis* shares features with similar practices in other contexts. In light of these commonalities, broader study of *askêsis* and asceticism provided a starting point for the analysis of prophetic *askêsis*. In the context of the ancient gymnasium, the term *askêsis* named a set of rigorous bodily disciplines that molded the body and person of the practitioner and, in the process, performed and transmitted cultural values. Already in antiquity the meanings of this term expanded to describe a set of bodily disciplines including self-denial, abstention, and withdrawal that sought to transform the self in order to achieve greater proximity to the divine. Ascetic practices could aim not only at personal transformations but also social and cosmic ones, sometimes emerging as a mode of resistance to dominant social norms and structures, at others promoting healing and harmony. Ascetic practices also had a mediatory function. They could prepare an individual for the work of mediation; they could also be revelatory and efficacious.

These mediatory functions came into clearer focus in the analysis of Moses' sojourns on Mt. Sinai, narrated in Exodus and Deuteronomy. In Exod 19, 24, and 34, Moses' ascent and withdrawal both set him apart and, paradoxically, forge links between people and deity. Rigorous ascent and abstention from food and water push his body across the limits of possibility. His body becomes a mediating bridge, spanning the gulf between God and human, life and death. The transformation of the prophet's body prepares the way for Israel's own transformations. His fasting prepares him to receive revelation and to speak and act on God's behalf. It also negates the commitments enacted by the people in their sacrifice to the golden calf (Exod 32:6), effecting a "reset" that will allow the people to enter into covenant relationship with YHWH even in the wake of idolatry. The atoning function of Moses' fasting is made explicit in Deut 9–10. Through embodied practices of mourning, Moses petitions YHWH to forgive the people's sin. Moreover, Moses' *askêsis* finds a parallel in the observance of the law he enjoins upon the people, such that his withdrawal and self-denial provides for them a model of diligent practice.

In prophetic *askêsis* the body enters a border-zone in order to mediate between divine and human realms. In the practice of incubation, or ritualized sleeping in a holy place in hope of encounter, healing, or revelation from a divine being, the body similarly occupies a liminal space, in between the boundaries of sleeping and waking, night and day, sacred and profane, divine and human, life and death. Biblical literature does not portray incubation as a characteristic practice of Israelite and Judean prophets. Yet multiple stories in the HBOT nonetheless share key formal features with incubation type-scenes found in other ancient West Asian sources. In the stories of Hannah and Samuel (1 Sam 1–3), incubatory practice is constructed as a liminal mediatory modality that accompanies and makes possible a reconfiguration of prophetic, cultic, and political leadership. God responds to Hannah's petition by opening her birth canal and granting her the gift of a child. She responds to this gift with a victory song that interpreters have frequently regarded as prophecy. The transformation of her body mirrors, prefigures, and enables broader social and mediatory transformations. Her actions and experience chart a mediatory border-zone that creates space for her son Samuel's leadership and the transitions it both instantiates and heralds. Samuel's own incubatory practice opens new prophetic channels, eliciting revelation on behalf of Israel regarding the end in store for their cultic leaders. The veracity of the oracles he receives at Shiloh confirm him as YHWH's prophet (1 Sam 3:20).

Closely related to *askêsis* and incubation is a third type of religious experience, namely ecstasy. Prophets could employ a range of techniques to induce states of ecstasy that made of their bodies and consciousness a mediating bridge between human and divine realms. It is to this transformative experience that we turn in Chapter 7.

7
Ecstasy

During the past century, scholars have vigorously debated whether and to what degree religious ecstasy is a feature of biblical prophecy. I argue that, while prophetic ecstasy is not *universally* attested in the literature of the Hebrew Bible and Old Testament (HBOT), it nonetheless emerges as a significant, albeit contested, feature. Insights from scientific study of altered states of consciousness (ASC's) and anthropological research on trance and possession shed light on these debates while also illuminating prophetic ecstasy's embodied and social dimensions.

While ascetic practice (examined in Chapter 6) presumes the possibility of personal, social, and cosmic transformation through sustained bodily discipline or repeated practice, ecstasy names a more fleeting transformation that combines a subjective experiential dimension with transient changes in physiology and behavior. Prophetic ecstasy describes a type of religious experience that accompanies a prophet's encounter with supernatural beings, revelatory visions, and auditory revelation. It also describes modes of behavior viewed as characteristic of prophets and permissible within the context of prophetic mediation but otherwise outside the boundaries of normally accepted social comportment. It is an experiential bridge to another world and its denizens. The behavior it produces similarly occupies either side of a boundary line between acceptable and unacceptable behavior. The individual is not the sole arbiter of their experience; rather, it is evaluated and interpreted within a preexisting but malleable and contestable contextual frame.

Ecstasy's multivalent, contestable nature helps explain the high degree of debate within biblical studies as to whether and to what degree ecstasy characterized the experience and behavior of prophets in the HBOT. In what follows, I first review debates in biblical studies regarding the existence and nature of ecstasy among prophets in the HBOT. I then shift to a discussion of religious ecstasy as a category of embodied phenomena with complex and varied biological, psychological, and social dimensions and map an area of considerable overlap between religious ecstasy and certain phenomena today considered a symptom of mental illness. This phenomenological complexity and overlap have a correlate in the wide range of alternate states of consciousness associated with prophetic activity in the HBOT and debates within biblical texts about their interpretation and assessment. Consistent with this diversity, biblical literature does not yield one unified profile of prophetic ecstasy. A distinctive feature found in some but not all portrayals of ecstasy is the use of induction techniques, including music and rhythmic movement (other techniques received attention in Chapter 6). After briefly assessing the evidence for these techniques, I examine evidence linking prophetic ecstasy in the HBOT to spirit possession, including 1 Sam 10 and 19 and the visionary experiences of Ezekiel (Ezek 1–3, 8–11, 37, 40–48) and Balaam (Num 24).

Anxious about Ecstasy: A Century of Debate, 1914–2017

More than a hundred years ago, Gustav Hölscher combined insights from comparative religious study, anthropology, and physiological psychology to argue that religious ecstatic behavior was part of the "essence" of prophetic performance (i.e., the mode in which oracles were publicly delivered) and part of a legacy inherited and adapted by Israelites from their Canaanite cultural environment.[1] While his theory of cultural borrowing did not gain wide traction, his study inaugurated vigorous and ongoing debates about the nature, existence, extent, and evaluation of ecstasy in biblical prophetic literature. Not long after, Bernhard Duhm attributed poetic and prophetic speech to ecstatic experience that linked poets and prophets to "higher beings."[2] Several decades later, Johannes Lindblom drew on then-current cross-cultural anthropological research to illuminate prophetic inspiration and ecstasy, which he viewed as existing along a continuum of intensity. He

---

[1] Hölscher's study begins with a broad claim for the universality of prophetic ecstatic experience before he narrows his focus on the relation between Canaanite and Israelite modes of prophetic mediation: "Die Seher und Profeten aller Zeiten und Völker, auch die der Hebräer, haben sich stets eigentümlicher seelischer Erfahrungen gerühmt, durch die sie vor anderen Sterblichen im Besitze übernatürlichen Wissens, göttlicher Offenbarungen waren, und eben dies hat von jeher als das eigentliche Wesen des Seher- und Profetentums gegolten" (Hölscher, *Profeten*, 1). Cf. Gunkel, "Einleitungen," xxi: "Das Grunderlebnis aller Prophetie aber ist die 'Ekstase'. Das ist ein dem gewöhnlichen Menschen der Gegenwart sehr entlegener und ihm nicht ohne weiteres verständlicher Zustand des Bewusstseins."

[2] Duhm, *Israels Propheten*, 95. On diverse techniques for inducing ecstasy, see Duhm, *Israels Propheten*, 82. On the link between prophetic poetry and ecstasy, see also Duhm, *Buch Jesaia*, 2, 51, 59, 126.

defined the more intense state of ecstasy as a form of monoideism (absorption in a single focus) characterized by a narrowing of awareness, cessation of "bodily senses," exaltation of consciousness above ordinary experience, and the expression of unconscious ideas through vision and audition.[3] Yet he also understood inspiration and ecstasy to be dynamic states that varied in form, duration, and intensity.[4]

Subsequent decades saw multiple challenges to the assumption that the HBOT portrayed forms of religious ecstasy, with critics variously emphasizing the uniqueness, rationality, and calm demeanor of Israel's prophets or asserting a dearth of evidence for ecstatic mediation in ancient West Asian and biblical literature.[5] Abraham Heschel, for example, critiqued Hölscher's flattening of biblical evidence into an ahistorical "medley" and rejected comparative methodology that presumed an analogy between Israel's prophets and mediatory figures from other cultures.[6] Heschel opposed what he viewed as a naturalistic bias that reduced the religious experience of the prophets to a psychological phenomenon. He drew a bright line between ecstatic practices and experiences documented in other cultures and periods and "the consciousness of the great prophets."[7] This consciousness could be inferred from prophecy's "noetic" character, evident in prophetic social analysis, critique, and persuasion, and had as its correlate a God whose plans for humanity were not mysterious but wholly transparent.[8] For Heschel, "no trace of ecstasy is found in [the] experiences" of "Moses, Amos, Hosea, Isaiah, and Jeremiah."[9] Israel's prophets opposed the "frenzy" characteristic of Baal prophets, used no techniques to induce altered states, and never sought union with the God they viewed as wholly other.[10] For Heschel, prophecy was purely a gift from God.[11] At the same time, the prophet remained fully conscious, present, responsive, and free in every act of prophecy.[12]

---

[3] Lindblom, *Prophecy*, 4.
[4] Lindblom, *Prophecy*, 4–46.
[5] Kelle, "Phenomenon," 283. Kelle asserts that "the model of ecstatic prophets has received numerous reexaminations and largely fallen out of favor over the last century" ("Phenomenon," 283).
[6] Heschel, *Prophets*, 349–51.
[7] Heschel, *Prophets*, 352.
[8] Heschel, *Prophets*, 359–60.
[9] Heschel, *Prophets*, 353.
[10] Heschel, *Prophets*, 354, 357, 359.
[11] Heschel, *Prophets*, 359. Heschel's insistence on the "gift" of prophecy nonetheless leaves open the possibility of creating conditions conducive to receiving it. Stökl focuses on divination more broadly but finds overlap between "the roles of ecstatic and prophet" ("Ready or Not," 126). "Triggers," he argues, "are widely used to bring prophets and other diviners into the right frame of mind to receive divine messages" (Stökl, "Ready or Not," 133).
[12] Heschel, *Prophets*, 357–8.

By contrast with Heschel, Robert Wilson insisted on the validity of cross-cultural comparison, but emphasized the importance of "native explanations." In the Hebrew Bible, for example, "the primary means of divine-human communication" is spirit possession, but not necessarily trance or ecstasy.[13] While in Wilson's view trance or ecstasy should not be ruled out across the board, he cautioned against generalizing from one or more examples to all instances.[14] But contrary to the objections of Heschel, Wilson insisted that trance states and/or ecstasy are not *a priori* incompatible with rational, comprehensible speech or writing.[15]

For Wilson and others, emphasis on "native explanations" prompted attention to terminology. Within the corpus of the Hebrew Bible, the denominative verbal root נבא* (derived from the noun נביא, "prophet") occurs in two conjugations, *niphal* and *hithpael*. *Niphal* forms from this root commonly denote the delivery of a prophetic oracle or similar prophetic speech-form and have the meaning "to prophesy." While some *hithpael* forms appear to function similarly, others appear to denote patterns of behavior that many have judged consistent with prophetic ecstasy. Some account for this range of meanings (i.e., both prophetic speech and ecstatic behavior) by proposing a chronological development in which the *hithpael* originally denoted ecstatic behavior but later semantically assimilated to the more common *niphal* form.[16] Wilson accepted the theory of chronological development but proposed that early forms of the *hithpael* (התנבא) did not narrowly denote ecstatic behavior but referred more broadly to "behavior characteristic of a *nābî'*."[17] Characteristic behavior would vary in form across groups and periods, sometimes referring to ecstasy or trance, but sometimes not.[18] Wilson was careful to note that the term is not evaluative: absent other evaluative clues, naming behavior as characteristic of a prophet neither confirms nor denies an individual's status as a prophet.[19]

Contra Wilson, Simon Parker argued that "Yahwistic prophecy in Israel does not involve possession of any kind."[20] Instead, possession trance arises "only marginally" as a feature of Phoenician prophecy and in derogatory

---

[13] Wilson, "Prophecy and Ecstasy," 325.
[14] Wilson, "Prophecy and Ecstasy," 337.
[15] Wilson, "Prophecy and Ecstasy," 328.
[16] Wilson, "Prophecy and Ecstasy," 329–30.
[17] Wilson, "Prophecy and Ecstasy," 336.
[18] Wilson, "Prophecy and Ecstasy," 336.
[19] Wilson, "Prophecy and Ecstasy," 330.
[20] Parker, "Possession Trance," 281.

discourse aiming to discredit prophets whose authority the speaker rejects. While the narratives in 1 Sam 10:5–7 and 19:20–24 do portray possession trance, Parker argued, these trances do not produce visions and are not mediumistic.[21] As such, they do not constitute recognizably prophetic activity. On these grounds, Parker proposed that in these passages *niphal* and *hithpael* forms of the root נבא* have the meaning "'to be in, or to fall into, a possession trance,' and ... have nothing to do with prophecy or divination." Other instances of these verb forms can refer to prophetic mediation *or* possession trance but "never both."[22] Parker's analysis of 1 Sam 10:5–7 and 19:20–24 helpfully cautioned against assuming the presence of mediating activity from forms of the root נבא* absent other contextual indicators of mediation. Yet Parker's explanation for how a denominative verb derived from the noun "prophet" comes to have a meaning entirely divorced from prophetic role expectations relies on a narrative of cultural influence (with regard to *terminology*, Phoenician cultural meanings shaped Hebrew usage) in the face of cultural opposition (with regard to *practice*, Israelite prophets wholly rejected Phoenician prophetic styles).[23] Specifically, Parker suggests that Israelites would use a form of the verb נבא* to name ecstatic behavior because among the Phoenician neighbors in whom they observed this behavior it had a prophetic function. This is possible, but what is less likely is that such cultural influence would affect language but in no instance affect associated concepts and practices. It further assumes an absolute distinction between Israelite and Canaanite-Phoenician religious roles and practices even as biblical narratives portray the opposite and archaeology provides evidence of cultural interaction and exchange within a "plural society ... in which several ethnic groups existed."[24] Parker's denial that *hithpael* forms of נבא* could refer to ecstatic prophetic activity in any biblical text overstates the case.[25]

These problems notwithstanding, David Petersen built on Parker's conclusions by appeal to role theorist Theodore Sarbin's scale of "organismic involvement" in "role enactment" to argue that ecstasy cannot be an

---

[21] Parker, "Possession Trance," 272–3.
[22] Parker, "Possession Trance," 274.
[23] "It would be natural for the Israelites to refer to [possession trance] by the same word with which they referred to mediumistic activity in their own culture, namely *nbʾ*—even though its function in Israel was generally unrelated to prophecy" (Parker, "Possession Trance," 274).
[24] Faust, "Ethnic Complexity," 21.
[25] See also Grabbe, *Priests, Prophets, Diviners, Sages*, 111. Michaelsen further critiqued what he viewed as Parker's overreliance on anthropological categorization of trance states ("Ecstasy and Possession," 42–3).

essential feature of prophecy in ancient Israel because it is not attested.[26] Petersen found four levels of organismic involvement portrayed within biblical prophetic literature, namely "ritual acting," "engrossed acting," "hypnotic role taking," and "histrionic neurosis." Petersen suggested that, while Ezekiel's commanded staging of a siege in miniature (Ezek 4:1–3) provides an example of ritual acting, engrossed action is more typical of Israel's prophets. Such action is voluntary, strategic, and committed; examples include occasions when the prophet interacts with an individual or group and speaks in their own voice rather than the deity's.[27] Vision reports are for Petersen an example of "hypnotic role taking" (behaving "as if" sensorimotor stimuli are present), while prophetic experience of the presence or "hand of God" in the form of illness, pain, or other physiologic and psychic distress provides examples of "histrionic neurosis."[28] Petersen did not find evidence of Sarbin's levels VI, "ecstasy," or VII, "bewitchment."[29] As Peter Michaelsen notes, however, Sarbin's levels chart a continuum of intensity with overlapping criteria that make it difficult to classify individual examples with certainty, particularly while analyzing a literary description.[30] Moreover, Petersen gives short shrift to the level of organismic involvement Sarbin labels ecstasy. Petersen characterizes it only as involuntary, a feature he does not find in Israelite prophecy, yet whether lack of volition is a primary marker of Sarbin's level VI is not at all clear from Sarbin's own analysis. Sarbin does write that "ecstasy . . . usually involve[es] suspension of voluntary action," but his examples, namely rites of passage, religious conversion, mystical experience, revival meetings, dance marathons, being caught up in a musical performance, and sexual climax, do not consistently bear this out.[31] This lack of clarity in Sarbin's own description of ecstasy and Petersen's heavily abridged summary of it render problematic Petersen's argument for the absence of ecstasy among Israel's prophets. Moreover, for the category to which Petersen assigns prophetic visionary experience (which other scholars would consider a form of ecstasy or trance), Sarbin's

[26] Sarbin, "Role Theory." Sarbin was particularly concerned to show that behavior of hypnotized subjects was a form of role enactment and did not result from a physiologically altered state of consciousness. Sarbin elsewhere writes that "'organismic involvement' is synonymous with the contemporary meaning of 'embodiment'" and applies this concept to analyze the experience of reading narrative (Sarbin, "Role of Imagination," 6).
[27] Petersen, *Roles of Israel's Prophets*, 30–2.
[28] Petersen, *Roles of Israel's Prophets*, 32–3.
[29] Petersen, *Roles of Israel's Prophets*, 31–3.
[30] Michaelsen, "Ecstasy and Possession," 30–3. See Sarbin, "Role Theory," 223.
[31] Sarbin, "Role Theory," 234–5.

social-cognitive theory rejects out of hand the presence of an altered state of consciousness.[32] That is, regardless of whether ecstatic *behavior* is found to be present, the methodology opposes the learned behavior of role enactment to the very supposition that an altered state of consciousness is part of the underlying mechanics. Appeal to Sarbin's work thus does not resolve debate but rather highlights disagreement within the fields of psychology and neurobiology. Whether hypnotic trance is in fact the appropriate category for prophetic visions is another question. In her study of Siberian shamanism, for example, while Anna-Leena Siikala argues that shamanic trance induction follows a process analogous to "Western hypnotic trance," she also emphasizes that these phenomena differ culturally, neurophysiologically, cognitively, and functionally and thus cannot be equated.[33]

A further challenge to earlier notions of prophetic ecstasy came from Gunnel André, who, echoing some of Heschel's arguments, maintained that prophets did not experience "union" with the deity but retained their sense of identity, rejected interpretive frames derived from the field of psychology, and emphasized the intelligibility of Israel's "true" prophets.[34] Like Parker, while André did find evidence of possession trance and argued that this is in several places the meaning of the *hithpael* forms of נבא*, she unyoked these forms from prophecy. The trance states indicated by these verb forms were not, as Wilson had argued, characteristic of prophets. Rather, they provided evidence that YHWH's spirit had possessed an individual to confirm their status as a leader.[35] Unlike Parker and Petersen, André did not deny that Israel's prophets experienced religious ecstasy, but she averred that their ecstasy was more tranquil than energetic. For André, "false and non-Israelite prophets" could exhibit "orgiastic, vigorous ecstasy," but the ecstasy of Israel's true prophets was "characterized by a calm, sometimes paralytically calm,

---

[32] Theodore R. Sarbin, "Hypnotic Behavior." He writes: "Hypnosis is a form of a more general kind of social psychological behavior known as role-taking. In the hypnotic experiment the subject strives to take the role of the hypnotized person; the success of his striving is a function of favorable motivation, role-perception, and role-taking aptitude. This orientation breaks completely with the tradition of looking on hypnosis as some strange phenomenon for which it is necessary to invent psychophysiological constructions" (Sarbin, "Hypnotic Behavior," 259). Lynn, Kirsch, and Hallquist write, "During the 1960s and 1970s, the altered state issue was acknowledged to be the most contentious issue in the field (Sheehan and Perry, 1976) . . . the controversy continues to simmer, if not boil . . . the claim that neurophysiological data resolve the altered state issue is not warranted by the available evidence" (Lynn, Kirsch, and Hallquist, "Social Cognitive Theories," 113). On this debate, see also Kihlstrom, who argues for a synthesis that recognizes the interaction of social, cognitive, and biological factors ("Is Hypnosis an Altered State?" 37).
[33] Siikala, "Siberian Shaman's Technique," 107.
[34] André, "Ecstatic," 190–1, 194, 200.
[35] André, "Ecstatic," 199.

seeing and hearing the word of YHWH."[36] In this contrastive portrait, foreign mediators are deceptive and out of control; the sexual undertones of the word "orgiastic" evoke caricatures of Canaanites as deviants whose religious rites incorporate immoral sexual behaviors. Moreover, for André, even in ecstasy, a true prophet does not encounter or mediate the presence or activity of an embodied deity but rather sees and hears the divine word. The ordering logic of the word is mirrored in the prophet's own regulated body.[37]

Responding to the critiques of Parker, Petersen, and André, among others, Lester Grabbe noted a terminological challenge: the term ecstasy has currency in religious studies, anthropologists speak of trance (and possession/possession trance), and psychologists and neurobiologists frequently, though not uniformly, consider trance states a subset of altered states of consciousness. A further challenge is difference across cultures. While ethnographic trance typologies group differing patterns for the sake of cross-cultural comparison, they do not provide hard and fast categorical distinctions. These differing vocabularies, foci, and methodologies in the study of overlapping but diverse phenomena across multiple fields erode confidence that scholars debating the existence and nature of prophetic ecstasy in the HBOT are in fact talking about the same things. Absent consensus about definitions or methodology, Grabbe found that those who deny the presence of prophetic ecstasy in the HBOT "have often used rather arbitrary criteria," excluding, for example, Ezekiel's experience of the hand and spirit of YHWH.[38] Motivated in part by a desire to protect Israel's prophets from association with foreign (especially Canaanite or Phoenician) mediators and forms of religious experience and practice viewed as wild, excessive, and irrational, these denials represented for Grabbe "willful attempts to bolster a partisan view of the 'classical' Israelite prophets."[39] Rather than the universal claims of Hölscher or Duhm, blanket rejections by Parker and Petersen, or stark cultural contrasts asserted by Parker and André, Grabbe argued for a more balanced approach that recognizes among Israelite prophets a range of prophetic experience and

---

[36] André, "Ecstatic," 200.
[37] Grabbe similarly observes a "blatant double standard applied to come up with such a clear distinction between the 'true' and the 'false' prophets based on ecstatic experiences" (*Priests, Prophets, Diviners, Sages*, 111).
[38] "If Ezekiel does not have ecstatic experiences, then we have no criteria to judge that *anyone* of antiquity had such experiences. We must either accept that the language of the OT text implies such experiences for some Israelite prophets or abandon the task of trying to determine whether such experiences are at all described in any ancient text for any prophetic figures" (Grabbe, *Priests, Prophets, Diviners, Sages*, 110).
[39] Grabbe, *Priests, Prophets, Diviners, Sages*, 110.

practice inclusive of but not uniformly characterized by various forms of religious ecstasy.[40]

In a similar vein, John Levison emphasized that ecstasy is not uniform.[41] While several of the studies considered above focus on 1 Sam 10–19, Levison examines Num 11:25, which employs a *hithpael* form of נבא* to describe the activity of seventy elders on whom the Lord confers part of the spirit that was on Moses so they may share his burden of leadership. Anthropologist I. M. Lewis distinguished between the differing forms and functions of peripheral and central possession, the former occurring among marginal social groups, the latter among those with recognized institutional power.[42] Levison argues that Num 11:25 describes a form of prophetic ecstasy that is neither "frenzy" nor "catatonic behavior" but "visionary experience within a controlled cultic setting intended to support Moses as he leads Israelites."[43] As such it is an example of Lewis's central possession in which the spirit "rests" on those present for a limited time within an authorized and authorizing social framework and "appointed locus of revelation."[44] Yet rather than generalize from this instance to all of Israelite prophecy, Levison urges attention to the diverse social locations, structures, contexts, and functions shaping instances of prophetic ecstasy. Treating ecstasy within the broader category of inspiration, Levison argues that "it is, accordingly, much more likely that differently occasioned experiences of inspiration should differ substantially from one another than that they should appear unvaryingly in the same guise."[45]

A social scientific framework similarly informed the approach of Richard Nelson, who affirmed that *hithpael* forms of the verb נבא* may denote trance behavior but questioned whether this entails an altered state of consciousness. Consistent with the approaches of Petersen and, to an extent, Levison, Nelson proposed that prophetic performance of ecstatic behavior was a form of stereotypical behavior that furnished social legitimation and a corresponding measure of public influence. Behaviors that are "eccentric and flamboyant" match a prophet's social role and experience as "mediator between the human and divine worlds." Yet while the "supernormal" character of prophetic experience and behavior can generate approval and influence, it

---

[40] Grabbe, *Priests, Prophets, Diviners, Sages*, 111–12.
[41] Levison, "Ecstatic Elders."
[42] Lewis, *Ecstatic Religion*.
[43] Levison, "Ecstatic Elders," 504–5.
[44] Levison, "Ecstatic Elders," 515.
[45] Levison, "Ecstatic Elders," 521. On the role of the spirit in relation to prophecy, see also MacDonald, "Spirit of YHWH."

can also lead to perceptions and accusations of social violation and even pathology.[46] Nelson's analysis moved away from a focus on religious experience to social performance of learned behavior.

Klaus-Peter Adam offered a similar assessment in his analysis of the *hithpael* form of נבא*. Adam affirmed a similar meaning for the *hithpael* to that proposed by Wilson, but with reference to perceptible status rather than discrete acts: "to put oneself in the status of a prophet / to act like a prophet." Yet Adam identified a depreciative bias attached to its use in most cases, with the result that it primarily designates not true prophetic behavior but its pretense.[47] Yet to whatever extent Adam is correct that the meaning of the *hithpael* stem is imitative, it must imitate known patterns of prophetic experience or behavior.[48]

By contrast with those who view ecstasy solely as performance, Martti Nissinen recognizes a combination of performative and experiential components, arguing that "an altered state of consciousness appears as a prerequisite of the prophetic performance in ancient Near Eastern, Greek and biblical texts."[49] Nissinen's approach resembles that of Hölscher and Lindblom in affirming the validity of cross-cultural comparison and adopting a broadly interdisciplinary approach. Yet Nissinen's analysis benefits from attention to ancient West Asian sources such as letters from the Mari archive that were not available to Hölscher and Lindblom as well as newer perspectives in anthropology and psychology that affirm the interdependence of social, psychological, and somatic factors. For example, texts describing the triggering practices, ritual context, and altered mind-states associated with the prophetic activity of the *muḫḫûm/muḫḫūtum* (Old Babylonian) and *maḫḫû/maḫḫūtu* (Neo-Assyrian) illustrate the function of ecstatic behavior within a patterned, ritual, mediatory performance that may be a precursor or analogue to some forms of biblical prophetic ecstasy.[50]

In what follows, I affirm that biblical literature frequently describes modes of prophetic experience and behavior that we may call ecstasy. Such ecstasy

---

[46] Richard D. Nelson, "Prophetic Lunacy," 116–17.
[47] Adam, "And He Behaved," 12, 22.
[48] Adam ("And He Behaved," 22) relies on the conclusions of Parker and Petersen to anticipate this objection. For reasons noted above, this does not resolve the question of prophetic ecstasy.
[49] Nissinen, *Ancient Prophecy*, 171.
[50] Nissinen, *Ancient Prophecy*, 173–80. See also Moran, "New Evidence from Mari"; Durand and Guichard, "Rituels de Mari." Strawn and Strawn consider the etymology of this Akkadian prophetic role label, from the verb *maḫû*, meaning "to rave, become frenzied, act crazy," as a possible parallel to the range of meanings for the Hebrew verb נבא*, particularly in relation to accusations of prophetic "madness" ("Prophecy and Psychology," 615).

takes a range of forms, and, anticipating modern debates, its meaning and function were frequently contested. Like Nissinen, I propose an approach to prophetic ecstasy that combines insights from neurobiology, psychology, anthropology, and religious studies. This multidisciplinary approach illumines its embodied character as a mode of experience and action.

A Multidisciplinary Approach

Religious ecstasy is widely recognized as an example of an altered or alternate state of consciousness, or ASC.[51] Albert Garcia-Romeu and Charles Tart define consciousness as "the subjective awareness and experience of internal and external phenomena," while "states of consciousness refer to the spectrum of ways in which experience may be organized."[52] Although an "ordinary waking state" is commonly considered to constitute a baseline state, individuals experience a variety of "discrete states of consciousness," each entailing "a unique, dynamic pattern or configuration of psychological structures."[53] Alternate states of consciousness differ from the baseline and include "dreaming, deep sleep, intoxication, hypnosis, and successfully induced meditative states," among others.[54] Such alternate states may be spontaneous, as in the case of sleepiness, daydreaming, or dreaming; may result from injury or illness; or may be induced by a variety of means including psychoactive substances, drumming, rhythmic movement, prayer, fasting, sensory deprivation, breathing techniques, relaxation, and meditation.[55]

To understand the embodied character of prophetic ecstasy requires attention not only to observable bodily techniques and behaviors, but also the embodied nature of consciousness itself and the changes in the body that accompany ASCs. Indeed, this embodied character of human consciousness is one factor enabling study of religious ecstasy across times, places, and cultural contexts. Dieter Vaitl and colleagues analyze the psychobiology of altered states along four phenomenological dimensions, namely activation (aroused v. relaxed), awareness span (wide v. narrow), self-awareness (present v. absent), and sensory dynamics (increased v. decreased). At a

---

[51] For a review of key terms and research on altered states of consciousness, see Garcia-Romeu and Tart, "Altered States."
[52] Garcia-Romeu and Tart, "Altered States," 123.
[53] Garcia-Romeu and Tart, "Altered States," 123.
[54] Garcia-Romeu and Tart, "Altered States," 123.
[55] Vaitl et al., "Psychobiology," 99–113.

biological level, they observe that the activation dimension correlates to "alterations of those brain systems responsible for the regulation of consciousness, arousal, and selective attention," while they associate awareness span and sensory dynamics with "breakdown of the connectivity between large groups of cell assemblies" within the brain.[56] These examples hint at the multifold connections between religious ecstasy and the body. According to Vaitl and colleagues, spontaneous and physically and physiologically induced ASCs typically exhibit a consistent phenomenological profile, as do states induced by sensory overload, relaxation, and rhythm. Trance-states induced by drumming and/or rhythmic movement, for example, commonly produce "distort[ed] time sense, unusual bodily sensations . . . , vivid imagery, and strong positive emotions."[57] Yet other ASCs, including those induced by meditation or hypnosis, exhibit phenomenological diversity.[58] This insight confirms the methodological caveat introduced by Wilson, Grabbe, and Levison, as it should not be assumed that prophetic ecstasy will have one, consistent, phenomenological profile.

Indeed, the ASC referred to as religious or spiritual ecstasy is itself a varied phenomenon and has been studied in relation to practices of mysticism and collective worship as well as mediatory roles such as shaman, spirit-medium, diviner, and prophet. In any given instance, the precise contours of ecstatic religious experience and behavior may be shaped by a range of factors including cultural frames, personal and social expectations, physiology, and techniques (if any) used to induce the ecstatic state.[59]

Moreover, a given instance of ecstatic experience and behavior may be subject to multiple, competing interpretations and valorizations even within a single cultural or communal context. These diverse shaping factors and interpretative frames notwithstanding, it has been proposed that a defining characteristic of *religious* ecstasy is a subjective experience of transcendence. Such transcendence may have intrapersonal, interpersonal, and/or transpersonal qualities. The intrapersonal quality denotes an interior dimension of experience that enables an individual to access greater insight, creativity, and self-knowledge. Interpersonal modes of transcendence link the person

---

[56] Vaitl et al., "Psychobiology," 115–16.
[57] Vaitl et al., "Psychobiology," 107.
[58] Vaitl et al., "Psychobiology," 115.
[59] Ludwig, "Altered States of Consciousness," 227. In her study of Siberian shamans, Siikala describes a "cumulative process" combining study, stimuli, affect, and attention with audience expectations, support, and participation ("Siberian Shaman's Technique," 111). This audience, according to Siikala, sometimes shares the mediating role with the shaman ("Siberian Shaman's Technique," 115).

to other individuals and/or to their environment, while transpersonal experience extends beyond the personal through expansive awareness of and connection to a reality greater than oneself.[60] This expansive awareness and connection may include an experience of union with a divinity, source of being, or cosmos.

This capacity of consciousness to transcend the felt boundaries of the self is expressed in the etymology of the Greek word from which "ecstasy" derives: ἔκστασις, literally "standing outside," applied to human consciousness, experience, and behavior thus implies "standing outside" the *self*, whether a movement of consciousness beyond the self or social performance divergent from a person's typical affect and social role. The Greek noun ἔκστασις can connote "displacement," "movement outwards," and "differentiation" and may apply to a range of states including distraction, wonder, excitement, and trance.[61]

Consistent with this etymological meaning, a commonly recognized component of religious ecstasy is a trance or trance-like state which may entail changes in perception, sensation, cognition, affect, volition, and behavior. In the study of religious ecstasy, social scientists distinguish between trance-states that are attributed to possession by a spirit or otherworldly being and those that are not.[62] Trance states not attributed to possession may still mediate supernatural encounter, as in the experience of transport to another dimension or realm.

Trance states characteristic of religious ecstasy are in many respects similar to trance states characteristic of certain forms of mental illness recognized within the field of psychiatry. I do not make this point in order to apply modern diagnostic criteria or models of mental illness to the study of ancient religious phenomena or their portrayals, but rather to highlight a parallel between modern and ancient debates, ambiguities, and uncertainties regarding the interpretation of these phenomena. In modern and ancient settings alike, the biological, psychological, and social complexity of the experience of ecstasy resists simple classification or uniform evaluation. These ambiguities further illuminate modern debates about prophetic ecstasy in the HBOT.

---

[60] Reed, "Theory of Self-Transcendence," 121.
[61] "ἔκστασις," LSJ, 520; "ἐξίστημι," LSJ, 595.
[62] On the distinction between possession trance and non-possession trance, see Bourguignon, "Framework for Comparative Study." Lewis is careful to note that experiences interpreted as possession do not always include a trance state (*Ecstatic Religion*, 25).

158   THE PROPHETIC BODY

For example, the Diagnostic and Statistical Manual of Mental Disorders, 4th edition (DSM-IV), included diagnostic criteria for Dissociative Trance Disorder (DTD), occurring in two subtypes.[63] The first, trance without possession, is characterized by

> temporary marked alteration in the state of consciousness or loss of customary sense of personal identity without replacement by an alternate identity, associated with at least one of the following:
> (a) narrowing of awareness of immediate surroundings, or unusually narrow and selective focusing on environmental stimuli
> (b) stereotyped behaviors or movements that are experienced as being beyond one's control.[64]

The second, possession trance, is, according to DSM-IV, comprised of

> a single or episodic alteration in the state of consciousness characterized by the replacement of customary sense of personal identity by a new identity. This is attributed to the influence of a spirit, power, deity, or other person, as evidenced by one (of more) of the following:
> (a) stereotyped and culturally determined behaviors or movements that are experienced as being controlled by the possession agent
> (b) full or partial amnesia for the event.[65]

The perceived phenomenological overlap between trance states characteristic of religious ecstasy and those considered symptomatic of mental illness led DSM-IV to include analysis of cultural and communal context among the diagnostic considerations for DTD. For example, DTD would not be indicated in settings where such trance is "accepted as a normal part of a cultural or religious practice" and if it does not cause a person "clinically significant

---

[63] The DSM (in any edition) is a cultural document and is here treated as such. It has been the subject of significant critique, e.g., with regard to the inclusion of "homosexuality" as a form of illness in DSM-I and DSM-II (Drescher, "Depathologizing Homosexuality"). On efforts to incorporate greater cultural awareness in DSM, see Lewis-Fernández and Aggarwal, "Culture and Psychiatric Diagnosis"; Mezzich et al., "Place of Culture."

[64] DSM-IV-TR, Appendix B, 783.

[65] DSM-IV-TR, Appendix B, 783. In their review of this definition, Emmanuel During et al. recommended removing the criterion of amnesia, which is not a prevalent diagnostic criterion, and including a reference to hallucinations ("Dissociative Trance and Possession Disorders," 240). This is an important corrective in light of Michaelsen's suggestion that the absence of amnesia would exclude any first-person narratives in Jeremiah and Ezekiel from consideration as examples of possession trance ("Ecstasy and Possession," 49–50).

distress or impairment in social, occupational, or other important areas of functioning."[66] Yet degree of distress or impairment can be difficult to assess, and contextual analysis does not always provide clear-cut answers, as social expectations and norms vary both across cultures and within communities.[67]

This example of phenomenological overlap and the attendant challenges of distinguishing symptoms of illness from a "normal" or "accepted" mode of religious experience and role performance in modern psychiatry illuminates debates in biblical studies surveyed above and mirrors a perennial concern within biblical texts, namely how to distinguish true from false prophets. Through ecstasy, a mediator could marshal powerful and potentially disruptive (or hegemonic) forces in contested social domains.[68] Charges of mental illness or social deviance furnished biblical writers and characters with ready ammunition by which to discredit mediators whose authority they rejected.[69] Defining and evaluating ecstasy was thus not a modern problem only, but also an ancient one.

In what follows I do not aim to differentiate true prophetic ecstasy from false, whether the latter be construed as deceptive, deviant, foreign, or pathological. Instead, I consider both the range of embodied experiences and behaviors attributed to prophets in the HBOT that suggest the presence of an alternate state of consciousness and the embodied practices that are occasionally used to produce such states. Prophetic ecstasy may produce trance states marked by decreased motor activity, altered time sense, narrowed attention, and selectively heightened senses. It may produce feelings of affliction or constraint. The prophet in ecstasy may be transported to other lands or experience visions of otherwise hidden realities. The body in ecstasy forms a bridge between places and times and between human and divine realities.

---

[66] DSM-IV-TR, Appendix B, 783. See discussion of criteria for dissociative trance/possession disorders (DTPD) in DSM-5 and ICD-11 as they relate to channeling of "discarnate entities" in Pederzoli, Tressoldi, and Wahbeh, "Channeling."

[67] During et al., "Dissociative Trance and Possession Disorders," 240. See also Bhavsar, Ventriglio, and Bhugra, "Dissociative Trance and Spirit Possession," 552–3: "Finally, there is the uncertainty regarding the extent to which this diagnostic category is responsible for the unnecessary pathologization of normative experiences. The relation between experiences diagnosed as dissociative trance/possession and those that are studied by anthropologists as 'spirit possession' is not clear. In the social sciences, across the categories of human experience regarded to be 'spiritual,' it is possession, the 'seizure of the spirit' by another, which has been the most arresting for observers. In this regard, dissociative trance states and possession states have, together, been of interest to both clinicians and anthropologists interested in the problem of making comparisons of mental illness between cultures."

[68] Lewis, *Ecstatic Religion*.

[69] Nelson, "Prophetic Lunacy"; Parker, "Possession Trance," 281–5; Strawn and Strawn, "Prophecy and Psychology."

Induction Techniques

Much of the prophetic literature records oracles or visions without detailed narrative framing and thus provides little evidence regarding possible techniques for inducing prophecy or altered states that may accompany it. Several passages nonetheless hint at embodied induction techniques. In Chapter 6, I considered ascetic practices such as fasting as one way that Israel's prophets might prepare themselves to be in the presence of the deity and/or receive revelation. I also considered a technique for inducing dream visions, namely incubation. Other techniques for inducing altered states of consciousness include music and rhythmic movement.[70]

The use of music as an induction technique is attested most clearly in 2 Kgs 3. The kings of Judah, Israel, and Edom together approach Elisha to seek an oracle regarding battle with Moab (2 Kgs 3:12). Reluctantly agreeing to inquire of the Lord on their behalf, Elisha commands them to get him a מנגן, a musician who plays a stringed instrument (vv. 14–15; cf. v. 11). The clause that follows this request, והיה כנגן המנגן ותהי עליו יד־יהוה, has been variously interpreted as a statement by the narrator reporting the sequence of events or a statement by Elisha describing the purpose of the musician.[71] In the first interpretation, the verb is past tense, and the narrator reports that while a musician was playing, the hand of the Lord came upon Elisha (v. 15).[72] This interpretation would be consistent with the aorist verb καὶ ἐγένετο in the LXX. In the second interpretation, Elisha describes a characteristic sequence in which a musician's playing would (frequently) produce this effect. Mordechai Cogan and Hayim Tadmor write that "syntactically, *wĕhāyâh* is frequentative and describes the recurring ecstasis which took hold of the prophet under the influence of music."[73] Jonathan Stökl notes further that "this reading leaves open the possibility that Elisha is claiming that prophets generally went into prophetic trance when music played."[74] Minimally, the passage portrays one instance in which a prophet used

---

[70] An additional technique attested in later Jewish tradition is weeping, which can also have a theurgic function (Idel, *Kabbalah*, 75–88, 197–9). Weeping was "a means for attaining revelations—mostly of a visual character—and/or a disclosure of secrets" (Idel, *Kabbalah*, 75).

[71] Stökl, "Ready or Not," 120.

[72] Many Hebrew manuscripts and the Targums preserve the reading "spirit" rather than "hand" (*BHS*, 622).

[73] Cogan and Tadmor, *II Kings*, 45.

[74] Stökl, "Ready or Not," 120–21.

this technique to elicit an oracle; maximally, it refers to a wider prophetic practice.[75]

Another narrative links music with prophetic activity in a manner that suggests music's use to induce prophetic ecstasy. Samuel tells Saul that Saul will meet a band of prophets who are מתנבאים while "before them" are harp, tambourine, flute, and lyre (1 Sam 10:5). The precise nature of the activity or state here described by מתנבאים is subject to debate, as noted in the discussion of terminology above, with proposals ranging from "prophesying" or "acting like prophets" to a state of prophetic ecstasy (see further below). Whichever the case, the phrase "before them" suggests that the prophets are accompanied by a group of musicians whose performance is integral to the activity or state in which the prophets are engaged. Comparison with 2 Kgs 3:15, examined above, raises the possibility that the music is intended to (help) induce an altered state of consciousness associated with prophetic activity.[76]

A tantalizing but inconclusive further example is Miriam's taking a tambourine in her hand as she sings and leads the Israelite women, who also play tambourines and dance (Exod 15:20–21). Yet, while from a phenomenological standpoint it is well established that the rhythmic percussion of tambourines and/or the rhythmic movement of dance can induce religious ecstasy, this short narrative provides insufficient detail to determine whether an altered state of consciousness is implied or whether the music and movement are used to induce such a state.[77] In sum, these examples affirm a strong correlation between music and prophetic activity, and one text explicitly

---

[75] Music's effect on states of consciousness brought about by or receptive to the influence of supernatural forces is elsewhere supported by the summoning of a מנגן to expel or assuage the evil spirit that afflicts Saul (1 Sam 16:16). Outside of the Hebrew Bible, two texts from Mari (Ritual of Ištar, Text 2 [FM 3 2]; Ritual of Ištar, Text 3 [FM 3 3], in Durand and Guichard, "Rituels de Mari") portray a ritual in which performance of a canonical city lament by a group of musicians aims to induce in the prophet (*muḫḫûm*) an altered state of consciousness that will enable some form of prophetic activity to take place (Nissinen, *Ancient Prophecy*, 176–9). Stökl ("Ready or Not," 122–3) argues, however, that the role of the *muḫḫûm* was not primarily prophetic but that they are instead "ecstatic cult functionaries" (123). In this case the link between music and ecstasy is affirmed, but their link to prophecy is less certain.

[76] An association between music and prophecy is elsewhere supported by the Chronicler's attribution of prophecy to the temple musicians who "prophesied with lyres, harps, and cymbals" (1 Chron 25:1) and by later designations of psalms as prophetic compositions. Yet the evidence is insufficient to establish whether in these cases music would have been viewed as or functioned as a technique for inducing altered states of consciousness. See Ko, *Levite Singers*, 151–82; Hilber, *Cultic Prophecy in the Psalms*; Bellinger, *Psalmody and Prophecy*.

[77] Stökl considers the use of rhythmic movement as a trigger among the Baal prophets in 1 Kgs 18 but is cautious in drawing conclusions ("Ready or Not," 125–6). He states that Miriam's music does not induce her prophecy but expresses it (Stökl, "Ready or Not," 123).

describes the use of music as a technique for inducing an altered state of consciousness that leads to delivery of a prophetic oracle.

Spirit Possession

Several texts portray what anthropologists refer to as spirit possession as a key component of prophetic experience and performance.[78] Frequently, the spirit (רוח) in question is identified as "the spirit of God," "the spirit of the Lord," or, when God speaks directly, "my spirit."[79] Other instances suggest a cohort of spirits that may interact with human beings. In 1 Kgs 22 a member of the heavenly court volunteers to be a lying spirit in the mouths of Israel's prophets (1 Kgs 22:21–23; 2 Chron 18:20–22; cf. 2 Kgs 19:7; Isa 37:7). "A spirit" twice enters a prostrate Ezekiel, raises him to his feet, and speaks to him (Ezek 2:2; 3:24); "the spirit" lifts him and carries him (3:12, 14; 8:3; 11:1, 24; 43:5). Spirit can also be transferred from one prophet to one or more others. God's distribution of spirit from "upon" Moses to the seventy elders leads them to "prophesy" (ויתנבאו Num 11:17, 25); the same spirit comes to rest on Eldad and Medad, who also "prophesy" (11:26; cf. 11:29). After Elisha asks for a double portion of Elijah's spirit, the assembled prophets he encounters declare that the spirit of Elijah rests upon him (2 Kgs 2:9, 15).[80] The broad association of prophets with spirit possession is further supported by a lament in Hosea, which places the phrase "man of the spirit" (איש הרוח) in poetic parallel with "prophet" (Hos 9:7).

As noted above, 1 Samuel portrays ecstasy or other prophetic state or activity likely induced by music. In multiple instances, this prophetic ecstasy or

---

[78] In a similar vein, Joseph and Daniel's gifts of dream interpretation are attributed to the spirit of God or gods in them (Gen 41:38; Dan 4:5, 6, 15 MT [4:8, 9, 18 NRSV]; 5:11, 14; cf. Dan 5:12; 6:4 MT [6:3 NRSV]). Joshua receives a spirit of wisdom when Moses lays hands upon him (Deut 34:9). Not all instances of spirit possession in biblical literature confer prophecy, knowledge, or wisdom. In the case of judges, possession confirms election to leadership, endows with superhuman strength, and energizes in the face of crisis (Judg 3:10; 6:34; 11:29; 13:25; 14:6, 19; 15:14). The spirit of the Lord similarly possesses David at the time of his anointing (1 Sam 16:13); at the same time it departs from Saul and an "evil spirit from the LORD" afflicts him (1 Sam 16:14–16, 23; 18:10; 19:9). In Isaiah, the spirit will rest on the shoot from the stump of Jesse (Isa 11:1–12) and God promises to put God's spirit upon the servant (42:1). For analysis of diverse syntactic constructions associated with spirit possession, see Carlson, *Unfamiliar Selves*, 94–122.

[79] "The spirit of God": Num 24:2–13; 1 Sam 10:10; 19:20, 23; 2 Chron 15:1; 24:20; Ezek 11:24; "The spirit of YHWH": 1 Sam 10:6; 2 Sam 23:2; 1 Kgs 18:12; 22:24; 2 Kgs 2:16; 2 Chron 18:23; 20:14; Isa 61:1; Ezek 11:5; 37:1; Mic 3:8; "The spirit of the Lord YHWH" (רוח אדני יהוה): Isa 61:1; "my spirit": Joel 3:1–2 MT; "his spirit": Zech 7:12.

[80] Elisha's own spirit travels outside his body to observe the actions of Gehazi (2 Kgs 5:26).

activity is linked to an experience of spirit possession that afflicts not (only?) the prophets but individuals who temporarily join their company. In the case of Saul, the resulting state is characterized by both transformed consciousness and observably altered behavior.

When Samuel meets the young Saul, he predicts that Saul will meet a band of prophets (חבל נבאים) before whom are harp, tambourine, flute, and lyre, and the prophets will be מתנבאים (1 Sam 10:5). As noted above, the appropriate translation of this *hithpael* participle is debated. NRSV translates "in a prophetic frenzy," CEB "caught up in a prophetic frenzy," NAB "in a prophetic state," NABRE "in prophetic ecstasy," NJPS "speaking in ecstasy," and ASV, ESV, Darby, NIV, and NKJV "prophesying" (cf. LXX προφητεύοντες). Wilson proposed above that they were demonstrating observable behavior characteristic of prophets, Parker exhibiting possession trance but not prophetic activity, and Adam "in the status of / behaving like prophets." Contextual clues suggest that in these passages the word enfolds multiple, interrelated aspects of prophetic experience and behavior that include a state of ecstasy. Samuel foretells that Saul will experience spirit possession that results in an altered state of consciousness: when Saul encounters the prophets, the spirit of the Lord will rush upon him, causing him also to "prophesy [or be in ecstasy/ behave prophetically, etc.] with them" (התנבית עמם) and to be transformed (literally "flipped" ונהפכת) into another man (לאיש אחר v. 6). As predicted, Saul meets the prophets and the spirit rushes upon him so that he prophesies (*hithpael*) in their midst (v. 10). The subsequent verse makes clear that his transformation is observable and marked: those who were familiar with him previously now witness his prophesying (*niphal*), ask each other what has happened to the man they knew, and coin a proverbial question about Saul's inclusion among the prophets (vv. 11–12). The use of *both* the *hithpael* and *niphal* stems of נבא* to describe Saul's activity while the spirit is on him frustrates any attempt to dissociate the meanings of these two stems in this passage.[81] As a result of his spirit possession, Saul enters an alternate state of consciousness that produces visibly altered affect and behavior characteristic of the prophetic role. He also, quite simply, "prophesies." The narrative collapses together the altered state and the activities it produces.

---

[81] Pace Stökl, who asserts that as a matter of linguistic principle the two stems cannot have the same meaning ("Ready or Not," 123). I suggest that in this passage their meanings are not entirely coterminous but overlap and interlock.

Repetition of the proverb in 1 Sam 19:24 links this first instance of Saul's prophetic possession with a second. In the second episode, at a time when Saul is hunting David to kill him, both Saul's messengers and Saul himself are possessed by God's spirit and prophesy. During the accompanying state of ecstasy Saul removes his clothing and falls to the ground for an entire day and night. The episode begins as Saul's messengers encounter the band of prophets led by Samuel. The narrator first describes the activity of the prophets using the *niphal* participle "prophesying" (*niphal* נבאים 1 Sam 19:20). As was previously the case with Saul, the messengers who encounter them are possessed by the spirit of God (ותהי על־מלאכי שאול רוח אלהים). As a result of their spirit possession, "even [the messengers] prophesied [or were in ecstasy/behaved prophetically, etc.]" (ויתנבאו *hithpael* v. 20). Cohort after cohort of messengers have the same experience, but in narrating this repeated event the narrator elides the detail of spirit possession into the state and activity named by the *hithpael* forms of נבא* (v. 21). Saul follows, and the narrator repeats the full sequence: "the spirit of God came upon him also, and he walked, prophesying [or in ecstasy/behaving prophetically, etc., *hithpael*] as he went," until he reached the destination he sought (v 23). When he arrived, Saul—"even he—stripped off his clothes, and he prophesied [or was in ecstasy/behaved prophetically, etc., *hithpael* again] before Samuel, and he fell naked for that entire day and night" (v. 24). This second instance of Saul's spirit possession begins when he is alone, absent any narrated trigger, social cues, or audience. When he arrives at Naioth, however, his prophetic state and actions take on a social and even cultic dimension. In removing his clothing he discards the visible signs and power of kingship, exposes his body to elements and scrutiny alike, and behaviorally positions himself outside of traditionally accepted social norms, as evidenced by the repeated proverb which questions his proper social role (v. 24). His ensuing state of extreme bodily calm, even catatonia, appears to entail altered time-sense, volition, and motor control, together redirecting his focus and intention, impeding his ability or desire to execute the actions he had intended and as a result creating a window of time in which David can escape unharmed (20:1).[82]

Although Saul's possession and resulting (proverbially questionable) status among the prophets is as much a puzzle to modern scholars as it was

---

[82] The possession of his messengers has the same effect for David. Chapman writes, "In this scene the power of prophecy takes the form of a spiritual army to protect David against Saul's murderous rage . . . all of Saul's strong men are portrayed as powerless before the action of God's spirit as it spreads through Samuel's band of prophets and overwhelms Saul's soldiers" (*1 Samuel*, 166).

to observers in the story, a more straightforward example of prophetic spirit possession is that of Ezekiel, to which he repeatedly attributes both visionary experience and supernatural transport.

Possession is first introduced in the book's superscription, which prefaces Ezekiel's chariot vision by stating that the hand of the Lord came upon him (Ezek 1:3). On the heels of this vision, a spirit enters Ezekiel, addressing him in audible speech while also moving his body, causing him to stand up (2:2; 3:24), lifting him, and eventually taking him to another location (3:12, 14–15).[83] The embodied character of this experience is emphasized by references to the prophet's sense of hearing (2:2, 8; 3:10) and multiple parts of his body (feet 2:2; 3:24; mouth, 2:8; 3:26, 27; forehead 3:9; heart, ears 3:10; tongue 3:26). This embodied dimension extends also to the deity, whose possessing power is characterized not only as spirit, but also as the "hand of the Lord" (3:14, 22; see also 8:1; 37:1; 40:1). By contrast with the possessions in 1 Sam 10 and 19, Ezekiel's possession is unambiguously accompanied by revelation, including a prophetic commission, a scroll of lamentation and judgment, and words that he must say to the people in exile.

Other instances of Ezekiel's spirit possession combine transport and prophetic vision (8:3; 11:1, 24; 37:1; 40:1–2; 43:5). Within the visions, the prophet is variously witness, interlocutor, and actor. While space does not permit examination of all the possession visions in detail, I here consider the possession-vision report that begins in 8:1 and concludes at 11:25.

As in the first instance, so here, the prophet's embodied experience is emphasized by reference to movement, senses, and parts of the body. Ezekiel recounts an experience of possession while seated among the elders of Jerusalem (8:1). This social setting resembles that of shamanic seances, in which the assembled audience plays the role of witness, support, participant, and anchor.[84] During this "session," the hand of the Lord God falls on the prophet (8:1) and he looks up to see an anthropomorphic figure (8:2). Threefold repetition of the noun מראה, meaning "sight, appearance, or vision," marks the inception of visionary experience. Yet this experience is also tactile and interactive, as the figure extends a hand and grabs Ezekiel by the hair. It is at this moment that the spirit again lifts him and carries him, "in visions," to a distant location (Jerusalem, 8:3). This journeying, according

---

[83] I examine prophetic transport in greater detail in Chapter 8. The spirit's capacity to effect movement is emphasized in the chariot vision as well (Ezek 1:12, 20–21).

[84] Siikala, "Siberian Shaman's Technique," 113, 115; Lewis, *Ecstatic Religion*, 46–7.

to Jan Tarlin, enacts a displacement that is also a dissolution of place. For Tarlin, in his ecstasy Ezekiel is "cut loose from all temporal and geographical mooring," an experience that eradicates all sense of security.[85] Yet the bodies of his angelic guide and the exiled community who surround him provide orientation and anchor as he assembles new configurations of reality and relationship across time and space.

In the first vision report that follows, Ezekiel performs commanded actions such as digging (8:8), but the sense of sight predominates. A command to lift his eyes is followed by the report "I lifted my eyes," the word "vision" is again repeated (8:4), and forms of the verb "to see" occur 13 times (8:2, 4, 6x2, 7, 9, 10, 12x2, 13, 15x2, 17). God's reference to the divine eye at the conclusion of this passage (8:18) forms a bookend with the earlier reference to the prophet's own eyes, directing the prophet's visionary experience toward the embodiment of divine mercy (withheld) and judgment (cf. 9:10).

As Ezekiel's visionary journey continues, the spirit carries him to another location within the vision-scape, moving from the temple's north gate to the east (11:1). He is commanded to deliver an oracle within the vision (11:5) and does so; its consequences are immediate and alarming (11:13). He is again charged to deliver oracles (11:16, 17) and witnesses the departure of God's glory from the temple before the spirit again lifts him and brings him back "in a vision by the spirit of God" to where he started among the exiles in Babylon (11:24). At this moment, he reports, the vision "went up from upon me" (11:24). The possession and vision are inextricably linked. In the geography of Ezekiel's possession experience, the hand and spirit fall on him from above, raise him into the upper realm, and place him down again. When the vision departs, it "goes up," in the same direction from which the hand and spirit came. The journey has had multiple stops but is ultimately a round trip, leaving the prophet among the assembled audience of exiles to whom he discloses the vision (11:25).

Body Overpowered, Eyes Uncovered

Spirit possession and other modes of religious ecstasy are sometimes accompanied by an experience of physical and/or psychic distress.[86] Ezekiel's

---

[85] Tarlin, "Utopia and Pornography," 181.
[86] On the relation between bodily affliction and spirit possession see Lewis, *Ecstatic Religion*, 59–89.

reported experience of the hand of the Lord as a force that grabs him, is "strong" upon, and falls on him partly reflects and intersects with usage in which the divine hand denotes illness or other bodily affliction attributed to divine power.[87] Elsewhere it is not the hand that falls but the prophet's own body (Ezek 1:28; 3:23; 9:8; 11:13; 43:3; 44:4). Ezekiel is not the only figure who falls in a state of prophetic or visionary ecstasy; others include Saul (1 Sam 19:24, examined above), Daniel (8:17–18; 10:9), and Balaam.[88] In Num 24:2, "the spirit of God came upon" Balaam, at which moment he delivers an oracle. He introduces the oracle by naming himself and describing the altered state in which he receives his visions. He is "the man whose eye is open . . . who hears God's words, who sees the vision of Shadday, who falls with eyes uncovered" (Num 24:3–4; 15–16). Balaam's repetition of this self-description and its function introducing his oracles suggests that the altered state he describes is both a characteristic and authenticating component of his prophetic visionary experience. The state is characterized by heightened visual and auditory senses, reduced motor activity and control, and narrowed focus on the words and vision of the deity. The two-fold description of the prophet's eye(s) as open and uncovered emphasizes the alteration of sight brought about by the spirit. The normal seeing eye is understood to be closed and covered. The open and uncovered eye sees dimensions of reality that others cannot.

Conclusion

For over a century, biblical scholars have debated whether biblical literature attributes religious ecstasy to the prophets of Israel and Judah. Some scholars, anxious to assert the uniqueness, rationality, or propriety of Israel's and Judah's prophets, have vigorously denied that ecstasy was a mode of prophetic experience. But while the experience of prophetic ecstasy is not portrayed as a universal feature of biblical prophecy, neither is it absent or marginal. It is also not monolithic. I have argued that this diverse and much debated phenomenon is best understood through a multidisciplinary

---

[87] See Roberts, "Hand of Yahweh." Note however that the hand sometimes empowers rather than afflicts (e.g., 1 Kgs 18:46, considered in Chapter 8). Ezekiel reports his experience of the hand of the Lord at Ezek 1:3; 3:14, 22; 8:1; 33:22; 37:1; 40:1.

[88] I consider Daniel's responses to his visions in Chapter 9.

approach that combines insights from neurobiology, psychiatry, anthropology, and religious studies. Though religious ecstasy may take a variety of forms, a common feature is a subjective experience of transcendence accompanying an altered state of consciousness (ASC). Characteristic physiologic changes have a counterpart in behaviors that push up against and sometimes cross normal boundaries of social comportment.

This altered state and its attendant behaviors are transient, temporarily opening a window that allows access to other times, places, and dimensions of reality. But this experience does not exist outside of cultural frameworks nor is it strictly individualistic. Context conditions both the experience and its interpretation. As prelude to, authorization for, or performance of prophetic mediation, ecstasy also commonly has a socially directed and efficacious component. Prophetic ecstasy might bolster or challenge existing structures of power. The ecstatic could make a spirit or deity present to gathered members of the community or disclose the hidden realities they witnessed. Like *askêsis* and incubation (see Chapter 6), the ecstatic body crosses boundaries in order to bridge a divide and, in so doing, affirm, reveal, or reconfigure the shape of the possible and the real.

Studies of religious ecstasy note the frequent use of induction techniques to produce altered states. Such techniques include fasting, meditation, sensory deprivation, drumming, and rhythmic movement. The story of Saul's encounter with a band of prophets and consequent ecstatic experience in 1 Sam 10 hints at the use of music as a technique to induce ecstasy. Second Kings 3 confirms the use of such a technique by the prophet Elisha. As discussed in the previous chapter, each such technique has a learned component, emerging from a cultural and, frequently, ritual matrix.

Within this cultural (and literary) framework, prophetic ecstasy was often understood and portrayed as a form of spirit possession. Frequently, the spirit is identified as belonging to YHWH/God. Spirit could be distributed and transferred; it enters and exits, rests and departs. It can feel like sickness or sweetness, or both at the same time. It can knock someone out or set them in motion. Possession could initiate a visionary experience or supernatural journey. It could also compel and empower prophetic speech. Possession could, for a time, turn one into another person entirely. Although Saul's prophetic status is questionable (proverbially so!), Samuel's description of Saul's ecstatic transformation surfaces the categorical "otherness" of the ecstatic body, consciousness, and behavior: Saul "flipped," becoming "another man" (1 Sam 10:6).

The ecstatic body mediates between realms, times, and places, between persons, between what *is* and what is *possible*, what has been and what must be. The preceding analysis of ecstasy and spirit possession sets the stage for Part IV of this book, "(E)Motion and Affect." Supernatural journeys were one way that prophets linked places, people, and God. The prophets' bodily movements were a further key to their mediation. Prophetic mobility and immobility, both physical and spiritual, are the subject of Chapter 8.

PART IV
(E)MOTION AND AFFECT

8
Mobility and Immobility

Prophets move.[1] On the surface, there is nothing very remarkable in this observation. Motility characterizes a vast number of animal species and thus fails even to distinguish a prophet from an amoeba. When we recognize that the prophetic body is also a body in motion, however, new dimensions of prophetic experience, mediation, power, action, and knowing come into view.

Perhaps more surprising than the fact of prophetic motion is that God commands it and does so often. Sometimes prophets must rise, sometimes descend.[2] But the verb of motion that appears most frequently in God's commands to prophets is simply "go" (הלך). While this common verb has numerous figurative uses, context typically makes clear that prophets who "go" are indeed on the move from place to place. YHWH's twin questions in Isaiah's temple vision, "whom shall I send and who will go for us?" (6:8) suggest that "to go" is not incidental or prefatory to prophetic mission, but constitutive of it: one who is sent is (ideally) one who goes.[3] More than pleonasm, the pairing of the two questions asserts synergy: "sending" is YHWH's causative, authorizing, and delegating action, "going" the prophet's acceptance and fulfillment of the mission by their own volition and agency and in their own body. The same responsive synergy is reflected in Jeremiah's commission: "Everywhere [or to everyone] I send you, you will go and

---

[1] Sometimes, of course, people move to get to prophets. See, e.g., 1 Sam 9:9–10: "Previously, in Israel, a person used to say—when they went to inquire of God—'come, let's go to the seer,' because the one we now call the prophet used to be called the seer. So Saul said to his servant, 'come, let's go,' and they went to the city where the man of God was." See also the Balaam inscription from Tell Deir ʿAlla: "and his people went up to him" (Combination I, l. 4, trans. Puech, "Balaʿam and Deir ʿAlla," 32). Puech comments, "'To ascend' to the diviner is quite acceptable as the movement of the heads of the people who want to meet him at the high place or *bamah*" ("Balaʿam and Deir ʿAlla," 34). Franken argues that the chamber where the inscription was found was itself the site to which inquirers would ascend ("Balaam at Deir ʿAlla").

[2] Rise, get up, or come up: Exod 19:24; 24:1; Num 22:20; 27:12; Deut 3:27; 9:12; 10:1; 32:49; 1 Kgs 21:18; 2 Kgs 1:3; Jer 13:4, 6; 18:2; Ezek 3:22; Jonah 1:2; 3:2; Descend: Exod 19:21, 24; 32:7; Deut 9:12; 10:11; 1 Kgs 21:18; 2 Kgs 1:15; Jer 18:2; 22:1. Cross: Exod 17:5. An angel directs Elijah's movements at 1 Kgs 19:5, 7, the "word" directs his movement at v. 11, and YHWH directs his movement at v. 15.

[3] For Kaplan, this pattern (God sends, the prophet goes) constitutes a "default model of moral agency" among prophets that is both subverted and reaffirmed in the book of Jonah ("Jonah and Moral Agency," 151–2, 156).

everything I command you, you will say" (Jer 1:7). Here, parallel syntactic structure supports the further conclusion that movement is not subordinate to speaking: they are coordinate tasks, each a necessary and vital component of the prophet's commission. Ambiguity in the first clause, עַל־כָּל־אֲשֶׁר אֶשְׁלָחֲךָ—is God sending Jeremiah to places or people?— is perhaps best resolved by answering, "both." As I discuss further below, the prophet's missional movement underscores the importance of place to prophetic mediation. But it is also the case that prophets move (and are told to move) to where people are. These are not competing destinations, as "place is the space where people exist as human beings."[4]

Mobilities: Catalyzing Dynamism in Relation to Deity, People, and Place

This link between people and place is key to the meanings and functions of mobility. Kevin Hannam and colleagues describe an "emerging mobilities paradigm" that "argues against the ontology of distinct 'places' and 'people.'" In this paradigm, places are "places of movement" and "proximities," constituted by "the bodily co-presence of people who happen to be in that place at that time, doing activities together."[5] Jørgen Ole Bærenholdt and Brynhild Granås similarly write, "mobility and place become together"; their relationships "are crucial in the making of societies."[6] For Tim Cresswell, "mobility is the dynamic equivalent of *place*" inasmuch as it is "socially produced motion" and thus movement "imbued with meaning and power."[7] Such an understanding of the interrelation of mobility with people and place informs Masao Kakihara and Carsten Sørensen's argument for "expanding the concept of mobility" to include not just movement through space and time but consideration of the social interactions such movement participates in and makes possible.[8] For Kakihara and Sørensen, mobility's contextual dimension requires attention not only to "where" and "when" but also "in what particular circumstance" and "towards which actor(s)."[9] The movement

---

[4] Prinsloo, "Place, Space and Identity," 3.
[5] Hannam, Sheller, and Urry, "Mobilities, Immobilities and Moorings," 13.
[6] Bærenholdt and Granås, "Places and Mobilities," 1–2. See also Carpio, *Collisions*; Verstraete and Cresswell, *Mobilizing Place*.
[7] Cresswell, *On the Move*, 3.
[8] Kakihara and Sørensen, "Expanding the 'Mobility' Concept," 33.
[9] Kakihara and Sørensen, "Expanding the 'Mobility' Concept," 35.

of bodies is attended, augmented, and supplemented by the movement of image and sound, ideas and objects (other theorists would add to this list affect, on which see Chapter 9), as well as mobilization and reconfiguration of space and place: "spatial mobility refers not only to extensive movement of people; it also signifies the global flux of objects, symbols, and space itself and as such evokes complex patterns of human interaction."[10] While Kakihara and Sørensen focus on modern information and communication technologies that temporarily "dissolve" boundaries of space and time, both the ancient technology of writing and the mediating body of the prophet function in the manner they describe. This is not to reduce the prophet to a communication technology, but rather to highlight ways in which the mobile prophetic body mediates and produces knowledge and relationship, dissolves and reconfigures boundaries, and shapes the space, places, people(s), and structures in, through, and to which it moves.

Contextual analysis of prophetic movement thus attends not only to where and when but, in Kakihara and Sørensen's words, "in what particular circumstances" and "towards which actor(s)," as well as what interactions and further movements it will make possible. While Jeremiah's commission, "Everywhere [or to everyone] I send you, you will go and everything I command you, you will say" (Jer 1:7) defers naming particular contexts in order to chart a general pattern of prophetic mobility, other instances illustrate the close link between prophetic mobility and particular people and places. The sequence "go" and "speak" is hardly unique to Jeremiah but occurs in divine direct address to numerous prophets, including Moses, Balaam, Nathan, Gad, Elijah, Isaiah, Ezekiel, Amos, and Jonah.[11] While this command sequence does not provide an exhaustive map of prophetic movements, where it occurs it signals that movement will create conditions for encounter and interaction in which spoken word will have its meaning and effect. As argued above, this does not subordinate movement to speech. Rather, the prophet's body plots and enacts vectors of divine intention. The dynamism

---

[10] Kakihara and Sørensen, "Expanding the 'Mobility' Concept," 34.
[11] E.g., Exod 3:16, 18; 7:26; 9:1; Num 22:35; Deut 5:30; 2 Sam 7:5; 24:12; 1 Kgs 18:44; 2 Kgs 1:3; 20:5; 1 Chron 17:4; 21:10; Isa 6:9; 22:15; 38:5; Jer 2:2; 3:12; 17:19–20; 19:1–3; 28:13; 34:2; 35:2, 13; 39:16; Ezek 3:1, 4, 11; Amos 7:15; Jonah 1:2; 3:2. Cf. 2 Kgs 1:15; Jer 22:1. Occasionally "go" or a different verb of motion precedes another commanded action but not commanded speech: Exod 4:21; 17:5; 19:10, 24; 32:7, 34; 33:1; Num 22:20; 1 Kgs 17:3, 9; 18:1; 19:15–16; Isa 20:2; 21:6; Jer 13:1, 4, 6; Hos 1:2; 3:1. Samuel is commanded to "go" after completing another action (1 Sam 16:1). Daniel is commanded to "go" and *not* speak but rest (12:9, 13). God forbids Balaam from going and speaking a curse (Num 22:12). A prophet can also send another prophet: 2 Kgs 9:1.

of the prophetic body in motion mirrors, responds to, and channels a divine dynamism that sets events and people in motion and prompts new realities into being.

Three examples, Moses, Balaam, and Jonah, illustrate the catalyzing dynamism of prophetic movement and its relation to deity, people, and place. Moses' identity as an Israelite by birth aligns him with the people to whom he is sent. His movements both participate in and catalyze the people's movements and mirror those of the deity. By contrast, Balaam's foreign identity sets him apart from the Israelites ethnically, culturally, and geographically. Divine ambivalence about his prophetic journey reflects a contest over who may direct this prophet's movements and actions and who will direct the movements of Israel. Balaam's journey parallels the future crossing of the Israelites and positions him to witness the dynamic future God has ordained for them. Jonah, meanwhile, resists divine commands to travel to Nineveh, capital of the foreign empire that will eventually destroy the kingdom of Israel. The movement and positioning of the prophet's body reflects a contest of wills between prophet and deity even as it underscores the importance of the prophet's movement for the implementation of divine plans.

Moses: Catalyst and Mirror

Moses' missional movements position him as a catalyst for the movement of the people. His movements also mirror, respond to, and instantiate the deity's own. God's self-introduction to Moses foregrounds divine movement—"I have come down" (Exod 3:8)—as a primary response to the people's suffering. The telos of God's motion is to liberate the people and "bring them up out of" Egypt "to a land flowing with milk and honey" (3:8). The sending and going of Moses have the same coordinates, direction, and purpose as God's actions: "So go: I will send you to Pharaoh so that you will lead my people, the Israelites, out of Egypt" (3:10). Moses' first of several objections to his prophetic calling pertains not to prophetic speaking (he objects to that later: 4:10) but prophetic going: "who am I that I would go to Pharaoh and that I would cause the Israelites to come out of Egypt?" (3:11). In these first articulations of Moses' mission, the prophet's movement is to be a causal force that triggers the liberating movement of the people from the place of slavery to the place God has chosen for their flourishing. As Moses recognizes, the force of Moses qua Moses would hardly mobilize a population or counteract Pharaoh's resistance.

Instead, the prophet's actions instantiate divine power to set a people in motion (3:17-22); Moses' movements mirror and participate in God's own as he/they lead the people by stages toward the destination(s) God determines.

Moses' movements mirror the deity's in a different way in the back and forth motion of mediation between people and God (Exod 17:5; 19:3, 10, 20-21; 24:1-18; 32:7, 15; 33:7-11; etc.). At Sinai, deity and prophet find a meeting point in the middle of the world: God descends from above, and Moses ascends from below (19:20). The tent of meeting similarly requires Moses to exit the camp and God to descend from the heavenly realm (33:7, 9). Sacred mountain and tent of meeting thus occupy spaces in-between, one the border of earth and heaven, the other the boundary between camp and wilderness. Each leaves their place—Moses his place with the people, God the heavenly realm—to encounter the other "face to face" (33:11), symmetrical vectors intersecting before returning to their points of origin. In this geography of mediation, the mirrored movements of prophet and deity traverse the spatial and ontological gulf between divine and human realms (Exod 19:24). The act of mediation emerges not as one, singular event, but as a sequence of coordinated movements and encounters.

At the conclusion of Moses' life, the Lord commands him to ascend a different mountain, Nebo, from which he will not descend (Deut 32:49). This final ascent does not fit the earlier pattern of mediating movement but marks its end. From the top of Mount Nebo Moses will behold the people's destination but he "will not enter it" or "cross over there" (32:52; 34:4); here his movements and mission end (34:5). His interment in a forgotten valley in Moab (34:6) houses his body in a border zone he will never leave, simultaneously marking the ceasing of his movement and his separation from deity and people alike.

Balaam: Witnessing to a Dynamic Future

Unlike Moses, Balaam is not Israelite. Thus from the beginning of his story Balaam is "placed" apart from the Israelite people, themselves portrayed as "dwelling apart" from the peoples around them (Num 23:9), and thus his movements do not directly participate in theirs. Yet just as the survival of Balaam traditions in the HBOT and at Deir 'Alla mark him as "a prophet who crosses cultural and religious boundaries,"[12] his narrated movements in

---

[12] Smith, *God in Translation*, 129.

Num 22–24 bring him to the geographical threshold of Israel's own fateful crossings. Their journeying (ויסעו) is the first word of the narrative unit, setting its events in motion even as the people themselves temporarily stop, making camp in Moab "across the Jordan from Jericho" (22:1). Balak, king of Moab, invites the prophet Balaam, who is in Pethor, "near the river" (22:5), to "come" curse the Israelites (22:6, 11). The king hopes that Balaam's arrival will empower Balak to "drive out" the Israelites who have recently "come out" of Egypt but now cover the earth and sit (dwell) opposite him (22:6, 11).

The position of the Israelites "across the Jordan"—language that anticipates their later crossing—mirrors the prophet's starting point "near the river."[13] Both are positioned at a site of liminality and flux. Many a poet has mined the paradoxical capacity of a river to occupy fixed points in space while constantly moving.[14] The river is both geographical boundary and physical instantiation of a perpetual dialectic between motion and fixity, container and excess, stasis and change. It is simultaneously path, mover, and propelling force. Both in "the Hebrew Bible and Mesopotamian prophetic texts," writes Martti Nissinen, "rivers in particular appear as liminal spaces, the crossing of which brings about destruction to enemies, and salvation for those under divine protection."[15] In a manner similar to Moses, the movement of Balaam is intended to trigger a movement of the people, yet the movement will be directed not by Balak, who intends their destruction, but by God, who promises to destroy their enemies (22:6; 24:8).[16]

The story repeatedly thematizes the prophet's travel, sometimes in puzzling ways. The Lord first refuses to allow Balaam's journey (22:13), then

---

[13] Near which river is a matter of debate. Balaam's association with Deir ʿAlla suggests that his home may be near the Jordan River, as Deir ʿAlla's location is "about eight kilometers east of the Jordan river, not far from the northern bank of the Yabbok/Zerka river" (Puech, "Balaʿam and Deir ʿAlla," 25). Yet his statement at 23:7 that "Balak made me come from Aram" suggests the river in question might be the Euphrates.

[14] E.g., Wallace Stevens, "This Solitude of Cataracts" ("Which kept flowing and never the same way twice, flowing / Through many places as if it stood still in one, / Fixed like a lake . . . " ll. 2–4; *Selected Poems*, 234) and "The River of Rivers in Connecticut" (its "propelling force" (l. 9) "flows nowhere" (l. 18); *Selected Poems*, 303); for Mary Oliver the river journeys perpetually: "And still, pressed deep into my mind, the river / keeps coming, touching me, passing by on its / long journey . . . " ("At the River Clarion," seventh stanza, ll. 1–3; *Evidence*, 54).

[15] Nissinen, "Sacred Springs," 48. Nissinen documents a further relation between water and divination in ancient west Asia, noting, e.g., that in later Jewish mystical texts "water not only appears as a ritual precondition for divine revelation, but also as the site where the revelation takes place, and, most notably, as a medium for inducing the altered state of consciousness" ("Sacred Springs," 35), but cautions that in the Hebrew Bible "water does not appear as a part of the oracular process" ("Sacred Springs," 48).

[16] Sals, "Hybrid Story," sees at the center of the story the question of who may direct movement and action.

commands Balaam to "rise, go" (22:20). Balaam saddles his donkey and begins the journey to Moab (22:21), but as he rides, God gets angry at Balaam for going (כי־הולך הוא) and an angel repeatedly blocks their path (22:22–26). The donkey tries to leave the road (v. 23) and presses against a wall (v. 25) before abandoning the prospect of movement all together and lying down (v. 27). The angel condemns the prophet's "way" (כי־ירט הדרך לנגדי v. 32) and Balaam offers to "return home" (v. 34), but the angel ultimately reissues the command to "go" (22:35).[17]

Intermittent divine opposition notwithstanding, a conversation between Balaam and his donkey at the climax of this contested journey suggests that travel was a frequent and long-standing component of Balaam's prophetic activity. The donkey points out that Balaam has ridden her his entire life; her behavior on this occasion differs from every other time they have traveled together (22:30). That is, the prophet's journeying is not itself unusual, but the habitual activity of a lifetime. Nor is it distance or route that distinguishes this journey from others before it but the prohibiting presence of an armed angel. Jan Bremmer identifies "geographical mobility" as a feature shared by seers in diverse settings in the ancient West Asian and Mediterranean world.[18] Eric Trinka similarly regards itinerancy, whether individually or in groups, as a characteristic of numerous prophets: "Across the biblical corpus, prophets such as Balaam, Elijah, Elisha, Amos, and Ezekiel are remembered as being highly mobile. Although the aforementioned prophets typically traveled alone or with a few companions, other texts indicate the normativity of troops of prophets moving about together (1 Sam 10:5)."[19] Combined with this broader evidence of prophetic patterns of itinerancy, the donkey's assertion supports the conclusion that travel was a normal feature of Balaam's prophetic service while highlighting the interactions of bodies, here including animal and angel, that both aid and hinder prophetic mobility.

---

[17] The reason for divine ambivalence about this journey is unclear. As Noort writes, "YHWH's anger ... in 22:22–35 is in no way derivable from the regular course of the narrative" ("Balaam the Villain," 9–10). Ashley similarly writes, "the most common question about this verse is the motive for God's anger with Balaam" (*Book of Numbers*, 454).

[18] Bremmer, "Balaam, Mopsus and Melampous," 51.

[19] Trinka, *Cultures of Mobility*, 195. Blenkinsopp regarded איש האלהים as an "itinerant" role (*Sage, Priest, Prophet*, 124). Focusing on a later period, Aune offered a typology of early Christian prophetic itinerancy, distinguishing "the prophet who traveled to a particular place to execute a divine commission," one "who traveled a circuit with some regularity," and "prophets whose wandering was an enactment of the ascetic values of homelessness, lack of family ties and the rejection of wealth and possessions" ("Social Matrix," 27).

In the encounter between Balaam, donkey, and angel, a Leitmotif and key factor in Balaam's im/mobility is vision (22:23–25, 27, 31, 33). After Balaam's arrival in Moab, narrator and characters alike continue to foreground Balaam's movements (22:36–39; 23:7) while further developing the thematic linkage between movement and vision.[20] When Balaam refuses to curse the Israelites, Balak invites Balaam to walk to other places, in hope that God would permit cursing from a different vantage point (23:13, 27). The logic of this perambulation is twofold, first that Balaam must travel to where he can see the camps of Israel with his own eyes, and second that he must travel to see them as Balak does. Balaam is thus invited to scout and survey from a height and distance (23:14, 28), a vantage point shared by kings and deities alike and thus a site of contest between royal and divine authority, agency, interests, and power (cf. Dan 4). Yael Avrahami explores the frequent twining of walking and seeing in the Hebrew Bible, noting their portrayal as interrelated modes of knowing through bodily exploration and examination that can also signal authority and control.[21] The prophet's movements and vision thus foreground the contest of power over people, place, and time being waged between Balak and God. While Balak hopes that the prophet's vision will align with his own, the prophet's vantage and vision instead align with the deity's. In reporting that "Balaam set his face toward the wilderness" and "looked up and saw Israel camping" (24:1–2) before delivering his third oracle, the narrator links Balaam's seeing the people's position with his vision of their future. References to seeing in each of the oracles (23:9, 21; 24:2–4, 15–16) gradually elide prophetic and divine seeing while privileging the latter. Though Balaam allows Balak to direct his movements, he sees not what Balak intends but what God intends. His movements make possible visions that (give) witness (to) the dynamic future God has ordained for Israel.

Jonah: Prophetic Distance

The journeys of a third prophet, Jonah, exhibit not divine ambivalence but the prophet's. Even as divine compulsion aligns the prophet's movements with the mission God has ordained, the positioning of the prophet's body betokens distance between God's plan for Nineveh's redemption and the

---

[20] On seeing as "mobile practice," see Adey, *Mobility*, 150–62.
[21] Avrahami, *Senses of Scripture*, 75–84, 160–2.

prophet's own hopes for the future. Jonah famously resists the divine command to "Rise, go to Nineveh" (Jonah 1:2) by securing passage on a boat going to Tarshish, "away from the Lord's face" (1:3).[22] In fleeing to the sea, mythic domain of chaos, Jonah attempts to find a space outside of the constellated relationships between God and people(s), where mediation is neither demanded nor needed.[23] He fails, as the sailors' plea to him to call on his God, their casting of lots, and his confession make clear (1:6–9). He is cast from the ship (1:15) only to be swallowed by a fish (2:1 MT/1:17 NRSV) who conveys him back to dry land (2:11 MT/2:10 NRSV). When the Lord again commands him to "Rise, go to Nineveh" (3:2), he rises and goes (3:3), then journeys into the city for one day to proclaim the oracle of Nineveh's overturning (3:4). The prophet then exits the city and sits to see what will happen in it (4:5). Though he again distances his body from the site of mediation, his lingering proximity preserves a line of sight and thread of connection between prophet and people.

Jonah's flight (Jonah 1:3), God's extraordinary efforts to corral and convey him (1:4; 2:1 MT/1:17 NRSV), fantastical transport in a great fish (2:1, 11 MT/1:17; 2:10 NRSV), and the twice iterated command to rise and go to Nineveh (1:1–2; 3:1–2) each emphasize the importance of the prophet's movement and presence to the mediatory task to which he is called. This calling to motion unsettles planned and anticipated futures (3:4, 8–10).[24] The very measure of Nineveh's size and importance is human movement: it is מהלך שלשת ימים "a three days' walk/journey" (Jonah 3:3; cf. Ezek 42:4), and Jonah begins his prophetic proclamation only when he has "entered the city a walk of one day" (3:4). The future that Jonah proclaims for Nineveh, meanwhile, is marked by a turbulent motion—overturning (נהפכת 3:4)—that equally might portend the city's destruction or self-directed reversal of repentance.[25] Whether God *could* have achieved the desired outcome without the prophet's traveling to Assyria and walking into its capital is beside the point of the story. In this instance, the prophet's journey, presence, and movement through the city is essential to fulfil the mission. Prophetic movement catalyzes the "turning" of

---

[22] While the location of Tarshish remains a matter of debate (for a recent proposal, see Castilio, "Tarshish"), Yafo (Jaffa), the port from which he departs, is located on the Mediterranean coast. Sasson observes, "Tarshish is obviously chosen for its location as the geographical and directional opposite of Nineveh" (*Jonah*, 79).

[23] On the symbolic and focal significance of the sea, see Prinsloo, "Place, Space and Identity," 14.

[24] Havea writes, "YHWH's words demand motion. Move. They aim to uproot Jonah from his ground and push him towards Nineveh . . . The story is in motion. Flowing. Meandering. Crisscrossing. Weaving" (*Jonah*, 20).

[25] Sasson, *Jonah*, 234–5, 267–8.

Ninevites (וישבו איש מדרכו 3:8) and God (מי־יודע ישוב 3:9) alike, altering the course of each: when God sees that they have "turned from the evil path," God abandons the plan to destroy them (3:10).

I argued above that a key to these prophetic movements and journeyings is the relation between mobility, place, and people. Moses was to lead the people from the place of enslavement to the place of promise. Moab, meanwhile, "is the place on the threshold of the Promised Land where the entire Torah is proclaimed during the final day of Moses' life. Moab is the site of a second Sinai."[26] It is also contested. While Moab is not their destination and the Israelites will leave without Balak's compelling it, they will later assert sovereignty over the space their camps now occupy. Jonah rejects his prophetic placement by fleeing to the fluid non-place of the sea; once re-placed he journeys not just to Nineveh but through it and outside it, positioning himself apart from people and city even as the deity attempts to draw the prophet's concern toward its inhabitants.

Supernatural Transport

In each example considered above, prophets move through space to place and people in order to achieve a bodily co-presence that is a precondition of their prophetic mediation.[27] In some instances movement was also a necessary component of prophetic visionary experience and knowledge. On occasion, the distance a prophet must traverse or the speed at which they must travel cannot be accomplished by "natural" means. The fantastical fish who fetches the fleeing prophet blurs the line between natural and supernatural conveyance. Elijah, Ezekiel, and Habakkuk also experience supernatural transport.[28] Elijah is impelled to superhuman speed and transported

---

[26] Noort, "Balaam the Villain," 6.

[27] People can also move to the prophet: see note 1 of this chapter. On the importance of physical co-presence for social life as it relates to patterns of mobility, see John Urry, "Social Networks." The pattern of "life involving strange combinations of increasing distance and intermittent co-presence" that Urry identifies in modern society ("Social Networks," 156) is suggestive for its parallels to prophetic mediation across distances and realms.

[28] Elisha's "heart," meanwhile, travels unseen, enabling him to see and hear events occurring at a distance while evading detection. When Elisha's assistant Gehazi has surreptitiously extracted payment from their Aramean petitioner, Naaman (2 Kgs 5:21–24), Elisha refutes Gehazi's assumption that his graft has escaped detection, asking, "did not my heart go when a man turned from his chariot to meet you?" (5:26). Paul Kissling links Elisha's knowledge of the future, ability to see invisible realities, and "knowledge of events from which he is spatially separated": each is a mode of prophetic knowing (Kissling, *Reliable Characters*, 173–8).

by whirlwind and flaming chariot. Ezekiel is grabbed by the hair and lifted by the spirit and hand of God as he is carried across distances, to Babylon, Jerusalem, and the valley of dry bones. Habakkuk is similarly transported from Judah to Babylon to provide sustenance to Daniel.

Elijah and the Chariots

Elijah's propensity for supernatural transport is portrayed as common knowledge. As the drought and famine plaguing Samaria are about to end, Elijah receives instructions from the Lord to present himself to king Ahab. On the way, he encounters the king's palace manager Obadiah, who falls on his face before the prophet. But when Elijah asks Obadiah to announce his presence to the king, Obadiah protests. He expects that by the time he reports to the king that he has found the elusive prophet, Elijah will have vanished before the king can meet with (apprehend?) him. "As soon as I have gone from you," he says, "the spirit of the LORD will carry you I know not where; so, when I come and tell Ahab and he cannot find you, he will kill me" (1 Kgs 18:12 NRSV). Richard Nelson refers to this statement by Obadiah as an expression of "flustered fears."[29] Yet as Obadiah takes pains to point out, up to this point in the narrative he has exhibited heroic courage, hiding one hundred prophets of YHWH in caves and providing them with food and water when his queen was hunting prophets to kill them (18:4, 13). While Elijah assures Obadiah that he will rendezvous with the king, a later narrative suggests that Obadiah's fears were nonetheless well-founded, as others later speak of Elijah's being whisked away by the spirit of the Lord as though it might be a frequent occurrence (2 Kgs 2:16).

Later in 1 Kgs 18, Elijah is endowed with superhuman speed, endurance, and agility that enable him to outpace the royal chariot.[30] When Elijah does speak with Ahab (Obadiah's fate is not disclosed), the prophet announces that the rain is finally coming. Elijah instructs the king to harness the horses, mount the chariot, and descend the mountain before the rain would stop him from reaching the plain of Jezreel, over twenty miles away. The king rides. Heavy rain comes (v. 45). "But the hand of the LORD was on Elijah; he

---

[29] Nelson, *First and Second Kings*, 115.
[30] Elijah also possesses superhuman sensory perception, hearing "the sound of rushing rain" before even a cloud is visible (1 Kgs 18:41).

girded up his loins and ran in front of Ahab [from the top of Mount Carmel] to the entrance of Jezreel" (18:46 NRSV).[31] The distance between the top of Mount Carmel and the plain of Jezreel is a few miles shorter than a marathon. The royal chariot would be drawn by a team of horses that are strong, sure, and fast, and its driver would no doubt be eager to avoid storm wind, driving rain, and the clogging churn of mud. Yet chariots are not designed for rough terrain, mountains, or mud. Chariots convey advantage when they enable flanking and pursuit.[32] Ahab's chariot accomplishes neither, for Elijah consistently outpaces it.[33] The hand that propels Elijah enacts a synergy of divine and human bodies, endowing the prophet with a superhuman admixture of speed and endurance.[34] Elijah's kinetic feat identifies the prophet's body as living conduit, storehouse, and demonstration of divine energy and power that exceed even the royal machinery of war. While the flashy but, here, impractical royal vehicle gets the king to his destination, the divinely propelled prophet proves both more powerful and more adaptable, able to maneuver through challenging conditions to arrive swiftly at the appointed destination.[35]

---

[31] McKenzie notes that the Elijah narratives refer to the hand of God only here. He argues that its use in this story is close to that in Ezekiel (1:3; 3:22; 33:22; 37:1; 40:1), where it describes, in the words of Greenberg, "extraordinary sensory experiences" (McKenzie, *1 Kings 16–2 Kings 16*, 136 quoting Greenberg, *Ezekiel*, 41–2).

[32] Archer, "Chariotry to Cavalry," 79.

[33] For Hauser, "Elijah the servant of Yahweh had been running in victory before Ahab's chariot as the king returned to Jezreel, apparently accepting the outcome of the contest." Though Elijah competes successfully, asserting "victory over death and Baal," the tables soon turn and he flees (Hauser in Hauser and Gregory, *Carmel to Horeb*, 62–3).

[34] Reading Jer 23:21 ("I did not send the prophets, yet they ran; I did not speak to them, yet they prophesied" NRSV) in conjunction with Zech 2:8 MT/2:4 NRSV (an angel tells another to "run and tell") and in the light of 1 Kgs 18, Strelan makes the case that running was a recognizably prophetic modality of movement that is, at least metaphorically but possibly more literally, parallel to, prefatory to, or component in the act of prophesying: "there are a few passages in the OT which suggest that running is characteristic of a prophet and conveys the notion of carrying out a divine commission . . . [Jer 23:21] explicitly understands running and prophecy as synonymous or at least as associated behavior" ("Running Prophet," 35). Strelan refers to Holladay, *Jeremiah 1*, 637, but note Holladay's comment there that "a connection [between Jer 23:21 and] . . . Elijah's "running" before Ahab's chariot (1 Kgs 18:46) seems wide of the mark." Holladay instead proposes that running might refer to "the unvarying performance of the manifestations of prophecy" (*Jeremiah 1*, 637).

[35] Archer documents the chariot's function both as technology of war and marker of status ("Chariotry to Cavalry," 57, 73). Even in periods when chariots were no longer popular in warfare, they "retained their position as the foremost prestige vehicle for kings and noblemen in Near Eastern and Mediterranean cultures for many centuries to come" (Archer, "Chariotry to Cavalry," 73). On the unsuitability of chariots for rocky, mountainous, and muddy terrain, see Archer, "Chariotry to Cavalry," 70–4. It is possible that the narrative portrays Elijah in a role similar to a "chariot runner," i.e., a tactically specialized member of or adjunct to the royal chariot team, that, according to Drews, was attested in the second-millennium BCE (*End of the Bronze Age*, 141–7). Archer is critical of Drews' reconstruction, however ("Chariotry to Cavalry," 64–5). A different parallel may be found in later sporting events (namely, the *apobates*) in Attica and Boeotia in which a hoplite runner dismounted from a chariot and possibly remounted in a demonstration of skill, speed, agility, and

At the end of his earthly life, Elijah no longer races the royal chariot: he becomes the passenger in a heavenly one. According to the narrator, the Lord plans to "take Elijah up to heaven by a whirlwind" (2 Kgs 2:1 NRSV). Elijah, Elisha, and the prophets of Jericho all have foreknowledge of this event (2:5, 10); rather than avoid his anticipated departure, they move toward it. Elijah and Elisha thus travel by foot from Gilgal to Bethel to Jericho to the river Jordan (2:1–8), ultimately retracing and reversing the path by which Joshua led Israel into the promised land. Elijah uses his mantle to part the waters, demonstrating not only his prophetic mobility but also, like Moses at the Reed Sea and the bearers of the ark at the first Jordan crossing, the power to create and alter media of movement. By reversing the path of Israel's entry into the land, he symbolically positions his body, like Moses' on Nebo, apart from the people at the moment when his prophetic mediation ceases. Here, at the site of crossing, "a chariot of fire and horses of fire" appear "and they divided the two of them, and Elijah went up in a whirlwind to heaven" (2:11; cf. Sir 48:9, 12). Elijah's cyclonic assumption provokes a cry from Elisha: "My father! My father! Israel's chariot and its horses!" (2 Kgs 2:12). Elisha then rends his garment in two, mimicking in his act of mourning the separation effected by the chariot and by Elijah's assumption.

Elisha's exclamation is identical to the phrase Jehoash will cry during Elisha's illness, shortly before his death (2 Kgs 13:14; cf. 6:17; 7:6). The repetition of the phrase suggested to Gerhard von Rad that the phrase originated in prophetic circles and named the role of prophet as mighty protector, revealing that prophecy "was not thought of only as an instrument of some sort of instruction—whether it be in messages of judgment or of consolation—but it was rather thought of as the guarantor of the protection of Israel against threats from outside."[36] Kristin Weingart agrees that the phrase highlighted prophetic military efficacy and argues that the title was originally associated with Elisha before also being applied to Elijah.[37] But it was applied to each in distinctive ways: In the case of Elisha, the phrase "the chariot of Israel and its horses" is a prophetic title; in the case of Elijah, it draws attention to the visible vehicle of prophetic transport. This malleable phrase and the imagery and symbolism it conveys thus weave together a rich set of

---

strength, though of course Elijah is not portrayed as dismounting or mounting the chariot. See Reed, "Chariot Race"; Crowther, "Apobates Reconsidered."

[36] Rad, *Holy War*, 100.
[37] Weingart, "Elisha's or Elijah's Title?"

associations pertaining to prophetic mobility. The prophet races the chariot, demonstrating the superior adaptability and power of divine locomotion; the prophet is the chariot, conferring strategic advantage in the face of enemies; the prophet rides in the chariot, traversing boundaries of space and time, earth and heaven. In each case, the power to direct the prophet's movements, the actions they cause, and the advantages they confer rests not with a temporal sovereign but with God.

Elijah's ascent implies the possibility of future descent. Although his spectacular rapture in a flaming chariot has no narrated precedent, the fifty "sons of prophets" who greet Elisha after Elijah's whirlwind assumption suspect it may be an instance of the same pattern of spirit-driven movement earlier mentioned by Obadiah. They propose a search, for "perhaps the spirit of the Lord has lifted him and thrown him on one of the mountains or into one of the valleys" (2:16). For these fifty men it did not defy imagination that a whirlwind would pick up the prophet Elijah, carry him elsewhere, and throw him down again. Their suggestion implies that Elijah was frequently taxied in this manner. With such a pattern of movement in view, they mistakenly rest their hope of finding him in the coverage afforded by fifty fit and mobile human bodies (חמשים אנשים בני חיל 2 Kgs 2:16). Yet their mobility is terrestrial only, and Elijah has now crossed into the zone of heaven. Like Moses', Elijah's body cannot be found. Unlike Moses', Elijah's transport to another realm leaves open the possibility that the departed prophet might yet return and, in so doing, cause others to turn (Mal 3:23–24 MT/4:5–6 NRSV; Sir 48:10). Later writers did look for the prophet, not in a nearby mountain or valley but in the future. Elijah's ascent was thus seen to cross not only spatial boundaries but also temporal ones. In so doing, it created and stored in the body of the prophet potential energy that could catalyze movements of people and God even in the distant future.

Ezekiel's Spirit Journeys

In Chapter 7, I considered Ezekiel's experience of spirit possession and supernatural transport as a form of prophetic ecstasy, with particular attention to his commissioning (3:12–15) and first temple vision (8:1–11:25). Ezekiel experiences supernatural transport on two other occasions. The "hand of the Lord" brings him out "by the spirit of the Lord" to the valley of bones, there leading him around the bones (37:1–2). The prophet is here brought to a valley of death to be an agent of restoration, commanding breath to enter into dry bones so that they may again live. Ezekiel's final narrated spirit journey has a similar orientation to the future. But the final journey focuses on the reconstitution not of human bodies, but of place. The "hand of the Lord" brings him "to the land of Israel" and sets him on a high mountain (40:1–2), where he sees a man building the temple (40:3). Fourfold repetition of causative forms of the verb בוא (hiphil: ויבא 40:1; הביאני 40:2; ויביא 40:3; hophal: הבאתה 40:4) emphasizes that divine embodied agency enables prophetic movement across boundaries of time and space that the prophet cannot otherwise traverse. The man (and/or the spirit 43:5) repeatedly directs the prophet's movements (40:17, 24, 28, 32, 35, 48; 41:1; 42:1, 15; 43:1; 44:1, 4; 46:19, 21; 47:1–4, 6), leading him around the space he is constructing and instructing him in the future disposition of the land that surrounds it. While other people are not present in the vision, their future movements and resettlement are paramount, as the unnamed tour-guide orients the prophet to spatial proprieties and allocations, points of access and egress, fixtures and flows.

Unlike Ezekiel's journey in 8:1–11:25, the final journey is not round-trip: although Ezekiel is instructed to tell the people what he has seen, his return is not narrated. Adriane Leveen argues that the temple vision/journey re-places his dislocated body in its proper location, the land of Israel.[38] As it does elsewhere in the book (see further "Ezekiel Bound" in the present chapter and "Ezekiel" in Chapter 9), so also here Ezekiel's body has a representative function. The emplacement of his body in the land and its orientation to the temple presages the people's restored relationship to place and deity. The position of the vision-report at the conclusion of the book makes this re-placing the book's telos and the reader's destination. While the temple is the focus of much of the vision, Ezekiel and the reader are also brought out of the temple and into the waters flowing from it (47:1–6) before being instructed as to the reapportioning of the land to the people of Israel. Final details regarding the dimensions of the city and its gates provide pathways for entry and offer assurance that this city will have room for all who return (48:30–35). The book's concluding word, "there" (שמה; cf. 40:1), points away from its starting point to this envisioned place that will be the destination of people and God alike.[39]

---

[38] Leveen, "Returning the Body."
[39] Leveen, "Returning the Body," 401, emphasizes the distance and deferral enacted by this final phrase.

188 THE PROPHETIC BODY

At the beginning of the book of Ezekiel, it is not the prophet that moves, but the deity. Ezekiel's chariot visions (chs. 1 and 10) portray a divine mobility that assures a people in exile of God's presence with them. For Jill Middlemas, Ezekiel's visions "indicate the mobility of the deity and God's ability to be in and outside of the homeland, thus among the covenant people."[40] The prophet's mobility mirrors that of the deity. If it is astonishing that the deity whose temple is in Jerusalem can nonetheless be present with a people in Babylon, it is similarly astonishing that the prophet can travel between a people in exile and their homeland. The prophet's mediating mobility links people and place across barriers of distance and time.

Habakkuk: Crossing and Dwelling

Ezekiel's supernatural transport bridges space and time in order to reimagine and reconstitute place and a shared future in the land for a people in Diaspora. In Greek Daniel, the prophet Habakkuk (Ambakoum) travels in a manner similar to Ezekiel: an angel lifts him by the hair, carries him from Judea to Babylon, then delivers him home again (Dan 14:36, 39 LXX; cf. Ezek 8:3; 11:24). While the route and mode of transport are the same, their itineraries are reversed. Exile has partitioned the people of Judea. The division in space is also a rupture within the community. The two prophets are placed on either side of this division, Ezekiel in Babylonia and Habakkuk in Judea (14:33). Each "confront[s] suffering by drawing on human and suprahuman forces to make homes and cross boundaries."[41] Ezekiel's travel mediates home to people and God through his visions of the new temple and restored Israel. Habakkuk's transport interrupts the quotidian work of home-making to enact translocal mediations of home in a space of exile and death.

For Thomas Tweed, religions consist of two types of spatial practice, "dwelling" and "crossing." Practices of dwelling "construct a home—and a homeland. They delineate domestic and public space and construct collective identity."[42] Religion's crossings, meanwhile, are "terrestrial, corporeal, and cosmic."[43] Before Habakkuk's travel, he is engaged in decidedly

---

[40] Middlemas, "Prophecy and Diaspora," 49.
[41] Tweed, *Crossing and Dwelling*, 54. The other function Tweed assigns religion, "to intensify joy," is less a focus in these particular texts, but note that Tweed employs joy and suffering merismically, encompassing the full spectrum of human emotion (*Crossing and Dwelling*, 70).
[42] Tweed, *Crossing and Dwelling*, 75.
[43] Tweed, *Crossing and Dwelling*, 76.

domestic work, preparing bread, stew, and wine (OG) to take to harvesters working in the field (14:33). Habakkuk's home-making is part of an interdependent cycle. The workers in the field bring home the grain for the bread; the bread he prepares nourishes the harvesters. In this way he sustains the workers who in turn make possible life in the land called home. The first detail provided about Habakkuk is his placement in the homeland (14:33); the places to which the angel directs him, meanwhile, Babylon and the lion's den, are places he does not know, for which he has no orientation and to which he has no prior connection (v. 35). By contrast with the home Habakkuk creates and maintains, Daniel occupies the anti-home: he is among the exiles in Babylon, but worse, he has once again been thrown into the lions' den (v. 31), an artificial habitat and space of death where human bodies can expect to be eaten. It is not even a good home for lions, who must rely on their keepers for provision (v. 32). Habakkuk's mission is simple and short: he must deliver the meal he has prepared not to the field workers, but to Daniel, materializing divine memory and love in the nourishment of Daniel's body (v. 38). Once this mission is accomplished and Daniel has eaten, the angel brings Habakkuk back home ("to his place" v. 39 Th). The intervention to deliver Daniel from death might have been accomplished by other means. In the fiery furnace, an angel intervened to repel the flames (3:49 LXX); an angel likewise intervened directly during Daniel's first sojourn among the lions. Habakkuk's intervention differs not just in the involvement of a human mediator, but also in its crossings that bridge homeland and exile, field and pit. Habakkuk's supernatural journey mediates place, history, identity, and future, temporarily translating a prophetic practice of home-making into the non-place of exile and death.

Immobilities

The flipside of mobility is immobility. Just as prophetic movement instantiates divine movement, catalyzes movement of the people, and bridges divisions of space, time, and relationship, prophetic stillness or immobility corresponds to divine inaction or restraint and to a human desire to limit the prophet's (and God's) dynamic, mobilizing power. It may also dramatize and presage the immobilizing inaction and captivity of the people and a corresponding rupture between people, place, and God.

Ezekiel Bound

In the case of Ezekiel, God and humans alike restrain the prophet. The spirit commands Ezekiel to enter and shut himself within his house (3:24), adding, "see, they have put cords on you and bound you with them so that you will not go out among them" (3:25). Ezekiel's immobilization concurs with his silencing: the spirit promises to cause his tongue to attach to his palate so that he cannot speak; if he cannot speak he cannot reverse the people's rebellion (3:26).[44] When the Lord is ready to speak to them again, the Lord will speak with the prophet and open his mouth so that he will again speak with the people (3:27; Ezekiel reports that God opens Ezekiel's mouth at 33:22). Following this instruction, Ezekiel is commanded to dramatize and embody the future God has planned for the people, first by staging a siege and setting his face against the "city" (4:3) and then by lying on his left side for 390 days and his right side for forty days, by which he is to bear in his body the punishment of Israel and Judah (4:4–6).[45] Echoing language, imagery, and action from 3:25, the spirit now declares, "see, I have put cords on you so that you will not flip (תהפך) from one side onto the other until you have finished the days of your siege" (4:8). We saw earlier in this chapter that in the book of Jonah the root הפך had a double meaning, referring to two possible futures, one a punishment, the other repentance. Here the punishment is already dramatized in the prophet's binding. But the cords prevent his "flipping" or "turning," movement that might embody transformation (cf. Exod 7:15, 17, 20; Job 38:14), a change or reversal of course (Exod 10:19; 1 Sam 25:12; 1 Kgs 22:34), or a change of heart (Exod 14:5; 1 Sam 10:9). The immobilized body of the prophet symbolizes a people prevented from altering a course they have already set for themselves.[46]

Brenda Farnell describes movement as "causal power"; social action is accomplished by *"moving* persons."[47] In such an understanding, the immobilized body can signify a loss of causal power and capacity for social action. The binding of the prophet here reflects both human constraint and

---

[44] On the silencing of Ezekiel, see Glazov, *Bridling of the Tongue*, 238–61. Glazov argues that the cleaving of Ezekiel's tongue to his palate is a "metaphor referring to the effects of grief" and "by extension it becomes, in prophetic literature, a metaphor for exile" (*Bridling of the Tongue*, 272).

[45] Tarlin ("Utopia," 182) writes that "Yahweh forces Ezekiel to undergo the fall of the southern kingdom in his own body. The all-sufficient priestly body is subjected to famine, shorn of its hair, and reduced to muteness and paralysis."

[46] Hornsby ("Ezekiel," 425) links Ezekiel's binding to the binding of war captives.

[47] Farnell, *Dynamic Embodiment*, 1–2.

divine restraint. The people in exile lack the freedom to return; for now, God declines to intervene or empower them. Yet as Margaret Odell argues, the people's participation in binding the prophet nonetheless allows them to claim a measure of ownership and agency as they simultaneously stage their captivity upon his body and secure him as their mediator:

> By binding Ezekiel and confining him to his house, the people allow him to symbolize their own situation in exile and thereby express their willingness to accept him as their representative. The cords with which Ezekiel is bound (*'ăbôtîm*) further signify Ezekiel's role as a representative.[48]

His binding by the spirit further identifies him not only with the people in exile but also with Jerusalem and its besieged inhabitants. The compression of time by which Ezekiel's 430 days will represent years of punishment matches the compression of space in his toy-sized model of the siege. In a similar way his own immobilized body offers a scale model of the people, his successive immobilities revealing their experiences of siege, captivity, loss of autonomy, and exile.[49] Yet because God and people alike have bound him in the role of prophetic mediator, his very binding presages the possibility of future movement by God and people.

Jeremiah, Incarcerated Pprophet

Ezekiel was not the only prophet whose immobilized body could dramatize Jerusalem's siege and the people's captivity. Jeremiah is restrained, imprisoned, and taken captive in efforts to curtail, control, manage, and even secure access to his prophetic activity. Yet these efforts fail. Instead, his confinement and captivity mirror and presage the siege of Jerusalem and the captivity of its ruler and inhabitants.[50]

---

[48] Odell, *Ezekiel*, 57. Note, however, that Odell states that because of his silencing "Ezekiel cannot act as mediator" (*Ezekiel*, 58). I maintain that Ezekiel continues to mediate, but what he mediates includes the divine refusal to alleviate the people's immobilizing punishment.

[49] McEntire writes that through his binding and silencing, "Ezekiel becomes Israel, suffering with and for the nation . . . Ezekiel's proclamations of judgment . . . are inflicted on him." ("Bound and Gagged," 335).

[50] On the importance of greater attention to incarceration within biblical texts and reading these texts in relation to contemporary carceral experiences and systems, see Jobe, "Carceral Hermeneutics."

The first instance of Jeremiah's immobilization occurs at the hands of the priest Pashhur, who places Jeremiah in stocks after hearing him prophesy (Jer 20:1–2). Elsewhere in Jeremiah, authorities are said to use stocks (מהפכת) and collar (צינק) to exert control over "madmen" posing as prophets (Jer 29:26).[51] The Chronicler similarly reports Asa's use of stocks to punish and restrain the seer Hanani (2 Chron 16:10). Stocks partly punish through humiliation. But they achieve this through a simultaneous public performance of the state's immobilizing power. The person so immobilized is presented for public viewing, insult, and even injury. The impossibility of retreating, hiding, or shielding one's body demonstrates the consequences and dangers of immobility and thus incentivizes compliance with the state. This performance is meant to reinscribe the state's power on the prophet's body through the forcible interruption of agency. If the state can immobilize at will, the performance further asserts that mobility and the agency it affords are contingent freedoms granted by the state.[52] Jeremiah's exercise of prophetic agency in his oracle to Pashhur (20:3–6; cf. 33:1) repudiates the state's claim to curtail or grant the prophet's power and freedom. Yet the lament that follows portrays the personal cost to Jeremiah of performing his prophetic office in the face of such opposition (20:7–18).

Mary Mills connects Jeremiah's confinement in stocks and subsequent lament to the fate of the people: "the grief felt by the prophet in the face of the mission is the equivalent of bodily marks, violently inflicted, which in turn signify the coming violent end of the community."[53] In this reading, the oracular body of the prophet portends the people's future. The parallel between Jeremiah's immobilities and the fate of city, people, and king is developed at greater length in chapters 32–33 and 37–40, where Jeremiah's incarcerations pointedly parallel the siege and capture of Jerusalem, its king's inaction and eventual captivity, and its people's exile.[54] The prophet's subsequent abduction to Egypt similarly presages the captivity of those who seek refuge there.

---

[51] Jong emphasizes the purpose of this practice "to undermine prophetic authority ... by humiliation and ridicule" ("Jeremiah and Prophetic Authority," 275). Based on the etymology of מהפכת "from the root word meaning 'to twist or distort,'" Jobe suggests further that "the twisting or distorting of Jeremiah's body might be read as Pashhur's attempt at retaliatory or proportional justice" for purported "distorting of theological truth" ("Jeremiah's Non-Burial Refrain," 474).

[52] A later verse illustrates this point well: "Jeremiah was coming and going in the midst of the people, for they had not [yet] put him in the house of confinement" (37:4). Other references to Jeremiah's confinement include 32:3, 8; 33:1; 37:15–16, 18–21; 38:4–13, 26, 28; 39:14–15; 40:1.

[53] Mills, *Alterity*, 119.

[54] Green ("Sunk in the Mud") analyzes parallels between Jeremiah and King Zedekiah, arguing that Jeremiah mirrors to the king his possible futures. See also Roncace, *Jeremiah, Zedekiah, and the Fall*.

Biblical law did not prescribe incarceration as a punishment. Instead, incarceration was primarily used to limit the movement of individuals awaiting trial and to limit the agency and curtail the influence of those regarded as political opponents. On multiple occasions, Jeremiah's incarceration is portrayed as a response to his prophetic activity (32:3-5; 38:1-4; cf. 37:12-16). Ironically, however, his imprisonment does not stop him from prophesying (e.g., 32:6-15; 33:1; 38:17-18, 20-23; 39:15-18) or prevent the future he heralds. The incarcerated prophet continues to speak. Moreover, when Jeremiah's restricted movement prevents him from completing prophetic tasks, he enlists the help of Baruch (32:12-14; 36:5).[55] In these instances, Baruch both helps complete actions commanded by God and records and proclaims oracles Jeremiah has dictated. The mobile body of Baruch acts for the immobilized prophet, transcending limits imposed by the state that aimed to curtail the prophet's mobilizing and mediating power.

Instead of curtailing Jeremiah's prophetic agency, Jeremiah's confinement has a different function: to reveal the future of city, king, and people. From the beginning of Jeremiah's imprisonment, his fate is tied to that of the city. The first reference to Jeremiah's imprisonment synchronizes his incarceration with the siege of the city: just as Jerusalem's inhabitants are shut within the city walls, so Jeremiah is shut within the palace, in the court of the guard (32:2). Later it is his proclamation about the city's fate that occasions his imprisonment (38:1-6). While Jeremiah's confinements are not presented in linear fashion, the conclusion of Jeremiah's imprisonment is similarly intertwined with the fate of the city, its king, and its inhabitants: "Jeremiah dwelled in the court of the guard until the day when Jerusalem was taken" (38:28). When the king is led away in fetters (39:7) and (some of) the people exiled to Babylon (39:9), Jeremiah is released from his bonds and granted freedom to settle in occupied Judah (39:11-14; see also 40:1-6). Yet he is unable to do so: he is freed from prison only to be taken captive to Egypt by his own people (43:5-7). Their efforts to control Jeremiah's prophetic power come to naught, as the fate he decrees to the refugees and pharaoh in Egypt parallel those of the people and king in Judah (44:12-14, 30). The prophet's captivity once again heralds captivity for people and ruler alike.

---

[55] In the second instance, Jeremiah is not incarcerated (at 36:19 the officials tell Baruch and Jeremiah to go into hiding, which they would not be able to do if he was in captivity), but nonetheless tells Baruch that he is עָצוּר: confined, restricted, or restrained such that he cannot enter the Lord's house (36:5).

The Costs of Mobility and Immobility

The example of Jeremiah draws attention to the ways immobility and mobility each leave traces on the bodies of prophets. I noted in the previous section the portrayal of personal cost incurred by Jeremiah during his confinement. The ill-effects of confinement and immobility on body and psyche are well-documented.[56] Mobilities are also costly. Bruno Latour calls attention to disparate ways that different kinds of travel affect bodies. Latour imagines the journeys of a pair of twins, one on foot through jungle, the other in the first-class car of a train. "Each minute, [the first twin] opens a few centimeters of pathway, she ages more than one minute. She sweats. Her body bears the traces of her efforts; each meter can be read in the bloody scars made by thorns and broken brush."[57] Her brother's journey costs him no comparable effort; time and space neatly fold to allow near effortless passage, leaving few traces in his body or memory. The first twin exemplifies the relation between transportation and transformation, while the second demonstrates the displacement of the mutating effects of mobility.[58] Latour observes, "That a mobile may travel without mutating is so rare, so miraculous, so expensive, that is has to be accounted for and explained in detail."[59] In cases where travel seems to leave no trace (or fewer traces) on the body of the traveler, the infrastructure required to produce such a seemingly effortless journey leaves its scars on the bodies of human workers and animals (e.g., Balaam's donkey), on the land, and within the ecosystem. While the costs of prophetic mobility and immobility may be distributed in various ways among prophet, God, people, nonhuman animals, and other nonhuman creation, their effects on the bodies of prophets should not be discounted.

In an analysis of the "transport" of information, Marshall McLuhan similarly argues that "each form of transport not only carries, but translates and transforms the sender, the receiver, and the message."[60] Latour's insights highlight the effects of mobility on the mover and the space through which they move. While the preceding analysis has shown that prophetic mobility accomplishes far more than the transmission of information, McLuhan's

---

[56] E.g., Wildeman and Andersen, "Disciplinary Segregation"; Guenther, *Solitary Confinement*; Gawande, "Hellhole." On the effects of immobility, see Bortz, "Disuse Syndrome."
[57] Latour, "Trains of Thought," 173.
[58] Latour, "Trains of Thought," 174.
[59] Latour, "Trains of Thought," 186.
[60] McLuhan, *Understanding Media*, 127. See further discussion in Näser-Lather and Neubert, "Traffic," 8–10.

observation nonetheless highlights important further effects of prophetic movement on each participant in the mediatory act and on the media and content of prophecy itself. Mobility and immobility are not merely adjunct to prophetic activity. They are a vital component of it. Bridge and barrier, catalyst and captive, the mobile and immobile body of the prophet mediates between people, place(s), and God, reshaping their present even as it augurs, directs, and announces their future.

Conclusion

Prophetic mobility is not subordinate or merely prefatory to other (i.e., verbal) aspects of prophecy, but is itself a component and modality of prophetic mediation. The terrestrial movements of Moses, Balaam, and Jonah catalyze movements of people. At times they also mirror the movements of God and make possible the interaction of God and people. Supernatural transport, meanwhile, enables Elijah, Ezekiel, and Habakkuk to cross spatial, temporal, and cosmic boundaries that they could not have traversed by solely human means. In the process, Elijah's catalyzing potential is deferred to the future, while Ezekiel and Habakkuk engage in translocal home-making that links homeland and Diaspora, present and future, people and God. The flipside of mobility is immobility. The mediatory power of prophetic mobility elicits efforts to curtail prophetic agency by immobilizing prophets. Yet prophetic immobility likewise mediates, embodying divine and human inaction and auguring captivity and exile.

Bodily movement through space and time finds a correlate in the circulation of affect: one facilitates and frequently aims at the other; they are also, partly, structurally analogous. The shared etymological root of motion and emotion testifies to this analogy, recognizing the capacity of affect and emotion to move through space, move in and through bodies, and touch, motivate, and move people, both singly and collectively.[61] In the final chapters I turn to affect and emotion as further dimensions of prophetic embodiment and means of prophetic mediation.

---

[61] On the interconnection of motion and emotion in human relationship and communication, see Foolen et al., *Moving Ourselves, Moving Others*.

9
Anger and Tears

"Coming to terms with affect implies coming to terms with the body."[1]

"As the mode of experience in which the embodied being lives its own excess, affectivity introduces the power of creativity into the sensorimotor body."[2]

Affect is a key component of prophetic embodiment. From Jonah's anger to Jeremiah's tears and from Ezekiel's devastation to Daniel's wonder, affect proves central to the prophets' embodied experience, action, and interaction and constitutes a vital part of what and how the prophetic body mediates between God and people.

In the past decade and a half, biblical studies have witnessed an explosion of interest in affect.[3] Central to this work is a recognition of the body's mediating role. In their introduction to the edited volume *Reading with Feeling: Affect Theory and the Bible*, Fiona Black and Jennifer Koosed write, "Religions move people in their bodies . . . Bodies touch, feel, sense, come together, and move apart as affects circulate. Affect theory gives us the conceptual tools to explore these movements, intensities, sensations."[4] The ferment that characterizes studies of affect both within and beyond biblical studies has produced varied understandings of affect and a corresponding diversity of approaches to its study. Yet the very phenomenological, biological, and social complexity of affect (including emotion) benefits from an interdisciplinary approach.[5]

---

[1] Wetherell, *Affect and Emotion*, 10.
[2] Hansen, "Affect as Medium," 208.
[3] See, e.g., Black and Koosed, eds., *Reading with Feeling*; Koosed and Moore, eds., "Affect Theory and the Bible"; Kotrosits, "How Things Feel"; Moore, *Bible after Deleuze*. The landmark essay that first applied affect theory to interpretation of the HBOT was Runions, "Rahab's Queer Affect."
[4] Black and Koosed, "Some Ways to Read with Feeling," 1–2.
[5] Cf. Charland, "Affect (Philosophical Perspectives)."

Understanding Affect: New Approaches and Relevance for Studying Prophetic Literature[6]

Affect has been variously defined or described as "felt bodily states,"[7] "emotional states and distinctive perturbations they cause in the body and mind,"[8] and an "umbrella term that includes related, and more familiar, words such as 'feeling' and 'emotion.'"[9] These understandings of affect largely focus on processes in the body and mind that produce various dynamic feeling-states in response to internal and external stimuli. Both culturally shaped and individually experienced, these responses are temporary, marked by shifting sensations and fluctuating intensities that are commonly experienced as a kind of movement or change within the body and mind. A related but much broader definition focuses not on bodily experience or feeling only but on processes that produce change more generally, yielding such descriptions of affect as "the process of making a difference" and "modes of influence, movement and change."[10] Even in this second understanding of affect, the body frequently plays a crucial role, but attention is given to the circulation and movement of affect not simply within bodies but also between and among them. My approach will integrate these understandings, attending to the embodiment of affect as a component of individual experience, social practice, and interaction, underscoring its power as a dynamic interpersonal force capable of producing personal and social change. Moreover, studies of emotion and affect increasingly recognize emotion as part of the bodily processes we call affect. I thus analyze the portrayal of culturally recognized emotions in the context of this wider set of affective processes and practices.

To construct the multidisciplinary framework that undergirds my analysis of prophetic affect, I draw on the work of three scholars in three fields: Klaus Scherer, Margaret Wetherell, and Sara Ahmed, in the fields of psychology and neurocognition, social science, and cultural studies respectively.

Among neurocognitive approaches, the work of Klaus Scherer has been influential for its mapping of the embodied complexities of affect in relation to cognition, volition, and action. Scherer proposes that affect be seen

---

[6] An earlier and shorter version of a portion of this section was published in Portier-Young, "Linking Emotion, Cognition, and Action," 60–1.
[7] Plantinga, *Moving Viewers*, 57. A succinct summary of differing approaches that resists simplistic categorizations can be found in Black and Koosed, "Some Ways to Read with Feeling," 2–5.
[8] Wetherell, *Affect and Emotion*, 2, referring to the object of study of "affective scientists."
[9] Cvetkovich, "Affect."
[10] Wetherell, *Affect and Emotion*, 2–3.

as a broader category to which emotion belongs. Its etymological root in the Latin verb *afficere* provides Scherer with a conceptual frame, encompassing as it does the meanings,

> 1) to bring somebody into a bodily or organic state, condition, or disposition, 2) to bring somebody into a mental or psychological mood, to excite or stimulate or to move or touch, 3) to attack, weaken, or exhaust someone.[11]

While definitions of the Latin verb are not determinative of the meaning of the English word "affect," for Scherer this range of meanings helpfully foregrounds the interrelation between bodily and mental or psychological processes (Scherer prefers "processes" to "states," as affect is more dynamic than static) that together constitute affect.

Emotions, for Scherer, refer to "clearly delineated, intensive patterns of affective processes" with four distinctive features: 1) They are elicited by the combination of event and appraisal, in which a person judges an event to be relevant to their "needs, goals, values, and general well-being;" 2) they "have a strong motivational force, producing states of *action readiness*" [italics original] and preparing a person "to deal with important events in their lives;" 3) "Emotions engage the entire person," including "somatovisceral and motor systems;" and 4) they exert considerable power in relation to behavior and experience.[12]

In this understanding, emotion includes not only subjective *feeling*, on which popular (and constructivist) understandings tend to focus, but also "elicitation processes, physiological symptoms, motor expression, and motivational changes."[13] As such, emotion, like the broader category of affect, is not divorced from reason and discernment, nor from body and action. It is fundamental to each.

Scherer's understanding focuses primarily on the individual person. Scholars working in social science and cultural theory look beyond the

---

[11] Scherer, "Nature and Function of Emotion," 298.
[12] Scherer, "Emotions are Emergent Processes," 3459, citing Frijda and Scherer, "Emotion Definitions." Compare Scherer's definition of emotion elsewhere as "an episode of massive synchronous recruitment of mental and somatic resources to adapt to and cope with a stimulus event that is subjectively appraised as highly pertinent to needs, goals, and values of the individual" (Scherer, "Unconscious Processes," 314). See further Scherer, "What Are Emotions?"
[13] Scherer, "Emotions Are Emergent Processes," 3461–2; see also Scherer, "Nature and Function of Emotion," 294, where he documents this as an emerging consensus view.

boundaries of the individual to consider social and cultural dimensions of affect.

Social scientist Margaret Wetherell adds to Scherer's understanding an emphasis on the interplay between individual and social domains, arguing that the study of affect must give greater attention to "interaction and intersubjectivity."[14] For Wetherell, affect is not the property of one individual. It is produced through interaction and collaboration. In her work, affect theory converges with practice theory, which recognizes the formative character of habitual actions on person and society alike.[15] "In affective practice," she states, "bits of the body ... get patterned together with feelings and thoughts, interaction patterns and relationships, narratives and interpretive repertoires, social relations, personal histories, and ways of life."[16] The theoretical concept of affective practice thus combines attention to affect's embodiment, the agency that accrues to it, the ongoing (re)formation of affective patterns through repetition and reflection, its interactive character, and a shaping socio-cultural matrix that is also shaped by these practices.[17] Among the affective practices examined by Wetherell are discursive ones. That is, crucial to her analysis is the "relation between affect and discourse," encompassing in the latter category utterance, embodied communication, diverse media, and social contexts, all of which she broadly characterizes as "language in action."[18] Rhetoric, she argues, has the power to "create and intensify" emotion.[19] Discourse "makes affect powerful, makes it radical and provides the means for affect to travel."[20] Discourse, broadly construed, is therefore a key to the interactive and collaborative character of affective practice.

Finally, Sara Ahmed's study of emotion as "cultural politics" argues that emotions simultaneously take shape within a social world and contribute to "world making."[21] Ahmed is interested in emotions not as the experiences of discrete individuals, but as forces that "*come from without and move inward*" through processes of social discourse, participation, and interaction.[22]

---

[14] Wetherell, *Affect and Emotion*, 25. See also p. 74.
[15] See especially Bourdieu, *Logic of Practice*.
[16] Wetherell, *Affect and Emotion*, 14.
[17] See further Wiesse, "Affective Practice."
[18] Wetherell, *Affect and Emotion*, 52. Wetherell understands affect as "embodied meaning making" (*Affect and Emotion*, 4).
[19] Wetherell, *Affect and Emotion*, 7.
[20] Wetherell, *Affect and Emotion*, 19.
[21] Ahmed, *Cultural Politics*, 12.
[22] Ahmed, *Cultural Politics*, 9.

As emotions circulate between subjects, they produce "surfaces and boundaries" of individual and social bodies alike, making "impressions" that carry the imprint of repetition, power relations, attachment and loss, and constructions of identity and difference.[23] Ahmed's attention to the interrelation between discourse, affect, bodies, and social worlds helps illuminate the interplay between affect, persuasion, and world-making in the prophetic literature, including the ways affectively-charged prophetic discourse and action aim to shape social identity, boundaries, and behavior through the production of affect among its audiences.

Indeed, the understandings of affect and emotion articulated by Scherer, Wetherell, and Ahmed yield several key insights and avenues for analysis of prophetic affect. First, prophetic affect and emotion arise at the nexus of embodiment, experience, cognition, volition, and action. Affect (including emotion) and cognition or "reason" are interrelated and interdependent. Emotion and affect are thus not opposed to reason but are necessary components of "rational" processes of perception, appraisal, and decision-making. A prophet's affective experience and practice emerges as a site of embodied learning, creativity, and social transformation.[24] Moreover, the relationship between affect and decision-making means that affect is not incidental to the prophetic work of persuasion but necessary to it.[25] Indeed, affect influences and shapes prophetic discourse and action, even as discourse, action, and interaction shape the affect of prophets, their interlocutors, and their audiences. For this reason the embodiment of affect is not limited to processes within an individual person, but encompasses social and discursive dimensions.[26] Affect does not reside in a subject but circulates between subjects. Divine affective practice shapes prophetic affect; prophetic discourse and action amplifies, transmits, and alters the affect of people and God. Collaborative affective practice, inter-affectivity, and the circulation of affect thus emerge as central components of prophetic experience and keys to prophetic mediation.[27] That is, these social, interactive, and intersubjective

---

[23] Ahmed, *Cultural Politics*, 10, 12.

[24] On creativity, see Hansen, "Affect as Medium."

[25] For a helpful review of rhetorical approaches to prophetic literature and an argument for the continued study of "rhetoric as persuasion" in this corpus, see Kelle, *Hosea 2*, 21–34.

[26] Wetherell, *Affect and Emotion*, 74: "Affect is pre-eminently a relational and social event, and the 'dialogic' activities involved need to be at the forefront of attempts to understand affective meaning-making."

[27] In the study of emotion, it is more common to speak of emotion regulation and co-regulation. On the interpersonal character of emotion regulation see Rimé, "Social Sharing."

aspects of prophetic affect are part and parcel of *how* the prophet mediates just as affect is itself part of *what* the prophet mediates.

When a prophet's role is reduced to transmitter of a verbal message, affect is similarly reduced to a supporting role. But affect is more than window dressing. It is entailed in decision-making. It motivates and facilitates learning and behavioral change. It plays a role in how words and events are evaluated in relation to the self. Thus, contrary to approaches that focus almost exclusively on prophecy's verbal component, even within the model of prophecy-as-message critiqued in Chapter 1, the affect of sender, messenger, and recipient would each play a critical role in the communication-event and its effects. But the analysis below will show that prophetic affect does more than facilitate or participate in the mediation of knowledge. It also mediates and negotiates relationship. It constitutes and transforms social practice, shapes identity and commitment, and opens into new realities.

Jonah: Transforming Affect

In the book of Jonah, affect is a site of tension and transformation. The book's first half is characterized by an affective arc from fear to gratitude. In the book's second half, Jonah's proclamation elicits affective reversal from the Ninevites; their reversal elicits God's in turn. It is at this moment of dramatic affective reversal that the book thematizes the *prophet's* affect. God counters Jonah's overwhelming anger and pain by eliciting and drawing Jonah's attention to the expanding scope of Jonah's attachment and concern. In this way God works to align Jonah's affect more closely with God's own and hints to Jonah that as prophet he already participates in God's affective practice toward the living beings God has created.

Toward the beginning of the book of Jonah, the dominant emotion is fear. Fear first grips the sailors in the face of the tempest God has hurled upon the sea, prompting them to cry out to their gods for help (1:5). Jonah also experiences fear, though it has prompted him not to cry out but to hide, for the object of his fear is not the wind but the deity who caused it: "I fear the LORD, the God of heaven" (1:9 NAB; cf. 1:16).[28] A cognate accusative construction

---

[28] LXX renders here σέβομαι, which captures the idiomatic association in Hebrew between fear and worship but accentuates an affective posture of reverence rather than fear. The lexical connection between Jonah's "fear" and that of the sailors that is present in MT is thus not retained in LXX.

and intensifying adjective demonstrate that Jonah's fear compounds and amplifies that of the sailors who harbor him (וייראו האנשים יראה גדולה 1:10), even as their attention remains focused on the raging sea (1:11).[29] Yet the futility of their efforts to quell the storm causes them finally to turn toward Jonah's god, attributing to the deity a very different emotion, namely "pleasure" or "desire" (חפצת 1:14). This disjuncture between human fear and divine desire helps to identify affect as a site of tension and transformation in Jonah. As the narrative unfolds, the narrator will thematize different sets of emotions and dispositions as God works to align the prophet's affect more closely with God's own.

In the scene that follows, Jonah begins to explore a broader emotional range than simply fear. In his psalm, Jonah first identifies his own state as one of distress, anxiety, and need (צרה 2:3). The narrow "straits" of his confinement in the innards or belly (במעי MT; κοιλίᾳ LXX 2:1) of the fish give fleshy form to the discomfort of his deliverance, even as they foreshadow a different kind of delivery. He declares that his return from the pit left his throat weakened (התעטף 2:8). The antidote was memory and mindfulness of God (2:8). The final note of his prayer is thanksgiving (תודה 2:10). The affective arc of the psalm thus moves from anxiety and recognition of dependence, through exhaustion and reflection, to gratitude.[30] Yet even as the prophet re-orients himself toward awareness of God's deliverance, in this scene he remains focused on his own journey from death to life.[31] In the book's concluding scene God will attempt to elicit a similar affective arc that would expand the scope of the prophet's concern.

At the conclusion of this scene, the fish—at the Lord's command—(r)ejects the prophet in a stream of vomit (2:11).[32] The fish's vomiting of the prophet may signify nothing more than a mechanism of disgorgement that

---

[29] Trible has noted that "this report prefaces a literary structure built on repetition: They designate major motifs, slow down the story, and build suspense" ("Jonah," 498). On "fear" as a major motif highlighted through repetition and use of the cognate accusative see also Trible, "Jonah," 476–7. Trible further argues that the sailors' "emotions . . . surround" Jonah ("Jonah," 499). In MT, the fear of the sailors and Jonah is matched by the attribution of corresponding but different affective states to the sea: presently it rages, but they seek action that will cause it to grow quiet/calm (1:11–13). The sea's "vexation" ceases when Jonah is hurled into it (1:15).

[30] Midrash Jonah traces a similar arc: God first ordains a male fish to swallow Jonah, so that in the fish's roomy interior Jonah will not feel anxious. But lacking anxiety, the prophet does not pray. So God appoints a second, female, pregnant fish to swallow Jonah, so that, crowded in with the excrement of 365,000 juvenile fish, he will be afraid and will therefore pray. Full text can be found in Eisenstein, אוצר מדרשים [Oṣar Midrashim], 217–23.

[31] Cf. Kamp, Inner Worlds, 145.

[32] For analysis of the motif of vomiting in this passage and Lev 18 and 20 and an application to the contemporary climate crisis, see Strawn, "On Vomiting."

allows the passenger to exit this fleshy vessel and continue his mission. But the book is replete with artful personifications and affords a dignity and agency to nonhuman animals that press us to consider the fish as subject. If Jonah's sojourn in the fish's belly has powerful effects on the prophet's affect, we might also ask how it affected the fish to hold this prophet, undigested, inside its body. Elsewhere in the Hebrew scriptures vomit carries connotations of rejection (Lev 18:25, 28; 20:22), filth (Isa 28:8), and humiliation (Jer 48:26). For humans, the experience of vomiting is associated with purgation, revulsion, disease or toxin, shock, and shame. In light of the book's affective and relational arcs, one interpretation might be that for the fish, Jonah's affective response to his commissioning, pursuit, and deliverance by God is not yet digestible and possibly toxic.[33] Jonah's prayer does not mention the fish who hosts him, possible evidence (from the perspective of the fish) that the scope of Jonah's concern has not yet expanded to include nonhuman creation. The fish's (r)ejection of the prophet forms a hinge between the two halves of the book. For Jonah, to be vomited is also to be born again. The prophet is spewed out for a do-over.

The book's third chapter foregrounds the affective practices of the Ninevites, who respond to prophetic proclamation with practices of humility, dependence, and grief and by turning from "their evil way" (3:8, 10).[34] Hearing Jonah's oracle elicits belief in God; belief elicits communal fasting and donning of sackcloth (3:5). The city's king further exemplifies this affective reversal as he abandons his throne to sit in a pile of ash (3:6) and resolves to abstain not only from food but also from water. He then calls for abstention, sackcloth, and crying out on the part of humans and animals alike and commands the people to turn from practices of evil and violence (3:7–8). The king grounds the motivation for these affective and behavioral reversals in the possibility that the deity might respond by turning from the anger (חרון) that would bring calamity upon them (3:9; cf. Exod 32:12).[35] This possibility is realized as God exhibits an affective and

---

[33] For the theme of indigestibility, see Strawn, "On Vomiting," 453.
[34] In *Pirkei de Rabbi Eliezer*, the Ninevites exemplify the power of תשובה, commonly translated repentance but literally meaning "turning" (*PRE* 43). The midrash elaborates that infants and mothers were separated, so that infants cried for their mothers' breasts and mothers cried to nurse their children. The merit of these weeping children saved the entire population.
[35] Lambert argues that rites of appeal through fasting and crying out and behaviors oriented toward justice are two distinct but necessarily paired sets of conditions for eliciting the divine reversal ("Mourning," 153–7).

204 THE PROPHETIC BODY

volitional reversal (וינחם; cf. Exod 32:14) corresponding and responding to that of the Ninevites (3:10).[36]

The book's final scene thematizes Jonah's affect.[37] The affective reversals of Ninevites and God hint at the possibility of the prophet's own affective transformation, even as God's reversal elicits from Jonah anger or pain "unto death." The scene's structure as a dialogue between Jonah and God suggests that Jonah's affect is not a private matter but closely related to Jonah's role as God's prophet.[38] As the dialogue unfolds, God works to "train" Jonah's affect to align more closely with God's own.

The ancient versions preserve slight variations in the portrayal of Jonah's affect, one foregrounding anger, the other pain. In the Masoretic Text (MT), Jonah is first portrayed as a grammatical object for or in whom circumstances generate feeling-states; in Old Greek (OG), passive verbs create a similar impression. God's repentance (וינחם 3:10) in response to that of the Ninevites is for Jonah a source of great distress (4:1); in response, according to MT, "it grew hot for him" (ויחר לו 4:1; see also 4:4, 9). In the latter, common Hebrew idiom, the physiological experience of heat is a metonym for the emotional experience of anger;[39] the idiom, moreover, portrays this autonomic response and, metonymically, anger itself, as something that happens "to" a person.[40] Old Greek foregrounds sorrow and confusion rather than anger: Jonah experiences great pain or grief (ἐλυπήθη . . . λύπην μεγάλην 4:1 OG; see also 4:4, 9), then is confounded, confused, or troubled (συνεχύθη 4:1). Underlying the meaning of confusion in the latter verb is the metaphor of substances being "poured together" and commingled. In the book

---

[36] Moberly characterizes God's change of heart as an instance of "divine responsiveness . . . to human attitude and action." ("Objectionable Mercy," 158). This responsiveness reflects the intersubjectivity/affective attunement that will be discussed in detail later in this chapter.

[37] Both Graybill and Bray draw on the work of Sara Ahmed to interpret Jonah as an "affect alien," using his affective refusals as an interpretive key. Graybill argues for an understanding of prophecy as a "practice of unhappiness . . . bound up with the practice of memory" ("Problem of Happiness," 110). Bray argues that "in his shamefully discontinuous self, Jonah opens alternate flows through the story that the mainstream has sought to dam/n up" (Bray, Grave Attending, 124).

[38] Indeed, for Rhiannon Graybill Jonah's defiance exemplifies prophecy as "practice of unhappiness" ("Problem of Happiness," 97, 101).

[39] Ekman, Levinson, and Friesen document changes in body temperature accompanying six emotions: anger, fear, sadness, happiness, and disgust. "The [temperature] change associated with anger was significantly different ($P < .05$) from that for all other emotions" ("Autonomic Nervous System"). Anger caused marked increase in temperature, while fear and disgust caused (less marked) decreases in temperature (Ekman, Levinson, and Friesen, "Autonomic Nervous System"). On the prevalence and function of this metonym across a wide range of cultures, see Kövecses, "Cross-Cultural Experiences of Anger."

[40] Fretheim links Jonah's anger in MT to Jonah's hopes and expectations regarding divine wrath ("Jonah and Theodicy," 228–9, 233–4). He writes, "Jonah by his anger demonstrates the only reaction he believes is truly God-like. He will be just if God will not" (Fretheim, "Jonah and Theodicy," 234).

of Joel, the earth responds this way (συγχυθήσεται, translating Hebrew רגזה "quaked") to an army of locusts; earth's disturbance parallels that of the heavens, which "shake" (σεισθήσεται Joel 2:10). In Nahum, meanwhile, the Greek verb συγχυθήσονται translates the affectively laden יתהוללו. In a context of human invasion, this Hebrew verb characterizes the wild, precipitous careening of chariots that "rush to and fro" (ישתקשקון) as "madness" (Nah 2:5). These uses of συγχέω in the OG translation of the Book of the Twelve suggest that Jonah's pain produces a feeling-state not simply "mixed," but turbulent, seismic, and out of control.[41]

The complaint of this turbulent prophet centers around well-known, even (says Jonah) predictable aspects of God's own affect and character: the Lord is "a compassionate and gracious God, slow to anger, abounding in kindness, renouncing punishment" (4:2 NJPS).[42] While the Ninevite king's reflection on the divine capacity for forgiveness (3:9) prompted his own affective reversal, Jonah's response to the same capacity in God prompts entrenchment, avoidance, and hostility.[43] Thomas Dozeman argues that Jonah's "misuse" of the familiar confession reveals that he did not "understand" it in the first place.[44]

But rather than lecturing Jonah on the divine traits, God works to cultivate and reveal the same traits within Jonah and thus elicit Jonah's reappraisal of God's actions and character. When Jonah asks for death (Jonah 4:3; cf. 4:8), God asks Jonah to evaluate his feeling-state (4:4).[45] God's questioning resembles the Socratic method used in portions of rational emotive behavioral therapy (REBT) and cognitive behavioral therapy (CBT). Developed in the twentieth century to treat such conditions as depression and anxiety disorder, these interventions proceed from recognition of causal and mutually shaping relationships between feelings, thoughts, and behaviors. Within

---

[41] Similar turbulence is reflected in Pseudo-Tertullian, "Carmen de Iona Propheta." Jonah declares: En ego tempestas, ego tota insania mundi, / In me, inquit, vobis aether ruit et mare surgit, / In me terra procul, mors proxima, nulla dei spes ("Carmen de Iona Propheta," ll. 73–75).

[42] Jonah's prayer alludes to and expands Exod 34:6 by way of Exod 32:12. Cf. Num 14:18; Neh 9:17; Ps 86:15; 103:8; 145:8; Joel 2:13; Nah 1:3; Mic 7:18. For discussion, see Thomas Dozeman, "Inner-Biblical Interpretation."

[43] Kamp notes that despite the focus on God's character, "In his relationship to YHWH Jonah determines the positions from a strongly egocentric point of view" (*Inner Worlds*, 145).

[44] Dozeman, "Inner-Biblical Interpretation," 217.

[45] Midrash Jonah attributes Jonah's desire for death to the conditions inside the fish: "Because of the great heat in the belly of the pregnant fish, Jonah's clothing, his jacket, and his hair were burned up, and flies, mosquitoes, ants, and fleas settled on him and made him so miserable that he wished he were dead." Cited in and translated by Limburg, *Jonah*, 112. Full text of Midrash Jonah may be found in Eisenstein, אוצר מדרשים [*Oṣar Midrashim*], 217–23.

REBT and CBT, the Socratic method of questioning aims at "cognitive restructuring"—revising attitudes, beliefs, and appraisals—through dialogue that aims to prompt reflection and facilitate behavioral change.[46] This interactive therapy relies on responsive participation by both parties. Just as the patient is prompted to answer the therapist's questions, so the therapist must assess whether a patient's answer moves the patient closer to the desired set of attitudes, beliefs, and actions. The therapist then responds with corresponding approval or disapproval, requests for clarification, and/or a new question. The parallel between REBT or CBT and God's interaction with Jonah helps call attention to the linking of emotion, cognition, and action in the narrative as well as the mutual, affective responsiveness of God and prophet.

Jonah's next action signals both ongoing rumination and refusal to let go of the outcome he has hoped for.[47] He builds a booth and sits in its shade to see what will happen to Nineveh (4:5). God meets action with action, causing a plant to grow over Jonah that will momentarily replace his anger or pain with a different emotion: joy. The physical comfort of the plant's shade "delivers" Jonah from the "evil," that is, from the negative feeling-state resulting from his appraisal of God's action. In the phrase, "he greatly rejoiced" (וישמח שמחה גדולה 4:6), a cognate accusative construction draws attention to Jonah's emotional response (cf. the similar construction in 1:10 and 4:1), while the adjective גדולה "great," repeated from 4:1, highlights the contrast between Jonah's previous and current feeling-states.

Jonah's experience of joy passes quickly, however. God appoints a worm that strikes the plant and a wind that strikes the prophet (4:7–8). God's strategy has shifted again, now incorporating tactics that might be construed as more aggressively confrontational and coercive.[48] They do not, however,

---

[46] Calero-Elvira et al., "Socratic Method."
[47] A similar point is made by Graybill, "Problem of Happiness," 106.
[48] Graybill argues that *each* aspect of YHWH's efforts to redirect Jonah's affective state, including not only the removal of the plant but also questioning, implicit promise, and encouragement, is coercive ("Problem of Happiness," 103–4). She writes, "YHWH is attempting to orient his prophet, to force him to find pleasure in certain appropriate objects and not in others. The violence that this lesson engenders—the nocturnal destruction of the plant by a worm—is supposed to go unmentioned. Jonah's preoccupation with the plant is a way of naming and calling out the otherwise unspoken process" ("Problem of Happiness," 104). This evaluation relies on an expansive understanding of coercion. It could be more useful to distinguish between aspects of coercion, manipulation, and rational persuasion (as distinguished, e.g., by Wood, "Coercion, Manipulation, Exploitation"; Gorin, "Interpersonal Manipulation"; Noggle, "Manipulative Actions") in analysis of the behavioral strategies God displays in this chapter. These determinations rely in part on whether and to what extent Jonah is free *not* to align his affect with God's. Graybill's affirmation of Jonah's freedom of refusal undercuts the broad claim of coercion ("Problem of Happiness," 109). This is not to ignore or

compel alignment between deity and prophet. Instead, a pattern of dialogue persists in which the prophet remains free to choose an affective practice and give voice to feelings that differ from the deity's. When the plant withers (4:7), Jonah's body becomes vulnerable to wind and heat. He grows faint and again asks for death, judging death better than life (4:8). In response, God again challenges Jonah with a question that invites Jonah to reappraise the situation and his feelings about it, yet the prophet declines to do so. Instead, Jonah affirms a causal connection between his intense negative feelings—anger (MT) or pain (OG)—and his desire for death (4:9).

The capacity for responsive turning—affective, volitional, and relational—exhibited by the Ninevites and God and thematized in Jonah's confession of God's character remains an obstacle for the prophet. In an earlier chapter Jonah began to experience an affective shift from anxiety to exhaustion to thanksgiving. In the book's concluding verses, God counters Jonah's overwhelming anger or pain by drawing Jonah's attention to a different shift, namely the expanding scope of Jonah's attachment and concern. In the process, God pointedly seeks to align Jonah's concern with God's. God's lesson to Jonah turns on the verb חוס, denoting a feeling of pity or compassion that prompts one person to spare or show mercy to another. Noting that the most frequent subject of the verb חוס is "eye" (in fifteen of twenty-four occurrences), Walter Moberly suggests that the verb has "primary resonances ... with the human phenomenon of a tear coming to the eye, the spontaneous and unpredictable bodily response to other creatures in need."[49] Drawing a parallel between God's feelings and actions toward the Ninevites, on the one hand, and Jonah's feelings regarding the plant, on the other, God emphasizes sympathy between deity and prophet and invites the prophet to extrapolate from his own affective experience in order to better understand God's (4:9–11).

The book's unresolved ending creates space for ongoing negotiation. Yet while God stops short of inviting Jonah to feel what God feels for Nineveh, God hints that Jonah already participates in God's affective practice toward the living beings God has created, whether Israelite, seafarer, or Ninevite, human, plant, or animal. Prophetic participation in God's responsive

---

exonerate the deity's manipulation of Jonah's affect and assault against the prophet's body through plant, worm, and wind.

[49] Moberly, "Objectionable Mercy," 166. Moberly draws on the analysis of Wolff, *Obadiah and Jonah*, 173). See also Wolff, *Studien zum Jonabuch*, 36.

affective practice builds outward from the prophet's concerns to God's. Just as gratitude displaced anxiety, here compassion has the capacity to counteract anger and pain. The prominence in the story of responsive affective reversals and transformations on the part of the prophet, Ninevites, and God, paired with God's persistent efforts to align Jonah's affect with God's own, highlights the signal importance of affect to the prophet's mediatorial role.[50]

Jeremiah

While the book of Jonah portrays God's effort to align a prophet's affect more closely with God's, the discourse of the book of Jeremiah constructs the prophet's body as a node of circulating affect. Clues regarding the prophet's affective experience and practice are found across a range of literary forms and subject positions: in first-person speech by the prophet, including the laments or "confessions" of Jeremiah; in second-person address to Jeremiah, with God as speaker; and in third-person narrative portrayals of the prophet. The book's most characteristic affective practice, lament, is fundamentally relational. Frequent ambiguity about who is speaking in Jeremiah's lament passages along with interdictions against intercession and shared practices of mourning highlight intersubjectivity and affective entanglement among prophet, God, people, and, in some instances, place.

It is in the book's direct discourse, frequently expressed in poetry, that we find the greatest density of affective language. But a distinctive challenge arises in interpreting poetic direct discourse in Jeremiah. In these passages, at times it is a simple matter to identify speaker and addressee. At other times, the identities of the speaker(s) and addressee(s) are not so clear. The discourse may have the form of a dialogue but lack dialogue tags to identify the sequence of speakers. Lacking such tags, interpreters analyze content clues that suggest that one speaker has concluded their turn and another has begun or that a new participant has entered the conversation, but interpreters often lack clarity or consensus about who those speakers are.[51]

---

[50] Graybill makes a similar point, urging interpreters to "tak[e] seriously the affective and emotional edges of prophecy as much as the message the prophet transmits" ("Problem of Happiness," 110). For Graybill the refusal of alignment (i.e., Jonah's status as "affect alien") is a practice of resistance that instantiates prophetic critique of the deity.

[51] On this phenomenon more generally in Jeremiah, see Glanz, *Participant-Reference Shifts*. Glanz refers to the shifts in question by the shorthand "PNG shift," indicating thereby observable shifts in the person, number, and gender of verbal and pronominal forms.

Contextual clues can further help interpreters assign discourse to speakers, but in the end, much ambiguity remains. The composer's choice not to mark speaking subjects reflects more than laconic writing or thoughtless editing.[52] It emerges as a characteristic feature of the poetic discourse in Jeremiah that highlights the prophet's affective, intersubjective entanglement with God, people, and even place. In this discourse, the sorrow, frustration, anger, and longing of God, Israel, Jerusalem, and Jeremiah blend and bleed into one another. This discourse constructs the prophet's body as a critical node for the intersecting affective experience and practice of God, people, city, and land.

A second, related feature of poetic discourses in the book of Jeremiah is a layered or concentric structure in which the speech of one party is nested within or interlocked with the speech of another. Consistent with the pattern noted above, the speaker of each speech-layer may be named or unnamed. This layering and variable attribution pattern constructs a dynamic, multi-party, interactive dialogue with permeable boundaries. Speakers and addressees may include figures past and present. In the process, the reader or hearer is also drawn into dialogue. In this dynamic dialogue, according to Oliver Glanz, no party is simply an observer and no party can rest, for each participant in the dialogue may be drawn in unexpectedly at any moment.[53] The intersubjective and inter-affective character of Jeremiah's speeches and dialogues is thus seen to be responsive, dynamic, and demanding, manifesting not only the relationality among the characters within the book but also between these characters and the audience.

Weeping, Lament, and Supplication

In the book of Jeremiah, one set of affective practices stands out in sharpest relief: weeping and lament.[54] Jeremiah's own weeping and lament so defined

---

[52] I acknowledge that these features of the text are in part a result of a complex compositional and editorial history, but I am interested here in the effects they produce and the understandings of prophecy and prophetic experience they construct. For studies that foreground the relation between this compositional history and the meanings produced by the text's composite form, see, e.g., Stulman, *Order Amid Chaos*; Biddle, *Polyphony and Symphony*.

[53] Glanz, *Participant-Reference Shifts*, 346–7.

[54] For a thought-provoking analysis of Jeremiah's crying in relation to body and gender, see Graybill, *Are We Not Men*, 71–95. Graybill reads the laments in Jer 11–20 by analogy with late nineteenth- and early twentieth-century studies of hysteria, arguing that "the prophet's use of sound defies the normative association of male voices and bodies" (*Are We Not Men*, 92; see also 72, 78–9). I am not persuaded, however, that the practice of lament is *not* a normatively male practice in the HBOT. While certain cultural practices of lament are associated with women's ritual performance

the portrait of his prophetic ministry in this book that tradents of another book, Lamentations, identified Jeremiah as singer of its poetic laments over the desolation of Jerusalem.[55] In its incipit, the Old Greek version of Lamentations supplies the narrative detail that "Ieremias sat [ἐκάθισεν] weeping [κλαίων] and lamented" (Lam 1:1a OG). In this narrative introduction, Jeremiah's seated posture draws the prophet down to the earth, the ruins, and the piles of corpses that the poem depicts as littering the streets of Jerusalem. The incipit further portrays Jeremiah in solidarity with the personified city, who at the poem's beginning sat (ἐκάθισεν) alone (Lam 1:1b). This embodied solidarity with the city Jerusalem finds parallels in the book of Jeremiah. There, weeping and lament are enacted by prophet, people, place, and God, establishing bonds of sympathy, identification, and mutually affecting relationship in the face of disappointment, devastation, and despair.[56]

This mutuality is well supported by studies of behavioral, developmental, and physiological aspects of weeping or crying. Judith Kay Nelson explains that crying is "interactive and relational," and argues that its function in adult humans can be traced to the relationship between infants and caregivers. In this early relationship, crying seeks a response of nurture, such that "crying and caregiving are mutual and intersubjective from the outset."[57] This intersubjectivity manifests not only at the level of conscious attunement, but at a physiological level as well.

Weeping, like other forms of crying, involves multiple bodily systems in the expression or performance of affect. Nelson observes that "Crying can never be approached dualistically: mind and body are always one in the act of shedding emotional tears. At the very least, crying involves five body systems: respiratory, cardiovascular, nervous, musculoskeletal, and

---

(Claassens, "Calling the Keeners"), the prevalence of lament within the psalter, e.g., supports the conclusion that in the HBOT lament was consistent with the performance of normative gender scripts *across* the spectrum of gender identities. Hysteria has frequently been defined with reference to "emotional excess." Implicit in such descriptions is a set of cultural expectations for what is "normal" and what is "excessive." Without detailed analysis of differences across cultural contexts and periods, comparison between the representation of Jeremiah's affective practice and modern discourse about hysteria risks retrojecting cultural expectations and affective scripts proper to one place and time onto another.

[55] Lee argues that Lamentations presents a musical dialogue between a Jeremianic voice and a woman she calls "Jerusalem's poet" (*Singers of Lamentations*).
[56] Mills argues that Jeremiah's "personal state forms an exact copy of the fragmentation and collapse of his community" (*Alterity*, 110–11).
[57] Nelson, *Seeing through Tears*, 19. On infant weeping in the HBOT and other ancient literature, see Bosworth, *Infant Weeping*.

endocrine."[58] Yet crying involves bodily systems of those who witness or hear it as well. Physiological responses that parents exhibit to the cries of their infant include elevated heart rate, diastolic blood pressure, and skin conductance as well as, for some mothers, milk ejection or let-down reflex.[59] With these and other physiological responses in view, Nelson writes, "infant crying goes straight to the parent's nervous system, heart, gut, and blood stream, literally."[60] Varied emotional responses, whether concern and caring or aversion and irritation (or a combination thereof), entail further, distinctive, embodied responses in turn.

Embodied responses to crying are shaped by a wider set of stimuli than just sound. The work of Allan Schore offers a model for understanding further aspects of this embodied interaction. In an analysis of positive mirroring behavior between infants and caregivers, Schore describes a thoroughly embodied, "interactive matrix" of mutual attention and response between infant and caregiver. Through "mutually synchronized attunement of emotionally driven facial expressions, prosodic vocalizations, and kinesic behaviors the dyad coconstructs a mutual regulatory system of arousal" that amplifies and affirms each member of the dyad.[61] While Schore is here focusing on arousal states with "positive valence," his inclusion of facial expression and movement apply equally to crying behavior and response, as does his understanding of a co-constructed "mutual regulatory system."[62]

While the bond between infant and caregiver has unique features not shared among other relationships, this early relationship is evolutionarily and developmentally formative to such a degree that outside of the infant/caregiver relationship, crying in adult humans remains a relational, intersubjective behavior.[63]

What does this mean for Jeremiah, or for study of weeping and lament in prophetic literature more generally? First, the prophet's weeping is not expressive in a strictly individualistic way. Rather, it embodies and effects attunement between prophet and God, people, and place. In so doing, it makes claims on those who hear or witness it.[64] David Bosworth applies Nelson's work on crying to a study of tears in the book of Jeremiah, highlighting

---

[58] Nelson, *Seeing through Tears*, 11.
[59] Nelson, *Seeing through Tears*, 20.
[60] Nelson, *Seeing through Tears*, 20–1.
[61] Schore, *Affect Dysregulation*, 96.
[62] Schore, *Affect Dysregulation*, 96.
[63] Nelson, *Seeing through Tears*, 23–5.
[64] Prophetic weeping may also have other, related functions such as protest and critique.

crying's function as a "social, rather than individual, behavior."[65] Bosworth highlights the desire of the one weeping for "empathy and support" as well as "proximity."[66] In the story of Jeremiah's commissioning, God's assertion that God's relationship with Jeremiah not only encompasses the prophet's infancy but precedes it (Jer 1:5), combined with Jeremiah's emphasis on his young age at the time of his calling, suggests a developmental frame for the relationship between prophet and God akin to that between infant and parent. Within such a frame, prophet and God respond to and resonate with one another, amplify and affirm each other, "coconstruct[ing] a mutual regulatory system of arousal."[67] I argue that this co-constructed system of arousal and intersubjectivity extends beyond the relationship between God and prophet to encompass people and place.

Circulating Lament: Jer 4:8, 4:19–21, and 8:18–21

Three examples of unattributed lament, 4:8, 4:19–21, and 8:18–21, contribute to the book of Jeremiah's construction of intersubjectivity and interaffectivity between prophet, God, people, and place.[68] The first example constructs a relationship between the lament of people and prophet and the anger of God.

> Because of this put on sackcloth,
> lament and wail:
> "The fierce anger of the Lord
> has not turned away from us." (4:8 NRSV; cf. 6:26)

The command in 4:8 combines instructions for embodied practice and for speech. The commanded practice of lament is to include binding ritual clothing to the body (חגרו שקים), howling (הילילו), and other publicly perceptible performances of grief (ספדו). A shift from second-person plural

---

[65] Bosworth, "Tears of God," 25.
[66] Bosworth, "Tears of God," 25.
[67] Schore, *Affect Dysregulation*, 96.
[68] Mills' analysis of the Confessions yields some similar conclusions to the present analysis of the unattributed laments and interdictions. She finds in them "a common theme, namely the fate of the prophet himself and the interlinking of his destiny with that of his fellow citizens and with the profile of the Deity" (*Alterity*, 118).

address to scripted direct speech enjoined upon the audience (cf. 4:5b–4:6a) further constructs the audience as speaker, now using a first-person pronominal form. The prescribed words of lament include explicit recognition of God's own affective state (characterized by anger) and its movement and orientation toward the people. This lament thus names and constructs the complex inter-affectivity of people and God.

Yet the absence of dialogue tags and the use of a first-person plural pronoun produces ambiguity regarding the prophet's own position within the relationship described above. To clarify the possibilities in play, it can be helpful to consider Erving Goffman's deconstruction of the role of "speaker." Goffman identifies three possible roles contained in the broader role of "speaker," namely animator, author, and principal. The "animator" refers to the person (and technology) that physically produces the talk, the person whose mouth moves and voice projects. "Author" reflects intention and design. The author has chosen the content of the utterance and arranged its words. The "principal" is the person or group "whose position is established by the words that are spoken, . . . whose beliefs have been told, . . . who is committed to what the words say."[69] In the example of a political campaign speech, the animator might be the candidate, the author might be a paid speechwriter, and the principal might shift throughout the speech between the candidate as an individual, the party they belong to, a group of voters the candidate seeks to align herself with, and a larger local, state, or national collective.

In the narrative world of 4:8, Jeremiah functions as animator. The identity of the author and principal is less clear. On one hand, this verse may be a continuation of a larger unit in which the dialogue tags "thus says the Lord" attribute the role of author and principal to the Lord (4:1, 3). Alternatively, the phrase "Because of this" may mark a shift in author and principal to Jeremiah himself. In 4:8b, meanwhile, the shift to scripted direct discourse assigns the role of principal to the people. The use of first-person plural within the scripted direct discourse raises a further question: does Jeremiah here include himself among the principals of this lament?

It is possible to construe the layering of discourse in 4:8 in a way that excludes the prophet from the group of addressees, such that the words of

---

[69] Goffman, *Forms of Talk*, 144–5. Goffman is analyzing talk "in real life" rather than literary representations of talk. I apply these categories by analogy to the roles and relationships implied by the structure of dialogue in Jer 4.

lament in 4:8b are understood as the words he enjoins the addressees to say but are not expressive of his own lament. Yet the layering and mixing of second- and first-person speech create a productive ambiguity, simultaneously constructing collective identity and personal distance. Timothy Polk argues that with the first-person pronoun "us" that concludes 4:8,

> the prophet is identifying himself with the people he addresses; ... what threatens them, threatens him. It belongs to his identity that this should be so, for the identification of the prophet with his people is ingredient in the very nature of intermediation and in the prophet's intercessory role in particular.[70]

Yet the shift in principal within the broader unit also creates distance, from the Lord and the people alike. Theodossia-Soula Pavlidou notes that first-person plural pronouns "prototypically index" "relational and collective aspects" of self-identification.[71] In continuous discourse, an indicator of identification with one group can be followed in swift succession by distancing from the first group and identification with another. As in the imagined political speech considered above, the referent of "we" may shift repeatedly throughout, reflecting an "inherent fluidity" in the indexing of self-identifications.[72] Jeremiah's identification with the people thus emerges as one thread in a web of relationships and identifications. Moreover, Jeremiah's identifications with God and people are never total but always entail the possibility of distance from one and identification with the other.[73]

---

[70] Polk, *Prophetic Persona*, 46. In my view, however, Polk is overly dismissive of physical dimensions of Jeremiah's language of "the heart" (as for example in analyzing Jer 4:19 in *Prophetic Persona*, 33–34), as Polk draws too sharp a contrast between emotional/psychic realities and physical, embodied ones.
By contrast with the identification Polk describes here, in the oracles against the nations the prophet typically has a greater affective distance from the addressee. An exception in Jeremiah occurs in the powerful and poignant oracle against Moab: "my heart moans for Moab like a flute, and my heart moans like a flute for the people of Kir-heres" (Jer 48:36 NRSV). In Ezekiel, the prophet is commanded to "raise a lamentation over Pharaoh king of Egypt" (Ezek 32:2) and "wail over the hordes of Egypt" (32:18). Yet throughout this oracle "I" clearly refers to God who brings judgment and "you" clearly refers to Egyptian addressees. There is no slippage or merging in the manner of Jer 4.

[71] Pavlidou, "Constructing Collectivity," 6.

[72] Pavlidou, "Constructing Collectivity," 7.

[73] This alternation of identity and distance is consistent with the liminality Mills attributes to Jeremiah's prophetic role and suffering body (*Alterity*, 112). Jeremiah stands "on the midline between God and people ... because his function is to convey the ultimate border of Otherness for the community, between continuing to exist as a city-state and annihilation by a foreign invader" (Mills, *Alterity*, 116).

The second unit, 4:19–21, is an unattributed lament that seems to actualize the mourning enjoined upon the people in 4:8. Here too a productive ambiguity obtains, this time including poetic identification between prophet and city.[74] As in Jonah 4:1, examined above, so here, MT and OG each contribute in distinctive ways to the portrayal of affect. I thus reproduce 4:19 in Hebrew, Greek, and, for each, English translation, analyze embodied and affective imagery in each version, and then ask, who is the speaker?

מעי מעי אחולה [אוחילה] קירות לבי המה־לי לבי לא אחריש כי קול שופר
שמעתי [שמעת] נפשי תרועת מלחמה

My womb, my womb—I am contracting—the walls of my heart—my heart is roaring at me! I will not be silent, because my throat has heard the voice of a trumpet, a battle alarm.

τὴν κοιλίαν μου τὴν κοιλίαν μου ἀλγῶ καὶ τὰ αἰσθητήρια τῆς καρδίας μου μαιμάσσει ἡ ψυχή μου σπαράσσεται ἡ καρδία μου οὐ σιωπήσομαι ὅτι φωνὴν σάλπιγγος ἤκουσεν ἡ ψυχή μου κραυγὴν πολέμου

My womb! I am hurting in my womb and the senses of my heart. My soul is excited, my heart shakes, I will not be silent, because my soul has heard the voice of a trumpet, a clamor of war.

In the Hebrew text, the opening interjection, repeated twice, interrupts the preceding discourse and draws attention to the body of the one who cries out. NRSV translates this interjection with the affective descriptor, "My anguish, my anguish!" and NJPS similarly renders it as "Oh, my suffering, my suffering!" (4:19). Yet the Hebrew word מעה and corresponding Greek translation κοιλία refer to the internal organs associated with the belly, including stomach and womb (cf. Jonah 2:1). The phrasing is indeed affectively charged. It is also vividly embodied (cf. NAB's translation, "my body, my body!"). The speaker identifies the vital organs in the softest, most vulnerable part of their body as the focal point of a pain that now grips the speaker in response to collective disaster.

---

[74] Marjo Korpel makes this argument in part by adducing evidence of ancient unit-delimitation from Septuagint and Vulgate versions. Once v. 22 is included in the speech-unit, the speaker's voice is more readily identified as the city's (Korpel, "Who is Speaking?").

Old Greek translates the subsequent verb as an expression of the speaker's feeling of pain; this pain overtakes not only the organs of the soft belly but also the "faculties" or senses of the heart, seat of perception and cognition. An eager quivering in the speaker's soul conveys the difficulty of self-restraint and is matched by a tearing open of their heart, suggesting that something is about to break forth.

In MT, by comparison, the speaker next describes the pairing of contraction and movement denoted by the verb חיל (here, "I am contracting"; NRSV, NAB, and NJPS translate "I writhe"). This verb frequently denotes the active labor of women giving birth (e.g., Jer 6:24; 22:23; 50:43; cf. Jer 4:31), suggesting (in a manner similar to OG) that the speaker's body labors to open to a new, emergent reality. Such labor is dangerous work, again marking a moment of vulnerability. MT then portrays the speaker's heart in architectural terms: it is walled, perhaps connoting constriction and confinement, but, in light of the preceding imagery, perhaps also suggesting that something is about to break through the confinement of its walls. This heart growls or moans: its audible reverberations turn speaker into an audience who must listen to the complaint of their own organs.[75]

In both MT and OG, as a result of this opening and breaking forth, the speaker will not or cannot remain silent. The next detail draws attention to the speaker's auditory sense, which is assaulted by the sound of a war-trumpet. Hebrew idiom produces catachresis in which the throat hears and is thus primed to respond in kind. The consequent announcement of disaster and the question "how long ... ?" (Jer 4:20–21) verbalize and give shape to the lament that has welled up within the speaker and overwhelmed their body.

Who, then, is the speaker who will not be silent? A lack of dialogue tags in the MT and OG versions of this passage makes it difficult to discern who is the speaker. Targum Jeremiah remedies this lack by explicitly identifying the prophet as speaker (אמר נביא). Polk, following numerous other interpreters, likewise attributes these verses to the prophet, but he links the prophet's lament to that of the people. For Polk, the prophet here undertakes the lament that the people are not yet capable of performing, enacting on their behalf and modeling for them a practice they must re-learn and do in order to be re-formed as God's people.[76] In a similar vein, Louis Stulman understands

---

[75] Schroer and Staubli interpret this verse as describing a heart attack (*Body Symbolism*, 42).
[76] Polk, *The Prophetic Persona*, 47. Others who identify the lamenting speaker as Jeremiah include Heschel, *Prophets*, 120; Lundbom, *Jeremiah 1–20*.

Jeremiah to be the speaker and subject of 4:19–21, noting that through his cry "he becomes the people's voice and their strong ally."[77]

Yet the lack of dialogue tags opens space for other interpretations. Based in part on the speaker's lament for "my tents" and the use of imagery of a woman in labor (cf. 4:31), Christl Maier argues that the speaker of 4:19–21 is Zion (cf. 6:24).[78] Applying the method of unit delimitation, Marjo Korpel arrives at the same conclusion.[79] And while Stulman identifies the speaker of 4:19–21 as Jeremiah, he argues that the divine first person pronoun at the beginning of v. 22 closely links the distress of the prophet (and people) to that of God: "Both Yahweh and Jeremiah are distraught over the people's wound."[80]

We might then answer the question, "who is the speaker?" in this way: lack of dialogue tags, layering of discourse, structure, word choice, and context together create an ambiguity that cannot be resolved.[81] As a result, the lament belongs equally to each of these possible principals, circulating between them, creating what Sara Ahmed calls an "affective economy" of lament. In Ahmed's terms, the sorrow of this lament does not "positively inhabit *anybody* or *anything*, meaning that 'the subject' is simply one nodal point in the economy, rather than its origin and destination."[82] In the book of Jeremiah pain does not *belong* to any one character. The lament's opening words ask for attention to the effects of this suffering in the most vulnerable parts of the speaker's body, but the pain is not static. The labor of lament contracts the bodies of prophet, God, people, and place, even as it prepares to push through walls. The catachreses of a hearing throat and a roaring heart give expression to the shocking and unsettling dynamism of a circulating sorrow that is responsive, transmissible, and shared.[83]

---

[77] Stulman, *Jeremiah*, 70.

[78] Korpel, "Who is Speaking?"; Maier, "Klage der Tochter Zion."

[79] Korpel ("Who is Speaking?" 89) acknowledges that "a prophet may identify himself with his people while using the first person singular," but argues that unit delimitation does not support identifying Jeremiah as speaker in this instance.

[80] Stulman, *Jeremiah*, 70. Stulman argues that the prophet Jeremiah "embodies a new spirituality and ethic" for audiences within the book and those who engage with it (*Jeremiah*, 35).

[81] Cf. the analysis of Hildebrandt, who argues that the ambiguity "compels the reader to hear the mourning of prophet, city, and God *all at once*—an acoustic panorama, a tri-dimensional lament, a cumulative response to the historical disaster of enemy takeover" ("Whose Voice?" 204).

[82] Ahmed, *Cultural Politics*, 46.

[83] Runions writes that "the ambivalences of a prophetic text like Jeremiah create openness to the contradictory possibilities of affect, in ways that might move people and thought beyond the expected" ("Prophetic Affect," 242).

218   THE PROPHETIC BODY

A third example of unattributed lament occurs at 8:18–21. An unidentified speaker declares,

> My joy is gone, grief is upon me, my heart is sick.
> Hark, the cry of my poor people
> From far and wide in the land:
> "Is the Lord not in Zion?
> Is her King not in her?"
> ("Why have they provoked me to anger with their images,
> With their foreign idols?")
> "The harvest is past, the summer is ended, and we are not saved."
> For the hurt of my poor people I am hurt,
> I mourn, and dismay has taken hold of me.
> Is there no balm in Gilead? Is there no physician there?
> Why then has the health of my poor people not been restored?
> O that my head were a spring of water,
> And my eyes a fountain of tears,
> So that I might weep day and night
> For the slain of my poor people. (Jer 8:18 – 9:1 NRSV)

The pericope concludes with a sentence that might be construed as a wish ("would that my head were water . . . ") or a question ("who will make my head water . . . ?").[84] This poetic imagery transforms the entire head, a body part symbolic of governance and authority and determinative of one's spatial orientation, into the very substance that gives bodily expression to grief.[85] Water brings with it associations of cleansing, purifying, source of life, and stimulus for growth, suggesting catharsis and a possibility of a new beginning.[86] The homology between eyes that weep and a fountain of water enables the poet to portray a seemingly inexhaustible grief that surpasses bodily limitations. A question remains: Whose grief does it describe?

---

[84] OG preserves the rhetorical question "who . . . ?" but interprets the idiom נתן ל literally as "give to" rather than expressing transformation, yielding the translation, "who will give water to my head, and a fountain of tears to my eyes?" that is, who will supply head and eyes with sufficient water to express the speaker's grief.
[85] On the symbolism of the "head," see Schroer and Staubli, *Body Symbolism*, 83–5.
[86] On the symbolism of such homology, see Patton and Hawley, "Introduction," 16. They further note the associations between tears, cleansing water, and repentance (Patton and Hawley, "Introduction," 16).

Kathleen O'Connor identifies the implied speaking subject of this vivid lament as God.[87] As O'Connor notes, the exclamation expresses a wish contrary to fact: "God wishes to become water," but none can effect this transformation on God's behalf. O'Connor finds in this passage an invitation to the people: God's vulnerability and desire to weep without ceasing summons God's people to an embodied response to pain and trauma that signals the re-emergence of feeling and recovery of affectivity.[88] Such an expression of vulnerability is a necessary step toward the healing of their wound.

Others identify the speaking subject as the prophet Jeremiah or recognize the merging of prophetic and divine subjectivity and embodied affect. David Bosworth, for example, argues that "In this passage, YHWH and Jeremiah both weep over the impending doom of the people as Jeremiah embodies the tears of YHWH in his own weeping."[89] In a similar vein, Terence Fretheim argues that Jer 8:18–9:1, along with 4:19, evinces "the prophet's embodiment of God's mourning."[90] Fretheim discerns a symbiosis between divine and prophetic mourning, which we might view as analogous to the mirroring, affirming, and amplifying attunement described by Schore, considered earlier in this chapter. The lament thus gives voice to the anguish of God and prophet alike, allowing the prophet to visibly and audibly manifest God's response to the pain, confusion, and sickness of God's people.[91] At the same time, the people's confusion and despair is also given voice, highlighting the intersubjectivity not only of God and prophet but also of God and people and prophet and people.[92] Divine and prophetic tears mirror the people's own despair, enacting solidarity, sympathy, and connection between them even in the face of inevitable and irreparable loss.

The discourse of these passages weaves together the affective practices and performances of people, place, prophet, and God, portraying a complex web of identification and inter-affectivity. Ambiguity and fluidity replicate for users of the text the destabilizing effects of shared grief in the face of anger, ruptured relationship, confusion, and loss, while also inviting the audience to participate in lament.

---

[87] O'Connor, "Tears of God and Divine Character"; see also O'Connor, *Jeremiah: Pain and Promise*, 62–3.
[88] O'Connor, *Jeremiah: Pain and Promise*, 63.
[89] Bosworth, "Tears of God," 34.
[90] Fretheim, *Suffering of God*, 160.
[91] Fretheim, *Suffering of God*, 161.
[92] See Stulman, *Jeremiah*, 100.

Interdictions

The inter-affectivity of God and prophet lies behind the repeated interdiction against Jeremiah's mediatorial affective practice. On three occasions God forbids Jeremiah to make supplication for the people of Judah (7:16; 11:14; 14:11). "As for you, do not pray for this people, do not raise a cry or prayer on their behalf, and do not intercede with me, for I will not hear you" (7:16 NRSV). Divine anger has led to a plan for destruction that eschews dialogue or mercy (7:16, 20; 11:14b, 17; 14:12). God's refusal to listen suggests that Jeremiah's supplication and lament would be efficacious. Kimberley Patton and John Hawley's observation about tears applies equally to the forbidden "cry" (רנה): "Often tears seem an expression of surrender before the inexorable, but myth and tradition repeatedly point in the opposite direction, stressing the view that weeping can actually transform what had seemed fixed forever."[93] Such tears or crying out may function theurgically, forming a bridge to the divine, drawing attention, seeking a response, and eliciting mercy. They might also voice protest and frame critique.[94] God's injunction against Jeremiah's affective practices of supplication and crying is here not about conserving the prophet's emotional and physical energies but aims to prevent the prophet from making a claim on God's mercy and drawing forth God's compassion for the people God has determined to destroy.[95] As Louis Stulman notes: "Jeremiah must do nothing to mitigate the sting of God's stance against the nation."[96]

This prohibition of supplication does not eliminate the possibility of lament. Following the first interdiction, even as Jeremiah is forbidden to make supplication to God, God nonetheless instructs the prophet to lament and perform God's rejection of the people of Judah:

> Cut off your hair and throw it away;
> Raise a lamentation [קינה] on the bare heights,

---

[93] Patton and Hawley, "Introduction," 1.
[94] Patton and Hawley, Introduction," 1–2; Nelson, *Seeing through Tears*, 34–38.
[95] In two passages Jeremiah's prayer and cry is implicitly identified with that of the people: "do not pray ... on their behalf, for I will not listen when they call on me ... " (11:14 NRSV); "do not pray for the welfare of this people. Although they fast, I do not hear their cry ... " (14:11–12 NRSV). The Lord's determination to resist God's own embodied response to prophetic supplication finds further expression at 15:1: "Though Moses and Samuel stood before me, yet my heart would not turn toward this people" (NRSV).
[96] Stulman, *Jeremiah*, 141.

> For the Lord has rejected and forsaken
> the generation that provoked [the Lord's] wrath. (7:29 NRSV)[97]

Why is Jeremiah commanded to lament when he is forbidden to intercede? Saul Olyan distinguishes four types of mourning in the Hebrew Bible: mourning for the dead, petitionary mourning (including penitence), non-petitionary response to "personal or communal disaster," and the isolating mourning of a person afflicted with skin-disease.[98] Prohibition of the prophet's intercessory cry thus does not preclude the performance of lament: the forbidden intercessory cry is an example of petitionary mourning, while the commanded lament is a non-petitionary response to communal disaster. They are closely related but not identical practices.

Olyan suggests that non-petitionary mourning in the face of disaster "aims to mark the calamity" and "serve as a way to express sorrow and horror."[99] Through the ritual behavior of lament and conventionalized modifications to physical appearance, it also "mark[s] those affected by the disaster off from others who are unaffected, and create[es] a ritual context in which they can enact and communicate their sorrow, shame, and personal or corporate diminishment."[100] In the lament commanded in Jer 7:29, poetic parallelism suggests that the bare head of the prophet mirrors the desolation that will come upon the land, while discarding the hair from his head mirrors the Lord's rejection of the people. Jeremiah will thus embody the Lord's rejection of the people, the death decreed for them, and the land's imminent devastation.

How might this performance of divine rejection, ritualized through embodied practices of mourning, including a funeral song, function for the prophet's audiences? Patton and Hawley argue that public, ritual weeping relates to individual expressions of grief in complex ways. Responding to collective trauma with the "work" of lament or weeping can "provide an outlet for depths of grief that might otherwise be overwhelming both to individuals and the communities in which they gather."[101] Beyond providing an outlet, ritual lament may help a community accept the reality of death and move toward connection and healing. It can also effect an "unbinding," a letting

---

[97] Stulman argues, however, that the addressee is Zion (*Jeremiah*, 95).
[98] Olyan, *Biblical Mourning*, 25–6.
[99] Olyan, *Biblical Mourning*, 26.
[100] Olyan, *Biblical Mourning*, 98.
[101] Patton and Hawley, "Introduction," 9. On the work of weeping women in Jeremiah, see Claassens, "Calling the Keeners."

go of a force or circumstance that has exerted pressure upon the community.[102] The explanation immediately following God's command to Jeremiah suggests that the circumstance that must now be "let go" or indeed rejected by the people includes child sacrifice in the valley of Ben-Hinnom, which is soon to be called the "Valley of Slaughter" (7:30–34). Jeremiah's commanded performance of divine rejection and funeral lament invites the Judahite community to grieve both the children they have killed and the devastation God will bring upon them and their land as a result, even as it hints at the possibility that this people will let go of their practices of child sacrifice and even now come together to heal as a community and repair the ruptures in their relationship with God, land, and one another.

Just as the first injunction against supplication is followed by a divine command to perform lament, so following the third injunction against praying for the people's welfare (14:11) Jeremiah is commanded to voice a lament for the people's wound:

> You shall say to them this word:
> Let my eyes run down with tears night and day, [103]
> and let them not cease,
> for the virgin daughter—my people—
> is struck down with a crushing blow,
> with a very grievous wound. (14:17 NRSV)

The lament that follows (14:19–22) includes confession of sins and hope in God, even as it interrogates God's feelings and actions toward Judah and Zion. As in 4:8, 4:19–21, and 8:18–9:1, analyzed earlier in this chapter, the identity of the principal(s) in 14:17–22 is not entirely clear. For J. A. Thompson, the words remain Jeremiah's, "who identified himself with the nation and confessed guilt on their behalf."[104] If this interpretation is correct, then the prophet is not deterred by the Lord's interdiction and instead persists in interceding for the people. Stulman offers a similar interpretation, stating that "Jeremiah refuses to acquiesce and relinquish his role as advocate for Israel."[105] Yet Stulman also observes that in this passage "the voices

---

[102] Nelson, *Seeing through Tears*, 35; Patton and Hawley, "Introduction," 1.
[103] On the role of tears in lament, see Lynch, "Ritual Tears." She writes, "Tears are as much a part of the syntax of lament as words" ("Ritual Tears," 68).
[104] Thompson, *Book of Jeremiah*, 386.
[105] Stulman, *Jeremiah*, 141.

of grief are so intertwined that any sharp distinction between Jeremiah and God risks misrepresenting the text."[106] Prophetic and divine lament thus merge into one, while simultaneously exhibiting a responsive dialogism that highlights the intersubjectivity of prophet, God, and people.

In a final instance of interdiction, God makes of Jeremiah a model and portent of the people's future affective practice. God forbids Jeremiah to marry or father children (Jer 16:2). Opening his life to marriage and children would mean forming social bonds of attachment in a place and community where death has been decreed. It would also entail communal celebration, but God has determined to "banish from this place, in your days and before your eyes, the voice of mirth and the voice of gladness, the voice of the bridegroom and the voice of the bride" (16:9 NRSV). God banishes not only the expression of joy, but the social connections formed through family-making, shared celebration, and communal grieving. For Stulman, this prohibition "symbolizes the end of community life as it was known. Jeremiah is to reveal in his body the woeful destruction of structured life, Judah's hour of darkness."[107] Jeremiah's personal asceticism and detachment is to be matched by a public moratorium on rites of burial, lament, and sitting, eating, and drinking with the bereaved. Prohibiting these embodied forms of social connection in the midst of grief and loss imposes a detachment upon and among the people that matches that imposed on the prophet and prevents the shared "work" of mourning that facilitates acceptance, comfort, and healing.[108]

These interdictions will be reversed in Jer 31 (cf. 33:11), in a portion of the book commonly referred to as the "little book of consolation." Where previously consolation and celebration were banished, now the people are to "keep your voice from weeping, and your eyes from tears" (31:16), not to prevent appeal to God's mercy (31:7), but because God has already promised reward (31:16). God's love for the survivors among God's people is a cause for their hope, gladness, and joy (31:3, 7, 13, 17).[109] Their future will hold the music of tambourines and "the dance of the merrymakers" (31:4b NRSV; cf. 31:13), and the people are now commanded to engage in activities that were previously forbidden, to raise a cry, sing and shout, and make supplication to the Lord (31:7). The Lord, meanwhile, now provides the very comfort, consolation, and nourishment the people had been forbidden to provide one another

---

[106] Stulman, *Jeremiah*, 144.
[107] Stulman, *Jeremiah*, 162.
[108] See Nelson, *Seeing through Tears*, 35.
[109] Stulman calls this love "the force behind God's act of renewal" (*Jeremiah*, 267).

(31:9a, 13, 25). On this occasion, the prophet "sees" this future from the intimate distance of a dream, a complex form of sight in which the observer may also be a participant. Jeremiah wakes and declares his sleep "pleasing" or "sweet" (31:26), hinting at a future consolation for the prophet as well.[110]

The frequent omission of dialogue tags and dynamic alternations among speakers in the book of Jeremiah contributes to the construction of a complex web of intersubjectivity and inter-affectivity. The performance of lament is seen to be relational, occurring within a "mutual regulatory system of arousal" that includes prophet, God, people, and place. Jeremiah's self-identification with the people allows him to participate in, model, and anticipate the laments of the people and Zion. The Lord's interdictions against Jeremiah's petitionary mourning further highlight the prophet's stake in the people's sorrow and the affective attunement between God and prophet. Although Jeremiah's function as animator and (at times) co-principal of divine speech also distances him from people and place, his experience of the dream vision in 31:26 locates him among those who will be consoled, emphasizing once more his self-identification and solidarity with the people of Judah.

Conclusion

Affect and emotion are central components of prophetic experience and mediation. Because affect is a biologically, socially, and culturally complex phenomena, my approach to the analysis of prophetic affect is eclectic, drawing insight from three interrelated fields: psychology and neurocognition, social science, and cultural studies. An understanding of affect and emotion's contribution to action-readiness, decision-making, and behavior; the concepts of collaborative affective practice; the circulation of affect and emotion; and affect's transformative social and political power provide a robust framework for analyzing the role of affect and emotion in prophetic mediation.

In the first chapter of Jonah, a disjuncture between human fear and divine desire identifies affect as site of tension and transformation. Jonah's psalm traces an affective arc from anxiety to gratitude but remains focused on his own journey from death to life. The fish he ignores in his prayer pukes him out, giving him a second chance at aligning his affect and the scope of his concern more closely with God's. In the book's third chapter, it is neither Jonah's

---

[110] The same collocation appears in Prov 3:24, where it is associated with absence of fear.

nor the fish's affect that occupies center-stage, but that of the Ninevites, who respond to Jonah's prophetic proclamation with a set of affective practices that display humility, dependence, and grief and mark their commitment to transformed patterns of behavior. The practices that mark and embody their transformation elicit a corresponding affective, volitional, and behavioral reversal from God, who accordingly abandons God's prior plan for their destruction. The book's final chapter shifts attention once again to the prophet's affect, using the device of dialogue with God to underscore that Jonah's affect is not merely private but is central to his mediating role as prophet. God's interactions with Jonah resemble modern-day rational emotive behavioral therapy (REBT), a therapeutic technique that uses dialogue to prompt reflection that leads to revising of attitudes, beliefs, and appraisals. God counters Jonah's anger and pain by calling Jonah's attention to Jonah's experience of joy and his expanding scope of concern. In so doing, God invites Jonah to perceive the analogy between the prophet's affective experience and God's. That is, God's pedagogical practice is not simply therapeutic. It aims to establish affective attunement between prophet and God.

The book of Jeremiah amplifies the portrayal of affective attunement but also portrays a more complex intersubjectivity that entails affective entanglement. The book's discourse constructs Jeremiah's body as a node of circulating affect between God, people, and even place. Two devices, the frequent omission of dialogue tags and the concentric or layered structure of discourse, draw the reader or hearer into an experience of dynamic dialogue that is richly interactive and intersubjective. Analysis of the book's most characteristic affective practices, weeping and lament, emphasized their social and embodied character. Unattributed laments in Jer 4:8, 4:19–21, and 8:18–21 articulate a responsive, circulating sorrow that is transmitted and shared between the bodies of prophet, God, people, and place. In so doing these unattributed laments construct solidarity and connection even in the face of rupture and loss. Divine interdictions against Jeremiah's intercession for the people further emphasize the attunement between prophet and God: God prohibits the prophet's supplication because God is moved by it. Yet even when he is forbidden to intercede, Jeremiah's affective practice variously performs divine rejection, models the people's ritual lament, and portends the future interruption of their shared work of mourning. Conversely, the reversal of interdiction and prophetic experience of sweet sleep in Jer 31 enfold the prophet into a vision of divine love and mercy that elicit consolation and joy expressed and transmitted through practices of dancing, percussion, shouting, and singing.

10
Devastation and Wonder

The synergy of word and body takes on further contours in the affective practices of Ezekiel and Daniel. The prophet who swallows the scroll absorbs into his body words of divine wrath and human sorrow, transforming body and word alike. Prophet becomes recipient, bearer, and performer of revelation across spatial distance, realms of being, rupture and repair, ending and beginning. Chapter 9 introduced a multidisciplinary methodological framework for the study of prophetic affect and emotion and analyzed affective attunement and entanglement in the books of Jonah and Jeremiah. While Jeremiah's prophetic experience is characterized by an excess of intersecting and overlapping subjectivities, Ezekiel's affect interacts with that of God and people from a greater distance. There is less focus on the interplay of affect between Ezekiel and God and a greater variety of affective interactions between Ezekiel and the people. Ezekiel's affective practices variously contrast, mirror, counteract, portray, presage, and shape those of the people to whom he is sent. These affective labors work *across* distances to manifest and inaugurate the future ordained by God. In the book of Daniel, the interdependence of affect and revelation helps expand our understanding of mediation. In the book's first half, Daniel's affective experience and practice of wonder help to open a pathway for the affective transformation and education of the king he serves. In the book's second half, the portrayal of Daniel's fear and paralysis in the face of revelation invites identification not from a king but from the book's audience. An angel mediates to Daniel—and the text mediates to the audience—affective experiences of divine favor and fortitude that are themselves part of the book's revelation.

Ezekiel: Devastated and Devastating

The book of Ezekiel opens with a report of a vision of the divine throne-chariot. In this vision report, the prophet is the subject of only three different verbs: "I saw" (1:1, 4, 15, 27, 28), "I heard" (1:24, 28), and "I fell" (1:28). That is, Ezekiel's sensory perceptions of the Lord's glory, both visual and auditory, culminate in one embodied response of humility, submission, reverence, and supplication: "I fell on my face" (1:28). Ezekiel exhibits this same response to the Lord's glory at 3:23, 43:3, and 44:4. In three of these instances (2:3; 3:27; 44:6), Ezekiel is subsequently commissioned to speak to the "rebellious house" of Israel. The prophet's somatic performance of submission and reverence thus contrasts with the affective practices of the people to whom he is sent.[1]

This contrastive affective practice generates an oppositional intimacy exemplified in Ezekiel's commissioning narrative, examined in part in Chapter 4. At the time of his prophetic commissioning, the prophet is told,

> And you, mortal, do not be afraid of them and do not be afraid of their words, because thorns and briars accompany you and you sit among scorpions. Of their words, do not be afraid, and by their faces do not be dismayed, because they are a house of rebellion. (Ezek 2:6)

Spiky hedges and venomous arachnids can here be interpreted either as a protective barrier between prophet and people or as a metaphor for the painful but (usually) nonfatal stings of their rejection.[2] But closer analysis highlights a further dimension of the relationship between prophet and people: the sharp point of the thorn, the spiny trichomes of bramble bushes, and the scorpion's stinger all pierce the skin.[3] They get under the surface and inject irritants into the body. They often do so even when a person tries to avoid them. Together they symbolize barriers and opposition as well as persistence, stickiness, and subtlety; they are also sharp, penetrating, and destabilizing. Whether the people are trying to get under his skin or God promises that he will get under theirs is unclear. But the pairing of an emphatic, threefold injunction against fear with three images of oppositional, persistent, and piercing intimacy highlights the dangerous and painful dance between

---

[1] Elsewhere, Ezekiel's falling accompanies an act of supplication (9:8; 11:13). On the contrast between Ezekiel and people, see also Graybill, *Are We Not Men*, 103–4.

[2] While the latter is the more common interpretation, Odell finds this "unlikely" (*Ezekiel*, 40) and argues that "it is more appropriate to understand the second half of the verse as the reason why Ezekiel should not be afraid" (*Ezekiel*, 43). For Odell, Ezekiel himself "possesses the qualities of briers and thorns and can therefore ward off any attack"; further, "he is nestled among the thorns of Yahweh's enveloping care" (*Ezekiel*, 43).

[3] For the argument that "scorpion" refers here to a plant rather than an animal, see Garfinkel, "Thistles and Thorns," 430–5.

people and prophet. They are two parts of an untamed ecosystem, organically connected to, dependent on, and susceptible to one another.

The injunction against fear is followed by a command not to be "dismayed" (Ezek 2:6; repeated at 3:9). Yet this command, אל־תחת, can also be translated "do not break," prescribing for the prophet an affective posture and practice, what Pierre Bourdieu calls "bodily *hexis*," that correspond to the divine commissioning and transformation of the prophet.[4] Using repetition, reversal, and wordplay (cf. Isa 7:9b), the compound command "do not fear . . . and do not break" enjoins equanimity and courage while rejecting bodily and psychic fragility.[5] In so doing, it circumscribes prophetic affect and underscores the link between the prophet's emotional experience, physical state, and mission. In this shared ecosystem, rather than break, the prophet must transform and adapt. To this end, botanical and zoological imagery will harden into strongest mineral.

This portion of Ezekiel's commissioning story shares two key features with Jeremiah's, introducing what Lauren Berlant refers to as "affective citation" between these prophetic books:[6] both are commanded not to be dismayed or not to break (Ezek 2:6; Jer 1:17) before the face of the people to whom they are sent and both are transformed into mineral by the Lord in order to withstand their adversaries. In Jeremiah's case, his transformation into an iron pillar and wall of bronze would convey a strength (cf. Deut 33:25 and Jer 15:12) to match and resist the destructive force of his enemies (Jer 6:28). Ezekiel's transformation similarly mirrors a quality of the people to whom he is sent in order that he may oppose or withstand them. They are "impudent and stubborn" (Ezek 2:4) and "rebellious" (2:5, 6, 7, 8; 3:9; cf. 2:3), and while Ezekiel is commanded not to be rebellious like them (2:8), yet God transforms his face and forehead to be "like the hardest stone, harder than flint" (3:9 NRSV), in order to be "hard against their faces . . . hard against their foreheads" (3:8 NRSV). This transformation heralds and makes possible embodied engagement between Ezekiel and his audience.[7] Face and forehead metonymically

---

[4] Bourdieu, *Outline of a Theory of Practice*, 93.

[5] In Jeremiah's case, the same command adumbrates the prophet's architectural transformation (Jer 1:18). For Jeremiah, the negative command is accompanied by a threat: if the prophet is dismayed before the inhabitants of the land (named in 1:14), if the prophet "breaks," God will in turn "dismay," "break," or "shatter" (אחתך) the prophet before them (1:17b). That is, if the prophet fails to maintain the affective disposition or *hexis* commanded by God, God will apply such emotive and percussive force to the person of the prophet as to render him incapable of performing his commission.

[6] Berlant, "Poor Eliza," 647.

[7] Graybill, by contrast, observes that "the promised transformation of Ezekiel's body . . . never seems to occur" (*Are We Not Men*, 104). Graybill interprets Ezekiel's sitting in 3:15 as reflecting a passive state. I offer a different interpretation later in this chapter.

represent this encounter's affective dimensions. Silvan Tomkins emphasized the unique role of the face in expressing affect to others and to self.[8] Building on Tomkins work, Mark Hansen adds that the face invites interaction and elicits affective responses from those who see it. This inter-affective role of the face operates across media precisely because it taps into bodily affective processes in the viewer.[9] Hansen's analysis suggests that Ezekiel's facial transformation does not simply allow him to butt his head against the people's like a ram. Rather, he becomes a mirror, reflecting back to the people he will address the very face they have presented to God. In so doing, he elicits an affective response from them in turn. That is, Ezekiel embodies their impudence, stubbornness, and rebellion in order to reflect, redirect, and reshape their affective practice (43:10–11).[10]

Ezekiel experiences a further transformation during his commissioning which will render him not only a mirror of the people's present affect but also a portent of their future affect. The hardening of Ezekiel's forehead to match the stubbornness of the people is preceded by a command to eat a scroll bearing the words "dirges and moaning and lamentation" (Ezek 2:10). One of these grief-words occurs elsewhere in Ezekiel; the other two do not. "Dirge" (קינה) occurs more times in Ezekiel than it does in all other biblical books combined.[11] It names a poetic and musical genre publicly performed so that a community may mark together the experience of death and misfortune. The קינה is thought by many to be characterized by a "limping" meter that replicates the dragging imbalance of grief; the embodied weakness and instability of sorrow is thus formalized and performed in song.[12] The second word, "moaning" (הגה), is less common. Rather than a genre label, it denotes

---

[8] Tomkins, *Affect, Imagery, Consciousness*, 1.113–33.
[9] Hansen, "Affect as Medium," 207, 214, 224.
[10] Indeed, on the final occasion of Ezekiel's falling (43:3), the prophet's posture of humility and submission, with face turned toward the ground, presages and models the affective outcome the Lord envisions for Ezekiel's prophetic mission: the Lord desires that the description of the new temple (43:10), filled with the Lord's glory (43:4), will elicit in Ezekiel's audience shame for their sins and, as a result of their shame, conformity with the ordinances and plan the Lord has laid out for it (43:11). See further Carvalho, "Finding a Treasure Map." Carvalho defines the shame the Lord seeks to elicit as "the recognition of the abuse of privilege that comes from an inadequate recognition of the true goal of worship" ("Finding a Treasure Map," 146). Consistent with the argument here, Carvalho notes that "what Ezekiel calls 'shame' is close to what Christian tradition calls the virtue 'humility'" ("Finding a Treasure Map," 147). See also Lapsley, "Shame and Self-Knowledge."
[11] It occurs three times as a genre-label for the lament over the princes of Israel in Ezek 19 (19:1, 14), four times in reference to Tyre (26:17; 27:2, 32; 28:12), and twice with reference to the lament over Pharaoh/Egypt (32:2, 16).
[12] The classic study of the *qinah* meter is Budde, "Hebräische Klagelied." The proposed characteristic meter is challenged by Hoop, "Lamentations."

a wordless but audible expression of grief, pain, or frustration marked by a constricted throat and slow but forceful passage of air across vocal cords. If the dirge denotes an artful literary and musical expression of grief intended for public ritual performance, the moan precedes art and bypasses reflection. In so doing, it also makes a different, more forceful claim on its hearer: it does not perform a shared grief but expresses an individual's pain and need.[13] The third word, הי, occurs only here in the corpus of the Hebrew Bible, making its meaning less certain, but it is possible to interpret it as an interjection.[14] If an interjection, the word on the page (soon to be in Ezekiel's stomach) does not name the thing, but is the thing. An interjection is a "functional noise" that typically conveys emotion.[15] Studies suggest that the shorter an interjection, the greater its emotional valence.[16] Its abrupt immediacy attempts to interrupt the hearers' state and yank them into that of the speaker.

In eating these three words, the prophet incorporates into his body a divine decree that summons into being diverse modalities of grieving.[17] They include ritualized communal practice, pre-reflective expression, and an interruptive appeal for emotional recognition and connection. Their combination suggests more than ornamental pleonasm. Rather, the grief God has ordained for the people will manifest in different registers, from the most basic of audible expressions to the most complex of social forms, interrupting the states and rhythms of life as the people know it and joining them to each other in the shared experience of pain and loss. The people's stubbornness will require from the prophet similarly multimodal affective practice. From the start, then, affective practices are constitutive of Ezekiel's prophetic ministry, as he assimilates into his body both the words of the decree and the practices they name.

The sense of taste mediates and expresses Ezekiel's conflicted experience of this incorporated commission: he finds the words sweet in his mouth (3:3; cf. Jer 15:16), like honey. This sweetness suggests that the scroll is satisfying and life-giving, contributing to survival. "Affect of taste" has been shown to be biologically "hard-wired" in human beings. Jacob Steiner's studies of infant

---

[13] Pell et al., "Preferential Decoding."
[14] Alternately, it may be an aphaeretic form of the noun נהי, meaning lamentation (GKC §19h).
[15] Stange, Acquisition of Interjections, 17.
[16] Stange, Acquisition of Interjections, 38.
[17] For the interpretation of the scroll as divine decree, i.e., "not *words* that he must speak but the judgment itself and its consequences," see Odell, "You Are What You Eat," 241–5 (quotation is from p. 244).

facial expressions observed, for example, that "the sweet stimulus leads to a marked relaxation of the face, resembling an expression of 'satisfaction.'"[18] This innate response has the positive function of disposing humans to eat nutritional foods that will contribute to growth and well-being. In the same way, bitter taste-stimuli cause infants to stick out their tongues, spit, and gag. It is theorized that humans evolved this aversive response to help the species avoid ingesting poisons. Both responses thus evolved as an aid to survival.[19]

Yet affect of taste can also be acquired, and both positive and negative affects can be transferred by association from one stimulus to another, particularly when highly charged circumstances accompany the act of eating. To understand Ezekiel's attribution of sweetness to the scroll, we might then look for clues in the circumstances in which he eats it. Meredith Warren includes Ezekiel's eating the scroll in a study of hierophagy, defined as "transformational eating" by which "characters in narrative cross boundaries from one realm to another through ingesting some item from that other realm."[20] Ezekiel's act of eating prepares his body to bridge the distance between heaven and earth, God and people. By eating the scroll, Ezekiel internalizes an external reality from the divine realm and becomes bound to that realm.[21] It is perhaps this binding that Ezekiel experiences as sweet, prompting a transferal of affect from the intimate experience of divine reality to the decree of judgment he ingests. In her analysis, Warren argues that associating an ingested object with a familiar but unexpected taste entails a "reorientation of categories" that attaches meaning to the eaten object.[22] This reorientation aligns with the evaluative conditioning described in studies of affect-transfer. Ezekiel's declaration that the scroll tastes sweet, despite its blandly fibrous material and the sorrowful words it contains, exhibits such a reorientation of affect, categories, and meaning.

Yet Ezekiel's initial act of meaning-making is confounded as he is transported to Tel-Abib by the river Chebar. This journey takes him away from the divine realm and toward the people he must confront. He calls his going "bitter" (מר 3:14). The combination of sweetness and bitterness

---

[18] Bartoshuk and Snyder, "Affect of Taste," 236. Quoted material is from Steiner, "Facial Expressions," 174.
[19] Bartoshuk and Snyder, "Affect of Taste," 237.
[20] This definition is from Warren (*Food and Transformation*, 152), who treats Ezekiel's eating the scroll as an example of hierophagy (*Food and Transformation*, 38, 68).
[21] "Food from another world, when eaten, binds the eater to that place" (Warren, *Food and Transformation*, 30).
[22] Warren, *Food and Transformation*, 13.

exemplifies the prophet's liminal status as a mortal gripped by God (3:14) who is transformed by ingesting words of judgment against his own people. Elsewhere in Ezekiel, the adjective "bitter" is associated with lament over another's fate (27:30–31). As Ezekiel travels from the divine to the mortal realm, the suffering in store for his people comes now to the fore. Its bitter aftertaste hints that the judgment he has ingested threatens not only the people's survival but also his own.

Ezekiel's journey to Tel-Abib by the river Chebar is characterized not only by bitterness but also by the "heat" of his spirit (בחמת רוחי Ezek 3:14). This first occurrence of the noun חמה in Ezekiel anticipates a major theme of the book: divine anger. In this book, in twenty-eight out of thirty-three occurrences of חמה, "heat" refers unambiguously to God's anger or wrath. In three instances the "heat" is not directly attributed to God, but God is identified as its cause (16:38; 23:25; 24:8). If we momentarily bracket this first occurrence, we find that every other instance of "heat" in Ezekiel portends destruction. With the exception of 19:12, which occurs in a parable lacking interpretive detail, that destruction is explicitly described as a consequence for violating the will of God. "Heat" in Ezekiel is thus a portent of divine judgment. This first occurrence is the only time in the book that it is explicitly attributed to someone besides the deity. Ezekiel's close linking of the heat of his spirit with the bitterness of his journey demonstrates that his bond with the divine realm is not broken as he journeys earthward. He participates in and contains within himself aspects of divine and human affect simultaneously. The pairing of bitterness and heat also activates another meaning of חמה, namely poison, highlighting the cost to the prophet of carrying divine judgment against his people within his body.

When Ezekiel arrives among the people at Tel-Abib, he sits in their midst, "appalling" or "appalled" (משמים 3:15 MT).[23] The *hiphil* participle מַשְׁמִים attested in MT would ordinarily convey active causation: "devastating," "appalling," that is, causing others to be dumbfounded or desolated (cf. Ezek 20:26; 32:10).[24] Some interpreters have found this meaning inappropriate to the context, however, and propose repointing the consonantal text משמים to yield a *polel* participle, מְשֹׁמֵם, with the stative meaning "appalled,"

---

[23] משמים בתוכם 3:15; OG here has a passive participle, "returned." On the form משמים and its possible range of meanings, see Block, *Ezekiel 1–24*, 137–9. For the interpretation "stunned" as reflecting a mute response to trauma, see Poser, "No Words," 30–2.

[24] GKC classifies this *hiphil* participle among intransitive forms that express action rather than a state (§67 p. 189).

"stunned," or "dumbfounded."[25] Yet the causative form preserved in MT is not out of place. Ezekiel *is* appalling. At various points in the book he will be commanded to engage in actions that portray or elicit specific affective practices on the part of his audience. One of the first such actions he must perform portrays future famine and drought; the Lord's explanation of this action uses the same root, שמם, to describe the people's consequent affect, as they drink "in devastation" (בשממון 4:16) and each person, together with their neighbor, experiences desolation (ונשמו 4:17). In Ezekiel's first prophetic encounter with the people, as he sits for seven days among the exiles, the decree of divine judgment has landed squarely in their midst.[26] His own liminal status and the poisonous verdict he has ingested may well elicit from them a sickening shock and horror that anticipates the desolation God has in store for them.

Later in the book, on three occasions, the Lord explicitly commands Ezekiel to dramatize this future affective experience.[27] Yet this dramatization is not like acting a part. Actors can leave the stage and resume their "normal" life. Ezekiel, bound to two realms, has no normal life. Instead, the prophet who has ingested divine judgment experiences, embodies and presages the traumas his people will experience. This proleptic affective work exacts an increasingly higher cost from the prophet: first he experiences terror, then a crushing of his loins, and finally the loss of his wife.[28]

First, as he eats and drinks, he must quake and tremble, exhibiting in the tension, contractions, and movement of his body the terror and dismay that will accompany the meals of God's people (12:17–19). Quaking and trembling are involuntary manifestations of fear and panic controlled by the autonomic nervous system, which does not respond to conscious effort. That is, Ezekiel cannot fulfill this command by "going through the motions." He must feel terror in order to (involuntarily) manifest it in his body. Such terror

---

[25] See examples in Block, *Ezekiel 1–24*, 138n.32. A close parallel that combines a *qal* form with the action of sitting on the ground occurs in Ezek 26:16.
[26] Note that Odell ("You Are What You Eat") argues that Ezekiel does not take on the role of prophet until after the seven days are completed. This argument responds in part to the perceived problem that Ezekiel has not yet been given words to speak (Odell, "You Are What You Eat," 233). Yet I argue that the prophetic mission includes diverse modalities not limited to words only.
[27] Contrast Ezek 4:12–15, where God grants Ezekiel a concession to prevent defilement.
[28] See detailed treatment of pain in Ezekiel in Mills, *Alterity, Pain, and Suffering*, esp. ch. 4. Mills analyzes the body as a "place of pain" (22) and maps the symbolic relationship between what Ezekiel experiences in his body and what the people must undergo (19), with Ezekiel's suffering "incarnating the severe pain experienced by the community as a whole" (80n54). In an analysis of Ezekiel's physical anguish, Graybill observes that, by contrast with Jeremiah, "Ezekiel never articulates his suffering" (*Are We Not Men*, 108).

displaces the enjoyment, satisfaction, and social bonding commonly associated with eating and drinking. In addition, as blood flow is directed to muscles, it is directed away from the digestive tract. The same activation of the autonomic nervous system that leads to trembling can inhibit the body's ability to digest food, causing "decreased gastric acid secretion, reduced blood flow to the stomach, inhibition of peristalsis, and reduced propulsion of food."[29] Ezekiel's body will thus presage the interruption and transformation of "normal" bodily processes and social practices of eating and drinking. Finally, food, memory, and emotion are closely linked.[30] By comparison with other senses, smell "trigger[s] the most vivid and emotional memories," while emotional arousal enhances memory formation, storage, and recollection.[31] Odors are thus "critical for learning" and "constitute efficient retrieval cues for the recall of emotional episodic memories."[32] The olfactory memory of this fearful meal will thus contribute to the embodied learning of prophet and people alike. Through smell and taste they will learn of a life shaped by terror.

On a second occasion, the prophet must "groan with crushing of loins and with bitterness (מרירות), groan before their eyes," then enter into dialogue with his audience about the future that is unfolding (21:6–7). His interactive performance is to warn of an inescapable grief that will afflict each person's heart, hands, throat, and knees (21:7). Yet, as in the fearful meal, so here, he is more than an actor in a play. In performing this future, the prophet will become the first mortal to experience it. He must commit and compromise his own body. In the crushing of his loins the prophet will become physically vulnerable and bear a wound in his body in order to show forth the future God has ordained (cf. 4:4–8).[33] His groaning in the sight of the people demands that they pay attention, challenging them to see the portrait of their future pain and devastation in the prophet's own.

The third and final instance is even more costly. God announces that God will take away the "delight" (מחמד) of Ezekiel's eyes (Ezek 24:16) but forbids the prophet to engage in publicly recognizable practices of mourning or expressions of grief. Even tears, frequently an involuntary response to loss, are forbidden (24:16–17; for analysis of their social dimension, see earlier in

---

[29] Insell et al., *Nutrition*, 126.
[30] See, e.g., Lupton, *Food, Body, and Self*, 32–6; Kita and Nakatani, "Smell-Based Memory."
[31] Saive, Royet, and Plailly, "Episodic Odor Memory," 25; Saive et al., "Odor Recognition," 45.
[32] Sullivan et al., "Olfactory Memory Networks," 5.
[33] Cf. Ezekiel's later immersion to his "waist" or "hips" (Ezek 47:4).

this chapter). The only expression allowed to him is a private one that cannot be heard: "moan, silence of dying ones" (24:17). God cannot forbid grief but does forbid ritual and relational practices that might elicit a response of solidarity, nurture, or comfort.[34] "Public ritual ... provides social validation, a public recognition of the loss that was experienced, and a collective reassurance of societal recognition and social support."[35]

The prohibition of conventional mourning practices has the additional effect of delaying or aborting the work of meaning-making. Robert Neimeyer has argued that "a central process in grieving is the attempt to reaffirm or reconstruct a world of meaning that has been challenged by loss."[36] When conventional and public expressions of grief are limited by external factors, creating what Kenneth Doka has called "disenfranchised grief," this process of reaffirming or reconstructing a world of meaning is also circumscribed.[37] Carlos Torres and Alfonso M. García-Hernandez highlight a further dimension of conventional and public grief-work:

> Rituals and memorialization practices exist within the social matrix and thus adhere to and reflect through symbolic behaviors the beliefs, values, and regulatory guidelines of a given society. However, rituals are not simply a show and tell of a culture's norms nor are the symbols meant to be passive reminders of values ... [T]he symbols and behaviors are entryways to direct contact and communication with the divine that remains unseen but energetically present in social life.[38]

That is, mourning practices link the bereaved and their community to the deity. Prohibition of mourning thus cuts off bonds within the community, inhibits the process of meaning-making and world-reconstruction, and severs critical channels of connection with God. Ritual connection to God is the very loss presaged by Ezekiel's loss of his wife.

That is, Ezekiel is to experience this loss and refrain from mourning in order to be a portent (מופת MT; τέρας LXX 24:24, 27) for the people,

---

[34] For a different interpretation, see Lipton, "Early Mourning?" Lipton argues that God prevents Ezekiel from petitioning for his wife's deliverance prior to her death.
[35] Doka, "Memorialization, Ritual and Public Tragedy," 184.
[36] Neimeyer, "Meaning Reconstruction," 80.
[37] This concept was first articulated in Doka, "Disenfranchised Grief," 3–11. Doka notes that disenfranchisement "may exacerbate ... bereavement ... [D]isenfranchising circumstances can intensify feelings of anger, guilt, or powerlessness ..." ("Disenfranchised Grief," 7).
[38] Torres and García-Hernández, "From Violation to Voice," 205. In this passage they cite the work of Turner, *Ritual Process*.

becoming what Zainab Bahrani has called a "mantic body" that bears, along with that of his wife, omens of a future decreed by God.[39] The translation "sign" (e.g., NRSV) does not adequately express the connotations of Ezekiel's function as portent. The Hebrew term מופת has the connotation of a wondrous thing or work, while the Greek τέρας has the connotation of anomaly or monster. Ezekiel's portent does not just provide information. By its very wondrous, anomalous, and monstrous nature it manifests a radical interruption and transformation of familiar realities.

While Daniel Block interprets God's instructions to Ezekiel to mean that "the prophet's personal feelings are beside the point," I argue to the contrary that Ezekiel's feelings, alongside the affective practices in which he engages and from which he refrains, are part of his somatic rendering of the future God plans.[40] That is, interruption and transformation are evident not *only* in the sudden death of Ezekiel's wife or the destruction of the temple. They are also embodied in Ezekiel's affective performance, which in turn provides a template for the people's affective responses to the temple's destruction and the death of their children. Just as Ezekiel's loss of his wife, the "delight of [his] eyes" (24:16), presages the people's loss of the sanctuary, "delight of [their] eyes and compassion of [their] heart" (24:21; cf. 24:25), so Ezekiel's affective practice prefigures their own. The people's question to Ezekiel interrogates precisely this relationship between Ezekiel's behavior and theirs (24:19). He responds by instructing them, "you shall do as I have done" (24:22; cf. 24:24). Though they will experience grief and groaning, they will not engage in the public, ritual, relational practices that would enable them to move forward as a community toward acceptance, consolation, and healing (24:23).[41]

This analysis has shown that affect proves central to Ezekiel's mission. Yet, unlike Jeremiah, Ezekiel's subjectivity does not merge with that of God or people. Instead, he becomes mirror, vehicle, and portent. In the book's first scene, the prophet's somatic response to divine glory exhibits humility, submission, and reverence, contrasting sharply with the people's posture of rebellion. His commission foregrounds an oppositional intimacy between prophet and people, as Ezekiel's own face is transformed to reflect, withstand, and reshape the people's affective practice. The sorrowful verdict he ingests

---

[39] Bahrani, *Rituals of War*, 75–99.
[40] Block, *Ezekiel 1–24*, 788.
[41] For Block, the reason the people will not grieve is because they will interpret the fall of Jerusalem as good news, signaling that judgment has been accomplished and is now in the past. What follows is not a time of sorrow but "a new era of hope and salvation" (*Ezekiel 1–24*, 794).

makes his body the bearer of divine anger and portent of the people's future. He is bound to the divine realm, but forcibly removed from it so that his people can encounter in him their own terror, pain, and disenfranchised grief. The prophet's affective labor does not illustrate or adorn a prophetic message, nor is it merely a byproduct of his mission. Rather, it does critical work of its own. The future God has ordained for the people is not reducible to propositional content. It reshapes their very lives. Ezekiel's affective practice manifests and inaugurates this future.

Daniel

The book of Daniel, commonly identified by scholars as apocalyptic rather than prophetic literature, arguably does not portray *prophetic* affect. Yet I treat the book of Daniel in this chapter because, while Daniel may not fit definitions of classical prophecy, interpreters both ancient and modern have nonetheless grouped them together.[42] Equally important for this chapter, the book of Daniel emphasizes Daniel's affective practice in relation to visionary experience and revelation of knowledge. This affective practice functions as a bridge, linking Daniel's response to revelation to that of characters in the narrative as well as readers and hearers of the text. In the process, Daniel's affect becomes a locus of mediation.

Over the course of the book, Daniel's affect is portrayed in relation to two different types of characters. In the first half of the book, Daniel's affect is primarily portrayed in relation to that of the earthly king, Nebuchadnezzar. Affective attunement between Daniel and Nebuchadnezzar helps expand the king's affective repertoire to include an attitude of wonder, helping him to acknowledge divine sovereignty. In the book's second half, Daniel's affect receives greater attention, but no longer interacts with that of an earthly king. Instead, Daniel's affect responds to angelic encounters, visions, and discourse about the future of Daniel's people and the empires that would rule them. The textual portrayal of these affectively charged interactions also becomes a medium that engages and shapes the affect of the book's audience. In each case,

---

[42] For example, although in the TaNaK the book of Daniel is included among the writings and not the prophets, in the Septuagint and Christian bibles, it numbers among the prophetic books. And while the book of Daniel does not call Daniel a prophet, he is called a prophet in 4QFlorilegium (4Q174 II.3–4), by Josephus (*Ant.* 10.266), and by Jesus in Matthew's Gospel (Matt 24:15). For more extended treatment of Daniel's status within and outside of prophetic canons, see Portier-Young, "Daniel and Apocalyptic Imagination," 225–7.

Daniel's affective practice has implications for others beyond Daniel himself. The book's treatment of Daniel's affective practice underscores that to receive revelation is not simply to see a vision or hear a discourse, nor does it culminate in understanding. The book binds vision, word, and cognition with affect, volition, and action.

The relationship between Daniel's affect and that of the king he advises progresses from contrast to sympathy. Near the book's beginning, Daniel's affect differs sharply from Nebuchadnezzar's: following his first dream vision, when faced with the limitations of his advisers' interpretive abilities, the king is overcome with rage; when faced with his own death sentence, Daniel exhibits equanimity (Dan 2).[43] Yet when the king shares the content of his second dream with Daniel, this contrast disappears (Dan 4). Nebuchadnezzar's second dream frightens and alarms or disturbs him.[44] Upon hearing its contents Daniel is appalled (אשתומם) and, like Nebuchadnezzar, he too is alarmed by his thoughts (יבהלנה רעינהי 4:16 MT=4:19 LXX, NRSV). Daniel's affect now mirrors the king's, highlighting Daniel's attunement to and sympathy for the king he advises (cf. 4:19b).[45] Yet this attunement is not static.

Among the three oldest versions of Daniel (MT, Th, and OG), the Old Greek version (OG) offers the most detailed treatment of Daniel's affective response to Nebuchadnezzar's dream report. More precisely, it offers Nebuchadnezzar's interpretation of Daniel's affective response. In MT and Th, the king urges Daniel not to let the dream and its interpretation alarm or press him.[46] His seemingly compassionate words fail to grasp the seriousness or urgency of the catastrophe that will soon overtake him. By comparison with MT and Th, OG places greater emphasis on the king's perception of Daniel's affective response, with the result that the king presents himself as more closely attuned to the prophet's affect. While in MT, OG, and Th alike, the story is presented as part of a letter by Nebuchadnezzar, in MT and Th the narrative within the letter portrays the king in the third person. In OG,

---

[43] Pleonasm portrays the king's rage as excessive: בנס וקצף שגיא MT; στυγνὸς γενόμενος καὶ περίλυπος OG; ἐν θυμῷ καὶ ὀργῇ πολλῇ Th Dan 2:12; cf. 3:19. Daniel, by contrast, responds "with counsel and judgment" (עטא וטעם MT 2:14; "prudence and discretion" NRSV).

[44] ידחלנני ... יבהלנני 4:2 MT; εὐλαβήθην καὶ φόβος μοι ἐπέπεσεν 4:5 OG; ἐφοβέρισέν με καὶ ἐταράχθην 4:5 Th.

[45] Proto-Theodotion preserves the lexical mirroring of Nebuchadnezzar's response in Daniel's own, as Daniel's response (συνετάρασσον 4:19) echoes that of the king (ἐταράχθην 4:5). Th further emphasizes the effects on Daniel's body: for one hour, he becomes mute (ἀπηνεώθη 4:19 Th).

[46] אל־יבהלך 4:16 MT; μὴ κατασπευσάτω σε 4:19 Th; cf. 5:10; 10:12, 19.

unlike MT and Th, the king narrates his experiences and actions in first-person throughout. The king is thus narrator of this episode from start to finish, with the result that descriptions of Daniel are not provided by an omniscient narrator but portray the king's perceptions and interpretations. In OG Nebuchadnezzar does not offer words of reassurance to Daniel. Instead, he describes at length Daniel's bodily experience of wonder, fear, and apprehension (Dan 4:19 OG): Daniel experienced great wonder (μεγάλως δὲ ἐθαύμασεν), a rush of foreboding (ὑπόνοια κατέσπευδεν αὐτόν), fear (φοβηθεὶς) and trembling (τρόμου λαβόντος αὐτὸν). The shaking of his head transformed his appearance (ἀλλοιωθείσης τῆς ὁράσεως αὐτοῦ κινήσας τὴν κεφαλὴν), and for an hour he "marveled much" (ἀποθαυμάσας). When he spoke, his voice was "gentle" (φωνῇ πραεία Dan 4:19 OG). Daniel's affect, as portrayed by the king, reveals concern for the fate of the king and responds to the miraculous inbreaking of divine agency and correction in the face of royal presumption. Daniel's wonder and fear shake his body, temporarily deprive him of the capacity of speech, and transform his appearance. The soothing, calm, or mild voice with which he finally speaks suggests that Daniel is concerned to modulate Nebuchadnezzar's fear response.

Nebuchadnezzar's detailed attention to Daniel's affect, meanwhile, signals a degree of attunement and sympathy on the part of the king that may eventually facilitate his education and restoration. His restoration will require him to open outward, to move from a belief in his sole agency and majesty to an understanding of his place in relation to God. His own initial response of fear and alarm[47] did not prompt in him greater awareness of divine power and majesty. While Daniel's response also exhibits fear and alarm, in OG the added emphasis on wonder opens a path forward for Nebuchadnezzar. It is a path of openness to social change, decentering the self, and moral and aesthetic growth. Drawing insight from Sara Ahmed, who finds in wonder a fundamental orientation of openness that manifests in bodies and attitudes alike, Maia Kotrosits comments on wonder's capacity to open toward social change: "Wonder involves a tacit acknowledgment that the trajectory of social life, however over-determined, is not an inevitable one."[48] In a similar vein, though more focused on the individual

---

[47] יבהלני, ידחלנני Dan 4:2 MT; 4:5 OG is comparable; 4:5 Th adds the experience of confusion: συνετάραξάν με.
[48] Kotrosits, "How Things Feel," 12, citing Ahmed, *Cultural Politics*, 183.

person, Robert Fuller has argued that wonder "stimulates intellectual, moral, and aesthetic growth,"[49]

> prompting us to modify our previous cognitive structures to include the ever widening contours of the environment as opposed to incorporating new experiences into the existing stock of ideas with which we fashion instrumental behavior. These changes help us to bring otherwise distant people and objects into our personal scheme of ends, helping us to have empathy and concern for the wider world. And, by prompting us to detect causal agencies that lie somehow behind or beyond observed events, wonder predisposes us to religious and metaphysical thought.[50]

It is ultimately not enough for the king to observe Daniel's wonder. His learning will also require his own decentering and humbling. Yet the conclusion to Nebuchadnezzar's story suggests that he has indeed gained a sense of wonder. He acknowledges and praises "the one who created the heaven and the earth and the seas and the rivers and everything that is in them," praising the Lord of lords "because he does signs and wonders" (4:34 OG NETS). His cognitive framework now encompasses a widened view of creation, and his confession of God's activity as creator and performer of "signs and wonders" points to an appreciation of what Fuller has named as "causal agencies that lie somehow behind or beyond observed events."

While, in Dan 4 (OG), Daniel's affective experience and practice of wonder help to open a pathway for the king's own affective transformation and education, in the second half of the book Daniel's affect relates more closely to that of the book's audience. Vivid symbolic imagery and detailed descriptions of Daniel's affect facilitate "emotional transportation" into the story, heightening the reader's or hearer's identification with Daniel and affective involvement with the story.[51] Jonathan Cohen describes such identification as "a process that consists of increasing loss of self-awareness and its temporary replacement with heightened emotional and cognitive connections with a character."[52] Such temporary identification has more lasting personal and social effects.[53] The reader's or hearer's temporary identification with Daniel

---

[49] Fuller, *Wonder*, 2.
[50] Fuller, *Wonder*, 147.
[51] On "transportation," see Fitzgerald and Green, "Narrative Persuasion."
[52] Cohen, "Defining Identification," 251.
[53] Oatley, "Fiction: Simulation of Social Worlds"; Bal and Veltkamp, "How Does Fiction Reading Influence Empathy?" While some may not be comfortable applying the genre label fiction to Daniel,

shapes their affect in turn. With Daniel, the audience experiences distress, fear, and weakness. They also receive assurance, courage, and strength. Such affective interactions between audience and text further shape audiences' interpretations of their own present realities and their future actions.[54]

Daniel's dream and visions of four beasts, one like a human, and the ancient of days (Dan 7) affect him similarly to the report of Nebuchadnezzar's dream in Dan 4, but in stages, culminating in desire for understanding. Upon seeing the initial dream/vision sequence, Daniel's breathing grows short or becomes distressed (אתכרית רוחי) within his body (בגוא נדנה) and he is again "alarmed" (יבהלנני) 7:15; cf. 4:2, 16 MT). In proto-Theodotion's translation, Daniel's spirit or breath shudders (ἔφριξεν) and the visions shake, agitate, or disturb him (ἐτάρασσόν), while in OG, Daniel is "exhausted" (ἀκηδιάσας 7:15).[55] His affective response prompts action: he enters into the very scene of the vision in order to speak with one of the myriads who serve the Ancient of Days and inquire as to the vision's truth and meaning. Daniel's inquiry is motivated also by desire (צבית MT; ἤθελον OG) for clarity (7:19). While the ancient versions emphasize different physiological experiences ranging from shortness of breath (MT) and shuddering (Th) to exhaustion (OG), each portrays the physical stress experienced by Daniel upon receiving the vision. This embodied stress response prompts volition, action, and interaction as Daniel pursues further knowledge about the content of the dream. That is, Daniel's affective response to the vision is an integral part of his quest for understanding, leading him to pursue further revelation.

Daniel's distress triggers a state of action-readiness that results in a conscious choice to retain the revelatory word within his body. At the conclusion of the vision report Daniel relates, "As for me, Daniel, my thoughts alarmed me (יבהלנני). My brightness changed [i.e., dimmed] upon me. And I kept [MT/Th]/fixed [OG] the word in my heart" (7:28 AT). Daniel here encapsulates the close relationship between vision, word, cognition, affect, body, and will. Sense perceptions, cognitive interpretations, involuntary

---

the key characteristics for facilitating reader's or hearer's emotional transportation apply to narratives more broadly; more vivid story-worlds and figurative language, including metaphor and metonym, produce heightened transportation (Oatley, "Meetings of Minds").

[54] Fitzgerald and Green survey outcomes of narrative transportation, including changes in beliefs and attitudes (both short-term and long-term), behavior and the inclination to behave in certain ways in the future, self-concept, and perceptions of risk ("Narrative Persuasion," 55–62).

[55] The divergent readings in OG and Th likely reflect different interpretations of the Hebrew idiom preserved in MT. Thomas interprets ἔφριξεν in Th as referring to goose bumps (*Anatomical Idiom and Emotional Expression*, 153; cf. Job 4:15).

embodied responses, and embodied acts of will follow in close succession. It is not only the vision that alarms him but also his own cognitive process of apperception or sense-making. His body further exhibits elements of the fight-or-flight response, as it prepares for immediate action. Specifically, the transformation of his brightness or radiance seems to refer to an excitatory fear response that is visible in a person's skin, including their face. This visible dulling or paling results from "contraction of blood vessels in the skin ... that increases blood pressure and redirects blood flow to where it is most needed," including muscles, brain, and heart.[56] The action-readiness signaled by his pallor produces an act of will that unites word and body. By "fixing" or "keeping" the word in his heart, the organ believed to be the seat of cognition, memory, and volition,[57] Daniel allows the vision and its interpretation to continue to shape him from within.

Daniel's affective experiences in response to the second vision (Dan 8) and the subsequent revelation of a "word" (Dan 10) are more interactive than those in response to the vision in chapter 7. In chapter 8, Daniel's liminal body-states correspond to a mediated revelatory encounter that exceeds the capacities of Daniel's body even as he is supernaturally empowered to receive further revelation. When Gabriel approaches Daniel to help him understand the vision, Daniel is terrified (MT), confused (OG), or amazed (Th), and falls on his face (Dan 8:17).[58] In each version, Daniel's affective response signals difficulty assimilating the new experience into Daniel's existing cognitive framework. His accompanying fall to the ground simultaneously conveys fear or reverence and incapacity. In MT and OG, this response deepens as the angelic mediator explains that the vision is for the end-times, causing Daniel to fall into a deep sleep (נרדמתי MT; ἐκοιμήθην OG), still face-down on the ground (8:18).[59] The *niphal* verb form נרדמתי is closely related to the Hebrew noun תרדמה, which refers to an unusually deep, trance-like sleep, sometimes with supernatural origins (e.g., Gen 2:21; 15:12; 1 Sam 26:12; Isa 29:10). Whether attributable to God or reflecting Daniel's autonomic response to encounter with the angel, this sleep-state embodies the liminality of his revelatory encounter. In this encounter Daniel comes to the edge of what his body/self can receive and do on his own. Bodily interaction with the

---

[56] Chamberlain and Meuret, "Fight or Flight Response," 1482.
[57] Schroer and Staubli, *Body Symbolism*, 41–55.
[58] "Terrified" נבעתי MT; cf. Isa 21:4; "confused" ἐθορυβήθην OG; "amazed" ἐθαμβήθην Th. For the response of falling on his face, cf. Ezek 1:28; 3:23; 9:8; 11:13; 43:3; 44:4.
[59] Th omits the reference to sleep and instead repeats the detail that Daniel fell upon his face.

angel allows him to continue to receive revelation: the angel's touch rouses him from sleep and raises him to a standing position that signals a renewed readiness and capacity for attention (8:18).

When their conversation concludes, Daniel is again left at the edge of his bodily capacity; bodily limitation here corresponds to epistemic limitation. He is sick or weak (ונחליתי MT; ἀσθενήσας OG; ἐμαλακίσθην Th) for a period of days (8:27).[60] While Daniel eventually recovers sufficient bodily strength to return to his work in service of the king, his narration draws attention back to his affective response to the vision. Immediately following the report of Daniel's illness, each version summarizes Daniel's response to the vision using slightly different affective language: it appalled him (ואשתומם MT), caused him to feel faint (ἐξελυόμην OG),[61] or amazed him (ἐθαύμαζον Th 8:27). As narrator, Daniel associates these affective responses with his inability to understand the vision's meaning (MT) or the absence of someone to explain it (OG, Th). That is, Daniel correlates his affect with his epistemic limitations.

Further dimensions of the relationship between affect and revelation come to the fore as Daniel twice draws on a cultural and religious repertoire of ritualized affective practices in order to resolve his epistemic limitation. On the first occasion Daniel turns his face to God, "seek[ing] [through?] prayer and supplications/mercies" (9:3).[62] On the second occasion he "giv[es] his heart [MT, Th]/ face [OG] to understanding and to humbling [him]self" (10:12). The specific practices he performs include fasting/abstention (9:3, 10:3), sackcloth and ashes (9:3), and refraining from anointing himself (10:3). By drawing on this cultural repertoire, Daniel is able to make petition both as an individual and as representative of and mediator for his people.[63] These practices have multiple, overlapping associations and functions: 1) ascetic preparation for divine encounter and/or revelation; 2) a self-humbling that may express relative powerlessness in hopes of eliciting

---

[60] This period of physical weakness is reminiscent of what is known in psychiatric literature as "quiescent immobility," a defense-response that "promotes rest and healing" in a place of safety following a traumatic or fear-inducing event (Kozlowska et al., "Fear and the Defense Cascade," 267).

[61] Threat-induced fainting can be an example of "collapsed immobility," "in which muscle tone is lost and consciousness is compromised secondary to bradycardia-induced cerebral hypoxia" (Kozlowska et al., "Fear and the Defense Cascade," 267).

[62] Grammatically, "prayer and supplications" may be a direct object or the means by which Daniel seeks. In the latter case the object of his seeking is not specified. Newsom and Breed (*Daniel: A Commentary*, 291) and Seow (*Daniel*, 140) identify God as the object of Daniel's seeking.

[63] The practices described here recognize the difference in power between people and God, partly reflecting "status/power effects in who gets to do what in emotional displays" (Wetherell, *Affect and Emotion*, 87).

divine mercy or aid; and 3) expression of grief. David Lambert notes that "such practices ... encod[e] suffering on the body."[64] They also display mortality, finitude, and dependence. Contextual clues support each set of associations listed above: Daniel "set his mind to gain understanding" (NRSV 10:12), "humbled himself" (10:12), confessed (9:4, 20), sought mercy or favor (9:20, 23), and "was mourning" (הייתי מתאבל 10:2).[65] Wetherell notes that "affective practice is continually dynamic, with the potential to move in multiple and divergent directions."[66] While it may be possible to assign different primary functions to Daniel's embodied practices in chapters 9 and 10, the range and placement of contextual cues suggest that the multiple functions described above are here interrelated.[67] Embodied practices of fasting, sackcloth, and ashes accompany confession and a petition for mercy, yet they receive a response of revelation. Preparation for revelation, meanwhile, includes practices of mourning and self-humbling. In both cases, the close connection between the visionary's affective practice and seeking or receiving revelation and understanding demonstrate that, in the case of Daniel, affect and experience of and access to revelation are mutually shaping and interdependent.

Daniel's affective practice is met with a corresponding demonstration and declaration of divine affect. In the book's concluding revelatory discourses, Daniel's angelic interlocutor three times declares Daniel to be "desired," "precious," or "beloved" (חמדות 9:23; 10:11, 19). The angel implicitly attributes to God the act of desiring or delighting in Daniel, grounding Daniel's identity in divine affect and esteem.[68] God's delight in Daniel, moreover, is presented as the reason for Daniel's receiving ongoing revelation in response to his supplication (9:23). The declaration of Daniel's status as one in whom God delights will later preface the commands to pay attention, be strong, and act (10:11, 19). That is, the affective relationship between Daniel and God, here mediated through an angel, both precipitates divine revelation and facilitates Daniel's capacity to receive and respond to it.

---

[64] Lambert, "Mourning," 165.
[65] Seow adds that fasting requires "complete dedication and focus"; "the fasting, sackcloth and ashes are manifestations of his earnestness" (*Daniel*, 140–1).
[66] Wetherell, *Affect and Emotion*, 13.
[67] Collins, e.g., identifies penitence as the focus in chapter 9 and preparation for revelation in chapter 10 (*Daniel*, 372).
[68] At 10:11 he is addressed as "Daniel, desired man" דניאל איש־חמדות. At 10:19 he is addressed solely by the epithet איש־חמדות. Elsewhere in Daniel, the term חמדות characterizes food from which Daniel abstains in order to humble himself (10:3) and treasures given and governed by the king of the North (i.e., Antiochus IV Epiphanes; 11:38, 43).

The second and third declarations of divine delight in Daniel respond not to supplication but to Daniel's embodied response of fear. In the first instance, in response to an angelophany, fear (MT, OG) or *ekstasis* (Th) falls upon Daniel's companions, causing them to flee and hide (MT; "run away in haste" OG; "flee in fear" Th).[69] Daniel does not flee. Instead, the appearance and roar of the "man clothed in linen" (10:5) causes him to lose strength. A startling turn of phrase portrays Daniel's visible paling in language that echoes the destruction Antiochus IV Epiphanes will wreak upon nations, humans, Jerusalem, and its sanctuary (שחת 8:24, 25; 9:26). Just as these would be destroyed, so Daniel's "splendor" is turned to "destruction" (למשחית 10:8). His autonomic fear response makes his body a mirror of peoples and place, momentarily reflecting their fate in his own visible transformation. As in his earlier encounter with Gabriel, so here, Daniel's hearing of the angel's words causes him to fall into a deep sleep (הייתי נרדם), with his face upon the ground (10:9). The angel's response to Daniel's trance-state is similar to that of modern-day clinicians who use a sequence of touch, movement and speech as "grounding interventions" that increase bodily awareness, including exteroception (awareness of external stimuli such as touch) and proprioception (awareness of the position and movement of one's own body) in order to bring a fearful person's attention back to the present moment.[70] The angel re-orients Daniel to the present moment gradually, first with touch, then with shaking that rouses Daniel to hands and knees, the auditory stimulus of speech, and a command to stand (10:10–11). This sequence is followed by an exhortation: "Do not fear" (10:12).

The angel's verbal and haptic response to Daniel's fear broadens Daniel's perceptual horizon and prepares him for action. Fear directs attention to the perceived source of threat. In so doing, it affects what and how one sees. While fear enhances aspects of visual perception, the narrowed attention fear produces leads the viewer to register only certain visual stimuli.[71] As seen above, fear also motivates behavior such as running, freezing, hiding, or avoiding.[72] The twice-repeated injunction "do not fear" (10:12,

---

[69] חרדה גדלה נפלה עליהם MT. In MT and Th Daniel's companions do not see the vision, while in OG they do.

[70] Kozlowska et al., "Fear and the Defense Cascade," 279. These interventions help a person to ease out of a state of tonic immobility.

[71] Susskind et al., "Expressing Fear"; Bayle, Henaff, and Krolak-Salmon, "Unconsciously Perceived Fear." Chronic stress can negatively influence sight. Bubl et al. demonstrate "dramatically lower retinal contrast gain" in people with depression, regardless of whether they are taking anti-depressant medication ("Seeing Gray," 205).

[72] Adolphs, "Biology of Fear," table 3; LaBar, "Fear and Anxiety," 753.

19) discourages Daniel from fleeing, freezing, or hiding as his companions had done. It helps him to stay in the present moment and choose action. It also expands the horizon of his seeing and understanding, preventing a narrow focus on the destructive actions of Antiochus IV Epiphanes and widening Daniel's focus to include the activity of angels who fight on behalf of Daniel's people (10:13, 20; 12:1) and the deliverance in store for the people at the "end of days" (10:14; 12:1–3).[73] Words are again accompanied by touch (10:16, 18) that restores to Daniel his capacity for speech (10:16) and strength (10:19).

The angel's exhortations—"do not fear" and "be strong" (10:19)—speak not only to Daniel, but also to his audiences, drawing them in to participate in the affective interaction between Daniel and the angel. "Daniel's weakness and trembling may resonate with what the reader already feels... The physical strength and ability the angel confers on Daniel can similarly become a part of the reader's experience."[74] For Daniel's audiences, then, the instruction "do not fear" may help to expand their frame of vision and counter processes of conditioning by which aspects of their current and past situations have become coupled to fear responses, habituating them toward avoidance, retreat, or inaction.[75] By revealing God's plans for resolving the crises Daniel's audiences will face, the angel redefines a seemingly uncontrollable situation as one that is under God's control, thereby making it possible for audiences to recover their own sense of agency.[76] The strength and courage the angel imparts to Daniel, enabling him to stand and speak, becomes strength and courage for the audience as well.

Throughout the book of Daniel, affect is closely tied to revelation. The interdependence of affect and revelation and the mechanisms and effects of audience transportation and identification help to expand our understanding of mediation. Nebuchadnezzar's account of Daniel's response to the king's dream in Dan 4 (OG) suggests a process of embodied learning through affective attunement between visionary and king. This embodied learning results in a heightened capacity for wonder, allowing the king to recognize

---

[73] See Izard and Ackerman, "Motivational, Organizational, and Regulatory Functions."
[74] Portier-Young, "Daniel and Apocalyptic Imagination," 238.
[75] "In unaware fear conditioning, conditioning effects are largely established through affective learning. This means conditioning develops in a context of aversive external and internal sensations, rather than through a change in conscious expectancy of the [unconditioned, i.e., threatening, stimulus]" (Raes and Raedt, "Interoceptive Awareness," 1399).
[76] See Amat et al., "Medial Prefrontal Cortex."

a sovereignty greater than his own. Affect thus helps to accomplish what the dream or its interpretation alone could not do.

In the book's second half, Daniel's interactions with the king recede from view as Daniel now interacts with heavenly mediators. With this shift, it must be acknowledged again that the book of Daniel is not representative of "classical prophecy." One development distinguishing Daniel (and other examples of apocalyptic literature) from classical prophecy is the role of an angelic mediator who provides (partial) knowledge and understanding to the visionary; another is explicit attention to the mediating role of a text that records revelation (Dan 9:2; 12:4, 9; cf. 4 Ezra 12:37–38; 14:46–47; *1 Enoch* 104:11–13).[77] The angelic mediator addresses the epistemic limitations of the visionary, while the text of Daniel addresses those of the reader or hearer. But they mediate more than knowledge. Affect plays a critical role at each level of mediation. The angel mediates to Daniel, and the text to the audience, affective experiences of divine delight, courage, and strength in response to self-humbling, fear, and weakness. These affective mediations cannot be extricated from the book's revelatory content; they are integral to it.

Conclusion

Ezekiel's affective practices variously contrast with, mirror, counteract, portend, and shape the people's own. His affective responses to his visions of God contrast with the people's rebellion through performance of humility, submission, and reverence. This contrast presages and produces a piercing intimacy in which Ezekiel and the people will be susceptible to one another even as they oppose each other. To overcome this susceptibility, the prophet's forehead is transformed to be hard like the people's: he becomes like them, embodying their stubbornness to resist and reshape it. By ingesting divine judgment, he also incorporates into his body practices of grieving that will

---

[77] "Classical" prophecy does not ignore textuality. Jeremiah 36 foregrounds the act of writing and the movements of the scroll. Sherwood and Brummitt argue that this story reflects "anxious[ness] about the transition from the living Prophet to the book of the Prophet" ("Fear of Loss," 54). On textual mediation in Daniel, see Portier-Young, "Daniel and Apocalyptic Imagination," 230. Two points should be noted here: 1) in Daniel, (earlier) prophetic text cannot mediate on its own. Daniel is confounded by Jeremiah's scroll until Gabriel interprets it for him (9:24–7); 2) the scroll or book the visionary writes (or is instructed to write) is in some measure a counterpart to (though not a complete copy of) heavenly writings. The man clothed in linen later promises to reveal to Daniel what is written in the "book of truth" (10:21) and refers to those whose names are "written in the book" (12:1). Both refer to heavenly writings. Cf. 7:10.

both constitute and respond to the future God has decreed for them. In a subsequent series of dramatic actions and experiences, Ezekiel's body and affect mediate and portend the resulting devastation: terror and trembling are followed by bitter groaning and the crushing of his body. Most devastating of all is the loss of his wife, the delight of his eyes, and the prohibition of ritual mourning. The prophet's performance and experience of disenfranchised grief presages and inaugurates a dissolution of communal bonds and structures, a loss of connection to the deity, and the inhibition of meaning-making in the face of disaster.

In the book of Daniel, the interdependence of affect and the revelation of knowledge expand our understanding of affect's mediating role. Moreover, the text itself emerges as a conduit for the synergistic mediation of knowledge and affect for the purpose of shaping interpretation and action. This mediation is developed in the portrayal of affective attunement and the circulation or transmission of affect between and among characters in the book. The tales in Dan 1–6 foreground not only Daniel's affect but also that of the human king Nebuchadnezzar. Through gradual affective attunement, their affective responses to shared revelation progress from contrast to sympathy. In OG, this attunement makes possible a further progression from alarm to wonder that signals a transformed awareness and capacity to acknowledge divine sovereignty. The book's second half shifts the object of attunement from king to audience. Vivid portrayals of Daniel's visionary experience and corresponding affect heighten the audience's experience of identification and emotional connection with the character Daniel, transportation into the story world, and affective involvement with the story. Such transportation and identification have been shown to have lasting social effects. By experiencing Daniel's fear and weakness, the audience also experiences his strengthening and summons to courage. This affective transformation is knit together with the experience of revelation; they shape the audience's interpretation of reality, decision-making, and actions not separately but synergistically.

Conclusion

Biblical scholarship has given great attention to the mediating and revelatory power of the prophetic word. Alongside the word and knit together with it, we find the body. I have argued that the body is not afterthought, container, or impediment to the work of mediation. It is necessary. The prophetic body mediates between divine and human realities. It is a locus of encounter, node of relationship, site of transformation. It is conduit, bridge, and portent.

I began this book with a story—an unusual one, to be sure, which scholars have more typically regarded as puzzle than paradigm, namely the story of the Judahite man of God and the old prophet from Bethel in 1 Kgs 13. But the story's underdetermined character combines with a density of vocabulary pertaining to word and body to allow the story to function as parable about the interrelationship between word and body in biblical prophecy. In addition to its portrayal of vital synergy between word and body, the story focuses attention at its conclusion on the burial of prophetic bodies. If we may read 1 Kgs 13 as parable or even cautionary tale about biblical prophecy, then these buried bodies may furnish a metaphor for the marginalization of the prophetic body in modern scholarship.

Analysis of selected modern definitions of prophecy reveals a predominantly word-centered understanding that foregrounds cognition, communication, and knowledge. A model of prophecy as message produces a messenger-prophet, mouthpiece, or interpreter. Yet modern scholars of biblical prophecy have also recognized the importance of a prophet's embodied religious experience and social performance and the relation between prophetic words and communal action. My burden, then, has not been to call attention to aspects of prophecy that no one has noticed before. Rather, I have sought to move these aspects of prophecy to the center of analysis, where, alongside the prophetic word, the prophetic body may also be recognized as a crucial and integral component of prophecy itself.

Certain features of the biblical prophetic literature have contributed to a logocentric bias. But to understand how biblical scholarship came to focus on the prophetic word to the near exclusion of the prophetic body also requires attention to intellectual and social history, both ancient and modern. A logocentric approach to biblical prophecy has roots in a persistent dualism that constructs a binary relationship between mind and body and links these to other binaries in a hierarchical system of value. In such a system, mind is associated with God, spirit, order, word(s); body with chaos, disease, passions, death. Mind and its correlates have great value; body and all that is associated with it are denigrated and subordinated. Ancient roots of this bifurcated system and its devaluing of the body can be found in the writings of Plato; equally important for understanding the history of Christian ideas about the body are Pauline writings and John's Gospel. In the early modern period, European colonial discourse and practice further developed and applied this dualistic framework to classifications of peoples, gender, religion, culture, and class. Alongside these developments, the Protestant Reformation articulated a theology of the word that was especially influential for understandings of prophecy. The rationalism of Enlightenment philosophers such as Descartes and Spinoza, and Romantic construction of the prophet-poet further elevated mind and word over body. Capitalism, industrialism, and the rise of artificial intelligence and virtual reality have exacerbated the dissociation of mind and body and attendant privileging of the word.

This history helps to surface the cost of such a dualism. The project of recovering the prophetic body aims at a revaluing and reintegration that ramifies beyond the biblical prophetic texts and into the worlds of its audiences.

The personae designated "prophets" by modern users of the HBOT range from characters labeled "prophets" in biblical narratives to the implied authors of books included within the corpora deemed prophetic by later tradents. In light of this diversity, my corrective to overly word-centered definitions of prophecy does not entail a similarly narrow but body-inclusive definition. Instead, my working definition of biblical prophecy is intentionally broad, seeking to encompass the diverse forms of mediation attributed to personae understood to be prophets in the texts of the HBOT and in their history of reception and modern study. Yet it must be acknowledged that more narrow constructions of biblical prophecy have biblical origins. Analysis of Deut 18:9–22 illuminates the norming power of a text that itself privileges verbal mediation even as it exposes the contested character, phenomenological complexity, and plural forms of prophetic mediation portrayed within biblical literature. A review of prophetic role labels used in the HBOT offers further insight into this diversity while beginning to surface key aspects of

CONCLUSION 251

prophetic embodiment. These labels do not produce a definitive portrait of prophetic embodiment or even prophecy itself, but they help to locate under the umbrella term "prophet" a range of mediatorial specialists. Other evidence reveals a matching diversity of the modes and content of prophetic mediation. Prophets mediate not only knowledge but also presence, power, agency, affect, and relationship. The very category of mediation, meanwhile, helps to focalize the body's central and necessary role.

The integrative understanding of biblical prophecy proposed in this book requires an interdisciplinary methodology. In biblical studies, a turn to the body and new critical approaches to the study of religious experience have paved the way for this kind of analysis. In the present study, the focus has been not primarily on lived realities "behind" the text but rather on the textual portrayals and constructions of prophets and prophecy in the HBOT. Yet to make sense of textual representations requires audiences to draw on experiential and cultural repertoires, even as these representations shape/d those repertoires in turn. This dynamic relationship between lived phenomena and their textual representations warrants a methodology that draws on a wide range of approaches, ranging from studies of embodied cognition, the senses, and affect to anthropology, linguistics, and literary and cultural theory.

Prophetic call or commissioning narratives provide an apt starting point for analysis of prophetic embodiment, for several reasons. First, they mark the moment when a character is charged with the prophetic role, thereby thematizing the scope and content of the prophet's mission and the nature of the role itself. In the process they contribute to the construction of the prophetic persona. They are also programmatic, functioning to introduce, frame, and interpret the narrative and oracular material that follows. The call narratives of Moses, Isaiah, Jeremiah, and Ezekiel, moreover, focalize the prophet's embodied experience, but not in a general sense. Rather, they portray the prophet's bodily encounter and interaction with the deity as a necessary preparation for the prophet's mediation between embodied God and embodied people. Coordination of body and word in the prophet's encounter with God lays the groundwork for a correspondingly synergistic prophetic mission.

In Exod 3–4, bodily movement and mutual seeing position Moses to mediate between a suffering people and a responsive but transcendent deity. In his encounter with God, Moses is charged and equipped to channel divine speech and power to and for a vulnerable people. Moses' hand and mouth function as metonyms for his mediatory agency, portraying vital synergies between body and word, action and speech. His hand is portrayed as a surrogate for the divine hand, channeling divine power to destroy, transform, and save. Yet his body also represents the people he will liberate and is marked with a sign of mortality to ensure that none mistake the prophet for God. In the process, Moses' mediating body is set apart from God and people alike. The perceived insufficiency of Moses' mouth focuses attention on God's agency, presence, and power in a way that does not negate Moses' agency but contextualizes it. God extends the boundary of the prophetic body to include another mediating body, that of Moses' brother Aaron; Moses' recruitment of the elders of Israel enlists additional partners in prophetic speech and action. The balanced pairing of speech and actions in the commission and in narrative summaries of its fulfillment further emphasizes the conjoining of word and body at the mission's heart.

The commissioning stories of Isaiah (Isa 6), Jeremiah (Jer 1:4–10), and Ezekiel (Ezek 1–3:15) share features with that of Moses, including the portrayal of bodily encounter between prophet and deity, synergy of word and body, and correspondence between the prophet's embodied experience of divine encounter and call and embodied dimensions of the mission itself. But their stories differ from Moses' in an important way, namely the use of first-person narration. Studies have shown that first-person narration heightens audiences' experience of transport and immersion in the story world, affective engagement, and even sensorimotor simulation. Through this literary technique, the text itself facilitates imaginative identification with the prophetic body and mediates a form of embodied encounter and commissioning to and for its audiences.

Temporal, spatial, and sensory details invite Isaiah's audience to experience with him the temple's transformation, the deity's glorious presence, and an interactive liturgy that accomplishes the prophet's purification, atonement, and dedication. In the commission, knowledge of God and right decision-making are predicated on sense perception; the senses are accordingly a pathway to relationship with God, healing, and social repair. While these forms of wellness are deferred to the future, the vision report provides coordinates and template for transformative encounter. In Jer 1, multiple speaking subjects invite the audience into a dialogue that thematizes encounter, relationality, and agency. Interembodiment forms the matrix of Jeremiah's call, such that divine and human bodies are mutually shaping and affecting. The prophet's body makes present both God and people, facilitating their encounter, interaction, and relationship. The theme of interembodiment is developed further in Ezekiel's commission. Mutual seeing paves the way for shared sight linked to both judgment and mercy. The prophet becomes host to God's spirit and words in order to incarnate God's judgment on the people and their future restoration.

A feature shared among the call narratives is bodily transformation. Such transformations can prepare the prophet for their mission; they can also mark the prophet's body as visibly other. Exod 34 and Num 12 narrate visible transformations of the bodies of Moses and Miriam that mark the prophetic body as liminal and even monstrous. Moses' altered face makes his body the meeting place of human, divine, and animal natures. Miriam's transformed skin positions her at the border between life and death. These transformations render both bodies monstrous, isolating them from the people and reinforcing the very boundaries they inhabit. But while Moses' transformation mediates divine glory, Miriam's evinces her shame. Together they inscribe a mediatory hierarchy upon the bodies of Israel's prophets.

A different kind of bodily transformation results from the forms of religious experience and practice referred to as *askêsis*, incubation, and ecstasy. While I do not aim to reconstruct actual religious experience from extant textual portrayals, the mutually affecting relationship between texts and lived religious and cultural realties highlights the simultaneously conventional and creative aspect of a prophet's transformative bodily praxis: by transforming the body in culturally specified ways, the prophet also claims power to transform social realities. The sustained and formative bodily disciplines of *askêsis* shape the prophet's very person. They may prepare the prophet to encounter the deity or receive revelation; they may be an efficacious component of prophetic intercession. Prophetic ascetic practice can strengthen, challenge, or reshape social relationships and structures and even alter the cosmos itself. In Exodus and Deuteronomy, Moses' *askêsis* pushes up to and beyond the limits of what is humanly possible, making his body a bridge between impossibility and possibility, human and divine, death and life. His resulting transformation presages and makes possible the people's. Incubation is less clearly attested among Israel's and Judah's prophets. Instead, in 1 Sam 1–3 this liminal practice emerges at a moment of national transition to inaugurate new structures of leadership and open prophetic channels of mediation that had previously been closed.

Ascetic practice and incubation both have the capacity to induce altered states of consciousness. Such altered states can also be a hallmark of prophetic ecstasy. Debates about the existence and nature of prophetic ecstasy in the HBOT owe in part to prior assumptions about the characteristics of biblical prophecy (and of Israelite religion more broadly) and in part to the phenomenological complexity and diverse forms of religious ecstasy. Modern debates are matched by polemics, conflicting assessments, and questions within the biblical texts. Despite such polemics, ecstasy is not a marginal feature of biblical prophecy. It was a means by which the prophet could bridge human and divine realities through the temporary alteration of their mind and body. Biblical evidence for the portrayal of induction techniques such as fasting, meditation, music, or rhythmic movement is mixed. More frequently attested is the interpretation of prophetic ecstasy as a form of spirit possession that could produce visions or supernatural transport. Like Moses' *askêsis*, these experiences made of the prophet's body a mediating bridge between times, places, and realms. Prophetic ecstasy had the power to make the deity present, reveal hidden realities, and reshape structures of power and possibility.

These diverse transformations highlight that the prophetic body is not static but dynamic. The prophetic body is also a body in motion. Such motion is not incidental or even prefatory to prophetic mission but a critical component of it. A corollary to prophetic movement is the importance of place, proximity, and bodily co-presence. Prophetic mobility mediates the production of knowledge and relationship. The mobilities of Moses, Balaam, and Jonah variously mirror and respond to divine mobility and channel divine power to catalyze movement and change. Elijah's supernatural transport defers this catalyzing potential to the future, while Ezekiel and Habakkuk bridge homeland and exile to mediate and re-create home across boundaries of time and space, place and non-place, life and death. A prophet's *im*mobility could also mediate. The binding of Ezekiel dramatizes the people's punishment, simultaneously embodying human constraint and divine inaction. Jeremiah's incarcerations similarly dramatize and portend the siege and captivity of Jerusalem. The oracular body of the prophet thereby frustrates attempts to curtail or manage the prophet's power by immobilizing his body.

A different type of movement is captured in the portrayal of prophetic affect, including emotion. A theoretical framework drawn from neurobiology, social science, and cultural studies illumines affect's embodied and social character while establishing its vital role in cognition, decision-making, and behavior, and its capacity to effect social change. In Jonah, affect is a site of negotiation and transformation. The book's concluding dialogue prompts critical reflection to increase affective attunement between prophet and God.

Consistent with the portrayal of interembodiment in Jeremiah's call narrative, the portrayal of affective attunement in the book of Jeremiah is more complex. Jeremiah's body emerges as a node of circulating affect. Unattributed laments, interdictions against prophetic intercession, and the reversal of interdiction reveal intersubjectivity and affective entanglement between deity, people, place, and prophet. Ezekiel embodies the people's affect in order to transform it; he also performs and experiences their impending devastation and sorrow. His affective practice is participatory, revelatory, and efficacious, portending, enacting, and shaping the fate he shares with God's people. I concluded my study with analysis of affect in the book of Daniel, a book that occupies the edges of biblical prophetic literature. Its portrayal of the transmission of affect among characters in the book mediates affect also to its audiences. From a pedagogy of wonder to imparting strength and courage in the face of fear, affective transformation accompanies verbal revelation and shapes its reception, demonstrating that the synergy of word and body at the heart of biblical prophetic mediation persists in early apocalyptic literature.

This book does not exhaust the topic of prophetic embodiment. It is a first sounding that regards the prophetic body as a starting point for a broader inquiry regarding the body's role in relation to biblical prophecy. Next steps in this broader project include more detailed investigation of a) biblical representations of *embodied prophecy* and b) biblical prophecy's *embodied reception*.

With the descriptor "embodied prophecy" I refer to diverse forms of prophetic activity ranging from the dramatic actions commonly referred to as symbolic actions or sign-acts to prophetic acts of provision, healing, and restoring life. Prophetic action invites participation, inaugurates new realities, reconfigures relationships, heals, feeds, destroys, and actualizes divine power and will. Many of these prophetic actions are also interactions, entailing bodily participation on the part of diverse actors. This bodily participation extends also to later audiences of prophetic texts, prompting a reframing of audiences' reception as embodied interaction. Thus while "embodied reception" can refer to the body's role in the reception of prophecy narrated within biblical prophetic literature, it also names the body's role in audiences' diverse interactions with prophetic texts and traditions, from reading and hearing to interpreting and actualizing, across a wide range of media, cultural settings, times, and places.

Leaning into these future studies, I conclude, finally, with another story. Ancient interpreters sometimes linked the tale in 1 Kgs 13 with another unusual tradition, one that asserted that even in death the prophetic body had efficacy and power. Second Kings 13:20–21 preserves a legend about the prophet Elisha. One day, sometime after Elisha had died and was buried, a group of Israelites were digging a grave to bury another man who had died. Before they could finish digging, they were ambushed by a band of raiders. As they prepared to flee, they threw the man's body into Elisha's tomb. This man's corpse there came into contact with the bones of the prophet. The narrator of 2 Kings reports that "when the body touched Elisha's bones, the man came to life and stood up on his feet" (2 Kgs 13:21 NIV). Around 200 BCE, ben Sira reflected on this tradition as he composed his praise of Israel's prophets. He wrote about Elisha: "Nothing was beyond his power, and from where he lay buried, his body prophesied" (Sir 48:13 NABRE).

For ben Sira, restoring life to a dead body was an act of prophecy. Elijah had done it during life, as had Elisha. For ben Sira this limit example of the power of Elisha's body to restore life even after his own death was evidence that a prophet's very body—בשר in Hebrew, σῶμα in the Greek translation—is an active partner in the work of prophecy. But if it was a limit example, ben Sira's hope was that it would not be unique. In what appears to be one of the earliest explicit reflections on the corpus of prophetic literature that would come to be included in the HBOT, ben Sira offered a prayer for the prophets whose work was memorialized in the Book of the Twelve, that their bones too could be a source of life, even after death: "May the bones of the twelve prophets send forth new life from where they lie, for they comforted the people of Jacob, and delivered them with confident hope" (Sir 49:10 NRSV). The work they did in life and the comforting and salvific effects of their prophetic ministry for the people of Israel and Judah give him cause to believe that their bodies, too, would continue to be efficacious.

The poem "Elisha's Bones" by Julie Moore captures the impact of the bodily interaction conveyed in 2 Kgs 13:20–21 and the capacity of the prophetic body to channel God's creative and life-giving power:

>What was it like
>in such premature burial,
>tossed into another's tomb,
>ears deaf to the men's shouts beyond you,
>feet numb to the pebbles pressing upon them,
>breath escaped like a
>prodigal son,

and eyes blind to
the prophet dead beside you?

Sudden and insane,
you collided with his frame,
lingering power of God
seeping from his side
infusing your soul,
and once again,
you heard your heartbeat
suffocating silence, you found breath
coughing dust from your chest, your toes
dug into the ground below them,
you saw light.
And you knew your place,
as though you were Adam
again emerging from clay,
the bones of Elisha having released you
from your grave.[1]

The prophetic body mediates power, presence, punishment, and possibility. It mediates relationship and home, ending and beginning, death and life. The transformations and movements of the prophetic body link God and people across boundaries of heaven and earth, space and time. Synergies of word and body reveal the prophet to be more than God's messenger and prophecy to be more than words. What ben Sira claims for the prophetic body in death is all the more true in life: the body also prophesies.

---

[1] Moore, Julie. "Elisha's Bones." *Christianity and Literature* 54:1 (2004), 122. © 2004 The Conference on Christianity and Literature. Reprinted with permission of Johns Hopkins University Press.

Bibliography

Ackroyd, Peter R. "יד *yād* [hand]." Pages 393–426 in *Theological Dictionary of the Old Testament*. Vol. 5. Edited by G. Johannes Botterweck and Helmer Ringgren. Translated by David E. Green. Grand Rapids, MI: Eerdmans, 1986.
Adam, Klaus-Peter. "'And He Behaved Like a Prophet among Them.' (1Sam 10:11b): The Depreciative Use of נבא *Hitpael* and the Comparative Evidence of Ecstatic Prophecy." *Die Welt des Orients* 39, no. 1 (2009): 3–57.
Addey, Crystal. "In the Light of the Sphere: The 'Vehicle of the Soul' and Subtle-Body Practices in Neoplatonism." Pages 149–67 in *Religion and the Subtle Body in Asia and the West: Between Mind and Body*. Edited by Geoffrey Samuel and Jay Johnston. London: Routledge, 2013.
Adey, Peter. *Mobility*. London: Routledge, 2010.
Adolphs, Ralph. "The Biology of Fear." *Current Biology* 23, no. 2 (2013): R79–R93.
Ahmed, Sara. *The Cultural Politics of Emotion*. New York: Routledge, 2004.
Ahmed, Sara and Jackie Stacey. "Introduction: Dermographies." Pages 17–37 in *Thinking through the Skin*. Edited by Sara Ahmed and Jackie Stacey. New York: Routledge, 2001.
Alsen, Carolyn. "Veiled Resistance: The Cognitive Dissonance of Vision in Genesis 38." Pages 59–81 in *Imagined Worlds and Constructed Differences in the Hebrew Bible*. Edited by Jeremiah W. Cataldo. New York: T&T Clark, 2019.
Amat, Jose et al. "Medial Prefrontal Cortex Determines How Stressor Controllability Affects Behavior and Dorsal Raphe Nucleus." *Nature Neuroscience* 8, no. 3 (2005): 365–71.
Anderson, Gary A. *A Time to Mourn, A Time to Dance: The Expression of Grief and Joy in Israelite Religion*. University Park: Pennsylvania State University Press, 1991.
André, Gunnel. "Ecstatic Prophesy [sic] in the Old Testament." Pages 187–200 in *Religious Ecstasy*. Edited by Nils G. Holm. Stockholm: Almquist and Wiksell International, 1982.
Archer, Robin. "Chariotry to Cavalry: Developments in the Early First Millennium." Pages 57–79 in *New Perspectives on Ancient Warfare*. Edited by Garrett Fagan and Matthew Trundle. History of Warfare 59. Leiden: Brill, 2010.
Ashley, Timothy R. *The Book of Numbers*. NICOT. Grand Rapids, MI: Eerdmans, 1993.
Asikainen, Susanna. "The Masculinity of Jeremiah." *BibInt* 28, no. 1 (2020): 34–55.
Aune, David E. "The Social Matrix of the Apocalypse of John." *BR* 26 (1981): 16–32.
Avalos, Hector. "Introducing Sensory Criticism in Biblical Studies: Audiocentricity and Visiocentricity." Pages 47–59 in *This Abled Body: Rethinking Disabilities in Biblical Studies*. Edited by Hector Avalos, Sarah J. Melcher, and Jeremy Schipper. SemeiaSt 55. Atlanta: Society of Biblical Literature, 2007.
Avalos, Hector, Sarah J. Melcher, and Jeremy Schipper, eds. *This Abled Body: Rethinking Disabilities in Biblical Studies*. SemeiaSt 55. Atlanta: Society of Biblical Literature, 2007.
Avrahami, Yael. *The Senses of Scripture: Sensory Perception in the Hebrew Bible*. LHBOTS 545. London: T&T Clark, 2012.
Bach, Alice. "Dreaming of Miriam's Well." Pages 151–8 in *Exodus to Deuteronomy*. A Feminist Companion to the Bible (Second Series) 5. Edited by Athalya Brenner. Sheffield: Sheffield Academic Press, 2000.

Bachelard, Gaston. *The Poetics of Space*. Translated by Maria Jolas. Boston, MA: Beacon Press, 1994.

Baden, Joel S. and Candida R. Moss. "The Origin and Interpretation of ṣāraʿat in Leviticus 13–14." *JBL* 130, no. 4 (2011): 643–62.

Bærenholdt, Jørgen Ole and Brynhild Granås. "Places and Mobilities: Beyond the Periphery." Pages 1–12 in *Mobility and Place: Enacting Northern European Peripheries*. Edited by Jørgen Ole Bærenholdt and Brynhild Granås. Aldershot: Ashgate, 2008.

Bahrani, Zainab. *Rituals of War: The Body and Violence in Mesopotamia*. New York: Zone Books, 2008.

Baker, William R. "Did the Glory of Moses' Face Fade? A Reexamination of καταργέω in 2 Corinthians 3:7–18." *BBR* 10, no. 1 (2000): 1–15.

Bal, P. Matthijs and Martijn Veltkamp. "How Does Fiction Reading Influence Empathy? An Experimental Investigation on the Role of Emotional Transportation." *PLOS ONE* 8, no. 1 (2013): 1–12.

Balfour, Ian. *The Rhetoric of Romantic Prophecy*. Stanford, CA: Stanford University Press, 2002.

Barrick, W. Boyd. *The King and the Cemeteries: Toward a New Understanding of Josiah's Reform*. VTSup 88. Leiden: Brill, 2002.

Bartoshuk, Linda and Derek J. Snyder. "The Affect of Taste and Olfaction: The Key to Survival." Pages 235–54 in *Handbook of Emotions*. Edited by Lisa Feldman Barrett, Michael Lewis, and Jeanette M. Haviland-Jones. 4th ed. New York: The Guilford Press, 2016.

Batluck, Mark. "Religious Experience in New Testament Research." *CurBR* 9, no. 3 (2011): 339–63.

Bayer, Oswald. *Martin Luther's Theology: A Contemporary Interpretation*. Translated by Thomas H. Trapp. Grand Rapids, MI: Eerdmans, 2008.

Bayle, Dimitri J., Marie-Anne Henaff, and Pierre Krolak-Salmon. "Unconsciously Perceived Fear in Peripheral Vision Alerts the Limbic System: a MEG study." *PLOS ONE* 4, no. 12 (2009): e8207, 1–9.

Beal, Timothy K. and David M. Gunn, eds. *Reading Bibles, Writing Bodies: Identity and the Book*. London: Routledge, 1996.

Becker, Eve-Marie, Jan Dochhorn, and Else K. Holt, eds. *Trauma and Traumatization in Individual and Collective Dimensions: Insights from Biblical Studies and Beyond*. SANt 2. Göttingen: Vandenhoeck & Ruprecht, 2014.

Becker, Uwe. "The Book of Isaiah: Its Composition History." Pages 37–56 in *The Oxford Handbook of Isaiah*. Edited by Lena-Sofia Tiemeyer. Oxford: Oxford University Press, 2020.

Bellinger, William H., Jr. *Psalmody and Prophecy*. JSOTSup 27. Sheffield: JSOT Press, 1984.

Bellmann, Simon. "The Theological Character of the Old Latin Version of Esther." *JSP* 27, no. 1 (2017): 3–24.

Belnap, Dan. *Fillets of Fatling and Goblets of Gold: The Use of Meal Events in the Ritual Imagery in the Ugaritic Mythological and Epic Texts*. Gorgias Ugaritic Studies 4. Piscataway, NJ: Gorgias Press, 2008.

Ben Zvi, Ehud. "The Prophetic Book: A Key Form of Prophetic Literature." Pages 276–97 in *The Changing Face of Form Criticism for the Twenty-First Century*. Edited by Ehud Ben Zvi and Marvin A. Sweeney. Grand Rapids, MI: Eerdmans, 2003.

Berlant, Lauren. "Poor Eliza." *American Literature* 70, no. 3 (1998): 635–68.

Berquist, Jon. "Prophetic Legitimation in Jeremiah." *VT* 39 (1989): 129–39.

Bhavsar, Vishal, Antonio Ventriglio, and Dinesh Bhugra. "Dissociative Trance and Spirit Possession: Challenges for Cultures in Transition." *Psychiatry and Clinical Neurosciences* 70, no. 12 (2016), 551–9.

Biddle, Mark E. *Polyphony and Symphony in Prophetic Literature: Rereading Jeremiah 7-20*. Studies in Old Testament Interpretation 2. Macon, GA: Mercer University Press, 1996.

Black, Fiona C. and Jennifer L. Koosed. "Introduction: Some Ways to Read with Feeling." Pages 1–12 in *Reading with Feeling: Affect Theory and the Bible*. Edited by Fiona C. Black and Jennifer L. Koosed. SemeiaSt 95. Atlanta: Society of Biblical Literature, 2019.

Black, Fiona C. and Jennifer L. Koosed, eds. *Reading with Feeling: Affect Theory and the Bible*. SemeiaSt 95. Atlanta: Society of Biblical Literature, 2019.

Blenkinsopp, Joseph. *A History of Prophecy in Israel*. Philadelphia: Westminster, 1983.

Blenkinsopp, Joseph. *Sage, Priest, Prophet: Religious and Intellectual Leadership in Ancient Israel*. Library of Ancient Israel. Louisville: Westminster John Knox, 1995.

Block, Daniel I. *Ezekiel 1-24*. NICOT. Grand Rapids, MI: Eerdmans, 1997.

Boase, Elizabeth and Christopher G. Frechette, eds. *Bible through the Lens of Trauma*. Atlanta: Society of Biblical Literature, 2016.

Boda, Mark J., Daniel K. Falk, Rodney A. Werline, eds. *Seeking the Favor of God*. Vol. 1, The Origins of Penitential Prayer in Second Temple Judaism. Vol. 2, The Development of Penitential Prayer in Second Temple Judaism. Vol. 3, The Impact of Penitential Prayer beyond Second Temple Judaism. EJL 21–23. Atlanta: Society of Biblical Literature, 2006–8.

Bortz, Walter M., II. "The Disuse Syndrome." *West J Med* 141, no. 5 (1984): 691–4.

Bosworth, David A. *Infant Weeping in Akkadian, Hebrew, and Greek Literature*. Critical Studies in the Hebrew Bible 8. Winona Lake, IN: Eisenbrauns, 2016.

Bosworth, David A. "Revisiting Karl Barth's Exegesis of 1 Kings 13." *BibInt* 10, no. 4 (2001): 360–83.

Bosworth, David A. "The Tears of God in the Book of Jeremiah." *Biblica* 94, no. 1 (2013): 24–46.

Bourdieu, Pierre. *The Logic of Practice*. Translated by Richard Nice. Cambridge: Polity, 1990.

Bourdieu, Pierre. *Outline of a Theory of Practice*. Translated by Richard Nice. Cambridge: Cambridge University Press, 1977.

Bourguignon, Erika. "Introduction: A Framework for the Comparative Study of Altered States of Consciousness." Pages 1–35 in *Religion, Altered States of Consciousness, and Social Change*. Edited by Erika Bourguignon. Columbus: Ohio State University Press, 1973.

Boyarin, Daniel. "The Gospel of the Memra: Jewish Binitarianism and the Prologue to John." *HTR* 94, no. 3 (2001): 243–84.

Boyarin, Daniel. *A Radical Jew: Paul and the Politics of Identity*. Berkeley: University of California Press, 1994.

Bray, Karen. *Grave Attending: A Political Theology for the Unredeemed*. New York: Fordham University Press, 2020.

Bremmer, Jan N. "Balaam, Mopsus and Melampous: Tales of Travelling Seers." Pages 49–67 in *The Prestige of the Pagan Prophet Balaam in Judaism, Early Christianity and Islam*. Edited by George H. van Kooten and Jacques van Ruiten. Themes in Biblical Narrative 11. Leiden: Brill, 2008.

Brenner, Athalya, ed. *Exodus to Deuteronomy*. A Feminist Companion to the Bible (Second Series) 5. Sheffield: Sheffield Academic Press, 2000.

Breuer, Heidi. *Crafting the Witch: Gendering Magic in Medieval and Early Modern England*. Studies in Medieval History and Culture. New York: Routledge, 2009.

Bridgeman, Valerie. "Womanist Approaches to the Prophets." Pages 483–90 in *The Oxford Handbook of the Prophets*. Edited by Carolyn J. Sharp. Oxford: Oxford University Press, 2016.

Britt, Brian. *Rewriting Moses: The Narrative Eclipse of the Text*. JSOTSup 402. Gender, Culture, Theory 14. London: T&T Clark, 2004.

Brueggemann, Walter. *The Prophetic Imagination*. 2nd ed. Minneapolis: Augsburg Fortress, 2001.

Brummitt, Mark. "Of Broken Pots and Dirty Laundry: The Jeremiah Lehrstücke." *BCT* 2, no. 1 (2006): 3.1–10.

Bubl, Emanuel, et al. "Seeing Gray When Feeling Blue? Depression Can Be Measured in the Eye of the Diseased." *Biological Psychiatry* 68, no. 2 (2010): 205–8.

Budde, Karl. "Das hebräische Klagelied." *ZAW* 2 (1882): 1–52.

Bundock, Christopher M. *Romantic Prophecy and the Resistance to Historicism*. Toronto: University of Toronto Press, 2016.

Burns, Rita J. *Has the Lord Indeed Only Spoken through Moses? A Study of the Biblical Portrait of Miriam*. SBL Dissertation Series 84. Atlanta: Scholars Press, 1987.

Burrus, Virginia. *The Sex Lives of Saints: An Erotics of Ancient Hagiography*. Philadelphia: University of Pennsylvania Press, 2004.

Bynum, Caroline. "Why All the Fuss about the Body? A Medievalist's Perspective." *Critical Inquiry* 22, no. 1 (1995): 1–33.

Bynum, Caroline Walker. *Holy Feast and Holy Fast: The Religious Significance of Food to Medieval Women*. Berkeley: University of California Press, 1987.

Calero-Elvira, Ana, et al. "Descriptive Study of the Socratic Method: Evidence for Verbal Shaping." *Behavior Therapy* 44, no. 4 (2013): 625–38.

Cameron, Euan. *Enchanted Europe: Superstition, Reason, and Religion, 1250–1750*. Oxford: Oxford University Press, 2010.

Cameron, Euan. "For Reasoned Faith or Embattled Creed? Religion for the People in Early Modern Europe." *Transactions of the Royal Historical Society* 8 (1998): 165–87.

Cannon, Katie Geneva. "Sexing Black Women: Liberation from the Prisonhouse of Anatomical Authority." Pages 11–30 in *Loving the Body: Black Religious Studies and the Erotic*. Edited by Anthony B. Pinn and Dwight N. Hopkins. New York: Palgrave Macmillan, 2004.

Carlson, Reed. *Unfamiliar Selves in the Hebrew Bible: Possession and Other Spirit Phenomena*. Ekstasis: Religious Experience from Antiquity to the Middle Ages 9. Berlin: Walter de Gruyter, 2022.

Carpio, Genevieve. *Collisions at the Crossroads: How Place and Mobility Make Race*. Oakland: University of California Press, 2019.

Carr, David M. *Holy Resilience: The Bible's Traumatic Origins*. New Haven, CT: Yale University Press, 2014.

Carvalho, Corrine L. "Drunkenness, Tattoos, and Dirty Underwear: Jeremiah as a Modern Masculine Metaphor." *CBQ* 80, no. 4 (2019): 597–618.

Carvalho, Corinne L. "Finding a Treasure Map: Sacred Space in the Old Testament." Pages 123–52 in *Touching the Altar: The Old Testament for Christian Worship*. Edited by Carol M. Bechtel. The Calvin Institute of Christian Worship Liturgical Studies Series. Grand Rapids, MI: Eerdmans, 2008.

Carvalho, Corinne L. "Sex and the Single Prophet: Marital Status and Gender in Jeremiah and Ezekiel." Pages 237–67 in *Prophets Male and Female: Gender and Prophecy in the Hebrew Bible, the Eastern Mediterranean, and the Ancient Near East*. Edited by Jonathan Stökl and Corrine L. Carvalho. Ancient Israel and Its Literature 15. Atlanta, GA: Society of Biblical Literature, 2013.

Carvalho, Corinne L. "Whose Gendered Language of God? Contemporary Gender Theory and Divine Gender in the Prophets." *Currents in Theology and Mission* 43, no. 3 (2016): 12–16.

Carver, Daniel E. "Vision Signals and the Language of Vision Descriptions in the Prophets." *JSOT* 45, no. 1 (2021): 1–17.

Castilio, Arcadio del. "Tarshish in the Book of Jonah." *RB* 114, no. 4 (2007): 481–98.

Chamberlain, Stephen and Alicia E. Meuret. "Fight or Flight Response." Pages 1481–3 in *The SAGE Encyclopedia of Abnormal and Clinical Psychology*. Edited by Amy Wenzel. Los Angeles, CA: SAGE Reference, 2017.

Chapman, Stephen B. *1 Samuel as Christian Scripture: A Theological Commentary*. Grand Rapids, MI: Eerdmans, 2016.

Charland, Louis C. "Affect (Philosophical Perspectives)." Pages 9–10 in *The Oxford Companion to Emotion and the Affective Sciences*. Edited by David Sander and Klaus R. Scherer. Oxford: Oxford University Press, 2009.

Claassens, L. Juliana M. "Calling the Keeners: The Image of the Wailing Woman as Symbol of Survival in a Traumatized World." *Journal of Feminist Studies in Religion* 26, no. 1 (2010): 63–77.

Clark, Elizabeth A. *Reading Renunciation: Asceticism and Scripture in Early Christianity*. Princeton, NJ: Princeton University Press, 1999.

Clark-Soles, Jaime. *Engaging the Word: The New Testament and the Christian Believer*. Louisville, KY: Westminster John Knox, 2010.

Clements, Niki Kasumi. *Sites of the Ascetic Self: John Cassian and Christian Ethical Formation*. Notre Dame, IN: University of Notre Dame Press, 2020.

Cogan, Mordechai and Hayim Tadmor. *II Kings*. A New Translation with Introduction and Commentary. AB 11. Garden City, NJ: Doubleday, 1988.

Cohen, Jeffrey Jerome. "Monster Culture (Seven Theses)." Pages 3–25 in *Monster Theory: Reading Culture*. Edited by Jeffrey Jerome Cohen. Minneapolis: University of Minnesota Press, 1996.

Cohen, Jonathan. "Defining Identification: A Theoretical Look at the Identification of Audiences with Media Characters." *Mass Communication and Society* 4, no. 3 (2001): 245–64.

Collins, John J. *Daniel: A Commentary on the Book of Daniel*. Hermeneia. Minneapolis: Fortress, 1993.

Conrad, Edgar W. "God's Visions and God's Eyes in Ezekiel's Surrealistic Imagery." *The Bible and Critical Theory* 9, nos. 1–2 (2013): 54–60.

Cook, Joan E. *Hannah's Desire, God's Design: Early Interpretations of the Story of Hannah*. JSOTSup 282. Sheffield: Sheffield Academic Press, 1999.

Couroyer, Bernard. "Le 'doigt de dieu,' (Exode, viii, 15)." *RB* 63 (1956): 481–95.

Crenshaw, James L. *Prophetic Conflict: Its Effect upon Israelite Religion*. BZAW 124. Berlin: Walter de Gruyter, 1971.

Cresswell, Tim. *On the Move: Mobility in the Modern Western World*. New York: Routledge, 2006.

Crowther, Nigel B. "The Apobates Reconsidered (Demosthenes lxi 23–9)." *Journal of Hellenic Studies* 111 (1991): 174–6.

Cryer, Frederick H. *Divination in Ancient Israel and its Near Eastern Environment: A Socio-Historical Investigation*. JSOTSup 142. Sheffield: Sheffield Academic Press, 1994.

Csordas, Thomas J. "Embodiment as a Paradigm for Anthropology." *Ethos* 18, no.1 (1990): 5–47.

Cvetkovich, Ann. "Affect." In *Keywords for American Cultural Studies*. Edited by Bruce Burgett and Glenn Hendler. 2nd ed. New York University Press, 2014.

Czachesz, István. *Cognitive Science and the New Testament: A New Approach to Early Christian Research*. Oxford: Oxford University Press, 2017.

Dame, Enid. "A Paradoxical Prophet: Jewish Women Poets Re-Imagine Miriam." *Bridges: A Jewish Feminist Journal* 12, no. 1 (2007): 4–11.

Davis, Ellen F. *Biblical Prophecy: Perspectives for Christian Theology, Discipleship, and Ministry*. Louisville, KY: Westminster John Knox, 2014.

Davis, Ellen F. *Swallowing the Scroll: Textuality and the Dynamics of Discourse in Ezekiel's Prophecy*. Bible and Literature 21. Sheffield: Sheffield Academic Press, 1989.

Descartes, René. *Meditations on First Philosophy*. With Selections from the Objections and Replies. A Latin-English Edition. Edited and Translated by John Cottingham. Cambridge: Cambridge University Press, 2013.

Descartes, René. *The Passions of the Soul and Other Late Philosophical Writing*. Translated with an Introduction and Notes by Michael Moriarty. Oxford: Oxford University Press, 2015.

Deutscher, Penelope. "Three Touches to the Skin and One Look: Sartre and Beauvoir on Desire and Embodiment." Pages 143–59 in *Thinking through the Skin*. Edited by Sara Ahmed and Jackie Stacey. New York: Routledge, 2001.

Doan, William and Terry Giles. *Prophets, Performance, and Power: Performance Criticism of the Hebrew Bible*. London: T&T Clark, 2005.

Doka, Kenneth J. "Disenfranchised Grief." Pages 3–11 in *Disenfranchised Grief: Recognizing Hidden Sorrow*. Edited by Kenneth J. Doka. Lexington, MA: Lexington Books, 1989.

Doka, Kenneth J. "Memorialization, Ritual and Public Tragedy." Pages 182–93 in *Living with Grief: Coping with Public Tragedy*. Edited by Marcia Lattanzi-Licht and Kenneth J. Doka. New York: Brunner-Routledge, 2003.

Dougherty, Raymond Philip. *The Shirkûtu of Babylonian Deities*. New Haven, CT: Yale University Press, 1923.

Douglas, Sally. *Early Church Understandings of Jesus as the Female Divine: The Scandal of the Scandal of Particularity*. London: Bloomsbury T&T Clark, 2016.

Dozeman, Thomas B. "Inner-Biblical Interpretation of Yahweh's Gracious and Compassionate Character." *JBL* 108, no. 2 (1989): 207–23.

Dozeman, Thomas B. "The Way of the Man of God from Judah: True and False Prophecy in the Pre-Deuteronomic Legend of 1 Kings 13." *CBQ* 44, no. 3 (1982): 379–93.

Drescher, Jack. "Out of DSM: Depathologizing Homosexuality." *Behavioral Sciences* 5, no. 4 (2015): 565–75.

Drews, Robert. *The End of the Bronze Age: Changes in Warfare and the Catastrophe ca. 1200 B.C.* Princeton, NJ: Princeton University Press, 1993.

Duhm, Bernhard. *Das Buch Jesaia*. Göttingen: Vandenhoeck & Ruprecht, 1914.

Duhm, Bernhard. *Israels Propheten*. 2nd ed. Tübingen: J. C. B. Mohr, 1922.

Dunn, Jacob E. "A God of Volcanoes: Did Yahwism Take Root in Volcanic Ashes?" *JSOT* 38, no. 4 (2014): 387–424.

Dunn, James D. G. *The Theology of Paul the Apostle*. Grand Rapids, MI: Eerdmans, 1998.

Durand, Jean-Marie and Michaël Guichard. "Les rituels de Mari (textes n°. 2 à n°. 5)." Pages 19–74 in *Florilegium marianum*. Vol. 3, Recueil d'études à la mémoire de Marie-Thérèse Barrelet. Edited by Dominique Charpin and Jean-Marie Durand. Mémoires de NABU 4. Paris, SEPOA: 1997.

During, Emmanuel, et al. "A Critical Review of Dissociative Trance and Possession Disorders: Etiological, Diagnostic, Therapeutic, and Nosological Issues." *Can J Psychiatry* 56, no. 4 (2011): 235–42.

Eastman, Susan Grove. *Paul and the Person: Reframing Paul's Anthropology*. Grand Rapids, MI: Eerdmans, 2017.

Egger-Wenzel, Renate and Jeremy Corley, eds. *Emotions from Ben Sira to Paul*. DCLY 2011. Berlin: Walter de Gruyter, 2012.

Eilberg-Schwartz, Howard. "The Problem of the Body for the People of the Book." Pages 34–55 in *Reading Bibles, Writing Bodies: Identity and the Book*. Edited by Timothy K. Beal and David M. Gunn. London: Routledge, 1996.

Eisenstein, J. D. אוצר מדרשים [*Oṣar Midrashim*]: *A Library of Two Hundred Minor Midrashim*. 2 vols. Edited by J. D. Eisenstein. New York: J. D. Eisenstein, 1915.

Ekman, Paul, Robert W. Levenson, and Wallace V. Friesen. "Autonomic Nervous System Activity Distinguishes Among Emotions." *Science* 221, no. 4616 (1983), 1208–10.

Erzberger, Johanna. "Prophetic Sign Acts as Performances." Pages 104–16 in *Jeremiah Invented: Constructions and Deconstructions of Jeremiah*. Edited by Else K. Holt and Carolyn J. Sharp. LHBOTS 595. London: Bloomsbury T&T Clark, 2015.

Exum, J. Cheryl. "Second Thoughts about Secondary Characters: Women in Exodus 1.8–2.10." Pages 75–87 in *A Feminist Companion to Exodus to Deuteronomy*. The Feminist Companion to the Bible 6. Edited by Athalya Brenner. Sheffield: Sheffield Academic Press, 1994.

Farnell, Brenda. *Dynamic Embodiment for Social Theory: "I move therefore I am."* Ontological Explorations. New York: Routledge, 2012.

Fauconnier, Gilles and Mark Turner. *The Way We Think: Conceptual Blending and the Mind's Hidden Complexities*. New York: Basic Books, 2002.

Faust, Avraham. "Ethnic Complexity in Northern Israel During Iron Age II." *Palestine Exploration Quarterly* 132, no. 1 (2000): 2–27.

Fischer, Georg. "Riddles of Reference: 'I' and 'We' in the Books of Isaiah and Jeremiah: The Relation of the Suffering Characters in the Books of Isaiah and Jeremiah." *OTE* 25, no. 2 (2012): 277–91.

Fischer, Irmtraud. "The Authority of Miriam: A Feminist Rereading of Numbers 12 Prompted by Jewish Interpretation." Pages 159–73 in *Exodus to Deuteronomy*. A Feminist Companion to the Bible (Second Series) 5. Edited by Athalya Brenner. Sheffield: Sheffield Academic Press, 2000.

Fischer, Irmtraud and L. Juliana M. Claassens, eds. *Prophetie*. Die Bibel und die Frauen 1.2. Stuttgart: Kohlhammer, 2019.

Fitzgerald, Kaitlin and Melanie C. Green. "Narrative Persuasion: Effects of Transporting Stories on Attitudes, Beliefs, and Behaviors." Pages 49–68 in *Narrative Absorption*. Edited by Frank Hakemulder, Moniek M. Kuijpers, Ed S. Tan, Katalin Bálint, and Miruna M. Doicaru. Linguistic Approaches to Literature 27. Amsterdam: John Benjamins Publishing Company, 2017.

Flannery, Frances. "The Body and Ritual Reconsidered, Imagined, and Experienced." Pages 13–18 in *Experientia*. Vol. 1, Inquiry into Religious Experience in Early Judaism and Early Christianity. Edited by Frances Flannery, Colleen Shantz, and Rodney A. Werline. SBLSymS 40. Atlanta: Society of Biblical Literature, 2008.

Flannery, Frances. "Esoteric Mystical Practice in Fourth Ezra and the Reconfiguration of Social Memory." Pages 45–70 in *Experientia*. Vol. 2, Linking Text and Experience. Edited by Colleen Shantz and Rodney A Werline. EJL 35. Atlanta: Society of Biblical Literature, 2012.

Flannery, Frances. "'Go, Ask a Woman's Womb': Birth and the Maternal Body as Sources of Revelation and Wisdom in *4 Ezra*." *JSP* 21, no. 3 (2012): 243–58.

Flannery, Frances with Nicolae Roddy, Colleen Shantz, and Rodney A. Werline. "Introduction: Religious Experience, Past and Present." Pages 1–10 in *Experientia*. Vol. 1, Inquiry into Religious Experience in Early Judaism and Early Christianity. Edited by Frances Flannery, Colleen Shantz, and Rodney A. Werline. SBLSymS 40. Atlanta: Society of Biblical Literature, 2008.

Flannery, Frances, Colleen Shantz, and Rodney A. Werline, eds. *Experientia*. Vol. 1, Inquiry into Religious Experience in Early Judaism and Early Christianity. SBLSymS 40. Atlanta: Society of Biblical Literature, 2008.

Flannery-Dailey, Frances. *Dreamers, Scribes, and Priests: Jewish Dreams in the Hellenistic and Roman Eras*. JSJSup 90. Leiden: Brill, 2004.

Flesher, Paul V. M. and Bruce Chilton. *The Targums: A Critical Introduction*. SAIS 12. Leiden: Brill, 2011.

Foolen, Ad, Ulrike M. Lüdtke, Timothy P. Racine, and Jordan Zlatev, eds. *Moving Ourselves, Moving Others: Motion and Emotion in Intersubjectivity, Consciousness, and Language*. Consciousness & Emotion Book Series 6. Amsterdam: John Benjamins Publishing Company, 2012.

Foster, Brett and Safwat Marzouk. "Horns of Moses." In *Encyclopedia of the Bible and Its Reception Online*. Edited by Constance M. Furey, Peter Gemeinhardt, Joel Marcus LeMon, Thomas Römer, Jens Schröter, Barry Dov Walfish, and Eric Ziolkowski. Berlin and Boston: De Gruyter, 2016.

Fraade, Steven D. "Ascetical Aspects of Ancient Judaism." Pages 253–88 in *Jewish Spirituality: From the Bible through the Middle Ages*. Edited by Arthur Green. Vol. 13 of World Spirituality: An Encyclopedic History of the Religious Quest. New York: Crossroad, 1986.

Franken, Henk. "Balaam at Deir 'Alla and the Cult of Baal." Pages 183–202 in *Archaeology, History and Culture in Palestine and the Near East: Essays in Memory of Albert E. Glock*. Edited by Tomis Kapitan. Atlanta: Scholars Press, 1999.

Fretheim, Terence E. "Jonah and Theodicy." *ZAW* 90, no. 2 (1978): 227–37.

Fretheim, Terence E. *The Suffering of God: An Old Testament Perspective*. Overtures to Biblical Theology 14. Philadelphia, PA: Fortress Press, 1984.

Friedlander, Gerald, trans. and ed. *Pirḳê de Rabbi Eliezer*. London: Kegan Paul, Trench, Truber & Co. Ltd., 1916.

Frijda, Nico H. and Klaus R. Scherer. "Emotion Definitions (Psychological Perspectives)." Pages 143–4 in *The Oxford Companion to Emotion and the Affective Sciences*. Edited by David Sander and Klaus R. Scherer. Oxford: Oxford University Press, 2009.

Fritschel, Ann. "Women and Magic in the Hebrew Bible." Ph.D. dissertation, Emory University, 2003.

Fuchs, Esther. *Feminist Theory and the Bible: Interrogating the Sources*. Lanham, MD: Lexington Books, 2016.

Fuller, Robert C. *Wonder: From Emotion to Spirituality*. Chapel Hill: University of North Carolina Press, 2006.

Gafney, Wilda C. *Daughters of Miriam: Women Prophets in Ancient Israel*. Minneapolis: Fortress Press, 2008.

Gager, John G. "Body-Symbols and Social Reality: Resurrection, Incarnation and Asceticism in Early Christianity." *Religion* 12, no. 4 (1982): 345–64.

Garber, David G. "'I Went in Bitterness': Theological Implications of a Trauma Theory Reading of Ezekiel." *RevExp* 111, no. 4 (2014): 346–57.

Garcia-Romeu, Albert P. and Charles T. Tart. "Altered States of Consciousness and Transpersonal Psychology." Pages 121–40 in *The Wiley-Blackwell Handbook of Transpersonal Psychology*. Edited by Harris L. Friedman and Glenn Hartelius. Chichester, UK: Wiley Blackwell, 2013.

Garfinkel, Stephen. "Of Thistles and Thorns: A New Approach to Ezekiel ii 6." *VT* 37, no. 4 (1987): 421–37.

Garroway, Kristine Henriksen. "Moses's Slow Speech: Hybrid Identity, Language Acquisition, and the Meaning of Exodus 4:10." *BibInt* 28, no. 5 (2020): 635–57.

Gatens, Moira. *Imaginary Bodies: Ethics, Power, and Corporeality*. London: Routledge, 1996.

Gawande, Atul. "Hellhole." *The New Yorker* (March 30, 2009), https://www.newyorker.com/magazine/2009/03/30/hellhole.

Glanz, Oliver. *Understanding Participant-Reference Shifts in the Book of Jeremiah: A Study of Exegetical Method and Its Consequences for the Interpretation of Referential Incoherence*. Studia Semitica Neerlandica 60. Leiden: Brill, 2013.

Glazov, Gregory Yuri. *The Bridling of the Tongue and the Opening of the Mouth in Biblical Prophecy*. LHBOTS 311. Sheffield: Sheffield Academic Press, 2001.

Goehring, James E. "Asceticism." Pages 127–30 in *Encyclopedia of Early Christianity*. Edited by Everett Ferguson with Michael P. McHugh and Frederick W. Norris. 2nd ed. New York: Routledge, 1999.

Goffman, Erving. *Forms of Talk*. Philadelphia: University of Pennsylvania Press, 1981.

Goffman, Erving. "The Neglected Situation." *American Anthropologist* 66, no. 6, part 2 (1964): 133–6.

Gold, Katherine J., et al. "Assessment of 'Fresh' versus 'Macerated' as Accurate Markers of Time Since Intrauterine Fetal Demise in Low-Income Countries." *International Journal of Gynecology and Obstetrics* 125, no. 3 (2014): 223–7.

Gordon, Robert P. "Prophecy in the Mari and Nineveh Archives." Pages 37–57 in *"Thus Speaks Ishtar of Arbela": Prophecy in Israel, Assyria, and Egypt in the Neo-Assyrian Period*. Edited by Robert P. Gordon and Hans M. Barstad. Winona Lake: Eisenbrauns, 2013.

Gordon, Robert P. and Hans M. Barstad, eds. *"Thus Speaks Ishtar of Arbela": Prophecy in Israel, Assyria, and Egypt in the Neo-Assyrian Period*. Winona Lake, IN: Eisenbrauns, 2013.

Gorin, Moti. "Towards a Theory of Interpersonal Manipulation." Pages 73–97 in *Manipulation: Theory and Practice*. Edited by Christian Coons and Michael Weber. New York: Oxford University Press, 2014.

Grabbe, Lester L. "'Her Outdoors': An Anthropological Perspective on Female Prophets and Prophecy." Pages 11–26 in *Prophets Male and Female: Gender and Prophecy in the Hebrew Bible, the Eastern Mediterranean, and the Ancient Near East*. Edited by Jonathan Stökl and Corrine L. Carvalho. Ancient Israel and Its Literature 15. Atlanta: Society of Biblical Literature, 2013.

Grabbe, Lester L. *Priests, Prophets, Diviners, Sages: A Socio-Historical Study of Religious Specialists in Ancient Israel*. Valley Forge, PA: Trinity Press International, 1995.

Grant, Deena E. *Divine Anger in the Hebrew Bible*. CBQMS 52. Washington, DC: Catholic Biblical Association of America, 2014.

Gray, William. "The Myth of the Word Discarnate." *Theology* 88, no. 722 (1985): 112–17.

Graybill, Rhiannon. *Are We Not Men? Unstable Masculinity in the Hebrew Prophets*. Oxford: Oxford University Press, 2016.

Graybill, Rhiannon. "Masculinity, Materiality, and the Body of Moses." *BibInt* 23 (2015): 518–40.

Graybill, Rhiannon. "Prophecy and the Problem of Happiness: The Case of Jonah." Pages 95–112 in *Reading with Feeling: Affect Theory and the Bible*. Edited by Fiona C. Black and Jennifer L. Koosed. SemeiaSt 95. Atlanta: SBL Press, 2019.

Green, Barbara, O.P. "Sunk in the Mud: Literary Correlation and Collaboration between King and Prophet in the Book of Jeremiah." Pages 34–48 in *Jeremiah Invented: Constructions and Deconstructions of Jeremiah*. Edited by Else K. Holt and Carolyn J. Sharp. LHBOTS 595. London: Bloomsbury T&T Clark, 2015.

Greenberg, Moshe. *Ezekiel 1–20. A New Translation with Introduction and Commentary*. AB 22. Garden City, NY: Doubleday, 1983.

Greene, John T. "The Old Testament Prophet as Messenger in the Light of Ancient Near Eastern Messengers and Messages." Ph.D. dissertation, Boston University Graduate School, 1980.

Grey, Jacqueline. "Embodiment and the Prophetic Message in Isaiah's Memoir." *Pneuma* 39, no. 4 (2017): 431–56.

Guenther, Lisa. *Solitary Confinement: Social Death and its Afterlives*. Minneapolis: University of Minnesota Press, 2013.

Guest, Deryn, Robert E. Goss, Mona West, and Thomas Bohache, eds. *The Queer Bible Commentary*. London: SCM, 2006.

Gunkel, Hermann. "Einleitungen." Pages xi–lxxii in *Die grossen Propheten*. By Hans Schmidt. Göttingen: Vandenhoeck & Ruprecht, 1915.

Habel, Norman. "The Form and Significance of the Call Narratives." *ZAW* 77, no. 3 (1965): 297–323.

Hagen, Fredrik. "New Kingdom Sandals: A Philological Perspective." Pages 193–203 in *Tutankhamun's Footwear: Studies of Ancient Egyptian Footwear*. Edited by André J. Veldmeijer. Leiden: Sidestone Press, 2011.

Hammer, Jill. "*Pirkei Imahot*/Sayings of the Mothers." Pages 46–7 in *The Book of Earth and Other Mysteries*. By Jill Hammer. Cincinnati, OH: Dimus Parrhesia Press, 2016.

Hamori, Esther J. "Childless Female Diviners in the Bible and Beyond." Pages 169–92 in *Prophets Male and Female: Gender and Prophecy in the Hebrew Bible, the Eastern Mediterranean, and the Ancient Near East*. Edited by Jonathan Stökl and Corrine L. Carvalho. Ancient Israel and Its Literature 15. Atlanta: Society of Biblical Literature, 2013.

Hamori, Esther J. *"When Gods Were Men": The Embodied God in Biblical and Near Eastern Literature*. BZAW 384. Berlin: Walter De Gruyter, 2008.

Hamori, Esther J. *Women's Divination in Biblical Literature: Prophecy, Necromancy, and Other Arts of Knowledge*. AYBRL. New Haven, CT: Yale University Press, 2015.

Hannam, Kevin, Mimi Sheller, and John Urry. "Editorial: Mobilities, Immobilities and Moorings." *Mobilities* 1 (2006): 1–22.

Hansen, Mark B. "Affect as Medium, or the 'Digital-Facial-Image.'" *Journal of Visual Culture* 2, no. 2 (2003), 205–28.
Harari, Yuval. "Ancient Israel and Early Judaism." Pages 139–74 in *Guide to the Study of Ancient Magic*. Edited by David Frankfurter. Leiden: Brill, 2019.
Hardtke, Thomas, Ulrich Schmiedel, and Tobias Tan, eds. *Religious Experience Revisited: Expressing the Inexpressible?* Studies in Theology and Religion 21. Leiden: Brill, 2016.
Harkins, Angela Kim. *Reading with an "I" to the Heavens: Looking at the Qumran Hodayot through the Lens of Visionary Traditions*. Ekstasis 3. Berlin: Walter de Gruyter, 2012.
Harrington, Daniel J. "The Apocalypse of Hannah: Targum Jonathan of 1 Samuel 2:1–10." Pages 147–52 in *"Working with No Data": Semitic and Egyptian Studies Presented to Thomas O. Lambdin*. Edited by David M. Golomb with Susan T. Hollis. Winona Lake, IN: Eisenbrauns, 1987.
Harrison, Carol. *The Art of Listening in the Early Church*. Oxford: Oxford University Press, 2013.
Hartenstein, Friedhelm. "Cherubim and Seraphim in the Bible and in the Light of Ancient Near Eastern Sources." Pages 155–88 in *Angels: The Concept of Celestial Beings: Origins, Development and Reception*. Edited by Friedrich V. Reiterer, Tobias Nicklas, and Karin Schöpflin. DCLY 2007. Berlin: Walter de Gruyter, 2007.
Hartung, Franziska, et al. "Taking Perspective: Personal Pronouns Affect Experiential Aspects of Literary Reading." *PLOS ONE* 11, no. 5 (2016): e0154732, 1–18.
Hauser, Alan J. and Russell Gregory. *From Carmel to Horeb: Elijah in Crisis*. Edited by Alan J. Hauser. JSOTSup 85. Bible and Literature 19. Sheffield: Almond, 1990.
Havea, Jione. *Jonah*. Earth Bible Commentary. London: T&T Clark, 2020.
Hecker, Joel. *Mystical Bodies, Mystical Meals: Eating and Embodiment in Medieval Kabbalah*. Detroit: Wayne State University Press, 2005.
Hens-Piazza, Gina. *1—2 Kings*. AOTC. Nashville, TN: Abingdon Press, 2006.
Heschel, Abraham Joshua. *The Prophets*. New York: Harper & Row, 1962.
Hilber, John W. *Cultic Prophecy in the Psalms*. BZAW 352. Berlin: Walter de Gruyter, 2005.
Hildebrandt, Samuel. "Whose Voice is Heard? Speaker Ambiguity in the Psalms." *CBQ* 82, no. 2 (2020): 197–213.
Hoffman, Paul. *Essays on Descartes*. Oxford: Oxford University Press, 2009.
Holladay, William Lee. *Jeremiah 1: A Commentary on the Book of the Prophet Jeremiah, Chapters 1–25*. Hermeneia. Minneapolis: Augsburg Fortress, 1986.
Hölscher, Gustav. *Die Profeten: Untersuchungen zur Religionsgeschichte Israels*. Leipzig: J. C. Hinrichs, 1914.
Holt, Else K. "The Prophet as Persona." Pages 299–318 in *The Oxford Handbook of the Prophets*. Edited by Carolyn J. Sharp. Oxford: Oxford University Press, 2016.
Hoop, Raymond de. "Lamentations: The Qina-Metre Questioned." Pages 80–104 in *Delimitation Criticism: A New Tool in Biblical Scholarship*. Edited by Marjo C. A. Korpel and Josef M. Oesch. Assen: Van Gorcum, 2000.
Hornsby, Teresa. "Ezekiel." Pages 412–26 in *The Queer Bible Commentary*. Edited by Deryn Guest, Robert E. Goss, Mona West, and Thomas Bohache. London: SCM Press, 2006.
Hornsby, Teresa. "Ezekiel Off-Broadway." *BCT* 2, no. 1 (2006): 2.1–8.
Hunt, Hannah. *Clothed in the Body: Asceticism, the Body, and the Spiritual in the Late Antique Era*. Ashgate Studies in Philosophy & Theology in Late Antiquity. Farnham: Ashgate, 2012.

Husser, Jean-Marie. *Dreams and Dream Narratives in the Biblical World*. Translated by Jill M. Munro. Sheffield: Sheffield Academic Press, 1999.
Idel, Moshe. *Kabbalah: New Perspectives*. New Haven, CT: Yale University Press, 1988.
Insell, Paul, et al. *Nutrition*. 6th ed. Burlington, MA: Jones & Bartlett Learning, 2017.
Izard, Carroll and Brian Ackerman. "Motivational, Organizational, and Regulatory Functions of Discrete Emotions." Pages 253–64 in *Handbook of Emotions*. Edited by Michael Lewis and Jeannette M. Haviland-Jones. 2nd ed. New York: Guilford Press, 2000.
Jasper, Alison. *Shining Garment of the Text: Gendered Readings of John's Prologue*. JSNTSup. 165. Gender, Culture, Theory 6. Sheffield: Sheffield Academic Press, 1998.
Jassen, Alex. *Mediating the Divine: Prophecy and Revelation in the Dead Sea Scrolls and Second Temple Judaism*. STDJ 68. Leiden: Brill, 2007.
Jeffers, Anne. *Magic and Divination in Ancient Palestine and Syria*. Studies in the History and Culture of the Ancient Near East 8. Leiden: Brill, 1996.
Jewett, Robert. *Paul's Anthropological Terms: A Study of Their Use in Conflict Settings*. Leiden: Brill, 1971.
Jobe, Sarah C. "Carceral Hermeneutics: Discovering the Bible in Prison and Prison in the Bible." *Religions* 10, no. 2 (2019): 101.1–14.
Jobe, Sarah C. "Jeremiah's Non-Burial Refrain." Pages 466–80 in *The Oxford Handbook of Jeremiah*. Edited by Louis Stulman and Edward Silver. Oxford: Oxford University Press, 2021.
Jobling, David. *The Sense of Biblical Narrative: Structural Analyses in the Hebrew Bible*. 2 vols. JSOTSup 7, 39. Sheffield: JSOT Press, 1986–1987.
Johnson, Elizabeth A. *Ask the Beasts: Darwin and the God of Love*. London: Bloomsbury, 2014.
Johnson, Luke Timothy. *Religious Experience in Earliest Christianity: A Missing Dimension in New Testament Studies*. Minneapolis, MN: Fortress, 1998.
Jong, Matthijs J. de. *Isaiah among the Ancient Near Eastern Prophets: A Comparative Study of the Earliest Stages of the Isaiah Tradition and the Neo-Assyrian Prophecies*. VTSup 117. Leiden: Brill, 2007.
Jong, Matthijs J. de. "Jeremiah and Prophetic Authority." Pages 267–81 in *The Oxford Handbook of Jeremiah*. Edited by Louis Stulman and Edward Silver. Oxford: Oxford University Press, 2021.
Junior, Nyasha and Jeremy Schipper. "Disability Studies and the Bible." Pages 21–37 in *New Meanings for Ancient Texts: Recent Approaches to Biblical Criticisms and Their Applications*. Edited by Steven L. McKenzie and John Kaltner. Louisville: Westminster John Knox, 2013.
Junior, Nyasha and Jeremy Schipper. "Mosaic Disability and Identity in Exodus 4:10; 6:12, 30." *BibInt* 16 (2008): 428–41.
Kakihara, Masao and Carsten Sørensen. "Expanding the 'Mobility' Concept." *ACM SIGGROUP Bulletin* 22, no. 3 (2001): 33–7.
Kalmanofsky, Amy. "Israel's Open Sore in the Book of Jeremiah." *JBL* 135, no. 2 (2016): 247–63.
Kalmanofsky, Amy. "Postmodern Engagements of the Prophets." Pages 548–68 in *The Oxford Handbook of the Prophets*. Edited by Carolyn J. Sharp. Oxford: Oxford University Press, 2016.
Kalmanofsky, Amy. *Terror All Around: The Rhetoric of Horror in the Book of Jeremiah*. LHBOTS 390. London: Bloomsbury T&T Clark, 2008.

Kamionkowski, S. Tamar and Wonil Kim. *Bodies, Embodiment, and Theology of the Hebrew Bible*. LHBOTS 465. London: T&T Clark, 2010.

Kamp, Albert. *Inner Worlds: A Cognitive Linguistic Approach to the Book of Jonah*. Translated by David Orton. Biblical Interpretation Series 68. Leiden: Brill, 2004.

Kaplan, Jonathan. "Jonah and Moral Agency." *JSOT* 43, no. 2 (2019): 146–62.

Kazen, Thomas. *Emotions in Biblical Law: A Cognitive Science Approach*. Hebrew Bible Monographs 36. Sheffield: Sheffield-Phoenix, 2011.

Keefe, Alice. *Woman's Body and the Social Body in Hosea 1–2*. JSOTSup 338. Gender, Culture, Theory 10. Sheffield: Sheffield Academic Press, 2001.

Keesing, Roger M. "Toward a Model of Role Analysis." Pages 423–53 in *A Handbook of Method in Cultural Anthropology*. Edited by Raoul Naroll and Ronald Cohen. New York: Natural History Press, 1971.

Kelle, Brad E. *Hosea 2: Metaphor and Rhetoric in Historical Perspective*. Academia Biblica 20. Atlanta: Society of Biblical Literature, 2005.

Kelle, Brad E. "The Phenomenon of Israelite Prophecy in Contemporary Scholarship." *CurBR* 12, no. 3 (2014): 275–320.

Kelman, Herbert C. "Violence Without Moral Restraint: Reflections on the Dehumanization of Victims and Victimizers." *Journal of Social Issues* 29, no. 4 (1973): 25–61.

Kessler, Rainer. "Micah." Pages 461–72 in *The Oxford Handbook of the Minor Prophets*. Edited by Julia M. O'Brien. Oxford: Oxford University Press, 2021.

Kessler, Rainer. "Miriam and the Prophecy of the Persian Period." Pages 77–86 in *Prophets and Daniel*. The Feminist Companion to the Bible (Second Series) 8. Edited by Athalya Brenner. Sheffield: Sheffield Academic Press, 2001.

Kihlstrom, John. "Is Hypnosis an Altered State of Consciousness *or What?*" *Contemporary Hypnosis* 22, no. 1 (2005): 34–8.

Kim, Koowon. *Incubation as a Type-Scene in the 'Aqhatu, Kirta, and Hannah Stories: A Form-Critical and Narratological Study of KTU 1.14 I–1.15 III, 1.17 I–II, and 1 Samuel 1:1–2:11*. VTSup 145. Leiden: Brill, 2011.

Kissling, Paul J. *Reliable Characters in the Primary History: Profiles of Moses, Joshua, Elijah and Elisha*. JSOTSup 224. Sheffield: Sheffield Academic Press, 1996.

Kita, Yusuke and Yoshio Nakatani. "Smell-Based Memory Recollection and Communication Support." Pages 128–34 in *Haptic and Audio Interaction Design*. 6th International Workshop, HAID 2011, Kusatsu, Japan, August 25-26, 2011, Proceedings. Edited by Eric W. Cooper et al. Berlin: Springer, 2011.

Knafl, Anne K. *Forming God: Divine Anthropomorphism in the Pentateuch*. Siphrut 12. Winona Lake, IN: Eisenbrauns, 2014.

Knauf, Ernst Axel. "Prophets That Never Were." Pages 451–6 in *Gott und Mensch im Dialog. Festschrift für otto Kaiser zum 80. Geburtstag*. Edited by Markus Witte. Berlin: Walter de Gruyter, 2004.

Ko, Ming Him. *The Levite Singers in Chronicles and Their Stabilizing Role*. LHBOTS 657. London: Bloomsbury T&T Clark, 2017.

Koosed, Jennifer L. "Moses: The Face of Fear." *BibInt* 22, nos. 4–5 (2014): 414–29.

Koosed, Jennifer L. and Stephen D. Moore, eds. "Affect Theory and the Bible." Special Issue. *BibInt* 22, nos. 4–5 (2014).

Korpel, Marjo C. A. "Who is Speaking in Jeremiah 4:19–22? The Contribution of Unit Delimitation to an Old Problem." *VT* 59, no. 1 (2009): 88–98.

Kotrosits, Maia. "How Things Feel: Biblical Studies, Affect Theory, and the (Im)Personal," *Brill Research Perspectives in Biblical Interpretation* 1, no. 1 (2016): 1–53.

Kövecses, Zoltán. "Cross-Cultural Experiences of Anger: A Psycholinguistic Analysis." Pages 157–75 in *International Handbook of Anger: Constituent and Concomitant Biological, Psychological, and Social Processes*. Edited by Michael Potegal, Gerhard Stemmler, and Charles Spielberger. New York: Springer, 2010.

Kozlowska, Kasia, et al. "Fear and the Defense Cascade: Clinical Implications and Management." *Harvard Review of Psychiatry* 23, no. 4 (2015), 263–87.

Kuch, Hannes. "The Rituality of Humiliation: Exploring Symbolic Vulnerability." Pages 37–56 in *Humiliation, Degradation, Dehumanization: Human Dignity Violated*. Edited by Paulus Kaufmann et al. New York: Springer, 2011.

LaBar, Kevin. "Fear and Anxiety." Pages 751–73 in *Handbook of Emotions*. Edited by Michael Lewis, Jeannette M. Haviland-Jones, and Lisa Feldman Barrett. 3rd ed. New York: Guilford Press, 2008.

Laffin, Michael Richard. *The Promise of Martin Luther's Political Theology: Freeing Luther from the Modern Political Narrative*. Enquiries in Theological Ethics. London: Bloomsbury, 2016.

Lakoff, George and Mark Johnson. *Metaphors We Live By*. Chicago, IL: University of Chicago Press, 1980.

Lakoff, George and Mark Johnson. *Philosophy in the Flesh: The Embodied Mind and its Challenge to Western Thought*. New York: Basic Books, 1999.

Lambert, David A. *How Repentance Became Biblical: Judaism, Christianity, and the Interpretation of Scripture*. Oxford: Oxford University Press, 2016.

Lambert, David A. "Mourning over Sin/Affliction and the Problem of 'Emotion' as a Category in the Hebrew Bible." Pages 139–60 in *Mixed Feelings and Vexed Passions: Exploring Emotions in Biblical Literature*. Edited by F. Scott Spencer. Resources for Biblical Study 90. Atlanta, GA: SBL Press, 2017.

Lapsley, Jacqueline E. "Shame and Self-Knowledge: The Positive Role of Shame in Ezekiel's View of the Moral Self." Pages 143–73 in *The Book of Ezekiel: Theological and Anthropological Perspectives*. SBLSymS 9. Edited by Margaret S. Odell and John T. Strong. Atlanta, GA: SBL, 2000.

Latour, Bruno. "Trains of Thought—Piaget, Formalism and the Fifth Dimension." *Common Knowledge* 6, no. 3 (1997): 170–91.

Launderville, Dale. *Celibacy in the Ancient World: Its Ideal and Practice in Pre-Hellenistic Israel, Mesopotamia, and Greece*. Collegeville, MN: Liturgical Press, 2010.

Lawrence, Louise J. *Sense and Stigma in the Gospels: Depictions of Sensory-Disabled Characters*. Oxford: Oxford University Press, 2013.

Lee, Margaret E., ed. *Sound Matters: New Testament Studies in Sound Mapping*. Biblical Performance Criticism 16. Eugene, OR: Cascade, 2018.

Lee, Nancy C. *The Singers of Lamentations: Cities under Siege, from Ur to Jerusalem to Sarajevo*. Biblical Interpretation 60. Leiden: Brill, 2002.

Legaspi, Michael C. *The Death of Scripture and the Rise of Biblical Studies*. Oxford: Oxford University Press, 2010.

Leon-Sarmiento, Fidias E., Edwin Paez, and Mark Hallett. "Nature and Nurture in Stuttering: A Systematic Review on the Case of Moses." *Neurological Sciences* 34, no. 2 (2013): 231–7.

Leveen, Adriane. "Returning the Body to Its Place: Ezekiel's Tour of the Temple." *HTR* 105, no. 4 (2012): 385–401.

Levison, John. "Prophecy in Ancient Israel: The Case of the Ecstatic Elders." *CBQ* 65, no. 4 (2003): 503–21.

Lewis, I. M. *Ecstatic Religion: A Study of Shamanism and Spirit Possession*. 3rd ed. London: Routledge, 2003.
Lewis-Fernández, Roberto and Neil Krishan Aggarwal. "Culture and Psychiatric Diagnosis." *Advances in Psychosomatic Medicine* 33 (2013): 15–30.
Leyerle, Blake and Robin Darling Young. "Introduction." Pages 1–8 in *Ascetic Culture: Essays in Honor of Philip Rousseau*. Edited by Blake Leyerle and Robin Darling Young. Notre Dame, IN: University of Notre Dame Press, 2013.
Limburg, James. *Jonah: A Commentary*. OTL. Louisville: Westminster John Knox, 1993.
Lindblom, Johannes. *Prophecy in Ancient Israel*. Philadelphia: Fortress, 1962.
Linnell, Per. *The Written Language Bias in Linguistics: Its Nature, Origins, and Transformations*. Routledge Advances in Communication and Linguistic Theory. London: Routledge, 2005.
Lipton, Diana. "Early Mourning? Petitionary versus Posthumous Ritual in Ezekiel XXIV." *VT* 56, no. 2 (2006): 185–202.
Littlemore, Jeanette. *Metonymy: Hidden Shortcuts in Language, Thought, and Communication*. Cambridge: Cambridge University Press, 2015.
Lloyd, Genevieve. *The Man of Reason: "Male" & "Female" in Western Philosophy*. 2nd ed. London: Routledge, 1993.
Lo, Yuk Ming Dennis, et al. "Two-Way Cell Traffic between Mother and Fetus: Biologic and Clinical Implications." *Blood* 88, no. 11 (1996): 4390–5.
Løland Levinson, Hanne. "The Never-Ending Search for God's Feminine Side: Feminine Aspects in the God-Image of the Prophets." Pages 393–409 in *The Bible and Women. An Encyclopedia of Exegesis and Cultural History*, Vol. 1.2, Prophecy and Gender in the Hebrew Bible. Edited by L. Juliana Claassens and Irmtraud Fischer with the assistance of Funlola O. Olojede. Atlanta: SBL Press, 2021.
Ludwig, Arnold M. "Altered States of Consciousness." *Archives of General Psychiatry* 15, no. 3 (1966): 225–34.
Lundbom, Jack R. *Jeremiah 1–20*. A New Translation with Introduction and Commentary. AYB 21A. New York: Doubleday, 1999.
Lupton, Deborah. *Food, the Body, and the Self*. London: Sage Publications, 1996.
Lupton, Deborah. "Infant Embodiment and Interembodiment: A Review of Sociocultural Perspectives." *Childhood* 20, no. 1 (2012): 37–50.
Lynch, Gay Ord Pollock. "'Why Do Your Eyes Not Run Like a River?' Ritual Tears in Ancient and Modern Greek Funerary Traditions." Pages 67–82 in *Holy Tears: Weeping in the Religious Imagination*. Edited by Kimberley Christine Patton and John Stratton Hawley. Princeton: Princeton University Press, 2005.
Lynn, Steven Jay, Irving Kirsch, and Michael N. Hallquist. "Social Cognitive Theories of Hypnosis." Pages 111–40 in *The Oxford Handbook of Hypnosis: Theory, Research, and Practice*. Edited by Michael R. Nash and Amanda Barnier. Oxford: Oxford University Press, 2008.
MacDonald, Nathan. "The Spirit of YHWH: An Overlooked Conceptualization of Divine Presence in the Persian Period." Pages 95–120 in *Divine Presence and Absence in Exilic and Post-Exilic Judaism*. Edited by Nathan MacDonald and Izaak de Hulster. FAT 2/61. Tübingen: Mohr-Siebeck, 2013.
Mackie, Scott D. "The Passion of Eve and the Ecstasy of Hannah: Sense Perception, Passion, Mysticism, and Misogyny in Philo of Alexandria, De ebrietate 143–52." *JBL* 133, no. 1 (2014): 141–63.

Macwilliam, Stuart. *Queer Theory and the Prophetic Marriage Metaphor in the Hebrew Bible*. Sheffield: Equinox, 2011.

McCall, Robin C. "The Body and Being of God in Ezekiel." *RevExp* 111, no. 4 (2014): 376–89.

McEntire, Mark. "From Bound and Gagged to Swimming in the Water of Life: How God Breaks and Heals Ezekiel." *RevExp* 111, no. 4 (2014): 329–36.

McKenzie, Steven L. *1 Kings 16 – 2 Kings 16*. IECOT. Stuttgart, W. Kohlhammer, 2019.

McLuhan, Marshall. *Understanding Media: The Extensions of Man*. Corte Madera, CA: Gingko Press, 2003.

Maier, Christl M. "Feminist Interpretation of the Prophets." Pages 467–82 in *The Oxford Handbook of the Prophets*. Edited by Carolyn J. Sharp. Oxford: Oxford University Press, 2016.

Maier, Christl M. "Die Klage der Tochter Zion." *BThZ* 15, no. 2 (1998): 176–89.

Maier, Christl M. and Carolyn J. Sharp, eds. *Prophecy and Power: Jeremiah in Feminist and Postcolonial Perspective*. LHBOTS 577. London: Bloomsbury T&T Clark, 2013.

Martin, Craig and Russell T. McCutcheon, with Leslie Dorrough Smith, eds. *Religious Experience: A Reader*. Critical Categories in the Study of Religion. New York: Routledge, 2014.

Martin, Dale B. and Patricia Cox Miller, eds. *The Cultural Turn in Late Ancient Studies: Gender, Asceticism, and Historiography*. Durham, NC: Duke University Press, 2005.

Mathews, Freya. "The Dilemma of Dualism." Pages 54–70 in *Routledge Handbook of Gender and Environment*. Edited by Sherilyn MacGregor. London: Routledge, 2017.

Mathews, Jeanette. *Performing Habakkuk: Faithful Re-enactment in the Midst of Crisis*. Eugene, OR: Pickwick, 2012.

Mellinkoff, Ruth. *The Horned Moses in Medieval Art and Thought*. Eugene, OR: Wipf and Stock, 1997.

Merleau-Ponty, Maurice. *Phenomenology of Perception*. Translated by Donald Landes. New York: Routledge, 2012.

Merwe, C. H. J. van der. "A Cognitive Linguistic Perspective on הִנֵּה in the Pentateuch, Joshua, Judges, and Ruth." *HS* 48 (2007): 101–40.

Meyer, Birgit. *Religious Sensations: Why Media, Aesthetics and Power Matter in the Study of Contemporary Religion*. Amsterdam: Vrije Universiteit, 2006.

Meyers, Carol. *Exodus*. New Cambridge Bible Commentary. Cambridge: Cambridge University Press, 2005.

Mezzich, Juan E., et al. "The Place of Culture in DSM-IV." *The Journal of Nervous and Mental Disease* 187, no. 8 (1999): 457–64.

Michaelsen, Peter. "Ecstasy and Possession in Ancient Israel: A Review of Some Recent Contributions." *SJOT* 3, no. 2 (1989): 28–54.

Middlemas, Jill. "Prophecy and Diaspora." Pages 37–54 in *The Oxford Handbook of the Prophets*. Edited by Carolyn J. Sharp. Oxford: Oxford University Press, 2016.

Miles, Margaret R. *Carnal Knowing: Female Nakedness and Religious Meaning in the Christian West*. Boston, MA: Beacon Press, 1989.

Milgrom, Jacob. *Leviticus: A Book of Ritual and Ethics*. Continental Commentary. Minneapolis, MN: Fortress Press, 2004.

Miller, Patricia Cox. "The Blazing Body: Ascetic Desire in Jerome's Letter to Eustochium." *JECS* 1, no. 1 (1993): 21–45.

Miller, Patricia Cox. *The Corporeal Imagination: Signifying the Holy in Late Ancient Christianity*. Philadelphia: University of Pennsylvania Press, 2009.

Miller, Patricia Cox. "Desert Asceticism and 'The Body from Nowhere.'" *JECS* 2, no. 2 (1994): 137–53.

Miller-Naudé, Cynthia L. and C. H. J. van der Merwe. "הִנֵּה and Mirativity in Biblical Hebrew." *HS* 52, no. 1 (2011): 53–81.

Mills, Mary E. *Alterity, Pain, and Suffering in Isaiah, Jeremiah and Ezekiel*. LHBOTS 479. New York: T&T Clark, 2007.

Minnich, Nelson. "Prophecy and the Fifth Lateran Council (1512-1517)." Pages 63–87 in *Prophetic Rome in the High Renaissance Period*. Edited by Marjorie Reeves. Oxford: Oxford University Press, 1992.

Mirguet, Françoise. *An Early History of Compassion: Emotion and Imagination in Hellenistic Judaism*. Cambridge: Cambridge University Press, 2017.

Mirguet, Françoise and Dominika Kurek-Chomycz, eds. "Emotions in Ancient Jewish Literature: Definitions and Approaches." *BibInt* 24, no. 4–5 (2016).

Mittman, Asa Simon. "Introduction: The Impact of Monsters and Monster Studies." Pages 1–14 in *The Ashgate Research Companion to Monsters and the Monstrous*. Edited by Asa Simon Mittman with Peter J. Dendle. London: Routledge, 2017.

Moberly, R. W. L. "Jonah, God's Objectionable Mercy, and the Way of Wisdom." Pages 154–68 in *Reading Texts, Seeking Wisdom: Scripture and Theology*. Edited by David F. Ford and Graham Stanton. London: SCM, 2003.

Moore, Julie. "Elisha's Bones." *Christianity and Literature* 54, no. 1 (2004): 122. © 2004 The Conference on Christianity and Literature. Reprinted with permission of Johns Hopkins University Press.

Moore, Stephen D. *The Bible after Deleuze: Affects, Assemblages, Bodies without Organs*. New York: Oxford University Press, 2023.

Morales, Rodrigo. *The Spirit and the Restoration of Israel: New Exodus and New Creation Motifs in Galatians*. WUNT 282. Tübingen: Mohr Siebeck, 2010.

Moran, William L. "New Evidence from Mari on the History of Prophecy." *Biblica* 50, no. 1 (1969): 15–56.

Moravec, Hans. *Mind Children: The Future of Robot and Human Intelligence*. Cambridge, MA: Harvard University Press, 1988.

Morris, Wayne. *Theology without Words: Theology in the Deaf Community*. Aldershot: Ashgate, 2008.

Morrison, John. "Spinoza on Mind, Body, and Numerical Identity." Pages 293–336 in *Oxford Studies in Philosophy of Mind*. Vol. 2. Edited by Uriah Kriegel. Oxford: Oxford University Press, 2022.

Moss, Candida R. and Jeremy Schipper, eds. *Disability Studies and Biblical Literature*. New York: Palgrave MacMillan, 2011.

Moss, Candida R. and Joel S. Baden. *Reconceiving Infertility: Biblical Perspectives on Procreation and Childlessness*. Princeton, NJ: Princeton University Press, 2015.

Nagler, Michael N. "Towards a Generative View of the Oral Formula." *TPAPA* 98 (1967): 269–311.

Näser-Lather, Marion and Christoph Neubert. "Traffic—Media as Infrastructures and Cultural Practices: Introduction." Pages 1–27 in *Traffic: Media as Infrastructures and Cultural Practices*. At the Interface / Probing the Boundaries 88. Leiden: Brill | Rodopi, 2015.

Neimeyer, Robert A. "Meaning Reconstruction in Bereavement: Development of a Research Program." *Death Studies* 43, no. 2 (2019): 79–91.

Nelson, Judith Kay. *Seeing through Tears: Crying and Attachment*. New York: Routledge, 2005.

Nelson, Richard D. *First and Second Kings.* Interpretation: A Bible Commentary for Teaching and Preaching. Atlanta: John Knox Press, 1987.

Nelson, Richard D. "Priestly Purity and Prophetic Lunacy: Hosea 1.2–3 and 9.7." Pages 115–33 in *The Priests in the Prophets: The Portrayal of Priests, Prophets, and Other Religious Specialists in the Latter Prophets.* Edited by Lester L. Grabbe and Alice Ogden Bellis. LHBOTS 408. London: Bloomsbury T&T Clark, 2004.

Neufeld, Dietmar. "Eating, Ecstasy, and Exorcism (Mark 3:21)." *BTB* 26, no. 4 (1996): 152–162.

Newman, Judith H. *Before the Bible: The Liturgical Body and the Formation of Scriptures in Early Judaism.* Oxford: Oxford University Press, 2018.

Newman, Judith H. "Embodied Techniques: The Communal Formation of the Maskil's Self." *Dead Sea Discoveries* 22, no. 3 (2015): 249–66.

Newsom, Carol A. *Songs of the Sabbath Sacrifice: A Critical Edition.* HSS 27. Atlanta: Scholars Press, 1985.

Newsom, Carol A. with Brennan W. Breed. *Daniel: A Commentary.* OTL. Louisville, KY: Westminster John Knox, 2014.

Niditch, Susan. *Oral World and Written Word: Ancient Israelite Literature.* Library of Ancient Israel. Louisville, KY: Westminster John Knox, 1996.

Nielsen, Bent Flemming. "Ritualization, the Body, and the Church: Reflections on Protestant Mindset and Ritual Process." Pages 19–45 in *Religion, Ritual, Theatre.* Edited by Bent Holm, Bent Flemming Nielsen, and Karen Vedel. Frankfurt: Peter Lang, 2009.

Nijf, Onno Martien van. "Athletics, *Andreia* and the *Askêsis*-Culture in the Roman East." Pages 263–86 in *Andreia: Studies in Manliness and Courage in Classical Antiquity.* Edited by Ralph M. Rosen and Ineke Sluiter. Mnemosyne: Bibliotheca Classica Batava Supplementum 238. Leiden: Brill, 2003.

Nikolsky, Ronit, et al., eds. *Language, Cognition, and Biblical Exegesis: Interpreting Minds.* London: Bloomsbury Academic, 2019.

Nissinen, Martti. *Ancient Prophecy: Near Eastern, Biblical, and Greek Perspectives.* Oxford: Oxford University Press, 2018.

Nissinen, Martti. "Comparing Prophetic Sources: Principles and a Test Case." Pages 3–24 in *Prophecy and Prophets in Ancient Israel.* Proceedings of the Oxford Old Testament Seminar. Edited by John Day. New York: T&T Clark, 2010.

Nissinen, Martti. "Prophecy as Construct: Ancient and Modern." Pages 11–35 in *"Thus Speaks Ishtar of Arbela": Prophecy in Israel, Assyria, and Egypt in the Neo-Assyrian Period.* Edited by Robert P. Gordon and Hans M. Barstad. Winona Lake: Eisenbrauns, 2013.

Nissinen, Martti. *Prophetic Divination: Essays in Ancient Near Eastern Prophecy.* Berlin: Walter de Gruyter, 2019.

Nissinen, Martti. "Prophetic Intermediation in the Ancient Near East." Pages 5–36 in *The Oxford Handbook of the Prophets.* Edited by Carolyn J. Sharp. Oxford: Oxford University Press, 2016.

Nissinen, Martti. "Prophetic Madness: Prophecy and Ecstasy in the Ancient Near East and in Greece." Pages 3–30 in *Raising Up a Faithful Exegete: Essays in Honor of Richard D. Nelson.* Edited by Kurt L. Knoll and Brooks Schramm. Winona Lake: Eisenbrauns, 2010.

Nissinen, Martti. "Sacred Springs and Liminal Rivers: Water and Prophecy in the Ancient Eastern Mediterranean." Pages 29–48 in *Thinking of Water in the Early Second Temple Period.* Edited by Ehud Ben Zvi and Christoph Levin. BZAW 461. Berlin: Walter De Gruyter, 2014.

Nissinen, Martti and Francesca Stavrakopoulou. "Introduction: New Perspectives on Body and Religion." *Hebrew Bible and Ancient Israel* 2, no. 4 (2013): 453–7.

Noggle, Robert. "Manipulative Actions: A Conceptual and Moral Analysis." *American Philosophical Quarterly* 33, no. 1 (1996): 43–55.

Noort, Ed. "Balaam the Villain: The History of Reception of the Balaam Narrative in the Pentateuch and the Former Prophets." Pages 3–24 in *The Prestige of the Pagan Prophet Balaam in Judaism, Early Christianity and Islam*. Edited by George H. van Kooten and Jacques van Ruiten. Themes in Biblical Narrative 11. Leiden: Brill, 2008.

Noth, Martin. *Könige*. BKAT 9/1. Neukirchen-Vluyn: Neukirchener, 1968.

Oatley, Keith. "Fiction: Simulation of Social Worlds." *Trends in Cognitive Sciences* 20, no. 8 (2016): 618–28.

Oatley, Keith. "Meetings of Minds: Dialogue, Sympathy, and Identification in Reading Fiction." *Poetics* 26, no. 5–6 (1999): 439–54.

O'Connor, Kathleen M. *Jeremiah: Pain and Promise*. Minneapolis: Fortress, 2011.

O'Connor, Kathleen M. "The Tears of God and Divine Character in Jeremiah 2–9." Pages 387–401 in *Troubling Jeremiah*. Edited by A. R. Pete Diamond, Kathleen M. O'Connor, and Louis Stulman. JSOTSup 260. Sheffield: Sheffield Academic Press, 1999.

Odell, Margaret. "You Are What You Eat: Ezekiel and the Scroll." *JBL* 117, no. 2 (1998): 229–48.

Odell, Margaret S. *Ezekiel*. Smyth & Helwys Biblical Commentary. Macon, GA: Smyth & Helwys, 2005.

O'Donoghue, Keelin. "Fetal Microchimerism and Maternal Health During and After Pregnancy." *Obstetric Medicine* 1, no. 2 (2008): 56–64.

Oliver, Mary. *Evidence: Poems*. Boston, MA: Beacon, 2009.

Oliver, Sophie. "Dehumanization: Perceiving the Body as (In)human." Pages 85–97 in *Humiliation, Degradation, Dehumanization: Human Dignity Violated*. Edited by Paulus Kaufmann et al. New York: Springer, 2011.

Olson, Dennis T. *Numbers*. Interpretation: A Bible Commentary for Teaching and Preaching. Louisville, KY: John Knox, 1996.

Olyan, Saul M. *Biblical Mourning: Ritual and Social Dimensions*. Oxford: Oxford University Press, 2004.

Olyan, Saul M. *Disability in the Hebrew Bible: Interpreting Mental and Physical Differences*. Cambridge: Cambridge University Press, 2012.

Oppenheim, A. Leo. *The Interpretation of Dreams in the Ancient Near East, with a Translation of an Assyrian Dream-Book*. Transactions of the American Philosophical Society, New Series 46, no. 3. Philadelphia: American Philosophical Society, 1956.

Orlov, Andrei A. *Embodiment of Divine Knowledge in Early Judaism*. Routledge Studies in the Biblical World. New York: Routledge, 2022.

Orlov, Andrei A. *The Glory of the Invisible God: Two Powers in Heaven Traditions and Early Christology*. JCTCRS 31. London: Bloomsbury, 2019.

Oschman, James L., Gaétan Chevalier, and Richard Brown. "The Effects of Grounding (Earthing) on Inflammation, the Immune Response, Wound Healing, and Prevention and Treatment of Chronic Inflammatory and Autoimmune Diseases." *J Inflamm Res* 8 (2015): 83–96.

Overholt, Thomas W. *Channels of Prophecy: The Social Dynamics of Prophetic Activity*. Minneapolis, MN: Fortress, 1989.

Page, Sophie. "Medieval Magic." Pages 29–64 in *The Oxford Illustrated History of Witchcraft and Magic*. Edited by Owen Davies. Oxford: Oxford University Press, 2017.

Pak, G. Sujin. *The Reformation of Prophecy: Early Modern Interpretations of the Prophet and Old Testament Prophecy*. Oxford Studies in Historical Theology. Oxford: Oxford University Press, 2018.

Papeo, Liuba, Corrado Corradi-Dell'Acqua, and Raffaella Ida Rumiati. "'She' Is Not Like 'I': The Tie between Language and Action Is in Our Imagination." *J Cogn Neurosci* 23, no. 12 (2011): 3939–48.

Parker, Simon B. "Possession Trance and Prophecy in Pre-Exilic Israel." *VT* 28, no. 3 (1978): 271–85.

Patton, Kimberley Christine and John Stratton Hawley. "Introduction." Pages 1–23 in *Holy Tears: Weeping in the Religious Imagination*. Edited by Kimberley Christine Patton and John Stratton Hawley. Princeton, NJ: Princeton University Press, 2005.

Pavlidou, Theodossia-Soula. "Constructing Collectivity with 'We': An Introduction." Pages 1–22 in *Constructing Collectivity: 'We' across Languages and Contexts*. Edited by Theodossia-Soula Pavlidou. Pragmatics and Beyond New Series 239. Amsterdam: John Benjamins Publishing Company, 2014.

Pederzoli, Luciano, Patrizio Tressoldi, and Helané Wahbeh. "Channeling: A Nonpathological Possession and Dissociative Identity Experience or Something Else?" *Cult Med Psychiatry* 46 (2022): 161–9.

Pell, Marc D., Kathrin Rothermich, Pan Liu, Silke Paulmann, Sameer Sethi, and Simon Rigoulot. "Preferential Decoding of Emotion from Human Non-linguistic Vocalizations versus Speech Prosody." *Biological Psychology* 111 (2015): 14–25.

Perkins, Judith. *The Suffering Self: Pain and Narrative Representation in the Early Christian Era*. London: Routledge, 1995.

Petersen, David L. *The Prophetic Literature: An Introduction*. Louisville, KY: Westminster John Knox, 2002.

Petersen, David L. "Rethinking the Nature of Prophetic Literature." Pages 23–40 in *Prophecy and Prophets: The Diversity of Contemporary Issues in Scholarship*. Edited by Yehoshua Gitay. SemeiaSt 33. Atlanta: Scholars Press, 1997.

Petersen, David L. *The Roles of Israel's Prophets*. JSOTSup 17. Sheffield: JSOT Press, 1981.

Pettersen, Christina. *From Tomb to Text: The Body of Jesus in the Book of John*. London: T&T Clark, 2017.

Philo. *The Works of Philo Judaeus, the Contemporary of Josephus, Translated from the Greek*. 4 vols. Translated by C. D. Yonge. London: Henry G. Bohn, 1854–5.

Phinney, D. Nathan. "Call / Commission Narratives." Pages 65–71 in *Dictionary of the Old Testament: Prophets*. Edited by Mark J. Boda and J. Gordon McConville. Downers Grove, IL: IVP Academic, 2012.

Piantadosi, Claude A. *The Biology of Human Survival: Life and Death in Extreme Environments*. Oxford: Oxford University Press, 2003.

Plantinga, Carl. *Moving Viewers: American Film and the Spectator's Experience*. Berkeley: University of California Press, 2009.

Plato. *Phaedo*. Translated by Hugh Tredennick. In *Plato: The Collected Dialogues*. Edited by Edith Hamilton and Huntington Cairns. Princeton, NJ: Princeton University Press, 1961.

Polak, Frank. "Theophany and Mediator: The Unfolding of a Theme in the Book of Exodus." Pages 113–47 in *Studies in the Book of Exodus: Redaction, Reception, Interpretation*. Edited by Marc Vervenne. BETL 126. Leuven: Leuven University Press, 1996.

Polk, Timothy. *The Prophetic Persona: Jeremiah and the Language of the Self*. JSOTSup 32. Sheffield: JSOT Press, 1984.

Portier-Young, Anathea E. "Commentary on Exodus 3:1–15." *Workingpreacher.org* (August 31, 2014), https://www.workingpreacher.org/commentaries/revised-common-lectionary/ordinary-22/commentary-on-exodus-31-15-5.

Portier-Young, Anathea E. "Daniel and Apocalyptic Imagination." Pages 224–40 in *The Oxford Handbook of the Prophets*. Edited by Carolyn J. Sharp. Oxford: Oxford University Press, 2016.

Portier-Young, Anathea E. "Linking Emotion, Cognition, and Action within a Social Frame: Old Testament Perspectives on Preaching the Fear of the Lord." *International Journal of Homiletics* 4, Supplementum (2019): 42–62.

Poser, Ruth. *Das Ezechielbuch als Trauma-Literatur*. VTSup 154. Leiden: Brill, 2012.

Poser, Ruth. "No Words: The Book of Ezekiel as Trauma Literature and a Response to Exile." Pages 27–48 in *Bible through the Lens of Trauma*. Edited by Elizabeth Boase and Christopher G. Frechette. Atlanta: SBL Press, 2016.

"The Previous Fasts." *The Indian Express* 11, no. 86 (March 4, 1943): 1. https://news.google.com/newspapers?id=LLw-AAAAIBAJ&pg=4995,4559107&dq=.

Prinsloo, Gert. "Place, Space and Identity in the Ancient Mediterranean World: Theory and Practice with Reference to the Book of Jonah." Pages 3–25 in *Constructions of Space V: Place, Space and Identity in the Ancient Mediterranean World*. Edited by Gert T. M. Prinsloo and Christl M. Maier. LHBOTS 576. London: Bloomsbury, 2013.

Propp, William Henry. *Exodus 1–18*. A New Translation with Introduction and Commentary. AYB 2. New York: Doubleday, 1999.

Propp, William Henry. "The Skin of Moses' Face: Transfigured or Disfigured?" *CBQ* 49, no. 3 (1987): 375–86.

Pseudo-Tertullian. "Carmen de Iona Propheta." Pages 769–771 in *Quinti Septimii Florentis Tertulliani Quae Supersunt Omnia*. Editio maior vol. 2. Edited by Francis Oehler. Lipsiae: T. O. Weigel, 1854. https://www.tertullian.org/latin/carmen_de_iona_propheta.htm.

Puech, Émile. "Balaʿam and Deir ʿAlla." Pages 25–47 in *The Prestige of the Pagan Prophet Balaam in Judaism, Early Christianity and Islam*. Edited by George H. van Kooten and Jacques van Ruiten. Themes in Biblical Narrative 11. Leiden: Brill, 2008.

Rad, Gerhard von. *Holy War in Ancient Israel*. Translated and edited by Marva J. Dawn. Grand Rapids, MI: Eerdmans, 1991.

Raes, An K. and Rudi De Raedt. "Interoceptive Awareness and Unaware Fear Conditioning: Are Subliminal Conditioning Effects Influenced by the Manipulation of Visceral Self-Perception?" *Consciousness and Cognition* 20, no. 4 (December 2011): 1393–402.

Rao, Anupama and Steven Pierce. "Discipline and the Other Body: Humanitarianism, Violence, and the Colonial Exception." Pages 1–35 in *Discipline and the Other Body: Correction, Corporeality, Colonialism*. Edited by Steven Pierce and Anupama Rao. Durham, NC: Duke University Press, 2006.

Raphael, Rebecca. *Biblical Corpora: Representations of Disability in Hebrew Biblical Literature*. New York: T&T Clark, 2008.

Rapp, Ursula. *Mirjam: Eine feministisch-rhetorische Lektüre der Mirjamtexte in der hebräischen Bibel*. BZAW 317. Berlin: Walter de Gruyter, 2002.

Rappaport, Roy A. *Ritual and Religion in the Making of Humanity*. Cambridge: Cambridge University Press, 1999.

Raz, Josefa. "Jeremiah Before the Womb: On Fathers, Sons, and the Telos of Redaction." Pages 86–100 in *Prophecy and Power: Jeremiah in Feminist and Postcolonial Perspective*.

Edited by Carolyn J. Sharp and Christl M. Maier. LHBOTS 577. London: Bloomsbury T&T Clark, 2013.

Reed, Nancy B. "A Chariot Race for Athens' Finest: The *Apobates* Contest Re-Examined." *Journal of Sport History* 17, no. 3 (1990): 306–17.

Reed, Pamela G. "Theory of Self-Transcendence." Pages 119–45 in *Middle Range Theory for Nursing*. Edited by Mary Jane Smith and Patricia Liehr. 4th ed. New York: Springer, 2018.

Reif, Stefan C. and Renate Egger-Wenzel, eds. *Ancient Jewish Prayers and Emotions: A Study of the Emotions Associated with Prayer in the Jewish and Related Literature of the Second Temple Period and Immediately Afterwards*. DCLS 26. Berlin: Walter de Gruyter, 2015.

Renberg, Gil H. *Where Dreams May Come: Incubation Sanctuaries in the Greco-Roman World*. 2 vols. Religions in the Graeco-Roman World 184. Leiden: Brill, 2017.

Rensberger, David. "John." Pages 339–58 in *Theological Bible Commentary*. Edited by Gail R. O'Day and David L. Petersen. Louisville, KY: Westminster John Knox, 2009.

Rimé, Bernard. "Emotion Elicits the Social Sharing of Emotion: Theory and Empirical Review." *Emotion Review* 1, no. 1 (2009): 60–85.

Roberts, J. J. M. "The Hand of Yahweh." *VT* 21, no. 2 (1971): 244–51.

Roncace, Mark. *Jeremiah, Zedekiah, and the Fall of Jerusalem: A Study of Prophetic Narrative*. JSOTSup 423. New York: T&T Clark, 2005.

Roshwalb, Esther H. "Jeremiah 1.4–10: 'Lost and Found' in Translation and a New Interpretation." *JSOT* 34, no. 3 (2010): 351–76.

Rousseau, Philip. "The Structure and Spirit of the Ascetic Life." Unpublished typescript.

Rowland, Christopher. "The Visions of God in Apocalyptic Literature." *JSJ* 10, no. 2 (1979): 137–54.

Rowland, Christopher with Patricia Gibbons and Vicente Dobroruka. "Visionary Experience in Ancient Judaism and Christianity." Pages 41–56 in *Paradise Now: Essays on Early Jewish and Christian Mysticism*. Edited by April D. DeConick. SBLSymS 11. Atlanta: Society of Biblical Literature, 2006.

Runions, Erin. "From Humor to Disgust: Rahab's Queer Affect." Pages 45–74 in *Bible Trouble: Queer Reading at the Boundaries of Biblical Scholarship*. Edited by Teresa J. Hornsby and Ken Stone. Atlanta: Society of Biblical Literature, 2011.

Runions, Erin. "Prophetic Affect and the Promise of Change: A Response." Pages 235–42 in *Jeremiah (Dis)Placed: New Directions in Writing/Reading Jeremiah*. Edited by Louis Stulman and A. R. Pete Diamond. New York: T&T Clark, 2011.

Rutz, Matthew. *Bodies of Knowledge in Ancient Mesopotamia: The Diviners of Late Bronze Age Emar and Their Tablet Collection*. Ancient Magic and Divination 9. Leiden: Brill, 2013.

Saive, Anne-Lise, Jean-Pierre Royet, Nadine Ravel, Marc Thévenet, Samuel Garcia, and Jane Plailly. "A Unique Memory Process Modulated by Emotion Underpins Successful Odor Recognition and Episodic Retrieval in Humans." *Frontiers in Behavioral Neuroscience* 8, no. 203 (2014): 37–47.

Saive, Anne-Lise, Jean-Pierre Royet, and Jane Plailly. "A Review on the Neural Bases of Episodic Odor Memory: From Laboratory-Based to Autobiographical Approaches." *Frontiers in Behavioral Neuroscience* 8, no. 240 (2014): 24–36.

Sals, Ulrike. "The Hybrid Story of Balaam (Numbers 22–24): Theology for the Diaspora in the Torah." *BibInt* 16, no. 4 (2008): 315–35.

Sanders, Seth. "Old Light on Moses' Shining Face." *VT* 52, no. 3 (2002): 400–6.

Sarbin, Theodore R. "Contributions to Role-Taking Theory: I. Hypnotic Behavior." *Psychological Review* 57, no. 5 (1950): 255–70.

Sarbin, Theodore R. "The Role of Imagination in Narrative Construction." Pages 5–20 in *Narrative Analysis, Studying the Development of Individuals in Society*. Edited by Colette Daiute and Cynthia Lightfoot. London: Sage, 2004.

Sarbin, Theodore R. "Role Theory." Pages 223–58 in *Handbook of Social Psychology*. Vol. 1. Edited by Gardner Lindzey and Elliot Aronson. Reading, MA: Addison-Wesley, 1954.

Sarna, Nahum. *Exodus*. The JPS Torah Commentary. Philadelphia: Jewish Publication Society, 1991.

Sasson, Jack M. "Bovine Symbolism in the Exodus Narrative." *VT* 18, no. 3 (1968): 380–7.

Sasson, Jack M. *Jonah*. A New Translation with Introduction and Commentary. AB 24B. New York: Doubleday, 1990.

Schellenberg, Annette and Thomas Krüger, eds. *Sounding Sensory Profiles in the Ancient Near East*. Ancient Near East Monographs 25. Atlanta, GA: Society of Biblical Literature, 2019.

Scherer, Klaus R. "Emotions are Emergent Processes: They Require a Dynamic Computational Architecture." *Philosophical Transactions of the Royal Society B: Biological Sciences* 364, no. 1535 (2009): 3459–74.

Scherer, Klaus R. "On the Nature and Function of Emotion: A Component Process Approach." Pages 293–317 in *Approaches to Emotion*. Edited by Klaus R. Scherer and Paul Ekman. Hilsdale, NJ: Erlbaum, 1984.

Scherer, Klaus R. "Unconscious Processes in Emotion: The Bulk of the Iceberg." Pages 312–34 in *Emotion and Consciousness*. Edited by Lisa Feldman Barrett, Paula M. Niedenthal and Piotr Winkielman. New York: The Guilford Press, 2009.

Scherer, Klaus R. "What Are Emotions? And How Can They Be Measured?" *Social Science Information* 44, no. 4 (2005): 695–729.

Schipper, Jeremy. *Disability and Isaiah's Suffering Servant*. Oxford: Oxford University Press, 2011.

Schipper, Jeremy. *Disability Studies and the Hebrew Bible: Figuring Mephibosheth in the David Story*. New York: T&T Clark, 2006.

Schlimm, Matthew Richard. *From Fratricide to Forgiveness: The Language and Ethics of Anger in Genesis*. Siphrut 7. Winona Lake, IN: Eisenbrauns, 2011.

Schmidt, Bettina, ed. *The Study of Religious Experience: Approaches and Methodologies*. Sheffield: Equinox, 2016.

Schmidt, Brian B. *The Materiality of Power: Explorations in the Social History of Early Israelite Magic*. FAT 105. Tübingen: Mohr Siebeck, 2016.

Schnackenburg, Rudolf. *The Gospel according to St. John*. Vol. 1, Introduction and Commentary on Chapters 1–4. Translated by Kevin Smyth. New York: Herder & Herder, 1968.

Schniedewind, William M. *The Word of God in Transition: From Prophet to Exegete in the Second Temple Period*. JSOTSup 197. Sheffield: Sheffield Academic Press, 1995.

Schore, Allan N. *Affect Dysregulation and Disorders of the Self*. New York: W. W. Norton & Co., 2003.

Schroeder, Caroline T. *Monastic Bodies: Discipline and Salvation in Shenoute of Atripe*. Philadelphia: University of Pennsylvania Press, 2007.

Schroer, Silvia and Tomas Staubli. *Body Symbolism in the Bible*. Translated by Linda M. Maloney. Collegeville, MN: Liturgical Press, 2001.

Seely, David. "The Image of the Hand of God in the Book of Exodus." Pages 38–54 in *God's Word for Our World*. Vol. 1. Biblical Studies in Honor of Simon John De Vries. Edited by Deborah L. Ellens et al. LHBOTS 388. London: T&T Clark International, 2004.

Seidl, Theodor. "Mose und Elija am Gottesberg Überlieferungen zu Krise und Konversion der Propheten." *BZ* 37, no. 1 (1993): 1–25.

Seidler, Ayelet. "'Fasting,' 'Sackcloth,' and 'Ashes'—From Nineveh to Shushan." *VT* 69, no. 1 (2019): 117–34.

Seow, Choon Leong. *Daniel*. Westminster Bible Companion. Louisville: Westminster John Knox Press, 2003.

Shantz, Colleen. "Opening the Black Box: New Prospects for Analyzing Religious Experience." Pages 1–15 in *Experientia*. Vol. 2, Linking Text and Experience. Edited by Colleen Shantz and Rodney A. Werline. EJL 35. Atlanta: Society of Biblical Literature, 2012.

Shantz, Colleen. *Paul in Ecstasy: The Neurobiology of the Apostle's Life and Thought*. Cambridge: Cambridge University Press, 2009.

Shantz, Colleen and Rodney A. Werline. *Experientia*. Vol. 2, Linking Text and Experience. EJL 35. Atlanta: Society of Biblical Literature, 2012.

Sharp, Carolyn J., ed. *The Oxford Handbook of the Prophets*. Oxford: Oxford University Press, 2016.

Shaw, Teresa M. *The Burden of the Flesh: Fasting and Sexuality in Early Christianity*. Minneapolis: Fortress, 1998.

Shemesh, Abraham O. "'And God Gave Solomon Wisdom': Proficiency in Ornithomancy." *HTS Teologiese Studies*, 74, no. 1 (2018): 1–9.

Sherwood, Yvonne. "Prophetic Scatology: Prophecy and the Art of Sensation." *Semeia* 82 (1998): 183–224.

Sherwood, Yvonne, ed. "Prophetic Performance Art." Special Issue. *BCT* 2, no.1 (2006).

Sherwood, Yvonne. *The Prostitute and the Prophet: Reading Hosea in the Late Twentieth Century*. London: T&T Clark, 1996.

Sherwood, Yvonne and Mark Brummitt. "The Fear of Loss Inherent in Writing: Jeremiah 36 as the Story of a Self-Conscious Scroll." Pages 47–66 in *Jeremiah (Dis)placed: New Directions in Writing/Reading Jeremiah*. Edited by A. R. Pete Diamond and Louis Stulman. LHBOTS 529. London: T&T Clark, 2011.

Siikala, Anna-Leena. "The Siberian Shaman's Technique of Ecstasy." *Scripta Instituti Donneriani Aboensis* 11 (1982): 103–21.

Simms, Eva M. *The Child in the World: Embodiment, Time, and Language in Early Childhood*. Detroit, MI: Wayne State University Press, 2008.

Simon, Uriel. *Reading Prophetic Narratives*. Translated by Lenn J. Schramm. Bloomington, IN: Indiana University Press, 1997.

Siquans, Agnethe. "'She Dared to Reprove Her Father:' Miriam's Image as a Female Prophet in Rabbinic Interpretation." *JAJ* 6 (2015): 335–57.

Smith, Jonathan Z. "Religion, Religions, Religious." Pages 269–84 in *Critical Terms for Religious Studies*. Edited by Mark C. Taylor. Chicago, IL: University of Chicago Press, 1998.

Smith, Mark S. *God in Translation: Deities in Cross-Cultural Discourse in the Biblical World*. FAT 57. Tübingen: Mohr Siebeck, 2008.

Smith, Mark S. "The Three Bodies of God in the Hebrew Bible." *JBL* 134, no. 3 (2015): 471–88.

Smith, Mark S. *Where the Gods Are: Spatial Dimensions of Anthropomorphism in the Biblical World*. AYBRL. New Haven, CT: Yale University Press, 2016.
Solevåg, Anna Rebecca. *Negotiating the Disabled Body: Representations of Disability in Early Christian Texts*. ECL 23. Atlanta, GA: Society of Biblical Literature, 2018.
Sommer, Benjamin D. *The Bodies of God and the World of Ancient Israel*. Cambridge: Cambridge University Press, 2009.
Spencer, F. Scott, ed. *Mixed Feelings and Vexed Passions: Exploring Emotions in Biblical Literature*. Resources for Biblical Study 90. Atlanta, GA: Society of Biblical Literature, 2017.
Spinoza, Baruch. *Theological-Political Treatise*. Gebhardt edition. Translated by Samuel Shirley. Introduction and Annotation by Seymour Feldman. 2nd ed. Indianapolis, IN: Hackett Publishing, 2001.
Staalduine-Sulman, Eveline van. *The Targum of Samuel*. Studies in the Aramaic Interpretation of Scripture 1. Leiden: Brill, 2002.
Stacey, David. *Prophetic Drama in the Old Testament*. London: Epworth Press, 1990.
Stackert, Jeffrey. *A Prophet Like Moses: Prophecy, Law, and Israelite Religion*. Oxford: Oxford University Press, 2014.
Stange, Ulrike. *The Acquisition of Interjections in Early Childhood*. Hamburg: Diplomica Verlag, 2008.
Steiner, Jacob E. "Facial Expressions of the Neonate Infant Indicating the Hedonics of Food-Related Chemical Stimuli." Pages 173–87 in *Taste and Development: The Genesis of Sweet Preference*. Edited by James W. Weiffenbach. Bethesda, MD: U.S. Department of Health, Education, and Welfare, 1977.
Stevens, Wallace. *Selected Poems*. Edited by John N. Serio. New York: Alfred A. Knopf, 2011.
Stökl, Jonathan. *Prophecy in the Ancient Near East: A Philological and Sociological Comparison*. Leiden: Brill, 2012.
Stökl, Jonathan. "Ready or Not, Here I Come: Triggering Prophecy in the Hebrew Bible." Pages 115–33 in *Prophecy and Its Cultic Dimensions*. Edited by Lena-Sofia Tiemeyer. Berlin: Vandenhoeck & Ruprecht, 2019.
Stökl, Jonathan and Corrine L. Carvalho, eds. *Prophets Male and Female: Gender and Prophecy in the Hebrew Bible, the Eastern Mediterranean, and the Ancient Near East*. Ancient Israel and Its Literature 15. Atlanta, GA: Society of Biblical Literature, 2013.
Stone, Allucquère Rosanne. *The War of Desire and Technology at the Close of the Mechanical Age*. Cambridge, MA: MIT Press, 1996.
Strathern, Andrew. "Why is Shame on the Skin?" *Ethnology* 14, no. 4 (1975): 347–56.
Strawn, Brent A. "Moses' Shining or Horned Face?" *TheTorah.com* (2021), https://thetorah.com/article/moses-shining-or-horned-face.
Strawn, Brent A. "On Vomiting: Leviticus, Jonah, Ea(a)rth." *CBQ* 74, no. 3 (2012), 445–64.
Strawn, Brent A. and Brad D. Strawn. "Prophecy and Psychology." Pages 610–23 in *Dictionary of the Old Testament: Prophets*. Edited by Mark J. Boda and J. Gordon McConville. Downers Grove, IL: IVP Academic, 2012.
Streeck, Jürgen, Charles Goodwin, and Curtis LeBaron. "Embodied Interaction in the Material World: An Introduction." Pages 1–28 in *Embodied Interaction: Language and Body in the Material World*. Edited by Jürgen Streeck, Charles Goodwin, and Curtis LeBaron. Learning in Doing: Social, Cognitive, and Computational Perspectives. Cambridge: Cambridge University Press, 2011.

Strelan, Rick. "The Running Prophet (Acts 8:30)." *NT* 43, no. 1 (2001): 31–8.
Stulman, Louis. *Jeremiah*. AOTC. Nashville: Abingdon, 2005.
Stulman, Louis. *Order Amid Chaos: Jeremiah as Symbolic Tapestry*. Biblical Seminar 57. Sheffield: Sheffield Academic Press, 1998.
Stulman, Louis. "Prophetic Words and Acts as Survival Literature." Pages 319–33 in *The Oxford Handbook of the Prophets*. Edited by Carolyn J. Sharp. Oxford: Oxford University Press, 2016.
Styers, Randall. *Making Magic: Religion, Magic, and Science in the Modern World*. Oxford: Oxford University Press, 2004.
Sullivan, Regina M., Donald A. Wilson, Nadine Ravel, and Anne-Marie Mouly. "Olfactory Memory Networks: From Emotional Learning to Social Behaviors." *Frontiers in Behavioral Neuroscience* 9, no. 36 (2015): 5–8.
Susskind, Joshua M., Daniel H. Lee, Andrée Cusi, Roman Feiman, Wojtek Grabski, and Adam K. Anderson. "Expressing Fear Enhances Sensory Acquisition." *Nature Neuroscience* 11, no. 7 (2008): 843–50.
Sweeney, Marvin A. *Isaiah 1–39, with an Introduction to Prophetic Literature*. FOTL 16. Grand Rapids, MI: Eerdmans, 1996.
Tan, Tobias. "The Corporeality of Religious Experience: Embodied Cognition in Religious Practices." Pages 207–26 in *Religious Experience Revisited: Expressing the Inexpressible?* Edited by Thomas Hardtke, Ulrich Schmiedel, and Tobias Tan. Studies in Theology and Religion 21. Leiden: Brill, 2016.
Tarlin, Jan William. "Utopia and Pornography in Ezekiel: Violence, Hope, and the Shattered Male Subject." Pages 175–83 in *Reading Bibles, Writing Bodies: Identity and the Book*. Edited by Timothy K. Beal and David M. Gunn. London: Routledge, 1996.
Tart, Charles T. "Mind Embodied: Computer-Generated Virtual Reality as a New, Dualistic-Interactive Model for Transpersonal Psychology." Pages 123–37 in *Cultivating Consciousness: Enhancing Human Potential, Wellness, and Healing*. Edited by K. Ramakrishna Rao. Westport, CT: Praeger, 1993.
Taves, Anne. *Religious Experience Reconsidered: A Building-Block Approach to the Study of Religion and Other Special Things*. Princeton, NJ: Princeton University Press, 2009.
Tervanotko, Hanna. *Denying Her Voice: The Figure of Miriam in Ancient Jewish Literature*. Göttingen: Vandenhoeck & Ruprecht, 2016.
Thaden, Robert H. von, Jr. *Sex, Christ, and Embodied Cognition: Paul's Wisdom for Corinth*. Emory Studies in Early Christianity. Atlanta, GA: Society of Biblical Literature, 2017.
Thiering, Barbara. "The Biblical Source of Qumran Asceticism." *JBL* 93, no. 3 (1974): 429–44.
Thomas, Angela. *Anatomical Idiom and Emotional Expression: A Comparison of the Hebrew Bible and the Septuagint*. Hebrew Bible Monographs 52. Sheffield: Sheffield Phoenix Press, 2014.
Thompson, J. A. *The Book of Jeremiah*. NICOT. Grand Rapids, MI: Eerdmans, 1980.
Tigay, Jeffry. "Heavy of Mouth and Heavy of Tongue: On Moses' Speech Difficulty." *Bulletin of the American Schools of Oriental Research* 231 (1978): 57–67.
Tilford, Nicole L. *Sensing World, Sensing Wisdom: The Cognitive Foundation of Biblical Metaphors*. Ancient Israel and Its Literature 31. Atlanta: Society of Biblical Literature, 2017.
Tomkins, Silvan. *Affect, Imagery, Consciousness*. 2 vols. New York: Springer, 2008.
Torres, Carlos and Alfonso M. García-Hernández. "From Violation to Voice, from Pain to Protest: Healing and Transforming Unjust Loss through the Use of Rituals and Memorials." Pages 202–12 in *Handbook of Social Justice in Loss and Grief: Exploring*

Diversity, Equity, and Inclusion. Edited by Darcy L. Harris and Tashel C. Bordere. New York: Routledge, 2016.

Trible, Phyllis. "Bringing Miriam Out of the Shadows." Pages 166–86 in *A Feminist Companion to Exodus to Deuteronomy*. The Feminist Companion to the Bible 6. Edited by Athalya Brenner. Sheffield: Sheffield Academic Press, 1994.

Trible, Phyllis. "Jonah." Pages 461–529 in *The New Interpreter's Bible*. Vol. 7, Introduction to Apocalyptic Literature, Daniel, The Twelve Prophets. Edited by Leander E. Keck. Nashville, TN: Abingdon, 1996.

Trimm, Charlie. "God's Staff and Moses' Hand(s): The Battle against the Amalekites as a Turning Point in the Role of the Divine Warrior." *JSOT* 44, no. 1 (2019): 198–214.

Trinka, Eric M. *Cultures of Mobility, Migration, and Religion in Ancient Israel and Its World*. Routledge Studies in the Biblical World. Abingdon: Routledge, 2022.

Turner, Victor W. *The Ritual Process: Structure and Anti-Structure*. Chicago, IL: Aldine, 1969.

Tweed, Thomas A. *Crossing and Dwelling: A Theory of Religion*. Cambridge, MA: Harvard University Press, 2006.

Uhlig, Torsten. *The Theme of Hardening in the Book of Isaiah: An Analysis of Communicative Action*. FAT 2/39. Tübingen: Mohr Siebeck, 2009.

Urry, John. "Social Networks, Travel and Talk." *British Journal of Sociology* 54, no. 2 (2003): 155–75.

Vaitl, Dieter, Niels Birbaumer, John Gruzelier, Graham A. Jamieson, Boris Kotchoubey, Andrea Kübler, Dietrich Lehmann, Wolfgang H. R. Miltner, Ulrich Ott, Peter Pütz, Gebhard Sammer, Inge Strauch, Ute Strehl, Jiri Wackermann, and Thomas Weiss. "Psychobiology of Altered States of Consciousness." *Psychological Bulletin* 131, no. 1 (2005): 98–127.

Valantasis, Richard. "Constructions of Power in Asceticism." *JAAR* 63, no. 4 (1995): 775–821.

Valantasis, Richard. *The Making of the Self: Ancient and Modern Asceticism*. Eugene, OR: Cascade, 2008.

Vásquez, Manuel A. *More Than Belief: A Materialist Theory of Religion*. Oxford: Oxford University Press, 2011.

Vayntrub, Jacqueline. *Beyond Orality: Biblical Poetry on Its Own Terms*. London: Routledge, 2019.

Verrips, Jojada. "Body and Mind: Material for a Never-ending Intellectual Odyssey." Pages 21–39 in *Religion and Material Culture: The Matter of Belief*. Edited by David Morgan. London: Routledge, 2010.

Verstraete, Ginette and Tim Cresswell. *Mobilizing Place, Placing Mobility: The Politics of Representation in a Globalized World*. Amsterdam: Rodopi, 2002.

Vos, Nienke and Paul van Geest, eds. *Early Christian Mystagogy and the Body*. Leuven: Peeters, 2022.

Waetjen, Herman C. "Logos πρὸς τὸν θεόν and the Objectification of Truth in the Prologue of the Fourth Gospel." *CBQ* 63, no. 2 (2001): 265–86.

Wagner, Andreas. *Emotionen, Gefühle und Sprache im Alten Testament: Vier Studien*. KUSATU 7. Waltrop: Hartmut Spenner, 2006.

Wagner, Andreas. *God's Body: The Anthropomorphic God in the Old Testament*. Translated by Marion Salzmann. London: T&T Clark, 2019.

Wahlde, Urban C. von. *Gnosticism, Docetism, and the Judaisms of the First Century: The Search for the Wider Context of the Johannine Literature and Why It Matters*. LNTS 517. London: Bloomsbury T&T Clark, 2015.

Warren, Meredith J. C. *Food and Transformation in Ancient Mediterranean Literature.* Writings from the Greco-Roman World Supplement Series 14. Atlanta, GA: SBL Press, 2019.

Warrior, Robert Allen. "Canaanites, Cowboys, and Indians: Deliverance, Conquest, and Liberation Theology Today." *USQR* 59, no. 1–2 (2005): 1–8.

Way, Kenneth. "Animals in the Prophetic World: Literary Reflections on Numbers 22 and 1 Kings 13." *JSOT* 34, no. 1 (2010): 47–62.

Weber, Max. *The Protestant Ethic and the Spirit of Capitalism.* Translated and introduced by Stephen Kalberg. London: Routledge, 2001.

Weber, Max. *The Sociology of Religion.* With an Introduction by Talcott Parsons. Translated by Ephraim Fischoff. Boston, MA: Beacon Press, 1993.

Weems, Renita. *Battered Love: Marriage, Sex, and Violence in the Hebrew Prophets.* Minneapolis, MN: Fortress Press, 1995.

Weingart, Kristin. "'My Father, My Father! Chariot of Israel and Its Horses!' (2 Kings 2:12 // 13:14): Elisha's or Elijah's Title?" *JBL* 137, no. 2 (2018): 257–70.

Weippert, Manfred. "Prophetie im alten Orient." Pages 196–200 in *Neues Bibel-Lexikon.* Vol. 3. Edited by Manfred Görg and Bernhard Lang. Zürich: Benziger, 2001.

Werline, Rodney A. "Assessing the Prophetic Vision and Dream Texts for Insights into Religious Experience." Pages 1–15 in *"I Lifted My Eyes and Saw": Reading Dream and Vision Reports in the Hebrew Bible.* Edited by Elizabeth R. Hayes and Lena-Sofia Tiemeyer. London: Bloomsbury T&T Clark, 2014.

Werline, Rodney A. "The Experience of Prayer and Resistance to Demonic Powers in the Gospel of Mark." Pages 59–71 in *Experientia.* Vol. 1, Inquiry into Religious Experience in Early Judaism and Early Christianity. Edited by Frances Flannery, Colleen Shantz, and Rodney A. Werline. SBLSymS 40. Atlanta, GA: Society of Biblical Literature, 2008.

Wetherell, Margaret. *Affect and Emotion: A New Social Science Understanding.* London: Sage, 2012.

Wevers, John William. *Exodus.* Septuaginta 2.1. Göttingen: Vandenhoeck & Ruprecht, 1991.

Wheeler, Brannon M. *Prophets in the Quran: An Introduction to the Quran and Muslim Exegesis.* Comparative Islamic Studies. London: Continuum, 2002.

Wiesse, Basil. "Affective Practice." Pages 131–9 in *Affective Societies: Key Concepts.* Edited by Jan Slaby and Christian von Scheve. Routledge Studies in Affective Societies 3. London: Routledge: 2019.

Wildeman, Christopher and Lars Højsgaard Andersen. "Long-term Consequences of Being Placed in Disciplinary Segregation." *Criminology* 58, no. 3 (2020): 423–53.

Williams, Jennifer J. "Queer Readings of the Prophets." Pages 527–47 in *The Oxford Handbook of the Prophets.* Edited by Carolyn J. Sharp. Oxford: Oxford University Press, 2016.

Williams, Michael Allen. *Rethinking "Gnosticism": An Argument for Dismantling a Dubious Category.* Princeton: Princeton University Press, 1996.

Wills, Lawrence M. "Ascetic Theology Before Asceticism? Jewish Narratives and the Decentering of the Self." *JAAR* 74, no. 4 (2006), 902–25.

Wilson, Andrew D. and Sabrina Golonka. "Embodied Cognition Is Not What You Think It Is." *Frontiers in Psychology* 4, no. 58 (2013): 1–13.

Wilson, Brittany E. *The Embodied God: Seeing the Divine in Luke-Acts and the Early Church.* Oxford: Oxford University Press, 2021.

Wilson, Robert R. "Prophecy and Ecstasy: A Reexamination." *JBL* 98, no. 3 (1979): 321–37.

Wilson, Robert R. *Prophecy and Society in Ancient Israel.* Philadelphia, PA: Fortress, 1980.
Wolff, Hans Walter. *Obadiah and Jonah: A Commentary.* Continental Commentary. Translated by Margaret Kohl. Minneapolis: Augsburg, 1986.
Wolff, Hans Walter. *Studien zum Jonabuch.* BibS 47. Neukirchen-Vluyn: Neukirchener Verlag, 1965.
Wolfson, Elliot R. *Through a Speculum that Shines: Vision and Imagination in Medieval Jewish Mysticism.* Princeton, NJ: Princeton University Press, 1994.
Wood, Allen W. "Coercion, Manipulation, Exploitation." Pages 17–50 in *Manipulation: Theory and Practice.* Edited by Christian Coons and Michael Weber. New York: Oxford University Press, 2014.
Wordsworth, William. *The Prelude. The Four Texts (1798, 1799, 1805, 1850).* Edited by Jonathan Wordsworth. London: Penguin, 1995.
Yoo, YeonHee (Yani). "A Community That Participates in the Healing of Stigma and Trauma: Listening to Miriam (Num. 12)." *KJOTS* 27, no. 4 (2021): 148–86.
Yoon, Man Hee. *The Fate of the Man of God from Judah: A Literary and Theological Reading of 1 Kings 13.* Eugene, OR: Pickwick, 2020.
Zarhin, Dana. "'You Have to Do Something': Snoring, Sleep Interembodiment and the Emergence of Agency." *The British Journal of Sociology* 71, no. 5 (2020): 1000–15.
Zimmerli, Walther. *Ezekiel 1: A Commentary on the Book of the Prophet Ezekiel, Chapters 1–24.* Translated by Ronald E. Clements. Hermeneia. Minneapolis: Fortress, 1979.

Index of Modern Authors

For the benefit of digital users, indexed terms that span two pages (e.g., 52–53) may, on occasion, appear on only one of those pages.

Adam, Klaus-Peter, 154
Ahmed, Sara, 9–10, 197, 199–201, 217, 239–40
Alsen, Carolyn, 108–9
André, Gunnel, 105, 151–53
Avrahami, Yael, 59, 180

Bærenholdt, Jørgen Ole, 174–75
Bahrani, Zainab, 235–36
Barrick, W. Boyd, 3
Beauvoir, Simone de, 90
Belnap, Dan, 133
Ben Zvi, Ehud, 47, 49–50
Berlant, Lauren, 228–29
Black, Fiona, 196
Blenkinsopp, Joseph, 42–43
Block, Daniel, 55–56, 236
Bosworth, David A., 211–12, 219
Bourdieu, Pierre, 44–45, 228
Boyarin, Daniel, 20
Bremmer, Jan N., 179
Brueggemann, Walter, 12–14
Brummitt, Mark, 10–11

Cannon, Katie Geneva, 16–17
Carver, Daniel E., 78–79
Clark-Soles, Jaime, 22–23
Cogan, Mordecai, 160–61
Cohen, Jeffrey Jerome, 107–8, 112–13
Cohen, Jonathan, 240–41
Conrad, Edgar W., 92–93
Cresswell, Tim, 174–75
Cryer, Frederick H., 34–36
Csordas, Thomas J., 44–45

Davis, Ellen F. 12–14, 105, 120
Descartes, René, 26–27

Deutscher, Penelope, 90
Doan, William, 10–11
Doka, Kenneth J., 235
Dozeman, Thomas B., 205
Duhm, Bernhard, 146–47, 152–53
Dunn, James D. G., 20, 21

Erzberger, Johanna, 10–11

Farnell, Brenda, 190–91
Fischer, Georg, 78–79
Flannery, Frances, 11–12, 45, 50, 121
Fraade, Steven D., 124–25
Fretheim, Terence E., 219
Fuchs, Esther, 113–14
Fuller, Robert C., 239–40

Garber, David G., 94
García-Hernández, Alfonso M., 235
Garcia-Romeu, Albert P., 155
Garroway, Kristine Henrikson, 69
Giles, Terry, 10–11
Glanz, Oliver, 209
Glazov, Gregory Yuri, 69
Goehring, James E., 124–25, 127
Goffman, Erving, 48–49, 213
Golonka, Sabrina, 45–46
Goodwin, Charles, 47–48, 49
Grabbe, Lester L., 152–53
Granås, Brynhild, 174–75
Gray, William, 22–23
Graybill, Rhiannon, 9–10, 67, 70–72, 108
Grey, Jacqueline, 84

Habel, Norman, 55–56
Hallett, Mark, 70–72
Hammer, Jill, 115–16

INDEX OF MODERN AUTHORS

Hannam, Kevin, 174–75
Hansen, Mark B., 228–29
Harari, Yuval, 35–36
Harkins, Angela Kim, 11–12
Harrington, Daniel J., 138–39
Hawley, John Stratton, 220, 221–22
Heschel, Abraham Joshua, 147–48, 151–52
Hölscher, Gustav, 146–47, 152–53, 154
Holt, Else K., 91
Hornsby, Teresa, 10–11
Husser, Jean-Marie, 136–37, 141

Jeffers, Anne, 39–40, 42–43
Jobling, David, 113–14
Junior, Nyasha 70–72, 105

Kakihara, Masao, 174–76
Kalmanofsky, Amy, 9–10, 87
Kelle, Brad E., 38–39
Kim, Koowon, 137–38, 141
Koosed, Jennifer L., 107–8, 109, 196
Korpel, Marjo C. A., 217
Kotrosits, Maia, 239–40

Lambert, David A., 243–44
Latour, Bruno, 194
Launderville, Dale, 125–26
LeBaron, Curtis, 47–48, 49
Leon-Sarmiento, Fidias E., 70–72
Leveen, Adriane, 187
Levison, John, 153–54
Lewis, I. M., 153
Lindblom, Johannes, 146–47, 154–55
Linnell, Per, 47–48
Lupton, Deborah, 88–89

McCall, Robin C., 94–95
McLuhan, Marshall, 194–95
Maier, Christl M., 217
Mathews, Jeanette, 10–11
Merleau-Ponty, Maurice, 44–45
Meyer, Birgit, 43–44
Meyers, Carol, 69
Michaelsen, Peter, 149–51
Middlemas, Jill, 188
Milgrom, Jacob, 66
Mills, Mary E., 10, 85, 192
Mittman, Asa Simon, 107–8

Moberly, R. Walter L., 207
Moore, Julie, 256–57
Morales, Rodrigo (Isaac), 21

Neimeyer, Robert A., 235
Nelson, Judith Kay, 210–11
Nelson, Richard D., 153–54, 183
Niditch, Susan, 96
Nissinen, Martti, 12–14, 47, 154–55, 178

O'Connor, Kathleen M., 10, 219
Odell, Margaret, 190–91
Olson, Dennis T., 113–14
Olyan, Saul M., 70–72, 134, 221
Oppenheim, A. Leo, 136–37
Oschman, James L., 60

Paez, Edwin, 70–72
Pak, G. Sujin, 25
Parker, Simon B., 148–53
Patton, Kimberley Christine, 220, 221–22
Pavlidou, Theodossia-Soula, 214
Petersen, David L., 33–34, 35–36, 40, 42–43, 149–54
Polk, Timothy, 91, 214, 216–17
Poser, Ruth, 10

Rad, Gerhard von, 185–86
Rappaport, Roy, 122
Raz, Josefa, 86–87
Renberg, Gil, 136
Rensberger, David, 21–22
Roberts, J. J. M., 94
Roshwalb, Esther H., 90–91
Rowland, Christopher, 120

Sanders, Seth, 105, 107–8
Sarbin, Theodore R., 149–51
Sartre, Jean Paul, 90
Scherer, Klaus R., 197–99, 200–1
Schipper, Jeremy, 70–72
Schore, Allan N., 211
Seely, David, 61–62
Shantz, Colleen, 25, 41–42, 45
Sherwood, Yvonne, 10–11
Siikala, Anna-Leena, 149–51
Simms, Eva M., 88–89
Smith, Mark S., 83

Sommer, Benjamin D., 58–59, 80–81, 83
Sørensen, Carsten, 174–76
Spinoza, Baruch, 26–27
Staalduine-Sulman, Eveline van, 139
Stacey, David, 10–11
Stackert, Jeffrey, 33–34, 35–36, 49–50, 56–57
Steiner, Jacob E., 230–31
Stökl, Jonathan, 39–40, 42, 47, 121–22, 160–61
Streeck, Jürgen, 47–48, 49
Stulman, Louis, 10, 91, 216–17, 220, 222–23
Styers, Randall, 24–25, 35–36

Tadmor, Hayim, 160–61
Tan, Tobias, 122
Tarlin, Jan William, 165–66
Tart, Charles T., 155
Thiering, Barbara, 127

Thompson, J. A., 222–23
Tomkins, Silvan, 228–29
Torres, Carlos, 235
Trinka, Eric M., 179
Tweed, Thomas A., 188–89

Vaitl, Dieter, 155–56
Valantasis, Richard, 125–28
Vásquez, Manuel A., 80–81

Waetjen, Herman C., 22
Warren, Meredith J. C., 231
Way, Kenneth, 5–6
Weber, Max, 27–28
Weingart, Kristin, 185–86
Werline, Rodney A., 11–12
Wetherell, Margaret, 197, 199, 200–1, 243–44
Wilson, Andrew D., 45–46
Wilson, Robert R., 40, 120–21

Index of Subjects

For the benefit of digital users, indexed terms that span two pages (e.g., 52–53) may, on occasion, appear on only one of those pages.

affect
  circulation of, 199–201, 208, 212
  in Daniel, 226, 237–47, 248
  definitions of, 197–99
  in Ezekiel, 226–37, 247–48
  in Jeremiah, 208–24, 225
  in Jonah, 201
  Moses', 130–31
  study of, 8–9, 196–200
  textual mediation of, 226, 237–38, 240–41, 247, 248
affective practice, 11–12, 199, 200–1, 237–38, 243–44
Aagency, 87–89, 93–95, 112, 114–15, 246
Altered (or Alternate) State of Consciousness
  definition, 155
  embodied character of, 155–56
  prophetic ecstasy and, 145, 149–51, 152–54, 156, 163
angelic mediation, 165–66, 188–89, 226, 242–43, 244–46, 247
angelophany, 58–59, 92–93, 178–80, 237–38, 245–46
anger, 201, 204–5, 206–7, 212–13, 232
anointing, refraining from, 243–44
anthropology, theological 20–23
artificial intelligence, 28
ASC. *See* Altered State of Consciousness
asceticism, 28, 123–28
ascetic practice. *See askêsis*
ashes, 243–44
askêsis
  definition of, 123–26, 127–28, 143
  Moses', 129–35, 143–44

  prophetic mediation and, 118–19, 122–23, 127–28, 129, 143–44
  revelatory character of, 126–27
  social transformation and, 125–26, 127–28
attunement, affective
  in Daniel, 226, 237–40, 246–47, 248
  in Jeremiah, 210, 211–12, 219, 224–25, 254–55
  in Jonah, 204–8, 254–55
authority, prophetic, 110–16

Balaam
  mobility of, 177
  portrayal of ecstatic experience, 166–67
birth
  interembodiment and, 88–89
  Jeremiah's lament regarding, 87
  linked to death, 112–13
  as metaphor, 216
  as mode of prophetic mediation, 31, 115–16
  of Samuel, 119, 138
  theological implications, 23
bones, 6–7, 186–87, 255–57
burial, 6–7, 255–57

call narratives, 55–77, 120, 173–76
capitalism, 28
Catholicism, 24–25
CBT, 205–6
chariot(s)
  Ezekiel's vision of, 92, 95, 188
  in Elijah and Elisha cycles, 183
  metaphor, 18–19
  as prophetic title, 185–86

cognitive behavioral therapy, 205–6
colonialism, 16–18, 23–25, 35–36
commissioning narratives, 55–77, 120, 173–76
communication, 12–15, 47–49, 174–75
co-presence, 174–75, 182–83
crying. *See* lament; tears; weeping

Daniel
    affect in book of, 226, 237–47, 248
    receiving food from Habakkuk, 188–89
death, 66, 67, 103–4, 112–13
delight, 234–35, 236, 244–45, 247–48
desire, 201–2, 241, 244
disability
    Moses as person with, 57–58, 68
    study of, 8–9
discourse
    affect and, 199–201
    in Jeremiah, 208–9, 212–19
divination, 11–12, 24, 32, 36–38, 39–40, 136–37
divine embodiment, 56–68, 80–82, 94–95
divine presence, prophetic mediation of, 103–4, 105, 109–10
divine speech, 5–6, 32–33, 93. *See also* word/Word
dreams
    incubation and, 135–37, 141, 160
    as mode of revelation, 110–11
    response to, in Daniel, 238–43, 246–47
    study of, 11–12
drinking, 4, 6, 7–8, 96, 223, 233–34
dualism, 16–23

eating
    illustrating synergy of word and action, 6, 7–8
    as prophetic action, 233–34
    as ritual practice, 130–31, 132–33
    scroll of lament, 96–97, 229–33
ecstasy, prophetic
    debate concerning, 145–46, 157, 167–68
    definition, 145
    denoted by "hand of the Lord", 93–95, 96–97, 149–51, 160–61, 165–67
    mediation and, 39–40, 41–42, 118, 145
    as performance, 149–51, 153–54
    techniques for induction, 160, 168

Elijah
    as "man of God", 40–41
    mobility of, 179, 183
    spirit of, 162
Elisha
    bones of, 255–57
    as "man of God", 40–41
    spirit possession in story of, 162
    use of induction technique by, 160–61, 168
embodied cognition
    biblical studies and, 11–12
    in portrayal of the deity, 58–59, 60–61, 75
    interactive model of, 45–46
    physiological and neuromotor responses to first-person narrative, 79–80
    religious experience and, 41–42, 122
    study of affect and emotion and, 197–98
    study of prophetic literature and, 46
emotion
    circulation of, 199–201
    study of, 8–9, 197–201
encounter with deity
    portrayal of, 77, 80, 95, 97–98, 177
    preparation for, 129–30
    in prophetic commission, 48–49, 56
    relation to prophetic mission, 58, 98
    textual mediation of, 97–99
Enlightenment, European, 26–27
experience. *See* religious experience
eye, eyes, 83, 85, 92–93, 95, 97–98, 166–67, 207, 218
Ezekiel
    affect of, 226–37, 247–48
    call or commissioning narrative of, 78, 79–80, 91, 98–99, 226–31
    immobility of, 190
    religious experience in book of, 119–20, 164–67
    spirit journeys of, 164–66, 186

face
    affective role, 228–29
    Moses', transformation of, 103–4, 105–10
fasting, 129, 131–35, 243–44
fear
    in book of Daniel, 226, 238–43, 245–46, 247, 248

in book of Jonah, 201–2, 224–25
enacted by Ezekiel, 233–34, 247–48
in response to Moses, 105–6, 108, 109–10, 111, 116–17
feminist interpretation, 9–10, 16–17
first person narration, 78, 86, 95, 98, 238–43
'flesh', 21–22
food. *See* eating; fasting

gender
  relation to mind–body dualism, 16–17, 21–22, 23–24
  study of prophetic literature and, 9–10
  veiling and, 108–9
glory
  Ezekiel's response to, 95, 226–27
  Isaiah's vision of, 80–81
  meaning of, 83
  Moses' mediation of God's, 103–8, 111, 116–17
Gnosticism, 20
grief
  disenfranchised, 234–37
  expressions of, 212–13, 218, 221–22, 229–30, 234–35, 243–44
  of prophet, 192, 204–5, 222–23
  See also lament; mourning; weeping

Habakkuk, mobility of, 188
hand
  of deity, 57–59, 61, 89–90, 93–95, 96–97, 149–51, 160–61, 165–67, 183–84
  of prophet, 57–59, 61
Hannah
  incubatory practice of, 135–36, 137–38, 140–41, 144
  quasi-prophetic role of, 137–41
healing, 85–86, 136, 138, 255
heat, 204–5, 232
hierarchy among mediators/modes of mediation, 103–4, 112–13, 115–17
hierophagy, 231
horns of Moses, 105–8

illness
  accompanying religious ecstasy, 94–95, 166–67, 168
  in response to revelatory vision, 243, 246

imagination, 12–14, 49–50, 57–58
immobility, prophetic, 177, 189–95
impurity. *See* purity
incarceration, 191
incarnation, 21–23, 91, 96–97, 98–99
incubation
  definition and typology of, 135–36
  as divinatory practice, 119, 140, 141–42
  in HBOT, 136–37, 144
  prophetic mediation and, 118, 119, 135–36, 142
  as therapeutic practice, 119, 138
  type-scene, 137–38, 141
industrialism, 28
intercession, 130–31, 134–35, 220–23, 243–44
interembodiment, 77–78, 88–89, 90, 91–99

Jeremiah
  affect in book of, 208–24, 225
  commissioning narrative of, 86, 173–76
  incarcerations of, 191
Jonah
  affect in book of, 201
  mobility of, 180
Judaism, early, influence of Hellenistic philosophy within, 20

lament, 87, 96, 192, 208–24, 225, 229–30, 235–37
learning, embodied, 200–1, 233–34, 240–41, 246–47
liminality
  of Hannah's body, 140–41
  of incubation, 119, 135–36, 137–38, 140–41, 142
  of prophetic body, 103, 107–10, 116–17, 231–33
  of river, 178
  of seraphim, 81–82
  of temple threshold, 82
lips. *See* mouth
logocentrism, 12–14, 16, 25, 29, 31, 47–48
logos, 21–23

'magic', 24–25, 27–28, 32–36, 39–40
'man of God' as prophetic role label, 4–5, 40–41

marriage, prohibition of, 223
masculinity, 9–10, 16–17
mediation, characteristics of prophetic, 12–14, 31–36
mental health or illness
 attributed to prophet in ancient literature, 119–20, 159
 attributed to prophet in modern study, 119–20
 cultural constructions of, 119–20
 phenomenological overlap with and differentiation from religious ecstasy, 157–59
message, prophecy as, 12–14, 27–28, 43
messenger, prophet as, 12–14, 36–38, 39–40
mind-body dualism. See dualism
Miriam, transformation of, 110
mobility
 cost of, 194
 linked to people and place, 173–75
 of prophets, 42–43, 175–89
monster, prophet as, 107–83, 110, 116–17
Moses
 call or commissioning of, 56–76, 176–77
 death of, 177
 mobility of, 176
 portrayal as prophet, 34, 36, 56–57
 visible transformation of, 104
motion
 commanded by God, 173–74, 178–79, 180–82
 of prophet and deity, 59, 93, 176–77
 running, 183–84
 verbs of, 6, 66–67, 177–78, 186–87
mourning, practice of, 134, 219, 221–22, 234–36, 243–44. See also grief; lament; weeping
mouth, 5–6, 57–58, 68, 83–85, 234–37
music
 as induction technique, 160–63
 as prophetic modality, 39–40
 celebratory, 223–24

narrative immersion, 78–80, 97
narrative transportation, 78–80, 97, 240–41, 246–47
neurocognition. See embodied cognition

nonhuman animals
 agency of, 202–113
 and body of Moses, 107–8, 116–17
 sacrifice of, 84–85, 132
 and transport of prophet, 178–79, 182–83, 194

orality, 10–11, 12–15, 49, 120

performance, 10–14, 49
philosophy, ancient, ideas about the human person, 18–20
place, mobility and, 173–82
portent, prophet as, 223, 229–30, 235–37
possession. See spirit: possession by
possession trance. See trance
presence, divine. See divine presence
prophecy, definitions of, 12–14, 26–27, 30–36, 47
prophet
 biblical terminology, 34–35, 38–43
 diverse roles, 30–31, 34, 38
prophetic speech, 14–15, 24
Protestant Reformation, 24–25
purity, 67–68, 83, 113–14

queer interpretation, 9–10

rational emotive behavioral therapy, 205–6
rationalism, 26–28, 119–20
REBT, 205–6
reception of prophecy, 15, 78, 255
religious experience
 evaluations of, 24, 119–20
 prophecy as, 12–14
 relation to texts, 50, 119, 142–43
 study of, 8–9, 11–12, 15–16, 44, 45, 119
 of transcendence, 156–57
revelation
 modes of, relative status, 110–11
 techniques for eliciting, 11–12
rite of bitter water, 96
ritual
 conventional character of, 122
 denigration of, 24–25
 lament, function of, 221–22, 234–35
 meal event, 130–31, 132–33
role labels, prophetic, 4–5, 39–43

INDEX OF SUBJECTS

Romanticism, 27–28
running, 183–84

sackcloth, 123, 203–4, 212, 243–44
    Samuel, incubatory practice of, 141–42, 144
Saul, ecstatic experience of, 162–65
scale disease. *See* skin
scroll, Ezekiel's swallowing of, 96–97, 226, 229–26
 See seeing.sight
seer, as prophetic role label, 41–43
senses
    divine sensory perception, 58–59, 60–61
    embodied cognition and, 46, 59, 70–72
    epistemology and, 22–23, 67–68
    mediation and, 44
    model of person and, 26
    prophetic role labels and, 41–43
    in prophetic vision report, 77, 79–80, 81–86, 95, 97–98, 226–27
    relevance for reception of biblical text, 22–23
    role of in response to prophecy, 15
    study of, 8–9, 11–12
    See also sight; smell; taste; touch
sensory criticism
    in biblical studies, 8–9
    relevance for study of religious experience, 11–12
separation, theme of, 109–10, 129–30, 177, 185
seraph, seraphim, 81–85
shamanism, 24, 149–51, 156, 165–66
shame, 103–4, 110, 113–15, 116
sickness. *See* illness
sight
    in encounter between prophet and deity, 59, 83, 94–95
    in fear response, 245–46
    mobility and, 180
    perception of suffering, 87
    in relation to disability, 69–70
    relevance for role of prophet, 41–43, 110–11
    shared by prophet and deity, 92–93, 98–99

    visionary experience and, 41–43, 165–67
sign-acts. *See* symbolic actions
sign, signs
    performed by Moses, 63–68
    prophet as, 96–97
skin
    of Miriam, affliction of, 103–4, 110, 111–15, 116–17
    of Moses' face, 105–6, 108, 116–17
    of Moses' hand, affliction of, 66–67
sleep, sleeping
    as ASC, 155
    Daniel's, 242–43, 245
    in incubation, 118, 119, 135–36, 137–38, 141, 142
    Jeremiah's, 223–24, 225
    smell, sense of, 233–34
spatiality
    in Ezekiel's visions, 93, 95, 166, 186–87
    in Habakkuk's journey, 188–89
    in Isaiah's temple vision, 80–83, 85–86
    in Jeremiah's commission narrative, 86–87
    mediation and, 114–15, 117, 129–30, 180–82
    mobility and, 174–75
spirit
    as animating force, 96–97
    entering body, 95–97
    possession by, 120, 148–49, 151–53, 157, 158–59, 162, 168
    transporting prophet, 93, 96–97, 183
spitting, 113–15
staff of Moses, 65, 70–72
'superstition', 24–25, 26–27
supplication, 220, 222, 223–24, 225, 243–45
symbolic actions, 10–12, 15–16, 255

taste, sense of, 230–32, 234
tears, 210–12, 218, 219, 220, 222, 234–35. *See also* lament; weeping
technology, modern, 28
temple, setting for prophetic vision, 80–83, 84–85, 92–93
temporality, 80–81, 85–87
terror. *See* fear

textuality, 14–15, 39–40, 47, 119, 142–43, 237–38
theological anthropology, 20–23
theophany, 80, 91–93, 130–31
tongue. *See* mouth
touch, 6–7, 77, 83–85, 89–90, 98, 245–46
trance, 148–54, 155–56, 157–61, 163, 245
transcendence, experience of, 156–57
transport, supernatural, 157, 162, 165–66, 182–89
transportation, narrative. *See* narrative transportation
trauma
 response to, 221–22
 study of, 8–9, 10
 witnessing to, 94
trembling, 233–34, 238–39, 241, 246

veiling of Moses, 108–10
vision. *See* dreams; sight
visionary. *See* seer
vision reports
 accompanying prophetic commissioning narrative, 91–93
 ecstasy and, 165–66
 function of first-person discourse in, 78–79, 95

incubation practices and, 136–37
prophetic experience and, 32–33, 42, 120, 149–51
vomiting, 202–3
vulnerability
 of God, 219
 of people, 134–35, 251–52
 of prophet, 89, 112, 206–7, 217, 234

weeping, 209, 219, 220, 221–22, 225
womanist interpretation, 9–10, 16–17
womb, 86–87, 96, 98, 215
wonder, 157, 226, 237–41, 246–47, 248
word/Word
 agency of, 3–6, 7–8, 93
 dissociation from body, 23
 embodiment of prophetic, 15
 in Gospel of John, 21–23
 historical development of role of prophet and, 39–40
 placed in prophet's mouth, 90–91
 in Protestant Reformation, 25, 26–27
 in thought of Spinoza, 26–27
 synergy of word and action, 3–8
 "word of the Lord", 3–8, 14–15, 93, 141
writing. *See* textuality
"written language bias", 47–48

Index of Ancient Sources

For the benefit of digital users, indexed terms that span two pages (e.g., 52–53) may, on occasion, appear on only one of those pages.

Tables are indicated by *t* following the page number

HEBREW BIBLE/OLD TESTAMENT
Genesis
  2:7 86–87
  2:21 242–43
  15:12 242–43
  15:17 82–83
  28:10–22 137n.60
  32:25 89–90
  41:38 162n.78
  49:24 61–62

Exodus
  3:1 59
  3:2–10 58
  3:2 58–59
  3:3 59
  3:4 58–59
  3:5 59
  3:7 60–61
  3:8–20 61, 73–74
  3:8 59, 61, 176–77
  3:9 60–61
  3:10 62, 63, 66–67, 73, 176–77
  3:11 66–67, 176–77
  3:12–15 62, 63
  3:12 42, 68n.42, 89
  3:14 73
  3:15 73
  3:16 60–61, 73, 74, 175n.11
  3:16–22 63, 176–77
  3:18 73, 74, 175n.11
  3:19 61
  3:20 61n.22, 62, 63, 65
  4:1–9 64–68, 75–76
  4:1 64

  4:2–8 62, 63–64
  4:2 65
  4:3–8 64
  4:3 65, 73
  4:4–30 73–75
  4:4 62, 63, 65, 73
  4:6 66–67, 73
  4:7 66–67, 73
  4:8 67–68
  4:9 64, 67n.41, 73
  4:10–16 68, 75–76, 89
  4:10 68–69, 176–77
  4:11 69–70
  4:12 56–57, 69–70, 74–75, 89
  4:13 63
  4:15 33n.5, 73, 74–75, 89
  4:16 37n.23, 69–70
  4:17 73
  4:20 65
  4:21 74–75, 175n.11
  4:22 74
  4:28 63n.28, 74
  4:30 15n.59, 68, 74
  5:22–7:7 57n.9
  5:22 63n.28
  6:1 61
  6:6–8 66–67
  6:12 69
  6:13 66–67
  6:26 66–67
  6:27 66–67
  6:30 69
  7:1 15n.59
  7:5 66–67
  7:15–20 65n.37

Exodus (*cont.*)
  7:15 190
  7:16 63n.28
  7:17–25 67n.41
  7:17 190
  7:20 190
  7:26 175n.11
  8:5 65n.37
  8:15 65n.34, 65n.36
  8:16 65n.37
  8:17 63n.28, 65n.37
  8:19 65n.34, 65n.36
  9:1 63n.30, 175n.11
  9:8–10 63n.30
  9:14 63n.28
  9:15 61n.22, 63n.28, 63n.30
  9:23 65
  10:13 65
  10:19 190
  12:17 66–67
  12:42 66–67
  12:51 66–67
  13:3 66–67
  13:5 66–67
  13:9 66–67
  13:11 66–67
  13:14 66–67
  13:16 66–67
  14:5 190
  14:8 81
  14:16 63n.30, 65
  14:21 63n.30
  14:26 63n.30, 65
  14:27 63n.30
  14:30 63n.30
  15:1–2 105–6
  15:2 81
  15:6 61–62, 105–6
  15:11 105–6
  15:17 66–67
  15:20–21 161
  15:21 105–6
  16:6 66–67
  16:7 105–6
  16:10 105–6
  17:5–6 65
  17:5 173n.2, 175n.11, 177
  17:9 65
  18:1 66–67
  19:3 129–30, 177
  19:4 66–67
  19:5–6 129–30
  19:10 175n.11, 177
  19:14–15 129–30
  19:18 82–83
  19:20 129–30, 177
  19:21 173n.2, 177
  19:24 173n.2, 175n.11, 177
  20:18 33n.6
  23:20 66–67
  23:23 66–67
  23:24 173n.2
  24:1–18 177
  24:1 173n.2
  24:1–2 130
  24:4–8 132
  24:9–13 130
  24:11 61n.22
  24:16–17 105–6, 130
  24:18 129, 130
  24:25 130
  29:43 105–6
  31:18 62
  32:6 133, 143–44
  32:7 173n.2, 175n.11, 177
  32:9–10 130–31
  32:12 203–4, 205n.42
  32:14 203–4
  32:15 130–31, 177
  32:19 130–31
  32:22 130–31
  32:30 130–31
  32:32 130–31
  32:34 175n.11
  33:1 175n.11
  33:3 133
  33:4–6 104
  33:7–11 177
  33:9 104, 176–77
  33:11–14 104
  33:12–17 105
  33:11 48–49, 56–57
  33:17 104
  33:18–20 105–6
  33:18–23 58–59
  33:22–23 62, 105

33:22 105-6
34:2 105, 131
34:5-7 131
34:6 105, 205n.42
34:9-28 131
34:15 133
34:18-22 133
34:25-26 133
34:28 105, 133
34:29 104, 105-6, 116-17
34:30-33 108
34:30 104, 105, 129
34:33 111
34:35 104, 105, 129
40:34-35 105-6

Leviticus
1:16 66
13:4 113-14
18:25 202-3
18:28 202-3
19:31 32
20:22 202-3

Numbers
5:2-4 67
5:11-31 96
6:1-21 127n.32
8:11 84-85
11:17 162
11:25-26 162
11:25 153
11:29 162
12:1 110-11
12:2 110-11, 117n.60
12:5 111
12:6 110-11
12:7 111
12:8 56-57, 110-11
12:9-10 111
12:10-15 67
12:11 112
12:12 66, 112
12:14 113-15
14:18 205n.42
20:1 117
21:8-9 65n.35
22:1 177-78

22:5-6 177-78
22:6 178
22:11 177-78
22:12 175n.11
22:13 178-79
22:20-27 178-79
22:20 173n.2, 175n.11
22:23-25 180
22:27 180
22:30 179
22:31 180
22:32 178-79
22:33 180
22:34 178-79
22:35 175n.11, 178-79
22:36-39 180
23:7 178n.13, 180
23:9 177-78, 180
23:13-14 180
23:21 180
23:27-28 180
24:1-4 180
24:2-4 166-67
24:8 178
24:2-13 162n.79
24:15-16 166-67, 180
26:51 117
27:12 173n.2

Deuteronomy
1:28 81
3:27 173n.2
5:4 56-57
5:30 175n.11
9:2 81
9:9-11 133-34
9:12 173n.2
9:18 133-35
9:25-29 134-35
10:1-5 134-35
10:1 173n.2
10:2 62
10:10 134-35
10:11 173n.2
11:18-22 133-34
18:9-22 31, 36-38
18:9-12 32
18:9 32-33

Deuteronomy (cont.)
18:12–13 33–34
18:14–15 32–33
18:15 33
18:18–22 32–33
18:19 33–34
24:8–9 67
24:9 112–13, 117
25:9–10 60n.19
32:49 173n.2, 177
32:52 177
33:25 228–29
34:4–6 177
34:10 33–34

Judges
3:10 162n.78
6:11–17 55n.1
6:34 162n.78
11:29 162n.78
13:25 162n.78
14:6 162n.78
14:19 162n.78
15:14 162n.78

Ruth
4:7–8 60n.19

1 Samuel
1:5 138
1:9 140
1:12 140
1:14 140
1:20 138
2:1–10 138–39
2:1 140–41
2:8 81
3:1–2 141
3:4 141n.71
3:6 141n.71
3:7 141
3:8 141n.71
3:9 141
3:9–14 141, 142
3:18 141
3:19–21 142
3:20 143–44
3:21 141
7:6 134n.49

8:2 139
9:1–10:16 55n.1
9:9–19 42–43
9:9–10 173n.1
10:5–7 148–49
10:5 161, 163, 179
10:6 162n.79, 163, 168
10:9 190
10:10–12 163
10:10 162n.79
15:16 141
16:1 175n.11
16:13–16 162n.78
16:16 161n.75
16:23 162n.78
18:10 162n.78
19:9 162n.78
19:20–24 148–49, 164
19:20 162n.79
19:23 162n.79
19:24 166–67
20:1 164
25:12 190
26:12 242–43
28:20 132n.43
31:13 134n.49

2 Samuel
1:12 134n.49
7:4 141
7:5 175n.11
12:22 134n.49
14:3 33n.5
14:19 33n.5
22:8–10 82–83
23:2 162n.79
24:11 42n.41
24:12 175n.11

1 Kings
3:4–15 136–37
12:22 5n.8
13:1–32 3
13:1–5 5–6
13:1 3–4, 6
13:2 6
13:4 3–4
13:6 3–4

INDEX OF ANCIENT SOURCES 303

13:8–9 6
13:9–11 4
13:9 5–6
13:10 6
13:11 7
13:14–19 4
13:15–19 6
13:16–17 6
13:17–18 5–6
13:18 4–5
13:20–21 5–6
13:22–23 6
13:22 4
13:24–25 4
13:26 5–6
13:28–31 4
13:28 6
13:32 5–6, 7
14:7 81
16:1 5n.8
16:7 5n.8
16:12 5n.8
16:34 5n.8
17:2 5n.8
17:3 175n.11
17:4–9 128
17:5 5n.8
17:8 5n.8
17:9 175n.11
17:16 5n.8
17:24 5n.8
18:1 175n.11
18:4 183
18:12–13 183
18:12 162n.79
18:22 41n.36
18:24 167n.87
18:36 41n.36
18:41 183n.30
18:44 175n.11
18:45–46 183–84
19:5 173n.2
19:7 173n.2
19:11 173n.2
19:15–16 175n.11
19:15 173n.2
19:16 41n.36
21:18 173n.2
22:21–23 162

22:24 162n.79
22:34 190

2 Kings
1:3 173n.2, 175n.11
1:9 41n.36
1:15 173n.2, 175n.11
2:1–8 185
2:9 162
2:10–12 185
2:15 162
2:16 162n.79, 183, 186
3:11 41n.36, 160–61
3:12 160–61
3:14–15 160–61
3:15 161
5:8 41n.36
5:21–24 182n.28
5:26 162n.80, 182n.28
6:12 41n.36
6:17 185–86
7:6 185–86
9:1 41n.36, 175n.11
9:26 5n.8
13:14 185–86
13:20–21 255–56
18:4 65n.35
19:7 162
19:33 5n.8
20:5 175n.11
22:19 5n.8
17:13 42
13:21 35n.14
23:18 35

1 Chronicles
6:16–17 139
6:33 139
9:22 42–43
15:17 139
17:3 5n.8
17:4 175n.11
21:9 42n.41
21:10 175n.11
25:1 139, 161n.76
25:5 42n.41
26:28 42–43
26:32 5n.8
29:29 42n.41, 42–43

304 INDEX OF ANCIENT SOURCES

2 Chronicles
9:29   42n.41
12:15   42n.41
15:1   162n.79
16:7   42–43
16:10   42–43, 192
18:20-22   162
18:23   162n.79
19:2   42n.41
20:14   162n.79
21:12   41n.36
24:20   162n.79
29:25   42n.41
29:30   42n.41
33:18   42
35:15   42n.41

Ezra
9:5   134n.49
10:6   134n.49
11:4   134n.49

Nehemiah
1:4   134n.49
9:17   205n.42

Esther
4:16   134n.49, 134n.51

Job
1:11   89–90
1:19   89–90
2:5   89–90
4:15   241n.55
19:21   89–90
38:5-6   70n.49
38:14   190
38:25   70n.49
38:36   70n.49
38:41   70n.49
39:5   70n.49

Psalms
8:3-4   62
18:8-10   82–83
69:10-11   134n.51
86:15   205n.42
103:8   205n.42
138:7   61n.22
145:8   205n.42

Proverbs
3:24   224n.110

Isaiah
6:1-13   79n.8, 80
6:1   81
6:3   83
6:4   82–83
6:5   83
6:7   83–85
6:8   173–74
6:9   85, 175n.11
6:10   84–85
6:11-12   85–86
6:11-13   81n.14
7:9   228
20:2   175n.11
21:6   175n.11
22:15   175n.11
28:8   202–3
29:10   42, 242–43
30:10   42
30:21   84–85
31:6   84–85
37:7   162
38:5   175n.11
42:1   162n.78
42:19   37–38n.24
42:22   66–67
51:16   33n.5
53:4   84
53:5-12   84–85
53:8   84
58:3   134n.49
59:21   33n.5
61:1   162n.79
65:4   135n.53

Jeremiah
1:4-10   86
1:4   86
1:5   86–88, 90, 211–12
1:6   89
1:7   173–74, 175–76
1:8   89

1:9 33n.5, 89–90
1:10 87–88, 90–91
1:14 228n.5
1:17 228–29
1:18 228n.5
1:19 89
2:2 175n.11
3:12 175n.11
4:1 213, 215
4:3 213
4:5–6 212–13
4:8 212–14, 215, 222–23, 225
4:19–21 212, 215, 216–17, 222–23, 225
4:19 214n.70, 215, 219
4:20–21 216
4:19 214n.70, 215, 219
4:22 215n.74, 217
4:31 216, 217
5:13–14 33n.5, 77n.1
6:14 91
6:24 216, 217
6:26 212
6:28 228–29
7:16 90, 220
7:20 220
7:29 220–21
7:30–34 221–22
8:11 91
8:18–21 212, 225
8:18–9:1 218, 219, 222–23
11:14 90, 220
11:17 220
13:1 175n.11
13:4 173n.2, 175n.11
13:6 173n.2, 175n.11
14:2 220
14:11 90, 220, 222
14:17–22 222–23
14:17 222
15:1 220n.95
15:12 228–29
15:16 230–31
16:2 128, 223
16:9 223
17:19–20 175n.11
18:2 173n.2
18:6–11 87–88
19:1–3 175n.11

19:1–15 87
20:1–18 192
20:7–18 87, 89–90
22:1 173n.2, 175n.11
22:23 216
23:21 184n.34
23:25 120
23:32 120
28:13 175n.11
29:26 119–20, 192
31:3–4 223–24
31:7 223–24
31:9 223–24
31:13 223
31:16–17 223–24
31:25–26 223–24
31:26 141, 224
32:2 193
32:3–5 188
32:3 192n.52
32:6–15 193
32:6 5n.8
32:8 5n.8, 192n.52
32:26 5n.8
33:1 192, 192n.52, 193
33:11 223–24
34:2 175n.11
35:1–19 134n.48
35:2 175n.11
35:13 175n.11
36:5 193
36:19 193n.55
37:4 192n.52
37:12–16 192n.52, 193
37:18–21 192n.52
38:1–4 193
38:1–6 193
38:4–13 192n.52
38:17–18 193
38:20–23 193
38:26 192n.52
38:28 192n.52, 193
39:7 193
39:9 193
39:11–14 193
39:14–15 192n.52
39:15–18 193
39:16 175n.11

Jeremiah (cont.)
- 40:1-6 193
- 40:1 192n.52
- 43:5-7 193
- 44:12-14 193
- 44:30 193
- 48:26 202-3
- 48:36 214n.70
- 50:43 216

Lamentations
- 1:1 209-10

Ezekiel
- 1:1-3:15 91
- 1:1 92-93, 226-27
- 1:3 93-94, 165, 167n.87, 184n.31
- 1:4 92, 226-27
- 1:4-28 95
- 1:7 92
- 1:12 165n.83
- 1:15 226-27
- 1:16 92
- 1:18 92
- 1:20-21 165n.83
- 1:22 92
- 1:24 226-27
- 1:27 92, 226-27
- 1:28 166-67, 226-27, 242n.58
- 1:26-28 94-95
- 2:1-2 95-96
- 2:2 96-97, 162, 165
- 2:3-8 228-29
- 2:3 226-27
- 2:6 227, 228
- 2:6-8 95-96
- 2:8 165
- 2:8-10 96
- 2:9 93-94
- 2:10 229-30
- 3:1 175n.11
- 3:3 96, 230-31
- 3:4 175n.11
- 3:8-9 228-29
- 3:9 228
- 3:9-10 165
- 3:11 175n.11
- 3:12 96-97, 162, 165
- 3:14 62n.23, 93-95, 96-97, 162, 165, 167n.87, 231-32
- 3:15 93-94, 165, 228n.7, 232-33
- 3:22 93-94, 165, 167n.87, 173n.2, 184n.31
- 3:23 166-67, 226-27, 242n.58
- 3:24-27 190
- 3:24 97n.61, 162, 165
- 3:26 165
- 3:27 165, 226-27
- 3:49 188-89
- 4:1-3 149-51
- 4:3-6 190
- 4:4-8 234
- 4:8 190
- 4:12-15 233n.27
- 4:16-17 232-33
- 8:1 93-94, 165-66, 167n.87
- 8:2-3 61n.22, 92-93
- 8:2 165-66
- 8:3 93-94, 96-97, 162, 165-66, 188
- 8:4 92n.50, 166
- 8:6-10 166
- 8:6-7 92n.50
- 8:9-10 92n.50
- 8:12 92-93, 166
- 8:13 92n.50, 166
- 8:15 92n.50, 166
- 8:17 92n.50, 166
- 8:18 92-93, 166
- 9:8 166-67, 227n.1, 242n.58
- 9:10 166
- 11:1 97n.61, 162, 165, 166
- 11:5 162n.79, 166
- 11:13 166-67, 227n.1, 242n.58
- 11:16-17 166
- 11:24 97n.61, 162, 188
- 11:24-25 165, 166
- 11:19 97n.62
- 12:1 5n.8
- 12:8 5n.8
- 12:17 5n.8
- 12:17-19 233-34
- 12:21 5n.8
- 12:26 5n.8
- 14:31-33 188-89

INDEX OF ANCIENT SOURCES 307

14:33 188
14:35 188–89
14:38–39 188–89
16:38 232
18:31 97n.62
19:1 229n.11
19:12 232
19:14 229n.11
20:26 232–33
21:6–7 234
23:25 232
24:8 232
24:16–17 234–35
24:16 236
24:19 236
24:21–22 236
24:24–25 236
24:24 235–36
24:27 235–36
26:17 229n.11
27:2 229n.11
27:30–31 231–32
27:32 229n.11
28:12 229n.11
32:2 214n.70, 229n.11
32:10 232–33
32:16 229n.11
32:18 214n.70
33:22 93–94, 167n.87, 190
36:26–27 97n.62
37:1–2 186–87
37:1 78, 93–94, 162n.79, 165, 167n.87, 184n.31
37:9–10 96–97
39:29 97n.62
40:1–2 93–94, 165
40:1 167n.87, 184n.31, 186–87
40:2–3 92–93, 186–87
40:4 92n.50, 186–87
40:17 186–87
40:24 186–87
40:28 186–87
40:32 186–87
40:35 186–87
40:48 186–87
41:1 186–87
42:1 186–87

42:4 181–82
42:15 186–87
43:1 186–87
43:3 166–67, 226–27, 229n.10, 242n.58
43:4 229n.10
43:5 162, 165, 186–87
43:10–11 228–29
44:1 186–87
44:4 166–67, 186–87, 226–27, 242n.58
44:6 226–27
46:19 186–87
46:21 186–87
47:1–4 186–87
47:1–6 187
47:6 186–87
48:30–35 187

Daniel
2:11–17 128
2:12 238n.43
2:14 238n.43
2:19 141
3:19 238n.43
4:2 [MT; 4:5 OG] 238n.44, 239n.47, 241
4:5 238n.44
4:5–6 162n.78
4:10 141
4:15 162n.78
4:16 [MT; 4:19 LXX] 238, 241
4:19 238–39
4:34 240
5:10 238n.46
5:11–12 162n.78
5:14 162n.78
6:4 162n.78
7:10 247n.77
7:15 241
7:19 241
7:28 241
8:17–18 166–67, 242–43
8:24–25 245
8:27 243
9:2 247
9:3 132
9:3–4 243–44
9:20 243–44
9:23 243–44

308 INDEX OF ANCIENT SOURCES

Daniel (cont.)
  9:24–27 247n.77
  9:25–26 245
  10:2–3 243–44
  10:3 244n.68
  10:5 245
  10:8–9 245
  10:9 166–67
  10:10–12 245
  10:11 244
  10:12–14 245–46
  10:12 238n.46, 243–44
  10:16 245–46
  10:18–20 245–46
  10:19 238n.46, 244, 246
  10:21 247n.77
  11:38 244n.68
  11:43 244n.68
  12:1–3 245–46
  12:1 247n.77
  12:4 247
  12:9 175n.11, 247
  12:13 175n.11
  14:36 188
  14:39 188

Hosea
  1:2 55n.1, 175n.11
  3:1 175n.11
  9:7 119–20, 162
  12:14 57n.8

Joel
  2:10 204–5
  2:12 134n.49
  2:13 205n.42
  3:1–2 162n.79

Amos
  2:6 60n.19
  7:12 42
  7:14–15 55n.1
  7:15 175n.11
  8:6 60n.19

Jonah
  1:1–4 181–82

  1:2–3 180–81
  1:2 55n.1, 173n.2, 175n.11
  1:5 201–2
  1:6–9 180–81
  1:9 201–2
  1:10 206
  1:11 201–2
  1:14 201–2
  1:15 199, 202n.29
  1:16 201–2
  1:17 [NRSV; 2:1 MT] 180–81
  2:1 181–82, 202, 215
  2:3 202
  2:8 202
  2:10 [NRSV; 2:11 MT] 180–82, 202
  2:11 202–3
  3:1–4 181–82
  3:2–4 180–81
  3:2 173n.2, 175n.11, 180–81
  3:5–10 203–4
  3:6–8 134n.49
  3:8–10 181–82
  3:9 205
  3:10 204–5
  4:1 204–5, 206
  4:2 205
  4:34 205–6
  4:4 204–5
  4:5–6 206
  4:5 180–81
  4:7–9 206–7
  4:8 205–6
  4:9–11 207
  4:9 204–5

Micah
  3:7 42
  3:8 162n.79
  6:4 110–11
  7:18 205n.42

Nahum
  1:3 205n.42
  2:5 204–5

Haggai
  1:13 36–38

Zechariah
    2:8 [MT; 2:4 NRSV] 184n.34
    7:12 162n.79

Malachi
    3:1 36–38
    3:23–24 [MT; 4:5–6 NRSV] 186
    3:23 41n.37

NEW TESTAMENT
Matthew
    4:2 129n.36
    17:1–8 129n.36
    17:2 109–10
    24:15 237n.42

Mark
    1:13 129n.36
    9:2–8 129n.36
    9:4 41n.37

Luke
    1:17 41n.37
    4:2 129n.36
    9:28–36 129n.36

Gospel of John 21–23
    1:1 22
    1:14 21–22
    3:6 21–22
    6:35 21–22
    6:48 21–22
    6:51 22
    6:63 21–22

1 Corinthians
    15:43–44 20
    15:50 20

2 Corinthians
    5:6 20

Galatians
    5:17 20

1 Thessalonians
    5:23 20

1 John
    4:2–3 23n.85

2 John
    1:7 23n.85

APOCRYPHA Sirach
    24:19–21 21–22
    48:1–11 41n.37, 41n.38
    48:9 185
    48:10 186
    48:12 185
    48:13 255–56
    49:10 256

2 Maccabees
    15:4 123n.15

2 Esdras
    15:1 33n.5

PSEUDEPIGRAPHA
Martyrdom and Ascension of Isaiah
    2:7–11 123
    5:7–14 123n.14

1 Enocih
    104:11–13 247

4 Ezra
    12:37–38 247
    14:46–47 247

4 Maccabees
    12:11 123n.15

DEAD SEA SCROLLS
4QFlor (4Q174)
    II.3–4 237n.42
4Q403
    frag 1 I.41 83n.20
    II.4–16 83n.20

HELLENISTIC JEWISH AUTHORS
Josephus
    Ant. 10.266 237n.42

Philo
   Ebr.
     1.147 140n.70
     1.152 140n.70
     1.484–5 140n.70

RABBINIC, TARGUMIC, AND CHRISTIAN SOURCES
Jerome
   Abacuc VI, 639 ad Hab. 3:4
     107n.16

Midrash Jonah 202n.30, 205n.45
Pirkei de Rabbi Eliezer
   43 203–4

Targum Pseudo-Jonathan 105–6, 138–39
   1 Sam. 2:1 139
   1 Sam. 2:5 139n.66

Talmud
   Meg. 14a 139
   Shabb. 97a 112n.37

CLASSICAL SOURCES
Plato 18
Phaedo
   §65–67 19–20
   §67 19
   §76 19
   §79 19–20
   §80–82 19

Phaedrus
   §245–46 18–19

Symposium
   §210 19–20

Pseudo-Tertullian
   "Carmen de Iona Propheta" ll. 73–75 205n.41

ANCIENT WEST ASIAN SOURCES
Mari
   Ritual of Istar
   Text 2 [FM 3 2] 161n.75
   Text 3 [FM 3 3] 161n.75